Clearing the Path

Editing: Elizabeth Licht
Cover and book design: David Spohn

ISBN 978-81-8037-115-8

Himalayan Yoga Publications Trust
Swami Rama Sadhaka Grama, Virpur Khurd, Virbhadra Road
Rishikesh, Uttarakhand - 249 203
info@yogapublications.org

This book is not intended to replace medical or behavioral health care. Neither the author nor the editor nor Ahymsa Publishers nor its affiliates shall be held liable should any harm result from applying the information contained herein. Please consult your doctor before beginning this or any other health or wellness initiative.

Clearing the Path

The Yoga Way to a Clear and Pleasant Mind: Patañjali, Neuroscience, and Emotion

Stephen Parker (Stoma), PsyD, E-RYT 500, YACEP
Edited by Elizabeth Licht

"Prisoner, tell me, who was it that bound you? . . . Who was it that wrought this unbreakable chain?" "It was I," said the prisoner, "who forged this chain very carefully. I thought my invincible power would hold the world captive, leaving me in a freedom undisturbed. Thus night and day I worked at the chain with huge fires and cruel hard strokes. When at last the work was done and the links were complete and unbreakable, I found that it held me in its grip!"

—RAVĪNDRANĀTHA THĀKURA (RABINDRANATH TAGORE),
Gitanjali, Song Offerings, 1912

In the heart of every man there is something—a drive?—which is already there when he is born and will haunt him unremittingly until his last breath. It is a mystery which encompasses him on every side, but one which none of his faculties can ever attain to or, still less, lay hold of. It cannot be located in anything that can be seen, heard, touched, or known in this world. There is no sign for it, but nevertheless it is the price of finding the treasure that is without name or form or sign. It is the unique splendor of the Self—but no one is left in its presence to exclaim, "How beautiful it is!"

—SWĀMĪ ABHISHIKTĀNANDA,
The Further Shore, 1984

Table of Contents

Figures

Tables

Table I
Abbreviations for Yoga Texts

Yoga Text	Abbreviation
Bhagavad-gītā	BhG
Haṭha-yoga-pradīpikā	HYP
*Upaniṣad*s	Up.
Yoga-sūtra	YS

Table II
Sanskrit Vowels and Their Pronunciation

Vowel	Pronunciation	Vowel	Pronunciation
a	as in *up*	*ā*	as in *father*
i	as in *dig*	*ī*	as in *glee*
u	as in *push*	*ū*	as in *rude*
ṛ	as in *grrr*[1]	*ṝ*	same as *ṛ*, twice as long
ḷ	as in *lllll*, as an exclamation of distaste[2]	*ḹ*	same as *ḷ*, twice as long
e (a + i)	as in *prey*	*ai*	as in *aisle*
o	as in *go*	*au* (*a*+*u*)	as in *sauerkraut*

Note. Alphabetical order is read horizontally across the grid. In the Kashmir Śaiva philosophy and science of mantra, each sound represents a sequential phase in the unfolding manifestation of the universe.

[1] This letter, a vowel version of *r*, is a sound not found in English or most Germanic or Romance languages. It appears in Slavic languages like Russian or Ukrainian and is pronounced correctly like a slight growl. Many people in North India and elsewhere tend to insert an *i* afterwards so that *Ṛg Veda* becomes *Rig Veda*. In South India many people insert an *u* sound: *Rug Veda*. Both are technically incorrect.

[2] This is another sound not found in most modern languages and somewhat rarely in Sanskrit. The sound is made by placing your tongue against the back of your upper teeth and then making sound from your throat. The long form of this vowel is not used in any written word and is included because it is one of the subtle sounds represented on the petals of the six *cakra*s (chakras).

Table III

Sanskrit Consonants and Their Pronunciation

(C)	Pronunciation	(C)	Pronunciation	(C)	Pronunciation
k	as in *kid*	*ś*	Pronounced with a slight hiss or whistle, as in the German *sprechen*	*dh*	as in *adhere,* off the back of your teeth
kh	as in *packhorse*	*ṭ*	as in *ducat,* touching the *bottom* tip of the tongue to the roof of your mouth	*n*	as in *ninny*
g	as in *go*	*ṭh*	as in *anthill,* touching the *bottom* tip of the tongue to the roof of your mouth	*l*	as in *lily*
gh	as in *doghouse*	*ḍ*	as in *drum,* touching the *bottom* tip of the tongue to the roof of your mouth	*s*	as in *sissy*
ṅ	as in *bungle*	*ḍh*	as in *roadhouse,* touching the *bottom* tip of the tongue to the roof of your mouth	*p*	as in *pin*
c	as in *church*	*ṇ*	as in *honor,* touching the *bottom* tip of the tongue to the roof of your mouth	*ph*	as in *uphill*
				b	as in *bowl*
				bh	as in *abhor*
				m	as in *mummy*
ch	as in *Churchill*	*r*	as in *roll*	*v*	as in *rove,* midway between *w* & *v.* The sound is made by bringing your lips together and making sound through them rather than by touching your upper teeth to your lower lip.
j	as in *jump*	*ṣ*	as in *shun*		
jh	as in *lodge house*	*t*	as in *bucket,* off the back of your teeth		
ñ	as in *cringe.* Often taught as resembling the Spanish *señor,* but the sound is much less like "nya."	*th*	as in *mythos,* off the back of your teeth		
y	as in *yes*	*d*	as in *detail,* off the back of your teeth	*h*	as in *hum*

Note. (C) = Consonant. Alphabetical order is read vertically down the grid. (Sanskrit organizes alphabetical order by where a sound is pronounced in the throat. The guttural consonants from the back of the throat are first, and the labials pronounced on the lips are last.)

The default stress in Sanskrit words is on the antepenultimate syllable, the third to the last. Most mispronunciations occur due to using the English custom of stressing the penultimate, the next to the last. Where there is a long vowel in the word and a short vowel in the antepenultimate position, the long vowel receives the preferred stress. Where there are two long vowels, the one in the antepenultimate position receives slightly more stress, as in *Rāmāyana.*

Note on plurals of Sanskrit words. Plurals in Sanskrit are formed by declined word endings. When used in an English context, the addition of *s* makes the word an Anglicization. As a compromise to the style manuals, when a Sanskrit word appears in italics, the main body of the word is presented in italics with the plural *s* ending unitalicized.

Gratitude, Gratitude, Gratitude:

To my guides on the path of light. What is light on the reader's path from this work is your gift. What is dark or dull is my own *tamas*, not yet transmuted into pure stability:

• To Swāmī Rāma of the Himalayas, who has been kind enough to guide from within what I was not prepared to learn from him when he was in the body.

• To Swāmī Veda Bhāratī, whom I first met in 1970 at the age of 19 and who has shaped my life more than any other person and continues to do so even after his *Mahāsamādhi.*

• To Bradford P. Keeney, my doctoral advisor, who encouraged me to keep my spirituality alive in my doctoral studies and profession and who was (and is) so much more than a professor.

To the Dutch teacher training student who, after a lecture on *citta-prasādana*, asked me when she would see my book. I made my usual excuses about how my busy schedule keeps me from writing, and she looked at me pointedly and said, "You know, no one has really written about this before!" which provided the Guru an opening to show me a clear intuition of this project. Since then it came ready to write itself, *voila!*

To Wesley Van Linda, whose experience in publishing was a welcome guide to this novice author in the process of producing, refining, and publishing this book.

To Elizabeth Licht, my very conscientious editor, whose relentless questions, thoughtful enthusiasm, advocacy for the reader's experience, careful suggestions, and substantive writing contributions, including expansions and reorganizations of several chapters and a number of exercises, references, and graphics, have made this a much better book.

To Jennifer Manion, whose minute editorial eye, broad experience, deep affection, and delicious cake brought a fine polish to the initial version of this project.

To David Spohn, our graphic designer, who gave thoughtful beauty to the appearance of the book and created a lovely cover.

To Anna Bajnok, MD, a graduate of the Himalayan Yoga Tradition Teacher Training Program in Hungary, for posing in the photos that appear in Exercises.

To all the students whose excitement about the idea of this book kept me finding time to work on completing it.

To all the spiritual sons and daughters who keep my heart open.

And, by way of bringing the *mālā* of blessings full circle back to the teachers again, to my husband of 23 years, Scott, whose beautiful heart has been the *ādhāra*, the spiritual and emotional foundation, of my ability to reach out in this work of love.

Introduction

In 2003 I attended an international conference on Tibetan Medicine in Washington, DC. Among the senior lamas at the conference was one of the last people trained in the same cohort of lamas as the Dalai Lama, by the same teacher. His name was Gelek Rimpoche, and I liked him enormously. His attire and demeanor reflected the practicality of his teaching. He wore a plain Brooks Brothers suit and spoke in ordinary language. At the end of the conference, Rimpoche ascended the stage to conduct an empowerment (meditative initiation) in the Yoga of the Medicine Buddha for all present. A little ways along, he stopped and looked quietly at the audience for a moment. Then he said, "I know you all want to save the world with Tonglen meditation,[1] but you really need to work on emotional purification first." Thus began his two-hour-long discourse on the necessity of cleansing one's own heart before undertaking any spiritual practice for the benefit of others. The risk, of course, is that the warps and impurities in the small waves of our own mindfields will invite the suffering energy we absorb from others to make us ill. It is no great trick to absorb others' pain and dis-ease (or to become trapped by our own); it is difficult to know how to handle that energy once we have absorbed it.

How many times had I heard this lecture from my own spiritual guides, Swāmī Veda Bhāratī (1933–2015) and Swāmī Rāma (1925–1996) of the Himalayas, over forty years?! I immediately sought out Rimpoche as he left the hall and thanked him for telling this truth so clearly—and for reminding me of my teachers.

Swāmī Rāma was taught from childhood by a legendary Yogi of the nineteenth and twentieth centuries, known variously as Mādhavānanda Bhāratī, Bāba Dharam Dās, Bāngla Bāba, Bengali

[1] Tonglen is a Tibetan Buddhist meditation practice of taking in the suffering energy in the world around us with the inhaling breath and offering friendliness (*maitri* in Sanskrit, *metta* in Pāli), compassion, joy, and well-being with the exhaling breath. See Appendix A, Exercise 2.6. For an alternative to Tonglen, see Appendix A, Exercise 2.5.

Baba, Mahārāj (ca. 1820–1981), and many other names. One day Bengali Baba took Swāmī Rāma into the mountains and showed him an enormous pile of gold and precious gems. He said, "'Take them. They're for you. You'll be the richest man in India. Now son, let me go. I want to go to the mountains far away'" (Rama, 1978, p. 181). Swāmījī was wounded to the core. Bengali Baba had raised him from early childhood. "'Are you telling me to accept these jewels instead of you?'" he cried (Rama, 1978, p. 181). Bengali Baba directed his attention to a column of fire that appeared nearby and said, "'If you can go through that fire you can follow me'" (Rama, 1978, p. 181).

When we disciples hear this story, we imagine ourselves standing in the fire with the master. But what do we really want from our practices and from our lives? We seem to want nice, peaceful meditations, quiet children, loving and agreeable spouses—don't those sound like the gems to you? These are beautiful and natural aspirations, but they stop short of the ultimate gift of Yoga. This is the difficulty with much of the practice of Yoga and meditation that happens in the West today. These desires reflect our deepest longing to connect with the Self, the joyful underlying Being and ultimate reality that unites us all. But we do not always recognize them as such. We think we want the quiet children and easy meditations and agreeable spouses. And we often try to avoid the necessary work of emotional purification to get them. We sidestep the disturbing aspects of our personality that we have defined as "not-me" and that have become, as it were, our emotional shadow. Conversely, when we do accept and take responsibility for the whole of our personality, we find that we progress on our path and can measure that progress with its positive "side effects": greater peace in our meditations and relationships. Having come this far through the fire, though, we can again be tempted to stop our work and to settle for those side effects, the gems, when the Ultimate is within reach.

Having taught in almost every corner of the world, I can testify that contemporary Yoga worldwide does not seem to have much space for this homely truth: The mind cannot concentrate and go deep, either to realize peaceful meditations or final liberation, when it is perturbed by emotional disturbances that create warps and knots in the mindfield, in the energy field, and, consequently, in our bodies. The work of cleansing our minds and hearts of these disturbances, of learning to walk joyfully through the fire, as it were, is a critical prerequisite to being able to enter the depth of meditation and open the gates of superconsciousness.

The purpose of this book is to explore the different domains of emotional purification and to provide a practical guide to the process. Before we proceed further, let's clarify what we mean by *purification*. Rather than a rigid or judgmental approach to morality, purification for our purposes refers to cleansing or untangling the knots in our mental, emotional, and energetic fields, which obstruct our ability to enter deep meditative states. We'll begin this process by understanding the relationship between emotions and the mind's ability to meditate. This will take us next into the sources of our emotions in instinctive drives, or four primary fountains, as they were identified by ancient Yoga practitioners. Our ability to transform our relationship to the fountains—and in the process to transform ourselves—is well supported by recent work in neuroscience on the phenomenon of *neuroplasticity*. The ability of the brain to change in even dramatic ways throughout our lifetime, neuroplasticity provides a biological explanation for the central role of awareness in Yoga practice. Awareness, whether we experience it during our waking or sleeping hours, as well as a special sort of awareness, mindfulness, is what makes everything in Yoga work and is what takes us from our first efforts to the doorstep of enlightenment. This is the foundation of our work together and is the core content of Part I.

Part II discusses a range of methods for applying mindful awareness to our everyday lives and Yoga practices. The application of mindfulness to the practices of Yoga is *tapas*, usually defined as austerity or asceticism. We will examine tapas in the context of the fountains above using a slightly different and more practical approach than that usually suggested by the word *austerity,* thus paving the way for making Yoga practice our greatest enjoyment. (In fact, it is a seldom recognized fifth fountain—our drive towards psychological growth, integration, and joy—that supports our practice, compels us towards it, and makes us most human.) In this largest part of the book, we will focus our attention primarily on transforming our own mind/body, which includes our physical structure as well as our mental, emotional, and energetic fields.

We will take each of the first four *aṅga*s, or limbs, of the eight-limbed *Rāja-yoga* of Patañjali and demonstrate how we can cultivate awareness in each of them. Patañjali is the Indian scholar-sage, thought to have lived during the second century BCE, who codified Yoga into the most commonly consulted Yoga text, the *Yoga-sūtra*. A series of short sayings (*sūtra*s) that can be memorized to facilitate practice, the *Yoga-sūtra* provides directions for achieving enlightenment, including the cultivation of emotional awareness. The Yoga path described within the text, already centuries old at the time Patañjali systematized it, has become known as *Rāja* ("Royal") *Yoga*, in that it aims to achieve the highest possible goal: realization of the Self.

By caring for our emotions through Patañjali's *yama* (ethical restraint), *niyama* (personal discipline), *āsana* (posture), and *prāṇāyāma* (practices for control and expansion of subtle energy), we can gradually cleanse and pacify the body and sensory mind of emotional disturbances. This leads us to pause at Patañjali's fifth limb, *pratyāhāra*, the transition from the outer to the inner limbs of Yoga. In pratyāhāra, our senses become stilled of their own accord, enabling various stages of meditation to unfold and encouraging us to draw ever closer to conscious recognition of the Self. We touch on this fifth limb in Part II but largely set it aside, along with the remaining meditative limbs, because our work with the first four indirectly causes, or rather invites, the last four to develop.

Note that Patañjali named the limbs carefully and intentionally. These are not simply sequential stages. Rather, the body needs all its limbs at once, and all the aṅgas of Yoga apply at every level of practice. The depth of our meditations improves our ability to exercise yama; our understanding of yama enhances our meditations. Through āsana and prāṇāyāma, we clear the warps and knots in our subtle body that distract us in meditation; through meditation, our subtle body is purified, increasing our enjoyment the next time we practice āsana and prāṇāyāma. We're always cycling through all the limbs. Our work in one aṅga stabilizes and propels our work in the others.

Thus experiences of meditative clarity and stillness (themselves affected by all the other limbs) impel the mind to realize the eighth and final aṅga, *samādhi*. As above, these meditative experiences do not cause samādhi; rather, they establish the conditions for samādhi to appear. In this limb, ineffable joy—pure consciousness, the one great Self—merges into us, superseding the personality's limited sense of self. But we cannot will our way there; we must await enlightenment by grace. In the meantime, we do the work that is ours to do. We clear our path.

Following our introduction to pratyāhāra, then, we will discuss how to experiment very pragmatically with managing the relationship between our emotions and thoughts. Learning to have a dialogue with one's own mind, either internally or in journal form, can be very helpful in the process of stabilizing emotions and in deepening meditation. We will consider a Yoga-based technique resembling cognitive behavioral therapy (CBT), and we will discuss the conditions under which psychotherapy is recommended to advance the process of stabilization. Witnessing the struggles and triumphs of our fellow human beings and seeing something of ourselves in their stories can assist us in our own growth. We will sometimes explore case histories from my psychotherapy practice as well as from the Yoga mat. I have omitted or changed names to respect the privacy of the individuals involved.

As we conclude, we will explore mantra recitation and silence practice and discuss how you can know whether you are making progress in your efforts. This is Part III, which provides tools for working with the deeper layers of the mindfield, including that which is nonphysical and even nonpersonal. Part III contains a section on the attitudes called *brahma-vihāra*s, or, in Buddhism, the *four great treasures*, or the *four immeasurables*. The brahma-vihāras will develop naturally in your mind and personality as you progress on the path. You can also undertake these as practices to invite them to arise. Finally, we will explore the nature of a strong and resilient mindfield and how it can positively affect your personality, relationships, and Yoga journey.

You will find a glossary of Sanskrit terms for your reference, as well as many annotations of books and scientific research articles that have helped me in my personal Yoga practice and in writing this book. I hope you will enjoy them. These sources and this book provide a theoretical understanding of the value of Yoga. They tell us how Yoga can assist us in initiating and sustaining personal growth and change. But to paraphrase a Buddhist proverb, "The finger pointing to the moon is not the moon." Although there are contemplative Yoga practices, and reading about Yoga influences the mindfield to a certain extent, the real benefits of Yoga derive not from reading about it, but from practicing it. For this reason, I have included a series of exercises from my own teaching over the years and from my teachers' teachings. These are found in Appendix A and are divided into three sections: 1. *Relaxation and Subtle Body Exercises*, 2. *Exercises for Awareness of Nāḍī*s, *Cakra*s, *and the Transpersonal Mindfield*, and 3. *Journaling Exercises.* My hope is that *Clearing the Path* will inspire you to do just that: to take up or deepen your own practice of Yoga so that you can clear your mindfield and know the Ultimate Ground of Being that you are, that we all are.

It is always a bit risky to practice Yoga simply from books, even when those books represent an authentic lineage tradition, as this text aims to do. But even as much of Yoga's real value lies in practical details maintained in its oral rather than written tradition, there is much that we can learn from self-guided study. As you read, rather than attach yourself to this book's theories and concepts or even to your own way of doing the exercises, let the theories and practices lead you to the experiential state of Yoga, to your (our) own true Self. And, if you are so inspired, consider initiating or strengthening your relationship with an authentic teaching lineage, as feedback from a teacher can be an invaluable tool in helping you to avoid pitfalls and to further personalize your Yoga practices, like the ones contained in these pages. May this material shed some light on your struggles with *sādhanā,* your personal spiritual practice, and help you to find a way out from wherever you may feel caught! May your wounds become your way into the clear light!

Swāmī Rāma Sādhaka Grāma
Rishikesh, India
Mahāśivarātrī, 10 March 2013

PART I

The Yoga View of Mind Is Increasingly the Neuroscience View of Mind

Chapter One

The Mind According to Yoga: Emotions, Mindfulness, and the Mind/Body

To engage the project of clearing our spiritual path of mental and emotional disturbances, we must first understand what we mean by *mind, mindfulness,* and *emotion.* Whereas we can discern some similarities across spiritual and secular definitions of mindfulness, scientifically mind and emotion have eluded precise and widely shared definitions for a very long time, even if we have some common-sense notions of what each of them means. The explanations in the Yoga system of thought and practice are clearer but have not always been translatable into the domain of scientific inquiry. At this moment in our history, however, changes in the field of neuroscience and the recognition of the therapeutic value of Yoga practice have made it much easier for the Yogi to approach the scientist in a friendly dialogue, and it is becoming increasingly clear that each can help the other understand these concepts in a much more holistic and complementary way.

The neuroscientist can explain many of the details of how the mind/body relationship works, and the Yogi can guide the scientist towards the intangible depths where experimental science has had difficulty following. What's more, explanations and insights from neuroscience, coupled with the tools and perspective of modern psychotherapy, can infuse Yoga practice and philosophy with relatable, practical information that makes sense to a contemporary Western mind. This blending of disciplines reveals their common ground and resembles the way in which spiritual practices across traditions share certain similarities, from prescribed outer conduct and inner attitudes to sometimes identical descriptions of various states of consciousness, which we can attain through mindfulness. Acknowledging these can help Yoga practitioners to reframe, refresh, and deepen our own practice of Yoga. Practice leads us ultimately to full psychological integration, whether we're using Yoga vocabulary to describe that integration (samādhi) or the language of neuroscience. So one might think of this book as an effort to bring Pātañjala Yoga together with contemporary neuroscience and modern psychotherapy in an introductory way, one that helps us understand how the systematic practice of Yoga constitutes a practical, holistic, and scientific approach to optimum mental and emotional health—and beyond.

The Mind/Body

Scientific work in the past several decades has made it clear that the old distinction in Western thinking between mind and body is obsolete and an obstacle to a clear understanding of their relationship. In psychology we now often speak of mind/body or body/mind.[2] California neuropsychiatrist Daniel Siegel, MD, in his 2010 book *Mindsight* makes the point that a generally agreeable scientific definition of mind has not existed until quite recently. He composed one in 1992 at the University of California, Los Angeles, where he is a professor of clinical psychiatry at the UCLA School of Medicine. In collaboration with an interdisciplinary panel of researchers from the sciences and other fields of study, he arrived at the following: "The human mind is a relational and embodied process that regulates the flow of energy and information" (Siegel, 2010, p. 52). This everyone could agree upon. (It's interesting that their definition of mind requires a body, and it requires relationships. We'll return to these ideas later.) So we may think of the physical

[2] In this book, we will generally use the term *mind/body* except where we are discussing the operations of the mind/body that are wholly within the nonpersonal or nonphysical part of this complementarity. In those cases, we will use the term *mindfield.*

body as the most concrete part of the mind. Yogis would say that the mind is the cause of the body, not the other way around. Increasingly, neurobiologists are beginning to say the same thing. But before we explore the neurobiology of mental function and how it parallels the observations of Yoga (the principal subject of Chapter 2), let's explore the Yoga view of mind in some detail.

The view of the Yoga system, articulated often by Swami Rama (2002), is this: "All of the body is in the mind, but all of the mind is not in the body" (p. 58). In Yoga, the mind contains the body but is not limited to it. Additionally, body and mind are not distinct. They

Table 1.1

Correlation Between Vedānta's Mind/Body Sheaths and Siegel's (2010) Definition of Mind

Mind/Body Sheath *(Koṣa)*	**Translation**	**Correlation to Siegel's (2010) Definition of Mind**[a]
Anna-maya-koṣa	the lowest and grossest mind/body sheath made of food	"…embodied process…"
Prāṇa-maya-koṣa	the mind/body sheath made of subtle energy	"…regulates the flow of energy…"
Mano-maya-koṣa	the mind/body sheath made of sensory mentation	"…and information"
Vijñāna-maya-koṣa	the mind/body sheath made of higher mentation (*buddhi,* intuition)	"relational and embodied process that regulates the flow of energy and information"
Ānanda-maya-koṣa	the highest and subtlest mind/body sheath made of reduced bliss[b]	n/a

[a] Siegel's (2010) interdisciplinary definition of mind is a "relational and embodied process that regulates the flow of energy and information" (p. 52). [b] The bliss of the ānanda-maya-koṣa is not the ultimate bliss of *Brahman,* the Vedāntin term for the Ultimate Reality, but is a reduction of that bliss. From the experience of embodied life, a practitioner can mistake this sheath for the Ultimate even though it is not.

exist on a continuum from gross to subtle. The physical body, or *anna-maya-koṣa,* literally the sheath or layer of our being made of food, is the grossest, most material level of the mind/body. There are also other levels according to Vedānta philosophy,[3] five in total, each subtler than the previous one (see Table 1.1). The first four are contained within Siegel's (2010) definition of mind, while the fifth lies beyond it.

To be clear, Siegel (2010) and his colleagues were not defining the mind/body in terms of Yoga or Vedānta, and the "energy" to which they refer is likely kinetic, rather than *prāṇik* (subtle life force energy, similar to Chinese *qi*). Still, it is interesting that Siegel describes four of the five sheaths of the Vedānta schema of mind/body, with only the subtlest layer yet to be identified. If we accept this definition with the term *energy* left open to both possibilities, then the two systems operate very much in harmony. And yet a primary difference remains: In the West, we are accustomed to collapsing any distinction between mind and consciousness so that we think of mind as consciousness in action. The Yoga view is quite the opposite. In the Yoga system, the mind is considered entirely material, having no consciousness of its own. It has the appearance of consciousness because the light of pure consciousness from the spiritual Self, *ātman* or *puruṣa,* shines into the mind through *buddhi,* our discriminative intelligence and decisive faculty. We only experience consciousness itself in the superconscious states of the deepest meditation (samādhi). When we are "yoked" to this state, we experience what Yoga (from the Sanskrit root √*yuj*, "join, yoke") really is.

Functions of the Mind/Body

The Yoga system distinguishes several different functions of mind/body, each reflecting consciousness without actually being

---

[3] Most Yoga teachers use the Vedānta schema of mind/body because it is more detailed than the threefold mind/body of Sāṃkhya-yoga: gross (physical) body (*sthūla-śarīra*), subtle (energy and lower mental) body (*sūkṣma-śarīra*), and causal body (*kāraṇa-śarīra*).

conscious. These also operate at different levels, which we can understand in concert with the sheaths discussed above (although at the higher levels the correspondences are not exact).

Manas. The grossest level of mental function is called *manas,* sensory and disputative mind; it occurs within the mano-maya-koṣa. This part of our mind/body continually gathers information through our cognitive senses (sight, hearing, taste, touch, and smell) and sends out impulses to act through our active senses in the anna-maya-koṣa (action in the hands, locomotion in the feet, speech in the tongue, reproduction in the genitals, and elimination in the anus). Note the parallels between function and bodily organs here; remember that in Yoga, the body is the densest part of the mind. Manas is also the disputative part of the mind/body, gathering information about and raising arguments on both sides of an issue. How many times have you found yourself unable to make a decision because your attention is mired in agitated, back-and-forth arguments and information in manas?! Manas has no ability to decide.

Ahaṁkāra. Literally the "I-maker," *ahaṁkāra* is the part of our mind/body that (falsely) identifies the consciousness of the spiritual Self with thoughts and external objects. This difficulty arises in part because ahaṁkāra does so much for us, governing four of the five koṣas from part of vijñāna-maya downwards through anna-maya. (Vijñāna-maya is partially transpersonal and partially personal; ahaṁkāra manages the personal "I.") As our I-maker, ahaṁkāra helps to maintain the functional integrity of our mind/body system and its participation in relationships, overseeing everything from our physical and subtle bodies to our senses, emotions, thoughts, and intuitions.

Although ahaṁkāra appears to be "in charge" of a lot, I like to refer to it in one way as the inner two-year-old because it actually functions quite similarly. A two-year-old person is in the process of forming a sense of psychological self by creating boundaries between him- or herself and the rest of the universe. One of the best ways to do this is for the child to say, "NO!!" To a two-year-old, "no" means "not-me," "not mine," and by saying this, he or she is also defining what is "me" and "mine." That's why two-year-olds often say "no" even when they mean "yes." The developmental drive of this age is very strong; it has to be for the child to form a sense of a distinct psychological self. However, we do not remain two years old forever, and ahaṁkāra's tendency to be overly concerned with its own identity eventually becomes developmentally inappropriate, an obstacle on our Yoga path.

The problem in spiritual practice is that, like the two-year-old, ahaṁkāra thinks of its roles as "Me" and "Mine"—the Self—when in truth the Self is none of this. Another metaphor illustrates this point. Ahaṁkāra often gets the idea that it is the chief executive officer—the spiritual Self, or ātman, the CEO—rather than just the general manager of the mind/body. So long as it is always aware of its true status, ahaṁkāra is a valuable function. My guru, Swāmī Rāma, had a very strong ahaṁkāra. He needed it to deal with running international organizations, managing large amounts of contributions, and dealing with the downsides and difficulties of his legions of disciples and students. But the moment that he needed to surrender his ahaṁkāra, he would remember his personal guru who represents the entire Guru lineage[4] and through whom any power flows. He would become like a young boy and would say, "I do nothing; my master does everything." The measure of one's humility lies not in a lack of strength in ahaṁkāra, but in how quickly and how completely one can surrender it when appropriate.

Sometimes people equate ahaṁkāra with ego as understood by modern psychology. This equation is only partially correct. The notion of ahaṁkāra goes well beyond the ego. For example, one must have an ahaṁkāra to have a body. This is one reason the common advice in some spiritual guidance to kill off, starve, dry up, or otherwise get rid of ahaṁkāra is ill conceived. To do so would be

[4] The Guru lineage includes all Self-realized beings from the primordial Guru (God, Spirit, Brahman, YHWH, Allah, I AM, or any other name for the Almighty) to masters (gurus) like the Buddha and Christ. The Christian notion of the Holy Spirit is a general equivalent.

to do violence to your mind/body, and you owe yourself the same gift of nonviolence that you would so readily offer to other creatures. It is a question of keeping one's ahaṁkāra in proportion, in balance, and in its proper role so that the mind/body can do its work skillfully and lovingly.

Buddhi. The subtlest and purest function of mind/body is buddhi, included partially within vijñāna-maya-koṣa and partially in the ānanda-maya-koṣa. It is the function that observes with awareness, discriminates, decides among options, creates intention *(saṁkalpa),* and receives intuition. It is roughly equivalent to the practice of mindfulness, to which we will return later in this chapter. Buddhi is like a two-way mirror. As mentioned above, the light of the spiritual Self shines into the mind through buddhi, giving the mind/body the appearance of consciousness. Meanwhile the operations of the mind all reflect in buddhi so that the spiritual Self, ātman or puruṣa, can witness and enjoy them. Most of our so-called "spiritual experience" in meditation up to the point of samādhi actually occurs in buddhi. These experiences are there for us just to observe, without a label of "mine." Until we reach samādhi, the experiences are not yet of pure consciousness.

Yet buddhi is an important intermediary. According to Yoga, the physical body receives its support from the prāṇa-maya-koṣa, which in turn is supported by the other koṣas, all of which the Self (ātman, puruṣa) intends into existence. Yet the Self is consciousness only, without action. In Kashmir Śaiva philosophy, which perceives reality as nondual, "not two," the personified deity Śiva represents the Self as the principle of pure consciousness and the first Guru. His feminine counterpart is Śakti, the Self's power to veil Itself in the form of the world and to manifest the universe. Śiva and Śakti are totally equivalent, yet only Śakti, *prakṛti,* acts; *kriyā-śakti* (action) is one of Her powers. Because prakṛti includes the manifest and unmanifest natural universe, we are part of Her, and through Her, the Self. It is important to remember that although we (as our

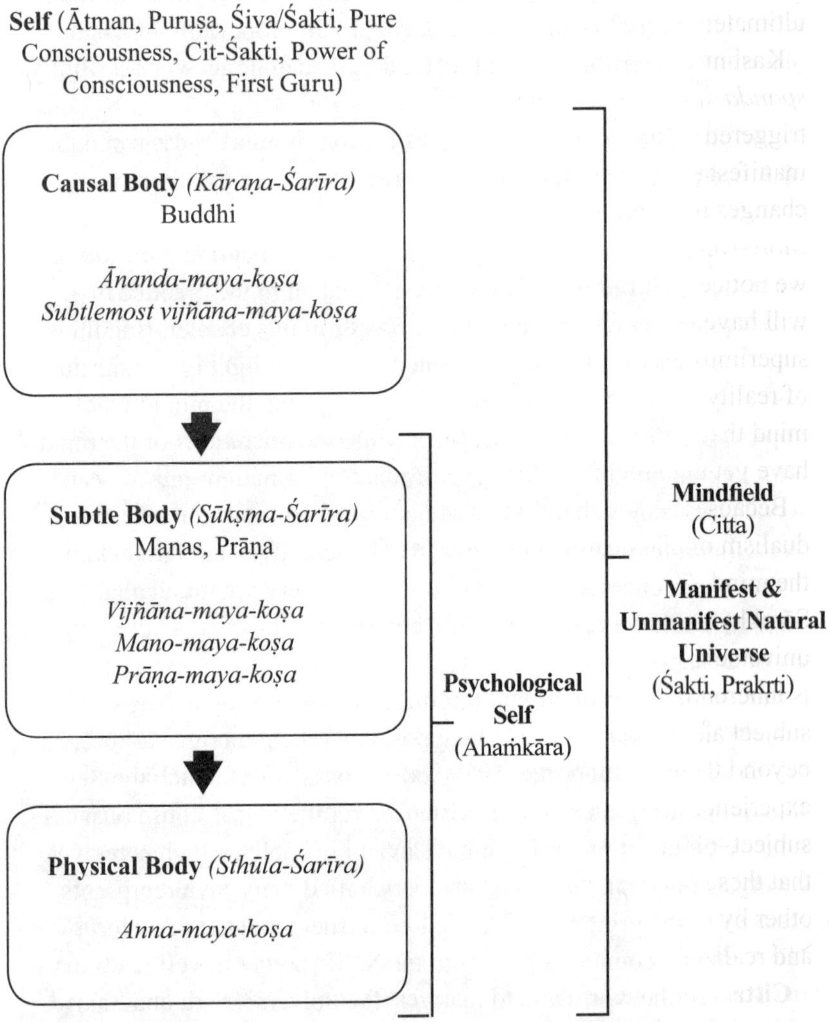

Figure 1.1. Dualist and Nondualist Views of Reality: The Sāṃkhya-Yoga Śarīras, Vedānta Koṣas, and Kashmir Śaivism

psychological selves) are the ones who undertake the various Yoga practices described in this book, it is the Self, through buddhi, who ultimately inspires our work.

Kashmir Śaivism would say that when we act, it is because *spanda,* a spontaneous pulsation of consciousness, has occurred and triggered an intuitive insight in buddhi, which then moves towards manifestation of energy and matter into form. The Self inspires the changes that buddhi then creates in our individual mind/bodies. Moreover, because pure consciousness devolves into matter, when we notice a change in our anna-maya-koṣa, all our other koṣas will have been affected. Figure 1.1 describes this relationship. It superimposes the nondual Vedānta and Kashmir Śaiva perspectives of reality with the dualist Sāṃkhya-yoga view and the functions of mind that we have discussed thus far. It also includes *citta,* which we have yet to explore.

Because the Vedānta system and Kashmir Śaivism collapse the dualism of classical Sāṃkhya-yoga to describe reality from beyond the mind, the material presented in Figure 1.1 is paradoxical. Sāṃkhya-yoga is dualistic in outlook because it describes the universe through the experience of the mind. (The domain of mind is inherently dualistic, due to the distinction it perceives between subject and object.) Kashmir Śaivism and Vedānta, however, move beyond the dualism of mind: beyond senses, language, thought, or experience. They offer the contemplative skills to harmonize the subject–object dichotomy and transcend it. In this way, we can say that these philosophies collaborate (rather than compete) with each other by offering a perspective from different levels of experience and realization. We will refer to each system throughout this text.

Citta. *Citta* can be defined in several ways. Manas, ahaṁkāra, and buddhi are functional descriptions. *Citta* is often used in this functional sense also to denote the personal unconscious, where the impressions of our experiences are stored in the form of *saṁskāra*s, or subtle *karmik* impressions with which we self-identify. These are impressions of each thought, feeling, or action that we have. They become the seeds of our future mental action *(vṛtti)*. We experience this mental action as a sort of emotional momentum at every moment that prompts us to act in a certain way. Through buddhi, we can choose to follow this momentum or perhaps do something different. This concisely describes the scope of human free will and is the central process in both the Yoga theory of *karma* and the neuroscience view that we can use our mind/body to gradually change our brain, ideas to which we will return.

Citta not only stores our personal karma but also houses the stories of all sentient beings. The great twentieth-century psychologist Carl Jung (1875–1961) observed that there appeared to be a part of most people's unconscious mind that they shared, even across time and cultures (Campbell, 1971, pp. 59–69). Jung noticed that all people seemed to incorporate symbols and certain energetic thought forms (archetypes) into their thought processes and especially into their dreams. This led him to the notion of a collective unconscious, the first intuition in modern psychology towards knowing citta in a much larger sense as the very substance of the mindfield, not only the personal mindfield but also the single great mindfield in which all the universes within universes (prakṛti) exist. Thus citta both lies beyond our personal mind/body and yet also envelops it, underlying all the koṣas without being limited to them. It is often described as an ocean in which some waves have formed and folded over on themselves temporarily, causing the waves, or parts of the mindfield within the ocean, to experience themselves as individual minds. The Śaiva and Vedānta philosophies would say that this is the veiling power of divinity, divine consciousness hiding from Itself. The experience of meditation eventually takes us beneath the surface of this ocean into the transpersonal depths of the universal mindfield, until finally divinity again "yokes" to Itself, and all that remains is samādhi.

Patañjali and the Mind/Body

Yoga's broad and all-encompassing definition of mind brings us to the work of Patañjali, who in about the second century BCE compiled into the *Yoga-sūtra* the system of Yoga practice that was already many centuries old by his time. The most authoritative commentator on these aphorisms was Vyāsa, who lived about 700 years later.

In the Yoga tradition, the *Yoga-sūtra* is usually read with Vyāsa's commentary as a single text. Vyāsa opens his commentary on the first sūtra by explaining that "Yoga is samādhi," the deep meditative state in which we experience pure consciousness. He goes on to say that this superconscious state is inherent within all our states of mind. In other words, we are actually in samādhi now, but we don't recognize it because the disturbances in our (individual) mindfields obscure it. He then describes five different levels *(bhūmis)* of disturbance, each one characterized by increasing clarity and pacification:

- *Mūḍham:* stupefied. This is a mindfield that cannot interpret the world around it accurately because of confusion, delusion, delirium, hallucination, or intoxication. It is a mindfield out of touch with "reality" as other people experience it.
- *Kṣiptam:* literally "tossed about," distracted. This is a mindfield whose attention is so scattered that it cannot settle down or concentrate at all. But this mindfield does interpret the world around it as others do.
- *Vi-kṣiptam:* less distracted. Here the mindfield, still distracted much of the time, begins to have some moments of concentration and meditation. This describes the majority of Yoga students.
- *Ekāgram:* "one-pointed." This mindfield has attained a one-pointed focus that allows it to move through the process of meditation and into the lower stages of samādhi: the samādhi with wisdom, or *saṁprajñāta.*
- *Niruddham:* "attenuated." This mindfield has ceased to function altogether, meeting the definition of Yoga, *Yogaś citta-vṛtti-*

> *nirodhaḥ,* "Yoga is the cessation of activities of the mindfield" (YS I.2). The aspirant has come to the final a-cognitive, or *a-saṁprajñāta,* samādhi. In the Vedānta and Tantra systems, this state is also called *a-mānasaka* Yoga: Yoga without, or beyond, mind. When it becomes the permanent state of a Yogi, he or she is liberated.

The process of Yoga, then, is to gradually reduce the level of disturbance in the mindfield so that the pure light of the spiritual Self (ātman) can shine through the mindfield undistorted, and eventually the light can shine "in its own nature" (YS I.3). In Yoga we use the mind/body as the means to deconstruct the mindfield so that it no longer obscures the light. Mind (including the body) is both the problem and the means to the solution!

The technical term in Yoga for this gradual process of mental purification and clarification is *citta-prasādana.* The word *prasādana* is from the Sanskrit verb root √*sad,* "settle, sit." The prefix *pra-* (same as the Latin *pro-*) means "forceful" and "complete." So a mind that is prasādana is one in which all its disturbances and impurities have settled out completely, like dirt settling out of a container of muddy water over time so that the water becomes clear and pleasant. Citta-prasādana means making the mind clear and pleasant, capable of stability and concentration. The same word, *prasāda,* also means "grace" because grace is that which settles down from above, from a higher state of being. So a clear and pleasant mind is also a mind that can receive and eventually transmit grace. Yoga refers to this process as *citta-śuddhi*, mental purification, or *citta-śānta,* mental pacification. Without this clarification and pacification of the mindfield, there can be no spiritual progress towards Yoga, whether we speak of Yoga as the final goal or any of its limbs leading up to the goal.

The mental disturbances. In sūtras I.30 and I.31, Patañjali and Vyāsa name the mental disturbances that hinder our progress towards Yoga. In YS I.30, they are called *citta-vi-kṣepa,* or mental distractions, the things that make the mindfield kṣiptam (tossed) or vi-kṣiptam (less tossed) (Arya, 1986, pp. 324–328). In the second chapter (YS II.3), they are called *kleśa,* or "afflicted," painful activities of the mindfield. Both terms refer to the same thing with a slightly different connotation (Bhāratī, 2001, pp. 30–35). *Kṣiptam* and *vi-kṣepa* connote disturbance; *kleśa* connotes affliction, pain. They summarize the suffering of the mind. In Chapter 2 of the *Yoga-sūtra,* the word *citta-prasādana* describes the thinning down of these painful mental operations (*kleśa-tanu-karaṇa,* "making the afflictions thin," YS II.2).

Sūtra I.30 lists the mental distractions (citta-vi-kṣepa) that prevent us from reaching samādhi:

- *vyādhi:* "illness," due to imbalances in the body;
- *styāna:* mental laziness, procrastination;
- *saṁśaya:* doubt;
- *pramāda:* negligence in cultivating the means to samādhi;
- *ālasya:* laziness, sloth due to inertia and heaviness in mind and body;
- *avirati:* not turning away from expending mental energy in outward sensuality;
- *bhrānti-darśana:* wrong views, confusion in one's philosophical map of Yoga practice;
- *alabdha-bhūmikatva:* failure to achieve a level (bhūmi) of realization in one's practice, especially samādhi; and
- *anavasthitva:* instability, inability to maintain a level of accomplishment that one has attained.

These might sound harsh, but Patañjali does not mince words. He calls a spade a *spade* and uses only one word to do so. Remember that he refers to the above as disturbances. They are not attributes of people, but just behaviors that need to be gradually changed.

Sūtra I.31 lists the *antarāya*s (conditions, illnesses, if you will) that result from the above disturbances:

- *duḥkha:* pain, physical and mental;
- *daurmanasya:* "bad mindedness," anger, anxiety, depression;
- *aṅgamejayatva:* physical and mental instability, literally, "trembling of the limbs";
- *śvāsa:* inhalation; and
- *pra-śvāsa:* exhalation.

We are likely familiar with some or most of these from our experience of difficulties in meditation. We know, for example, that if we are ill or physically or emotionally unstable, we will experience pain or perhaps a negative impact on our mood, or we will become restless in our meditation, and our breath will be disturbed.

It is very interesting here that inhalation and exhalation, which we usually think of as normal activities and part of the sustenance of life, are considered illnesses! If we look further on in the *Yoga-sūtra,* in the section on prāṇāyāma (subtle energy practices, including breathing exercises), Patañjali uses different terminology for exhalation and inhalation: *bāhya* (external, YS II.50), meaning exhalation, or *recaka,* and *abhyantara* (internal, YS II.50), meaning inhalation, or *pūraka.* We also find the terms *pūraka* and *recaka* used in the *haṭha-yoga*[5] texts 1000–1500 years later. Patañjali makes the point that there is a difference between ordinary breath subject to mental disturbances (pra-śvāsa, śvāsa) and breath in prāṇāyāma (bāhya, abhyantara): When we practice Yoga breathing exercises, or prāṇāyāma, we breathe consciously, with mindful awareness. This kind of focused attention is what makes all the difference in all the practices of Yoga and, more generally, in our thoughts, emotions, and behavior in our everyday lives.

[5] The term *haṭha-yoga* is often associated primarily with the physical practices of āsana and prāṇāyāma, though it actually refers to the effort to merge the opposite solar (*ha-*) and lunar (*-ṭha*) aspects of the subtle body. In meditation, this opens the *suṣumnā* channel (see Chapter 7) so that the practitioner can enter the deeper states and attain the final goal of haṭha-yoga, samādhi.

Emotion

We have covered how Yoga as a philosophical system classifies painful distortions of the light of consciousness in our mind/bodies, preventing us from entering the deeper states of meditation. But how do the distortions get there? The easy answer is that our emotions warp the "flow[s] of energy and information" that constitute the mind (Siegel, 2010, p. 52). Each emotion creates a "kink" or a "sticking point" in our mind/body that distorts the flow of pure consciousness from the Self.

The harder question to answer is this: "What is an emotion?" Just as Siegel (2010) describes the challenges of arriving at a scientific definition of mind, we see that the same problem applies to emotion. It is an elusive concept about which there is very little scientific agreement. This book proposes a theory of emotion that has four components: sensation, cognition, motivation, and saṁskāra (subtle impressions of habitual emotional momentum).

Sensation in Emotion

We might be tempted at first to say that emotions are feelings. But much that we feel isn't really an emotion. We may feel hot or cold or numb. We may feel nauseated or excited. While these may be related to emotion, they are not really emotions per se, at least not entirely. They are the body's physiological response to the environment or to the mind's thoughts. Together, our thoughts and sensations make every emotion a mind/body phenomenon. We can work with our body's sensations to pacify our emotions in two primary ways:
1. Our sensations can alert us to strong emotions, enabling us to become aware of how our emotional state might influence our behavior for better or worse. With awareness comes the choice to reframe our thinking and our actions. 2. The bodily sensations that accompany our strong emotions can remain outside of our awareness, even when we are very much aware of the emotions themselves. For example, we can know that we're angry without noticing the heat and tension that arise in our body. We might recognize that we're

nervous without being particularly aware of how short our breath has become. When these are the case, we can make an intention to watch what is happening in our body, to feel into what is going on. The act of paying attention shifts our awareness away from thoughts that might be fueling a strong emotion. Attending to our body also enables us to relax our emotion's physical components. When we can do this, the mind will often relax as well.

Cognition in Emotion

This is the domain of cognitive-behavioral psychotherapists, who work with people on changing the thought processes that modify and channel emotional energy. As above, this does not entirely define emotion but is only one facet of it. Additionally, there are many cognitions that we would not call emotions. Chapter 8 will explore this component of emotion in depth.

Motivation in Emotion

Emotion also has a quality of "motion." It implies motivation, a mental movement towards a goal. Thus it is useful to view emotions through the lens of our instinctive drives. These are our primary motivations in life, and they are important sources of energy for our embodied life: food, sleep, sex, and self-preservation. Swami Rama (1989) referred to these as the four "primitive fountains" (pp. 54–66). Many people feel that calling them primitive makes them sound bad in some way, something to be gotten rid of, which is a false assumption. Nevertheless, we will instead call them *primary fountains* since they are necessary to life, even if they also present us with some obstacles and challenges to our spiritual growth.

In the Yoga tradition, for example in *The Laws of Manu* (Bühler, 1886/1969), the primary fountains (although not named as such) are described as the basic desires that we share with all animal life. In the early days of psychoanalysis, Sigmund Freud (1856–1939) theorized in his own way about these drives, calling them collectively *libido*

(Dickson, 1991). He tended to consider libido primarily within the context of sexuality, but each of the primary fountains is actually an aspect of the libidinal energy that sustains our embodied lives. We try to stay alive (self-preservation) because we harbor the thought, "May I never cease to be." If we don't have food or water, our bodies begin to die after about two weeks. Without sleep, we begin to become psychotic generally within about 72 hours. We can live without sex, but its mental nature and the press for the continuation of the species do not make this easy or comfortable. All these drives are legitimate human needs. If we get too little of them, we begin to wither. If we overdo them, we risk illness or addiction.

The task for us in the first place is to have a balanced relationship with these drives so that we maintain our health and don't create obstacles for our spiritual growth. My recovering alcoholic and sexually addicted clients often tell me that for them, their addictions were their spirituality calling to them through the back door, as it were. Most addictions at their root are spiritual problems, no matter how biologically involved they may be.

Addictions, and our emotions in general, painful as well as pleasant, are usually driven in part by the intrinsic, instinctive motivations in life. When one of these basic desires (primary fountains: food, sleep, sex, or self-preservation) is frustrated, we ourselves often become frustrated and angry *(krodha)*. When a basic desire is satisfied, we feel pleasure, and our mind wants to move towards it; this is "e-motion" of the mind towards a desire *(kāma)*. Kāma is considered one of the legitimate aims of life because it is often where people begin on the spiritual path. The release we experience from our limited self at the height of sexual experience, for example, often clues us in to the greater Being that we are. People also awaken to their spirituality from the pursuit of any of the four primary fountains. They realize that a balanced relationship to the fountains stabilizes the mindfield, and no fountain itself provides lasting fulfillment. This we can only attain through experiencing our nature as Self.

Kāma, however, moves us away from these insights (and in a roundabout way back towards them) when we become attached, even addicted, to the pleasure of desire, identifying with that pleasure through our ego (ahaṁkāra). This may lead us to experience pride *(mada)* and to compare ourselves favorably to others. We may identify with our desire to such a degree that we believe the object of our desire belongs to the self ("mine") and is of the Self ("Mine"). This kind of misidentification of the Self with our desires is delusion *(moha)*. Finally, we may seek to maximize our possession of whatever we identify with (money, beauty, status, collections, etc.), and the e-motion of our mind/body turns to greed *(lobha)*. Of course, all this suffering will eventually lead us to realize how to avoid it, namely by having a balanced relationship to the fountains. This will in turn allow the mind to stabilize and to enter deep meditative states. So eventually we will come to know the Self, however painful the route may be.

The suffering of addiction, by pointing to what does not work, can eventually wake us up to what does, to the path towards freedom. This is the back door through which we might "pass" towards our spirituality. In another sense, though, all of it is already our spirituality because all of it is part of our path. We are always the Self, always in samādhi; we just don't know it. And even the suffering energy can help us come to know. This is a very classical explanation of painful emotions according to the Yoga system and is by no means exhaustive.

The twelve-step addiction recovery culture has a common-sense formula for identifying the connection between emotions born of the primary fountains, the impulse to addiction, and how these reflect our spiritual needs. It is referred to by the acronym HALT and happens to match the fountains exactly: hungry (food), angry (any of the above desires frustrated), lonely (sex, self-preservation), and tired (sleep). People tend to use their addictions to try to meet deeper spiritual needs when one or more of these conditions is present.

Human beings can find many ways to experience pain. If an object of our desire is lost, for example, we experience grief. If we lose contact with our deeper mind and spiritual Self, we often feel shame, a pervasive sense that we are hopelessly flawed and can never be made whole (and holy). If we become deeply deluded regarding our attachment to an object of desire, we may not only begin to hanker after the object that someone else possesses and become obsessed with our desire for it (envy), but we may also begin to believe that the object rightfully belongs to us (jealousy)!

All these manifestations of emotional pain can be traced back to our relationship with the four fountains. The key word here is *relationship*. It is a useful contemplative exercise to look at our pain in life through this lens to understand where it is coming from. What deeper spiritual need is motivating our desire as it arises? How can we relate to the desire skillfully to fulfill the spiritual need? For example, you feel an impulse to overeat. When you mindfully ask yourself what you feel (HALT?), you notice that you are actually tired and lonely. Then you have the choice to meet the real needs of your mind/body and get some rest and connect with a friend or a family member. If you choose instead to follow the impulse to overeat, then your needs don't get met, and afterwards you feel ashamed and even more lost.

We may not directly control the circumstances of our lives or our basic human condition as described by the primary fountains, but how we relate to these factors does make a difference in whether and how much we suffer. Even in the case of addiction, the saying applies, *Pain is inevitable; suffering is a choice*. We always have the choice to use our awareness (buddhi), perhaps with the help of therapy and/or medication, to reduce our dependence on the fountains and thereby reduce our suffering. We will return to this subject in our discussion of mindfulness below and in Chapters 3 and 4. Chapter 9 explores when working with a therapist may be helpful on our path.

Saṁskāra in Emotion

There is one final component of emotion: saṁskāra. These are the subtle mental impressions created in our mindfield (citta) by each of our thoughts, feelings, motivations, and actions. They exist in citta as seeds of our future action. When the time arises for these seeds to bear their fruit, they arise in the mindfield as a wave (vṛtti) of emotional momentum towards a certain action. Most often we simply act out these emotional momenta without awareness, creating another very similar seed of future action. In this way, we usually just recycle our saṁskāras, creating and reinforcing our emotional habit patterns and conditioning. If we remain intentionally, mindfully aware of this process unfolding in us, we have a chance to consider whether the incipient action is skillful in our current situation. This gives us a choice to do something different. Also, because we are aware of this process from the level of buddhi (rather than from ahaṁkāra), our self-identification with the impulse to action dissolves. It loses its momentum. We will discuss this aspect of emotional purification further in Chapter 5.

Mindfulness

The foundation of emotional purification, which allows us to transform our emotional conditioning (saṁskāras), is mindfulness. As we practice mindfulness, synonymous in Yoga with awareness, we clear our spiritual path. All the Yoga practices that Patañjali identifies (many of which we'll explore in this book) help us, through awareness, to create the space in which we glimpse and then fully know the Self.

Mindfulness Is the Awareness of Buddhi

Neurologically, we might describe awareness as focused, directed attention (the focus and direction may be conscious or unconscious) mediated through the activity of the middle prefrontal cortex of the brain. In truth, however, awareness also goes well beyond this neurophysiological process. Awareness is part of buddhi. It is the subtlest, purest aspect of mind, the part of our mind/body that is closest to our spiritual Self. All the other functions of buddhi—discrimination *(viveka)*, decision making and intention creating *(saṁkalpa)*, intuiting—are grosser functions than awareness. They exist at grosser levels of buddhi. Awareness exists at the interface between pure spirit and the material mind at its purest. Even when the rest of the mind is withdrawn, dissolved in its deepest, dreamless sleep, buddhi continues to observe the mind/body sleeping. It remains awake within the sleeping person. How do we know this? When you awaken, you always know whether you slept well or not! (See Vyāsa's commentary on YS I.10, Arya, 1986, p. 178.) Many of us have had the experience of our buddhi awakening us from deep sleep when there is, for example, an emergency or a baby crying or a phone call we must answer.

In the processes of both meditation and conscious, deep sleep *(yoga-nidrā)*, as well as when we are falling asleep, we seek to gradually relax the functions of the mind/body from the gross body and sensory mind up to the subtler I-maker (ahaṁkāra) and remain in a state where the active mind (manas) dissolves and essentially disappears. (Remember that in the Sāṃkhya and Yoga philosophies, the subtler aspects of matter are the source and origin of the grosser. Buddhi devolves into ahaṁkāra, which devolves into manas, elements, and cognitive senses. Meditation works this process of emanation backwards.) When we meditate, our personal sense of self moves into the background and disappears. Yet awareness remains! In the deepest state of yoga-nidrā, there is no thinking; we have only the awareness of pure being, awareness of the sensation of breath, and buddhi watches both the mind and the body sleeping. One might think this would be boring, but who ever got bored watching a baby sleep? Awareness comes from this innocent depth at the interface between the spirit (ātman) and the material mind.

In contemporary American usage, we can now recognize the word *mindfulness* as referring especially to the observing function of buddhi. As it has found its way into modern psychology and psychiatry, *mindfulness* has become a neutral term for both awareness and meditation that avoids the cultural and religious associations to which some people might object. Today's secular approaches follow the lead of many cultures, not only "major" but also indigenous, whose meditative practices have generally begun from the mindful observation of the breath. In Yoga and in Buddhism, breath awareness is synonymous with mindfulness, *smṛti-upasthāna* in Yoga, "the establishment of mindfulness," or *sati-paṭṭhāna* in the Buddhist traditions in the Pāli language.

Mindfulness Begins with Breath Awareness

Why this emphasis on breath? As a species, we are driven to promote and protect bodily life, and so we find ways to relax, often instinctively, by relying on our breath. (We are all familiar with the common folk wisdom to "take a deep breath" when feeling agitated or provoked.) Our ancestors faced quite a lot of stress just to stay alive. Because stress took its toll on the mind/body, peoples across time and continents developed ways to promote rest, rejuvenation, and cellular repair. As we'll discuss in Chapter 2, the keys to this healing repose are repetition and focus. What more repetitive activity exists than the constant inspiration and expiration of breath? This specific activity has been available to each of us, always, regardless of the relative scarcity or abundance of other resources. (Indeed, we have all, always, relied on it for our very lives.) As long as we are living embodied life, our breath is with us, so it is a useful, familiar, and ever-available object on which to place our concentration.

We also focus on our breath to respond to the call of our innate spirituality. In Yoga, we grow towards our fullest potential by learning to yoke mindful awareness to our every thought, feeling, and action so that we might make the most constructive and life-affirming choices, ultimately to purify our koṣas and prepare ourselves for superconsciousness. If we are to notice specific occurrences within a wide range of cognitive and behavioral possibilities, we must first calm the mind to attune ourselves to each mental activity as it arises—no easy task. So we begin with a simpler instruction: We intentionally focus on our breath. As the mind tethers itself to our breathing, both mind and breath slow down. When the usual background chatter of manas quiets somewhat, buddhi becomes more available to recognize manas's activities and habits, underscored by a backdrop of clarity not typically known to the mind. Manas's activities are then more easily identified in the moments when they take form as thoughts, feelings, or behaviors. Mindfulness thus often begins with breath awareness as the easiest and most natural starting point from which we can expand our attention into other arcas.

Mindfulness Is a State/Mindfulness Is a Practice

We've identified the breath as a common focus of mindful attention, indicated that mindfulness often expands beyond the breath, and defined mindfulness as the awareness of buddhi. But how exactly do we initiate and maintain mindful awareness? To answer this, let's explore the often-cited definition of mindfulness articulated by Jon Kabat-Zinn, PhD, professor of medicine emeritus and creator of the Stress Reduction Clinic and the Center for Mindfulness in Medicine, Health Care, and Society at the University of Massachusetts Medical School. For Kabat-Zinn (2005), "Mindfulness means paying attention in a particular way: on purpose, in the present moment, and nonjudgmentally. . . . The overall tenor of mindfulness practice is gentle, appreciative, and nurturing. Another way to think of it would be 'heartfulness'" (pp. 4–7). This definition includes the essential ingredients of mindfulness and, though secular, also captures much of what we're doing when we practice Yoga. It serves both as instruction for practice and as a description of the achieved state. As instruction, it gives manas, the thinking mind, something to do so that it can become still, and buddhi, the aware mind, can reveal itself. As description, it helps us to know what we're looking for in the attained state. Let's continue to examine Kabat-Zinn's mindfulness definition using the language of Yoga.

Mindfulness is on purpose. When we live and practice Yoga mindfully, we *intend* to pay attention. Because awareness happens from buddhi, mindfulness is inherently intentional. And because buddhi is beyond ahaṁkāra, the intention does not come from our personal sense of self (ego, if you will), but from deeper within. This is one interpretation of the process of *svādhyāya,* Self-study, coming to know the Self through all that it is not: the roles and functions of ahaṁkāra. When manas has been occupied in observing the flow of breath, buddhi is then free to observe the operations of our mind and heart, exercise its powers of discrimination, and dissolve self-identifications and conditionings, which disturb the mindfield and prevent our ability to concentrate and know the Self. This process prepares us to enter the deeper meditative states.

When we approach mindfulness with the intention to meditate, our process shifts according to our bhūmi of realization, though stabilizing the mindfield by concentrating on the breath first, and then the breath in conjunction with another object of focus, usually helps. We meditate "on purpose" (Kabat-Zinn, 2005, p. 4) by first using our buddhi—with its ability to intend attention to keep manas occupied—to focus on whatever we can access: our breath, physical sensation, a mantra, or even prāṇa or *nāda* (subtle, nonphysical sound). As tennis legend Arthur Ashe famously said, "Start where you are. Use what you have. Do what you can." We must emphasize, however, that if we interpret *on purpose* to mean that our personal self (ahaṁkāra) pays attention to one of these objects (for example, by mentally stating, "Now I am breathing out. Now I am breathing in. Now *x*. Now *y*."), this demand for verbalization stimulates manas, which we are trying to move into the background. Mindfulness is meant to be noncerebral: "There is nothing cold, analytical, or unfeeling about it" (Kabat-Zinn, 2005, p. 6). It is a gentle relaxation into pure witnessing. When we are the witness, there is no sense of a separate ahaṁkāra doing the practice, just an overall sense of Being. In the achieved state of mindfulness, only that Being remains, essentially merged with the object of focus. This is the state of *saṁprajñāta-samādhi* in Yoga and *śamathā* in the Buddhist practice of *Vipassanā,* insight meditation.

Mindfulness is near-present. The Yoga system holds that a true present exists only in samādhi, where past and future cease to exist. In our ordinary awareness, we are always a little in the past or a little in the future because the mindfield in its disturbed state is incapable of seeing anything as it is, in the true present. We can, however, intend to bring our attention nearer to the present through awareness. Here again we can understand Kabat-Zinn's (2005) definition as both instruction and description, and on multiple levels: In a basic sense, when we attempt to practice "in the present moment" (p. 4), we do not distract ourselves by thinking about, interpreting, or identifying with what we have just noticed. Rather, we continuously allow ourselves to witness what happens next (and next, and next, and next . . .). This is one reason breathing practices are so common. We can only notice ourselves breathing in as we're actually inhaling; we can only tune into the exhaling breath as it is leaving. In this way, the word *present* may seem to describe our felt experience and practical intention, but until we succeed at Yoga, we are not present in a real sense. Through mindfulness, we come closer to presence. We attempt it to encourage our mind/body to let go into it.

Mindfulness is nonjudgmental. Judgment is a function of thought, which occurs in manas, but because awareness originates in buddhi, mindfulness is by its nature nonthinking and nonjudgmental. When we attempt mindfulness practice, buddhi gives manas the task to observe the breath (rather than to judge ourselves, our skill at mindfulness, or the content of manas). In this way, we intentionally engage a spirit of nonjudgment. This quality is already present, even though in the beginning the judgmental voices in manas may try to reassert themselves. (Just keep watching and breathing!)

As we engage in emotional purification, we follow instructions to attend to ourselves and to our environments with an open heart, willing to see whatever arises. This is easier when we look nonjudgmentally as a relatively objective observer, suspending any assessment of what we observe as "good" or "bad." Siegel (2007) describes the flavor of nonjudgment beautifully when he refers to practicing in a state of "curiosity, openness, acceptance, and love (COAL)" (p. 15). With mindful awareness from buddhi, a gentle COAL approach—wonder—replaces assignment of good or bad, me or mine. Loving awareness just is.

Because mindful awareness is synonymous with the action of buddhi, and buddhi is the part of us that is curious, open, accepting, and loving (it is our calm presence), mindfulness relaxes us. It thus creates a window of opportunity in which we are attentive and receptive to change. From a place of peace, we feel courageous to notice the tendencies of thought and emotion from which we might otherwise turn away. Empowered, we are safe to question their constructiveness and whether and how accurately they reflect reality. As we'll see in Chapter 2, we feel supported by the very physiology of our mind/body and capable of facing what's difficult within us. Mindfulness thus provides the tools and the support, the instructions and the capacity, to allow us to choose new responses, again and again. This is how we grow; this is personal transformation and our spirituality at work. In the next chapter, we will explore the neurobiology of mindfulness and its role in changing even the structure of our brain and nervous system as we work with ourselves.

Final Thoughts

Mind is much more far-reaching than Western thought has traditionally conceived. As Siegel (2010) notes, the definition of mind continues to develop in the West, and many now postulate a complementary mind/body. Yoga further expands upon this idea to include even a mindfield, which encompasses both personal and nonpersonal "energy and information" (Siegel, 2010, p. 52) on the self and Self. This most complete definition of mind provides a foundation to appreciate our definition of emotion, comprised of four parts: 1. sensation, 2. cognition, 3. motivation, and 4. saṁskāra. At each level, we can employ the practice of mindful awareness to work with our emotions for psychological and spiritual growth. The further chapters of this book are designed to help us with just this.

Chapter Two

Yoga and Neuroscience Converge:
Mindfulness, Neuroplasticity, and the Relaxation Response

In the previous chapter, we discussed the Yoga view of the relationship between mind, body, and emotion, and we introduced the practice of mindfulness for relating skillfully to each. In this chapter, we will examine recent developments in neuroscience that explain the importance of mindfulness in the process of human growth and change. They parallel the explanations of the Yoga system beautifully, and they give us a modern, scientific way to articulate these explanations. For those who are averse to religious or spiritual language, neuroscience provides a way to understand how and why Yoga works as a method of personal transformation.

Mindfulness: A Brief Neuroscientific History

Today we know that at a physiological level, the positive influence of mindfulness on the mind/body is sweeping:

> It is of benefit to the mind in terms of emotional regulation, flexibility, and approaching rather than withdrawing from challenging events. Being mindful makes you more empathic and improves the health of relationships. And being mindful improves the health of the body in terms of enhanced immune function and increased telomerase—the enzyme that maintains the telomeres at the ends of chromosomes and thus enhances cellular longevity. Mindfulness also helps you have more resilience in the face of

chronic pain. (Siegel, 2012b, section 6, p. 3)

The discovery of the gifts of mindfulness has become possible with revolutionary changes in neuroscience over the last 30 years. Up until about the 1990s, the notion of a separation between mind and body and mind and brain remained for the most part intact, precluding the hypothesis that mindfulness could impact, let alone benefit, either. A neurologist would have explained that what we call *mind* is just the subjective experience of processes that occur physiologically in the cells of the brain and nervous system. In this way, it was argued, the brain caused the mind, and all mental experience could ultimately be reduced to electrical impulses and the chemical interactions of neurotransmitters and neuropeptides. The prevailing view of nervous system development at that time was that the number of newly created nerve cells (neurons) reached a peak in adolescence, and starting with the paring away of neurons that happens in late adolescence, the rest of the life of the nervous system was a story of gradual decline and reorganization. It was thought that neurons, once destroyed by trauma or aging, could not be replaced.

This turns out not to be true at all! How is this so? In the 1980s, a bird biologist observing a group of aged canaries noticed that even the old birds who were near death were learning new songs. He began to wonder whether they could somehow be generating new neurons. So he injected the birds with [3H]thymidine, a labeled form of glucose that only new neurons could absorb. When the birds died he examined their brain tissue via autoradiography and observed that, as he suspected, the birds had been generating new neurons (Goldman & Nottebohm, 1983). Even though evidence of neurogenesis (production of new neurons) in adult mammals had been found as early as 1962 (Altman), Goldman and Nottebohm rekindled interest in the question and its extension to humans. A number of investigators gradually established that adult neurogenesis does occur in the brains of both mammals and humans (e.g., see

Reynolds & Weiss, 1992; Eriksson et al., 1998; Imayoshi et al., 2008; Aimone, Wiles, & Gage, 2006). There have even been investigations of the potential therapeutic role of neurogenesis in neurological diseases like Alzheimer's disease and dementia (Mu & Gage, 2011; Foster, Rosenblatt, & Kuljiš, 2011), Parkinson's disease (Arias-Carrión, Freundlieb, Oertel, & Höglinger, 2007), and mental illnesses like depression (van Praag, Jacobs, & Gage, 2000) and schizophrenia (Reif, Schmitt, Fritzen, & Lesch, 2007). A thorough review of research on adult neurogenesis and its relationship to cognition can be found in Aimone, et al. (2014). The old notion of a finite number of neurons for life, which was accepted science during my training as a psychologist, has changed forever.

With these developments came a complete reassessment of how the brain and central nervous system operate. These discoveries coincided with the development of brain-scanning technologies that provided many different methods of visualizing the inner activity of the brain as it was happening. (We're now awash in a veritable alphabet soup of tools that have quickly become commonplace: computer-assisted tomography, CAT scan; magnetic resonance imaging and functional magnetic resonance imaging, MRI and fMRI; positron emission tomography, PET scan; magnetoencephalography, MEG; and more sophisticated electroencephalography, EEG.) Because of the finer resolution provided by these advancements, we have learned a great deal about the processes involved in what has come to be called neuroplasticity, the brain's enormous flexibility in its ability to adapt, recreate, and reorganize itself throughout our lives.

Prior to this, neuroscientists had investigated meditation for many years, noticing the peculiar way it appeared to change practitioners' mental and physical abilities well into the lifespan, something that should have been impossible. These investigations date back to the observation of Yogic demonstrations by an Indian-born, Western-trained physician in the British medical service, N. C. Paul, in 1851. An excellent review of the history of Yoga and meditation research is provided in Walsh and Shapiro (2006) and the annotated bibliography of Murphy and Donovan (1997), although neither limit themselves to neuroscientific studies. The Murphy and Donovan (1997) annotated bibliography is updated periodically by the Institute of Noetic Sciences and is accessible online (http://biblio.noetic.org/). An introductory PDF download is also available.[6] In addition to these, *New York Times* journalist William J. Broad (2012) offers an informative account of this history in *The Science of Yoga: The Risks and the Rewards,* notably his chapters on mood and healing.

Today the discovery of neuroplasticity, as well as the addition of some of the above brain imaging processes, has made the depth and resolution of meditation research much finer (Cahn & Polich, 2006; Davidson et al., 2003). As a result, there is a rapidly growing body of scientific literature on the effects of meditation and Yoga that supports the central role of awareness, and particularly of mindful awareness, in the nervous system's ability to reshape itself. Across the board these studies show over and over the critical activity of the middle prefrontal cortex in the process of meditation and its ability to help us rewire our neural networks (e.g., Miller & Cohen, 2001).

Up until the recent past, research attention has focused primarily on which parts of the brain are activated by a given task, like meditation. A very fruitful line of inquiry began in 2001 (Raichle et al.), which identifies the parts of the brain that go quiet when the brain focuses attention. The functioning that remains in the background has been called the "default mode network" (Raichle & Snyder, 2007), and it remains constant across many tasks. Some neuroscientists see this as a beginning to understanding the neurological correlates of the difference between me and I, theorized by William James, still one of the great psychological thinkers about spirituality more than a century after he lived and worked (Dor-Ziderman, Berkovich-Ohana, Glicksohn, & Goldstein, 2013; James, 1890). When we put James's theory into Yogic terms, "I" represents the being who

[6] Visit http://library.noetic.org/library/publication-bibliographies/physical-and-psychological-effects-meditation to access the PDF.

observes and experiences raw sensory data (buddhi), whereas "me" represents the psychological self who interprets and stores that data (ahaṁkāra). Me exists over time, through its narrative of memories and future projections. I exists in the present moment, or as much in the moment as it can, if you recall our definition of the present from Chapter 1. The default mode network likely represents me, at least in part. I is likely our function of mindful awareness, and as such, it is possible for I to take a step back to examine me. The next several decades are bound to produce a much deeper understanding of how these functions of (psychological) self interact to shape the brain. The neuroscience of awareness and its relationships to the theoretical notions of Yoga will probably not be far behind.

Neuroplasticity Is at Play, Whether We Realize It or Not

Sometimes me becomes lost in the past or future, and sometimes I is active in observing or even directing experience. Either way, as Canadian neuropsychologist Donald Hebb first put it in 1949, "Neurons that fire together wire together." When we engage a particular thought or behavior, our brains wire together a network of neurons, which helps us quickly and easily to revisit that same thought or behavior again in the future. The more often we repeat a behavior, the more we reinforce the network that represents it in our brain, and the more automatic the behavior becomes. Our networks are our short cuts; they prevent our needing to relearn how to drive our car every time we hit the road, and they enable us to walk, talk, think, and act in ways that others can predict based on our personality. When someone says, "It's so like him or her to do that!" he or she is recognizing our neural networks. Because the more well-trodden a neural pathway, the more likely we will be to take it again, we condition ourselves towards future behavior—one thought, one action at a time.

This process is continually at work, whether we are aware of it or not. Me's unconscious ruminations on something that me doesn't like predispose the brain to repeat these ruminations in the future in much the same way that I's mindful sensing of experience, focusing on what's positive, or taking a more constructive action increases the likelihood that the brain will pursue these again. Our minds continuously feed our brains with input, and over time the neural pathways used most often become the strongest. They wire into ever more advanced networks, such that our actual brain tissues even grow to reflect the amount of input they receive! So we must choose wisely how we direct our attention.

Brain-derived neurotrophic factor (BDNF). One important difference between the activities of I and me and their corresponding modes of brain function is illustrated when we look at a protein called *brain-derived neurotrophic factor (BDNF).* It was discovered in 1982 and is one of the principal substances that encourages the growth of new neurons and new synapses, or connections among existing neurons (for a review, see Binder & Scharfman, 2004). Exercising mindful awareness stimulates the activity of this protein, and its production is promoted by aerobic exercise. (We'll return to the importance of aerobic exercise shortly.)

To start, let's focus on how mindful awareness, directed by I, stimulates the activity of BDNF. The more demand for reorganization we place on our brains, the harder BDNF will work to generate neurons and synapses. (Think of how much brainpower is required to learn a new language or to master an unfamiliar dance. Compare this with how little mental effort we expend in mindlessly sweeping the garage floor. We can almost *feel* the activity of BDNF.) When me goes on autopilot, the brain will reinforce an existing network, but because nothing new needs to happen in the brain, BDNF will have little to do. When we're engaged in learning, however, BDNF (among other neurotrophic factors) will become very active, promoting the production of new neurons and networks.

Even when we are not learning in the usual sense, we can simulate the learning state—and thus actively engage neuroplasticity—

through mindfulness. Sometimes referred to as "beginner's mind," mindfulness by definition asks the brain to process our experience as if for the first time, requiring our brain to forge new neural connections rather than rely on existing pathways. When we practice mindfulness, it's as if we are learning. (And in a sense, we are.) So whether we like it or not, the brain is continually shaping itself based on the input it receives from me or I, but we can influence the trajectory of its development by using I to choose what we focus on. What we pay attention to matters.

If we're aware that we hate someone but do not examine why or choose a different response, we simply and sadly reinforce our hatred. This is how we unconsciously form habits of thought and emotion and solidify prejudice. Where our mind goes (whether through I or me), there our brain grows. Mindfulness, engaged by I, interrupts this process, breathing new life into our ability to be with our experiences as they actually unfold, rather than through the filters of me, which is conditioned by what has happened to it in the past. Through mindfulness, we can become aware of an experience by tuning into each component of emotion as it arises. We can thus more consciously direct our behavior and beliefs.

During a challenging interpersonal encounter, we can attend to our breath and body (sensation) to gain a measure of distance from our thoughts (cognitions) as they take form. We thus acquire a bit of space and time to acknowledge our felt experience and a moment to intuit how the other person seems to be thinking and feeling. We can then ask ourselves how accurate our interpretation of the situation is and how our own unmet needs may be (motivating) our response. We can consider the appropriateness of our response and how the other person is likely to react to our proposed action under the emotional momentum. If we don't like the potential outcome, we then ask whether there is a way to do things differently. Will our brain's habitual response (saṁskāra) solve the problem? If not, we choose something better. Each time we shine a light on our conditioned reaction and make a conscious choice instead of a reactive one, BDNF is stimulated, and our brains learn to move in a new direction. Thus we shape our brains over time until they acquire a new habit, with mindfulness itself the healthiest and most healing "habit" of all. (To practice with your emotions this way, see Appendix A, Exercise 3.1.)

While the learning state of mindfulness activates BDNF to stimulate the creation of new neurons and synapses (and, with these, our new selves), aerobic exercise plays an important role in creating BDNF in the first place. In 2013 researchers found that aerobic activity increased BDNF by 32% in healthy adult men, while sedentary control subjects experienced a 13% BDNF decrease (Schmolesky, Webb, & Hansen). This becomes particularly important when we consider that

> low circulating BDNF levels have been associated with a wide range of neuropsychiatric disorders including depression (Karege et al., 2002), bipolar disorder (Cunha et al., 2006), schizophrenia (Zhang et al., 2007) and neurodegenerative diseases (Yu et al., 2008), although no causal relationship has yet been established. Research over the past decade has investigated the factors that can acutely and chronically elevate brain levels of BDNF in animals and circulating levels of BDNF in humans, based on the assumption that elevated BDNF levels can lead to improved brain health. (Schmolesky, Webb, & Hansen, 2013)

Mindful awareness thus supports the health of the brain in two important ways. First, mindfulness can help us choose to incorporate aerobic activity into our lifestyle, even when we don't want to exercise. We can make a commitment to get our heart rates up on a regular basis, either as a therapeutic measure for our mental health (more on this in Chapter 9) or to simply support the creation of BDNF to keep us well. Second, mindfulness supports brain health by telling BDNF where to lay down neural tracks, assuming that we're choosing to condition ourselves towards healthy behaviors. This is the intentional use of neuroplasticity, and while physical Yoga (āsana) does not emphasize aerobic exercise, perhaps because Yoga originated at a time when most people were plenty active, mindfulness has been the core practice of Yoga for centuries. Through the ages Yogis have engaged in conscious personal change. With the discovery of neuroplasticity, we are now beginning to understand how.

Neuroplasticity Says the Body Is Part of the Brain

One of the fascinating findings of recent research on neuroplasticity concerns the fact that as we learn about the networks of relationships among groups of neurons, we can no longer say that the brain is limited to its location inside the skull. Because of the complex interconnections of neurons throughout the body, it becomes increasingly difficult to distinguish the brain from the rest of the nervous system. Even our muscles and bones, our cardiac and gastrointestinal organs, are connected to these networks and play a critical role in the formation and signaling of intuition. So the brain exists throughout the entire mind/body, from head to toe (see "Interoception" in Siegel, 2012b, section AI, p. 42). This is why we always incorporate the sensations of the body when we attend to our emotions. Not only do our bodily sensations give us important insight into our interactions with others and into our own emotional responses, but also the body's repeated responses to similar situations become part of the very network of neurons that wires together—from head to toe—to form our habits.

For example, the common fear of public speaking generally brings with it a long and well-known list of possible physical symptoms: shortness of breath, a dry throat, tightness in the neck and shoulders, a collapsed chest, sweaty palms, flushed face, "butterflies" in the stomach, and maybe a timid carriage of the body in space. Our thoughts about public speaking ("I'm no good at this, and my job depends on my performance" vs. "I am capable and prepared") can make a big difference in how we live in, and live from, our bodies in these moments. In a positive feedback loop, our anxious thoughts can increase our physical symptoms, our physical symptoms can reinforce our anxious thoughts, our thoughts can again amplify our symptoms, and so on. Or our thoughts of composure and their accompanying body sensations can do the opposite. Our bodies will continue to encourage the line of thinking that amped us up or calmed us down. Once activated, this pattern becomes "known" to the brain/body connection, and the brain/body will be more likely to select it again in the future. With repeated use, the pattern will become more and more ingrained in us until it becomes part of our belief system about ourselves and our world.

When we become aware of this process, eventually we come to know intimately that our bodies reflect our beliefs. While our attempts to restructure a belief can influence the body, sometimes the body does not believe our attempt. No matter how well intentioned and how well reasoned, we simply cannot think a phobia (or another strong emotion) away. This is because the emotion is wired not only into our brains but also into our bodies. Learning to physically relax the body through awareness training (Appendix A, Section 1), āsana (Chapter 6), and deep, diaphragmatic breathing (Chapter 7; Appendix A, Exercise 1.5) can break the cycle between thought and sensation. When we relax physically, we change our internal "climate," making it more amenable to a new perspective, more willing to believe a new thought, and more inclined to create a new internal "terrain." From within our "new" body, a new cognition can not only be conceived, but believed and integrated. Put another way, if we wish to interrupt our personality's habitual "programming" towards particular beliefs and replace it with something better, we must interrupt the whole mind/body pattern that wrote the program and provide in its place one that also includes our mind/body as a whole. This typically requires a bit of sustained attention and intentional self-talk, at least 30 seconds or so. (To read more on the role of the body in neuroplasticity and to experiment with it yourself, see Bo Forbes's 2011 book, *Yoga for Emotional Balance: Simple Practices to Help Relieve Anxiety and Depression.*)

If we now consider Siegel's (2010) definition of mind mentioned in the first chapter, we see reason to do away with the old idea that our minds are merely coincidental results of electrical or neurochemical brain activity. Recall that Siegel (2010) defines the mind as "a relational and *embodied process* [emphasis added] that regulates the flow of energy and information" (p. 52). Rather than a physical object, the mind is a dynamic and intangible process. Though it is embodied in that it occurs within the body, the process itself is only made material by the affects it leaves there. It relies on the relationship between mind and body to make its mark and to continually reshape its existence. What does this sound like to you? We're describing no less than neuroplasticity itself. The mind is not *neuroplastic*. The mind *is* neuroplasticity. As far as science can measure empirically, the mind is the observed process of continual change. (In Yogic terms, neuroplasticity is the ever-emerging anna-maya-koṣa. It's manas and buddhi and part of citta and prakṛti—all these definable components of the Yoga mind are in reality ever-changing processes—and the Self, puruṣa or ātman, is the unchanging witness, the source of them all who remains ever pure, ever radiant.) Because that which changes, neuroplasticity, relies on the dynamic interplay between itself and the body, and because the brain is molded by neuroplasticity, it seems clear that the mind, including the body, in fact creates and reshapes the brain!

The Human Brain and Its Capacities for Integration and Change

Rather than thinking of the brain as containing the mind, Yoga would say that the intangible mind (in its function as neuroplasticity) both acts on the brain and devolves into matter to contain the brain. Because the brain is the level at which the mind appears material, it will be useful to understand a bit about the structure of the brain and nervous system, how they work together as a single system, and how we can use our minds (as the process of neuroplasticity) to work with them.

Scientists sometimes liken the human brain to a series of Russian nesting dolls, roughly divided into three parts: the reptilian brain, early mammalian brain, and neocortex. Our nervous system embodies the whole history of neural evolution in its structure, just as the human body progresses through all these evolutionary neural developments in the womb. The anatomy of our brain reflects this. The newest (*neo-*) part of the brain to evolve is like the outermost nesting doll, in that it contains the next most recent evolutionary advancement, the early mammalian brain. This in turn contains the more ancient reptilian brain. While the nesting doll analogy leaves out many details, it is sufficient to help us understand some of the basic principles of neuroplasticity.

The Reptilian Brain

The reptilian brain is the deepest layer of the mind, the innermost nesting doll. It consists of the brain stem, cerebellum, and pons and is called *reptilian* because it is a remnant of the earliest brain structures in the history of our evolution as reptiles. The reptilian brain is responsible for maintaining the basic rhythms of life, for example breathing, heartbeat, and basal metabolism, among other functions. It also generates the fight, flee, or freeze response, which is the foundation of the stress response in humans. Because this response "lives" in the most subterranean, fundamental region of our brain, it is embedded deep within us and can be easily and automatically triggered. The reptilian brain is one group of structures that carries out some of what we experience as the "unconscious" functions of the Yogic manas. (From the Yogic perspective of consciousness, all manas's functions are technically unconscious in a spiritual sense; the Self alone is spiritually conscious. Here we differentiate those functions that also feel to us to be unconscious, i.e., the basic life rhythms that go on outside of our awareness and without our "conscious" control.)

The Early Mammalian Brain, or Midbrain

The nesting doll that contains the reptilian brain is known as the *early mammalian brain* because it developed in the earliest mammalian species as an evolutionary advancement from the brain and nervous system of reptiles. It consists of the structures of the midbrain, or limbic system, including the amygdala, hippocampus, and hypothalamus, among others. These, too, process the Yogic manas, but this time they include both "unconscious" and "conscious" functions, as we experience them. This is the main emotional center of the brain, as its several structures process and regulate both emotion and memory.

The amygdala. The amygdala helps with the interpretation of meaning, the initiation of emotional responses, and the perception of social cues. Importantly, it assists in formulating our fear responses. When we are traumatized, the amygdala takes a holistic "snapshot" of the experience, including images, cognitions, emotions, and sensations. It has an important evolutionary purpose. This fearful snapshot is a permanent imprint in the amygdala that is designed to help us avoid mortal danger. For example, when we walk along and see a poisonous snake, this part of the brain captures a terrifying collage of sensory, emotional, and cognitive data that helps us remember to avoid dangerous snakes in the future. However, when a traumatic experience remains trapped here, unintegrated by the action of the hippocampus and cerebral cortex, it returns to our awareness as a series of "flashback[s]" of events that always seem as if they are about to happen or are happening at the moment rather than occurring to us as a memory of something that took place in the past (Siegel, 2012b, section AI, pp. 33, 38).

The hippocampus. The hippocampus is primarily involved in the consolidation of memory. This consolidation process involves connecting sensations, images, and cognitions from the amygdala together with reason and language from the speech centers of the cortex to form a narrative, a story of our experiences. Many different parts of the brain that are connected to the hippocampus affect the construction of this narrative. Sensations and images sometimes exist cut off from this story, as illustrated above, and so are often difficult for one to integrate. Even cognitions about oneself at the time of a traumatic incident can remain unintegrated, for example, "There is nothing I can do," "I have no choice," or "This is happening because I am a bad person." All of the above can describe the struggle of people who have experienced severe trauma or who live in nervous systems that are highly skilled at dissociation for other reasons.

The hypothalamus. The hypothalamus performs several important functions. It helps to regulate body temperature in response to immune challenges. It is also a key player in maintaining homeostasis, the physiological stability that maintains the body's integrity. More importantly, it acts in cooperation with the master endocrine gland, the pituitary gland, to regulate the release of hormones in the body, especially the hormones that drive our stress response (cortisol and epinephrine) and our relaxation response (oxytocin). It is the hub of the nervous system's chemical communication system.

The Neocortex, or Cerebral Cortex

The most external nesting doll is the cerebral cortex. It is sometimes called the *neocortex* because in evolutionary terms, it is relatively new (*neo-*). The neocortex contains the centers that process speech and language. It also contains portions that process and coordinate our cognitive and active senses. (In addition to the familiar cognitive senses of sight, hearing, taste, touch, and smell, recall that Yoga describes active senses, motor senses, if you will, which comprise the ways we act on the world around us: locomotion in the feet, action in the hands, speech in the tongue and vocal organs, elimination in the anus, and reproduction in the genitals. Part of the neocortex enables the seemingly "conscious" function of the Yogic manas, even if Yoga would assert that neither the brain nor manas are themselves conscious.) To get an idea of how the sensory and motor functions are distributed across the cortex, you might look up "cortical homunculus" on Wikipedia or consult Penfield and Boldrey (1937).

The frontal lobes. Of particular importance are the frontal lobes of the neocortex. These very complex structures serve many different functions, integrating the disparate parts of the mind/body's systems and directing their activity. Their functions also include attunement to communication with others, maintenance of emotional balance, response flexibility (the ability to choose among behavioral options), fear moderation (keeping fear in a manageable range), insight and self-awareness, empathy ("com-passion," literally "feeling with" others and seeing things from another's perspective; Siegel, 2012b, section AI, pp. 16–17), morality (orienting behavior towards the welfare of the greater whole), and intuition (in the sense of *interoception,* a term from neuroscience for the perception of internal states; when we intuit, the whole body knows something in a nonrational way; see Siegel, 2012b, section AI, p. 42).

The middle prefrontal cortex. The integrative function of the middle prefrontal cortex is a vital force in the organization of neural activity and its expression in behavior. It is the most recent part of the cortex to evolve, and as such, we can say that it is the part of our brain that is the most uniquely human. It allows us to make choices in our responses to emotions arising out of our early mammalian midbrain and to choose our behavioral expression of those emotions. Mindful awareness stimulates this integrative function, which, as we discussed earlier, often begins with attention to the sensation of the breath. So simply focusing on our breathing activates the part of us that is most human, the part of us that allows for conscious behavioral choice.

It is the middle prefrontal cortex that directs the organization of budding neuronal networks and reorganizes networks that are no longer in use, all in the service of neuroplasticity. As a center through which buddhi operates physically, the middle prefrontal cortex effectively wires our mind/body's networks together. So we can say that our awareness (which comes from Self through buddhi) uses the mind (the process of neuroplasticity) to initiate and direct the integration of our brain-nervous-system-body-mind. As Yogis have described, mind shapes body. This integration occurs across a number of domains, summarized by Siegel (2012b) in his *Pocket Guide to Interpersonal Neurobiology,* which refers to the field of study that he both named and pioneered. Interpersonal neurobiology examines neural development (i.e., the ability of our brain to integrate its many roles) as a function of interpersonal relationships, including how others relate to us and how we relate to others. Each domain of psychological integration is important, and for the interested reader, I highly recommend Siegel's works. Here, let's examine how some of these domains parallel Yoga's observations of mental function.

Vertical integration. The vertical dimension of integration involves the coordination of the flows of inputs through all the evolutionary layers of the nervous system, from the reptilian brain to the neocortex, and the creation of connections between them. Through vertical integration, buddhi directs manas.

Bilateral integration. This involves the coordination between the right and left hemispheres of the brain. In Yoga we are quite familiar, for example, with the alternation of nostril activity, which goes by the physiological term *nasal cycle.* Freud began his early work as a neurologist with an interest in the nasal cycle but without the tools or the theoretical background to understand its true significance. Yoga studies this domain of integration through *svara,* the ancient science of subtle energy rhythms in the prāṇa-maya-koṣa, the body sheath made of subtle energy. The nasal cycle is the physiological result of these subtle rhythms. It reflects the fact that the two cerebral hemispheres are physically rather separate and communicate across a nerve "cable" that crosses the floor of the brain's grey matter called the *corpus callosum.*

The two hemispheres have very different ways of receiving and processing information and impulses to action. The right hemisphere, connected to sensory and motor functions on the left side of the body, is more holistic, visuospatial, and emotional; its cognitive style is creative, intuitive, and metaphorical. This mode of functioning is characterized by the activity of the left nostril and, in Yoga, the subtle *nāḍī, iḍā.*[7] The left hemisphere, connected to sensory and motor functions on the right side of the body, is more linear, logical, analytical, and linguistic. This mode of functioning is characterized by the activity of the right nostril and, in Yoga, the subtle nāḍī, *piṅgalā.* Balancing your checkbook goes most smoothly when the right nostril is active. When you need to write a book about emotional purification, writing will flow more readily when the left nostril is active. These are described in more detail in Siegel (2012b, section 41, pp. 6–7) and the *Svara-svarodaya* (Muktibodhananda, 1999), an ancient text on the science of rhythms in the breath and subtle body; it contains long lists of activities favorable to the dominant work of one hemisphere or the other. We will examine these systems in more detail in Chapter 7 of this book.

Integration of memory. This involves focusing our mindful awareness on discreet bits of information (implicit memory) so that they become coherent autobiographical facts that we can then experience as normal memories (explicit memory). Implicit memories include representations of our perceptions (i.e., instinctual cognitions that have not been subjected to reason, analysis, or perspective). They also include sensations, actions of our motor systems, and emotions—we might refer to these in Yogic terms as nonverbal saṁskāras. As previously described, before these impressions are integrated, they can occur without

[7] In the Yoga system, nāḍīs channel the mind/body's flow of sensory mind perceptions, subtle energy, and physical fluids. Chapter 7 examines the nāḍīs' relationship to the Yoga path.

a context in time in the form of a "flashback" or dissociated and/or repressed information (Siegel, 2012b, section AI, pp. 33, 38). Once our awareness has activated the hippocampus to assemble this information into a context, we experience it as memory in the usual sense. Memory integration involves connecting the centers of sensation and emotion in the midbrain with the centers for language in the cerebral cortex. This is the nature of much of the work done, for example, in hypnotherapy or in EMDR (eye movement desensitization and reprocessing) therapy. As we'll see, sometimes the mindful practice of Yoga postures (āsana) or breathing and subtle body practices (prāṇāyāma) can also integrate and heal traumatic memory. However, this observation comes with an important caveat: Most Yoga teachers are not trained therapists. If you wish to include Yoga in the deep work of healing trauma, it is essential to do so in conjunction with a qualified mental health care professional.

State integration. This involves recognition and coordination of states of attention and mood. There is coordination between states and within states. When I am trying to learn a new physical skill with my body, I don't want to be distracted by composing my shopping list or trying to learn Italian. Integration then means focusing my attention to increase the internal cohesion of a single state, in this case, a learning state. Integration also occurs across states: When I crave solitude, I don't feel my hunger for community. This coordination between two states, a contemplative mood and a sociable one, enables me to balance these needs in my life.

If states are well coordinated and balanced, a person is likely to be more skillful and creative. Some states coordinate well naturally (e.g., sex and play), while others conflict (e.g., compassion and aggression). In the latter case, I might simultaneously be irritated with someone, feel aggression towards him or her, and yet also desire to express compassion. When our states conflict in this way, we can employ mindful awareness to rearrange their relationship to each other and to bring ourselves into balance. For example, I can drop my story, the mental list of all the reasons I am irritated, and instead tune into my breath and bodily sensations. This would calm me down so that I would be able to think more clearly. My whole brain-nervous-system-body-mind would then get a chance to reconcile the conflict within me and determine a skillful response to the other person. The more well-coordinated our states, the more peaceful and joyful we will be. Here neuroscience and Yoga flow harmoniously in parallel; the *Bhagavad-gītā,* a text on Yoga from approximately the fourth century BCE, defines Yoga as *karmasu kauśalam,* "skill, wellness, and beauty in action" (BhG II.50). So we can understand the experience of Yoga, at least in part, as an experience of state integration.

Interpersonal integration. This is integration in relationship to others. We don't usually think of our relationships as playing an important role in the development of our nervous system, but they are crucial to its processes of integration, organization, and reorganization. In infancy, our attunement with our parents[8] and their attunement to us help us to set the processes of integration in motion. In effect, we borrow our parents' capacity for interpersonal attunement to begin organizing our mind/body and creating "maps" of "me," "you," and "we" (Siegel, 2012b, section AI, pp. 69–70). These are our stories, conscious and unconscious, about who we believe ourselves to be, how we perceive the significant others in our lives, and how we understand the nature of our relationships with those significant others. As we mature, our capacity for neurological attunement to the states of others is the necessary condition for cultivating compassion. Learning to "[feel] with" others helps us construct increasingly accurate you-maps and we-maps (Siegel, 2012b, section AI, p. 16). One emerging hypothesis is that people with disturbances in the ability to do this may experience, for example, varying degrees of autism. The cultivation of accurate empathy with others is the principal healing tool in the training of a psychotherapist.

---

[8] Throughout this text, the words *parent* and *parents* connote the individual(s) who assume primary responsibility in child rearing (e.g., a mother, father, grandparent, relative, foster parent, family friend, etc.).

Our interpersonal integration, our sense of community with others, is a vital part of our overall wellness both physically and emotionally. We can describe this dimension of integration in terms of patterns of attachment in relationships that, again, we learn in our early life with our parents. If, for example, we grow up neglected by our parents, we may develop an avoidant attachment pattern, where we may compensate for not being cared for by overvaluing our independence in an unbalanced way. This predisposes us to avoid relationships and to have an impoverished emotional life characterized by anxiety and depression. If, as we grow up, our significant others intrude on us and push their moods and emotions on us, we may develop an ambivalent or resistant attachment pattern in adult life that makes us either unable to open ourselves to relationships with others or unwilling to do so, with a rigid and inflexible sense of ourselves. Both patterns make it difficult to use relationships to manage the stress in our lives. Fortunately, through the mindful use of neuroplasticity, we can unlearn these patterns and replace them with more adaptive ones. In Chapter 5, we discuss the importance of relationships in Patañjali's *Rāja-yoga.*

Temporal integration. This concerns our ability to make internal maps of time. We are accustomed to thinking of time as an objective, absolute quality of the world around us. In actuality, according to Patañjali (YS III.13–16), our map of time consists of the perception of differences in the condition of objects. For example, when we move away from autopilot or habitual action to apply mindful awareness to a task, time takes longer, as it did when we were children. When we strongly dislike something, time can seem an eternity. It evaporates when we enjoy an experience and disappears when we're absorbed in concentration. Time has no absolute reality. Our maps of time, then, are highly dependent on the quality of our attention and awareness.

Out of *abhiniveśa,* our obsession with the continuity of our bodily life (YS II.9), our maps of time often reflect our yearning for certainty, permanence, and immortality. A careful examination of ourselves and the world reveals that we are in a perpetual process of change. Our bodies age, our personalities evolve, objects decay, mountains erode, oceans dry up, and people die. No desire for permanence can be fulfilled by our individual lives; we must come to terms with the facts of uncertainty, impermanence, and mortality. Hence Plato advised that we practice dying every day (*Phaedo,* 64a), and Jesus commanded, "He who would save his life must lose it" (Luke 9:24, 17:33; Matthew 6:25, 10:39). In our maps of time, we must accept our limited time, acknowledging our fears based on the impermanence of bodily life. The more directly we do this, the more we enjoy the time we have, and the less we fear the end of that time.

Transpirational integration. This concerns the degree to which our capacity to attune to others helps our sense of self, with its hunger for integration, grow beyond the boundaries of our skin. Through transpirational integration, we come to feel part of some larger sense of being in our lives, whether or not this has a social or religious expression. Some experience this as their spirituality. (For example, through the Yogic practice of self-study, svādhyāya, we come to know ourselves as the Self, ātman/puruṣa, connecting us to everyone and everything in manifest and unmanifest existence.) Others might come to feel that every child in the world is their child and act accordingly. Still others may feel a passionate commitment to environmental conservation. When this domain of integration is in balance, people can manage great works of social entrepreneurship and compassion (e.g., the work of Mother Theresa). When it is out of balance or is dominated by imbalances in the other domains, it can become the basis of megalomania (e.g., Nazism).

As we maximize our capacity for integration across these domains, there is a vital experiential reward: joy. It's what we feel when we grow, when we become more integrated. We might even characterize the meditative state of samādhi, which Swāmī Veda referred to as the ultimate harmonization of the mind, as an ultimate state of integration. The rewarding nature of joy assures that we continue to seek greater and greater integration in our effort to grow and evolve, both as individuals and as a species. So human beings have a drive for integration and joy as the most central feature of our growth. We will discuss this in more detail in Chapter 3, on the primary fountains.

The key to activating processes of integration is mindful awareness, which serves as the switch in the brain that turns on the integrative function of the middle prefrontal cortex and then directs its activity in the restructuring of the ever-emerging brain and nervous system. As we discussed in Chapter 1, attending to our breath is our most basic way to activate mindful awareness. And because mindfulness is the key to the integrative growth that we are all driven to seek, mindful awareness, especially of breath, plays a central role in all systems of meditation, regardless of their cultural origin.

Mindfulness Can Moderate Our Stress and Relaxation Responses

Integration is possible when we are relaxed; it is less so when we are under stress. Mindfulness thus becomes particularly important when we compare how easily the brain activates our stress response with how much more prodding the brain requires before it will galvanize our relaxation response. To access our integrative capacities on which spiritual growth depends, we purposefully cultivate the comfort and ease of the relaxation response through mindfulness. By contrast, when we do not practice mindful awareness, our mind/body may tend towards the stress response. For many of us, the latter can often hum in the background to create a low-grade feeling of discontent, a slightly jarring internal environment. Each physiological process has its implications for not only our spiritual well-being but also for our physical health. When we combine this with the distinguishing feature of our modern era—we live in times of anxiety and stress—it becomes imperative that we learn how to manage both sets of responses.

The Stress Response: Distress and Eustress

Change in every part of our lives happens faster than we can cope with it. Technology is multiplying the amount of information that we must process to a degree that is frequently overwhelming. The multiplication of media created by computing is conditioning human minds to move very quickly from subject to subject and contributing to the increasing incidence of attention deficit disorders (Weiss, Baer, Allan, Saran, & Schibuk, 2011). A hyperactive mind, due to excessive media consumption, has also been linked to mood and sleep disorders (Calabrese, Molteni, Racagni, & Riva, 2009; Han, Kim, & Shim, 2012). The impact of humans on the earth even reaches geologic proportions in the phenomenon of climate change, which has prompted some geologists to rename the current age the Anthropocene epoch, the period of humans and their stressful effect on the earth's environment (Syvitski, 2012). Do these influences sound a bit dis-integrating to you? Indeed, they disrupt our ability to be mindful, the very cornerstone of our integrative capacity.

We seldom face saber-toothed tigers in modern life, but unfortunately, as talented adapters, human beings have learned to associate psychological threats with physical threats through the primary fountain of self-preservation. As a result, for many people, the activation of their stress response is essentially continuous. In terms of a mental health diagnosis, we might call this generalized anxiety, and psychologists have long observed the evidence that this problem is becoming more widespread (May, 1980).

Yet stress is not necessarily a bad thing, at least not in the short term. Previously, we described the role of stress responses in protecting us from danger. They can also be powerful motivators of constructive change, ultimately leading to greater integration. The Canadian physician and medical researcher Hans Selye (1907–1982) who first wrote about stress called this constructive, motivational stress "eu-stress" (1974), in contrast to stress that is disorganizing and pathological, "dis-stress" (1978). For our purposes, we will focus our discussion on *the* stress response (both distress and eustress, "fight, flee, or freeze"), as distinguished from our mind/body's relaxation response ("rest and digest").

The stress response begins in the reptilian portions of the brain in the spinal cord and brain stem with the fight, flee, or freeze response. These impulses are then augmented in the midbrain's limbic system by emotional arousal (anxiety, fear, panic) and the release of the stress hormones cortisol and epinephrine (adrenalin). These prepare us to act decisively and give the body the energy it needs to respond quickly and forcefully. As these impulses continue to integrate with the rest of the brain and nervous system, the sympathetic branch of the autonomic nervous system begins to push the functioning of our vital organs towards readiness: Our heart beat increases, blood pressure rises, blood flow is shunted away from the periphery of the body and towards vital organs in the body's core, the liver releases more glucose into the bloodstream, and the pancreas makes more insulin so that sugar can be converted into energy for muscles and organs. These are just a few facets of the stress response.

Many of these physiological changes are mediated by the mind/body's principal stress hormone, cortisol, which is released through stimulation of the hypothalamus. Cortisol increases blood glucose, increases metabolism, suppresses immune function, and generally diverts energy in the body away from longer term processes to make it available for short-term action. Habitually high levels of cortisol have been implicated in many chronic disease states.

Stress can be useful and adaptive if the mind/body has a chance to rest, recover, and integrate. It is well documented, however, that if stress becomes continuous or unrelenting, the above changes begin to reach a point of diminishing positive return with serious health consequences: heart disease, hypertension, gastrointestinal disorders, and exaggerated inflammatory processes that contribute to cancers, arthritis, autoimmune disorders, chronic pain, and many other disease processes. Stress is a major factor in most chronic illnesses, which are a prime example of how the mind/body sometimes stores emotional energy (generalized anxiety) in the body, makes the body ill, and reduces our life span.

Because the stress response originates in the primitive parts of the brain and nervous system, its long evolutionary history in humans means that the processes of the stress response are relatively automatic. They needed to be to support human survival. Almost every other species has greater abilities than humans. Many animals have sharper eyesight, clearer hearing, and keener smell; they can run faster, jump higher, and act with greater strength than *homo sapiens.* In early humans, and in emergency situations today, a swift stress response saves lives. Yet our greatest survival skill was not and is not our physical abilities; it is our capacity to learn, adapt, and collaborate, skills that function best when the stress response is not activated. Humans rather use primarily the integrative capacities of our mind/body to meet evolutionary challenges.

The Relaxation Response

Over many millennia, humans developed a set of responses that help the mind/body to get the rest, re-creation, and integration it needs. In the 1970s, as scientists began to investigate meditation, Herbert Benson, MD, of Harvard Medical School coined the term *relaxation response* to describe this system of responses (Benson, 2000). Like mindful awareness, it is mediated through the middle prefrontal cortex of the brain and the parasympathetic branch of the autonomic nervous system. Because of its later evolutionary status, the relaxation response is less automatic than the stress response and requires more conscious intentionality to activate and sustain (though with repeated activation, as with repeating any behavior, it can become habitual). The ability to cultivate and sustain relaxation is one of the most important positive effects of mindful awareness, and we can train it in many ways. According to the Benson-Henry Institute for Mind Body Medicine,

> the necessary two basic steps to elicit the relaxation response are: the repetition of a sound, word, phrase prayer, or movement, and the passive setting aside of intruding thoughts and returning to the repetition. This can be done using any number of meditative techniques, such as diaphragmatic breathing, repetitive prayer, qi gong, tai chi, yoga, progressive muscle relaxation, jogging, even knitting.

Yoga triggers the relaxation response in multiple ways, for example through conscious attention to the sensation of breath as it flows repeatedly in and out of the nostrils (prāṇāyāma), through awareness of the continuous sensations of intentional movement (āsana), and through mantra repetition, among others. In each activity, practitioners set aside distracting thoughts and return to the practice. These methods stimulate the parasympathetic branch of the central nervous system, which operates in contrast to the sympathetic branch to produce a generally opposite set of physiological changes: reduced heart rate, lowered blood pressure, increased peripheral circulation of blood, and so forth.

The director of parasympathetic activity is the vagus nerve, which also regulates the functioning of our heart, lungs, and digestive system. Stimulating this nerve through slow, deep, diaphragmatic breathing, and especially through prolonged exhalation, activates the parasympathetic nervous system. Science does not yet fully understand how this works, but we can observe a phenomenon called *respiratory sinus arrhythmia (RSA),* where our heart pumps more quickly as we inhale and more slowly as we exhale. Additionally, parasympathetic activity increases as we breathe out, perhaps because the upward movement of the diaphragm during the exhalation phase of the breath stimulates the vagus nerve, thereby activating the parasympathetic nervous system and slowing the heart rate. Individuals who have had part of this nerve removed exhibit a faster resting heart rate than their healthy counterparts, suggesting that less vagal stimulation from the process of breathing causes less parasympathetic activity and more heart beats per minute (bpm). (Compare 100 bpm in a vagotomized heart with 60–70 bpm in an average heart.) This altering of parasympathetic activity may affect the heart only, however, and not the other organs that the vagus nerve innervates (P. Emerson, personal communication, November 5, 2016). In short, we don't know why our breath slows our heart rate to help us feel more relaxed, only that it does.

Deep, diaphragmatic breathing for relaxation was axiomatic in Swāmī Veda's teaching about breath awareness, and it is the basis for gradually extending the exhalation phase of the breath to ratios of 2:1, 3:1, and further (i.e., exhaling for two counts and inhaling for one; exhaling for three counts and inhaling for one). He went so far as to say that, with the exception of spontaneous breath retention (see Chapter 7), only the exhalation phase of the breath allows for meditation. Yoga, with its emphasis on both breath awareness and the mindfulness practices described above, activates the relaxation response particularly well.

Oxytocin. When we relax deeply, as in meditation, deep breathing, āsana, or mantra repetition, the relaxation response also stimulates the hypothalamus to begin the secretion of oxytocin. This hormone's important effects correct the chronic problems caused by excessive stress activation. In telling the story of oxytocin, the paragraphs below cite quite a few studies for those who wish to read more deeply into the science.

Oxytocin was first described as the hormone that initiates the process of labor in pregnant mothers and stimulates the cervical dilation necessary for birth to occur. Researchers also noticed that oxytocin would flood a mother's bloodstream at birth, even after the labor process had nearly finished. They discovered that it provides a biochemically driven flood of affectionate feelings in the mother towards her new baby and starts the process of relational bonding of parent with child with a bang! (For a review of the research on mother–infant attachment and bonding, see Galbally, Lewis, Ijzendoorn, & Permezel, 2011.) No one thought to investigate oxytocin in males for some time. Gradually as these investigations occurred, they revealed that oxytocin appears to play a role in the pair bonding of reproductive partners. Males experience a rush of oxytocin at the moment of sexual orgasm (Murphy, Seckl, Burton, Checkley, & Lightman, 1987). They also experience a similar flood of oxytocin when a child is born, demonstrating that fathers share in the intense initial affectionate bonding with their child (Carmichael et al., 1987; Marazziti et al., 2006).

As investigators looked more closely at this hormone, they discovered a whole host of ways oxytocin encourages human bonding and healing (Lee, Macbeth, Pagani, & Young, 2009). It assists in the recognition of familiar faces and promotes a sense of affection, security, and well-being around people who are familiar. This helps to build families and larger familial social units (e.g., tribes) and enhances social collaboration (Guastella, Mitchell, & Dadds, 2008; Kosfeld, Heinrichs, Zak, Fischbacher, & Fehr, 2005; Marsh, Yu, Pine, & Blair, 2010; Rimmele, Hediger, Heinrichs, & Klaver, 2009). Oxytocin inhibits processes of inflammation, and specifically the action of the carbohydrate metabolites called *cytokines,* both of which play a role in inflammation and chronic disease. It also inhibits the release of the stress hormones cortisol and vasopressin (Heinrichs, Baumgartner, Kirschbaum, & Ehlert, 2003). Oxytocin even moderates the formation of dose tolerance to opiates, that is, the need for more and more of a medication or a recreational drug to achieve the same intoxicating effect. Because such tolerance leads to addiction, oxytocin's ability to moderate it may explain part of the healing power of social networks in recovery for addicts (Kovács, Sarnyai, & Szabó, 1998). Physical wound healing, too, occurs with increased secretion of oxytocin, which itself is associated with positive social interaction (Gouin et al., 2010). A 2003 study found that oxytocin can reduce anxiety and stress responses both directly and indirectly by bolstering the stress-buffering effects of social support (Heinrichs et al., 2003).

It is clear that our participation in relationships—and I would emphasize participation in nurturing, affirming relationships focused by mindful awareness—promotes the functioning of oxytocin, thus positively impacting mind/body function. The mind/body truly is a "relational . . . process" (Siegel, 2010, p. 52). Looked at another way, increasing oxytocin production through cultivating the relaxation response may strengthen our potential to form intimate and meaningful human relationships. As many Yoga practitioners know, when we're relaxed at the end of a Yoga practice, we're perhaps more open and more vulnerable, and we often treat ourselves and the people in our lives with more compassion and honesty. Thus, through Yoga, there is great potential to improve the depth and quality of our relationships—and the accuracy of our me-, you-, and we-maps—over time.

Final Thoughts

By discussing the scientific discovery of oxytocin and the remarkable mechanisms of the brain and nervous system, I do not mean to suggest that human relationships can be reduced to neurochemistry. Nor do I wish to imply that the mind or mindfulness can be reduced to brain activity. Rather, I hope to share the perspective of advanced Yogis: The brain and body are physical devolutions of consciousness that receive and reflect pure consciousness. The clearer the mind, the greater its ability to transmit pure consciousness accurately. Swāmī Rāma had purified his mind to an extraordinary degree, and in the 1970s he demonstrated the existence of the deeper mindfield scientifically (Green & Green, 1977, pp. 210–211). However, at times the measurement tools were not able to detect the subtle forces at work in his demonstrations, and at other times, scientists refused to believe their own observations. Once Swāmī Rāma produced two cysts on his arm as a group of German physicians watched. He asked that biopsies be taken and predicted which was malignant and which was not. He then made the cysts disappear. Later, laboratory reports confirmed his diagnosis, but no one published anything about it for fear they would not be believed. Their observations simply did not confirm existing models of the relationship between mind and body and mind and matter. Thus, while science continues to reveal more and more about mental function, a complete understanding of mind can be impeded, both by the limited tools of empirical science and by the reluctance to take in something that challenges what one believes out of habituation (scientism as religion rather than science as epistemology).

I hope you will consider this possibility: Our bodily processes and neuroplasticity promote the growth and development of the mind/body, but they do so following inspiration from the Self's mindful awareness through buddhi. Even more so, I hope you will experiment with this possibility for yourself, through your own deepening Yoga practice. As we think about all the neurophysiological processes we discussed in this chapter, we can see how Yoga, with its emphasis on mindful awareness of all areas of our life and being, takes full advantage of developing the integrative capacities of the brain and nervous system. We can also delight in Yoga's promotion of the relaxation response and all the benefits that process brings in terms of stress reduction, healing, and the promotion of loving, healing human relationships.

In the next chapter, we will discuss the Yoga view of the four primary fountains (drive systems) introduced in Chapter 1. These sustain our lives, motivate human behavior through desire, and sometimes hinder our growth. We will discuss the application of mindful awareness to these drives and the result (desireless joy), which allows us to gradually lessen our dependence on the drives. Because mindfulness results in desireless joy and induces our relaxation response, these three concepts are intrinsically connected: 1. Our ability to get "in the zone" or to be "in flow" through repetition and focus induces the relaxation response; 2. These experiences also describe the learning state of mindfulness, which consciously engages the mind (as neuroplasticity) to help us grow; and 3. With integrative growth comes joy. In this way, we can understand the relaxation response as joy's physical precursor. (It is a precursor because relaxation yields to joy, and joy can accompany high levels of arousal that even extend well beyond our physical being.) The middle prefrontal cortex, as the interface between our physical and nonphysical selves, mediates the relationships between buddhi (as mindfulness) and mind (as neuroplasticity), between growth and integration, and between relaxation and joy.

PART II

Working with the Mind/Body:
Meet Your Manas, Know Thy Ahaṁkāra

Chapter Three

Our Instinctive Energies: The Four Primary Fountains (and a Fifth!)

In the first chapter, we mentioned the four primary fountains: food, sleep, sex, and self-preservation. We described these drives as perennial sources of desire that support the life of the body if we manage to keep our relationship with them in balance. They can also easily become the source of our painful emotions and motivations in life, even our addictions—all obstacles and opportunities on the Yoga path. We can consider all these drives to be facets of what Freud called *libido,* the etymology of which is desire or lust, from the Latin *libere,* "to please." *Libido* then refers to the pleasure of satisfying a desire. Yoga, too, defines pleasure as the satisfaction of desire (YS II.7).

Freud tended to equate libido with *eros,* meaning the instinctive drive to life and growth (Dickson, 1991). He interpreted this primarily in terms of sexual desire, and much of his psychoanalytical method for understanding behavior focused on finding the sexual motivations in our emotions. Many people accused him of being obsessed with sex and dismissed his thinking for this reason. But his psychoanalytic method had and still has considerable explanatory power, and many of his contributions are still evident a century or more later. (For example, his concept of transference, the tendency of clients to transfer onto the therapy relationship aspects of their own important relationships, is a phenomenon that most theoretical schools accept.) So we might say that in the case of emotions, Freud didn't go far enough, missing the behavioral motivations from drives other than sexuality.

Freud (1922/2009) also formulated the idea that human beings have a countervailing instinctive drive to death, which he called by the Greek word *thanatos,* a seeking for an experience of merger into something greater than oneself. He equated this with a presumed drive to "lead organic life back into the inanimate state" (Freud, 1989, p. 38), to go backwards in life towards the beginning, towards the origin. As a physician and scientist, he understood the beginning of life to be biological birth, and so the merger towards which we are headed, he reasoned, is the end of our biological life, death. He saw the drives for life and death, eros and thanatos, existing in a tension with each other, particularly with reference to the role of religion. However, he had a lot of difficulty making this explanation work with any clarity or success, and many analytical thinkers criticized or discarded the idea. What Freud was trying to articulate, I suspect, was this:

> The desire for a return to the womb has its origin not in a desire . . . but in a recognition we all have of our origins being in a very, very deeply, eternally silent place. When we are in that eternally silent place . . . it is the truly silent night. (Bharati, 2004, p. 27)

This yearning is for the experience of divine presence, our spiritual Selfhood, which is an experience of absolute silence. Freud had a strong interest in religion and spirituality, and because he understood these as expressions of this tension between the drive for life and the presumed drive towards death, he believed the goal of religion was to sublimate these drives by rechanneling their energies into higher and more constructive purposes. While this may be partially correct, it seems clearer to consider the tension to be between the desirous basis of our embodied life and the drive towards spiritual development and realization of the Self, characterized not by death, but by ultimate joy, silence, and Self-realization.

The Fifth Fountain

If the so-called primary fountains are libidinal drives, energy sources that we share with animals, then what is it that makes us human? There is actually a fifth fountain. Different writers call it by different names. Some refer to this fifth fountain as *dharma,* right behavior or natural order. Swāmī Veda has described natural drives in human beings towards peace, silence, and meditation (Bharati, 2013a). All of these can be characterized as a single drive towards ultimate integration, self-completion, and spiritual Self-realization, in which we feel ultimate joy *(ānanda)*. For this reason, we can call this fifth fountain of positive motivation in humans the fountain of joy.

Joy is what we feel when we grow in any way. (Remember the phenomenon of integration described in the previous chapter.) When your two-year-old child has gone through thousands of experiments with walking and has fallen over and over again into tears of frustration, when he or she finally balances on two feet and then takes one step and then a second step, what is the next reaction? An exclamation of joy! "Look Mom!!" "Look Dad!!" It is no different when we are adults and we achieve some growth that we have never managed before. We feel a similar thrill of joy. The more we grow, the deeper, broader, and more intense this joy becomes until it becomes the joy of harmonization in ultimate Being, ānanda.

At those moments, do we feel happy? Perhaps that is part of the picture, but as the great English poet and spiritualist William Blake (1790–1793) wrote in *The Marriage of Heaven and Hell,* "Excess of sorrow laughs; excess of joy weeps" (51). People who are deeply joyful are often tearful. We cry at weddings! How many pictures have we seen of Yogis and saints weeping in states of ecstasy? So joy is more than mere, ordinary happiness.

Is joy pleasure? It is certainly pleasing. But it isn't really the fulfillment of a desire *(rāga)* in the ordinary sense of pleasure *(sukha)*, which has inherent in it a germ of suffering about the possibility that we might lose the pleasure (YS II.7). So joy is clearly more than mere pleasure.

Joy isn't really an emotion, either, because there is no desire-based motivation in it, and when people are joyful, they are often in touch with the entire range of human emotion at once. Joy greets each moment of growth and development and makes the activities that draw us towards our growth seem appealing, exciting, and even erotic. We are accustomed to using this last word in relationship to sexuality alone. But in its ancient Greek sense, eros is a continuous pull towards our growing edge in life that makes the next step in our development "sexy" enough—compelling enough—for us to want to overcome the inertial forces of habituation and the psychobiological imperative of homeostasis, the tendency of the mind/body to remain stable. Only when we are sufficiently motivated to change can a new development and the necessary reorganization occur in our nervous system and consequently in our personality. At the age of two, saying "No!" is erotic. At the age of ten, learning the rules of social interaction on the playground is erotic. In adolescence, sex is erotic. In our early adult life, love and skillful work are erotic. And as we prepare for the transition from our mind/body, spirituality often becomes erotic. At each stage, we welcome disruption in our mind/body's status quo as our brain and nervous system change to accommodate our newest growth.

All the while, we are driving towards greater and greater physical and psychological integration, until these find completion in the joyful ānanda of Self-realization. This ultimate joy then satisfies, pacifies, all the other instinctive desires that arise from the four fountains. The great eighth-century text *Yoga-vāsiṣṭha* (I.74.40–44) sings,

> Rāma! When the multitude of desires is verily abandoned by the mind, a man, arriving at his inherent beauty like the moon, attains to joy! . . . Desirelessness is the greatest happiness—greater than even sovereignty, the heaven, the moon, or union with a lovely woman. (as cited in Atreya, 2005, pp. 396–397)

It is this drive towards the ultimate joy of Self-realization that makes us most human and distinguishes our humanity from our animal nature. Animals live according to their instinctive drives. Humans make choices, as the *Kaṭha-upaniṣad* (II.1–2) says, between the genuinely auspicious and beautiful—joyful, *śreyas*—and the merely pleasant, *preyas*. As humans, we turn to our drive of joyful Self-realization in the fifth fountain of human motivation to readjust, to balance, our relationship to the four primary fountains of our instinctive drives.

Cultivating the Fifth Fountain

Somewhat counterintuitively, we reach true ecstasy by calming our desires. Recall from the last chapter that the relaxation response can be considered a physical precursor of joy, that through repetition and focus (the learning state of mindfulness) we can induce the relaxation response. This leads to a new level of integrative growth, which produces joy. We get a taste of the ultimate joy each time we reach a developmental milestone. When our nervous systems toil to integrate a new experience, awkwardly at first, and then with greater refinement over time, they do so perhaps because we first experience some motivating eustress, and then because we're able to explore our challenge through repetition and focus, until a new way of being emerges. In these cases, we focus our attention outwardly on the task at hand and are rewarded with joy.

By contrast, the final joy asks us to go inside. Here we also employ mindful awareness, but the object of our mindfulness matters less than our awareness itself. Rather than focus attention on how to solve the problems and obtain the skills of a developmental milestone (e.g., how to interact on the playground, how to secure a date for the prom), we focus attention on living from mindfulness as often as possible. Whatever we're doing and whatever primary fountain is involved, we "[pay] attention . . . on purpose, in the present moment, and nonjudgmentally" (Kabat-Zinn, 2005, p. 4). The point isn't to enhance the pleasure of a primary fountain desire that is fulfilled or to dwell on one that isn't. The purpose is to calm the mind to a point where we can notice our awareness of the fountain. We then dwell not on the pleasure we derive from what is observed but on its transcendent beauty (divine presence) and on the joy of the one who sees. Mindfulness thus allows us gradually to "slough off" our primary fountain dependence, as a snake sheds a skin it no longer needs. One-pointedness then follows, creating the stability necessary to enter the deep meditative states, where we fully realize desireless joy. In this way, our relaxation response is a gateway to ecstatic, nonphysical absorption in Spirit.

Relying on the Fifth Fountain

As joy calls us towards itself, we "relax away" our dependence on the fountains. We then gradually come to rely on this refined joy and its relationship to the flow of prāṇa to sustain our lives. The masters are known for a considerable reduction in their dependence on the four primary fountain drives. In fact, near-independence from those drives is one definition of mastery. How many stories have we heard of the great Yogis who, having developed the fifth fountain of joyful Self-realization, sustain themselves on very little, whether it be sleep or food? When he did sleep, Swāmī Rāma slept only two hours per day. For much of his adult life, Swāmī Veda kept a similar schedule. In the process of replicating his master's experiments with yoga-nidrā, Swāmī Veda was observed by Dean Radin, PhD, of the Institute of Noetic Sciences to remain in a state of deep sleep even when moving around and talking. As they were having a conversation before commencing an experiment, Radin had already attached Swāmī Veda to an electroencephalogram (EEG), turned it on, and, as they talked, observed to his great surprise that Swāmījī was producing the delta brain waves of deep, dreamless, non-REM sleep (Bharati, 2006, p. 69). Recent measurements of Swāmī Veda as he entered an extended period of silence also confirm this result (G. Prabhu, PhD, Meditation Research Institute, personal communication, 2013).

The ability to access yoga-nidrā while waking becomes possible when practitioners have reached a certain meditative acuity. This itself depends upon the clarity and pacification of the mind, arrived at through emotional purification, that is, less dependence on the primary fountains. This process is self-reinforcing: Not only can we turn to the fifth fountain of joy to help us relax away our agitating emotions, but also the fifth fountain reveals itself as our emotions settle. We can witness the results of this process in other adept Yogis. For example, when the master Bengali Baba would take food or drink, it was never more than a glass of hot milk at midday or perhaps a bit of water. Paramahansa Yogananda (1971) records a female Yogi, Giri Bālā, who had taken neither food nor water for more than 50 years. Such Yogis have used the process of tapas, which we'll explore in the next chapter, to reduce their dependence on food as an object of mental desire, and they have refined their ability to absorb and expand prāṇa to a degree that they no longer require food (or even breath) as a vehicle for prāṇa. Through processes of tapas, Yogis can absorb subtle energy directly, and the result is a reduction in dependence on physical sustenance, accompanied by an ever-growing joy.

Final Thoughts

Two important, twin aspects of emotional purification, citta-prasādana, are the gradual reduction in our reliance on the primary fountains of food, sleep, sex, and self-preservation (our diverse libidos), as well as the accompanying reduction of emotional conflicts that result from those motivations. To the extent that practitioners have deeply refined their practices of tapas and prāṇāyāma, they can reduce their needs for physical survival by learning how to absorb prāṇa directly. Because joy results from these practices, and because these are practices of emotional purification, we can say that the pursuit of emotional purification is also the cultivation of joy. Ultimately, like the Yoga masters, we, too, can grow less dependent on the objects of desire—and even free ourselves from desire itself—through our own relaxed cultivation of greater and greater joy.

Chapter Four

The Process of Kriyā-Yoga: Tapas, Svādhyāya, and Īśvara-Praṇidhāna

The first half of the *Yoga-sūtra*'s second chapter describes the means for thinning down the painful (*kliṣṭa*, "afflicted") operations (*vṛtti*s) of the mind. The technique, called *Kriyā-yoga,* consists of three processes: *tapas* (ascetic practice), *svādhyāya* (self-study), and *īśvara-praṇidhāna* (practice of divine presence). Each of these techniques can bring us to the doorway of Self-realization, assisting us in its own way in decreasing our dependence on the primary fountains. Empowering each practice is mindful awareness, and through this, we experience deepening joy. Joy not only reduces our dependence on the primary fountains but is also one of the results, fulfilling us in place of desire. Kriyā-yoga is therefore essentially a set of mindfulness practices that help us to cultivate the ultimate (and permanent) satisfaction of joy.

Tapas

The first component of Kriyā-yoga, *tapas,* derives from the Sanskrit root √*tap,* meaning "burn." It is usually translated as "austerity" or "asceticism" and tends to be interpreted in much writing about spirituality as a series of practices that ask us to endure self-denial. Authors will often describe burning up desire, drying up the body, and the like. Do these ideas sound a bit violent to you? As we discussed in Chapter 1, many people approach ascetic practice in a way that essentially denies themselves the same commitment to nonviolence that they so easily give to other beings. Remember that you are also one of those beings! Swāmī Veda explains it this way:

> However, if tapas were mere drying up of the body by long fasts, etc., it would be contrary to the practice of yoga because such extreme asceticism causes imbalances of the body's constituents *(dhātu-vaiṣhamya)* and consequently brings about disturbances of the mind, which opposes the principle of fostering mental pleasantness *(chitta-prasādana)*. (Bhāratī, 2001, p. 67)

We have the story of Buddha reduced nearly to death by severe fasting. He was lying near a riverbank when down the river came a boat carrying an old music teacher giving a lesson to his young student on a stringed instrument: "If the string is not tight enough, it will make no sound; if it is too tight, it will break." Hearing this, it dawned in the mind of Buddha that one can only succeed on a middle path between the extremes of indulgence and self-denial because making progress requires a clear and pleasant mind, not a mind deprived of the energy it needs to do the work of sādhanā.

Within the Himalayan Yoga tradition, we often describe the practices of tapas as the "five pillars of sādhanā": stillness, silence, fasting, celibacy, and conquest of sleep.[9] One can easily see a relationship between these practices, the four primary fountains, and the fountain of joy. Stillness helps us overcome the motivation of self-preservation (the desire to move to escape danger) specifically, as well as the general characteristic of the mind to remain in motion. In addition, silence addresses all the fountains in that the desires born of them preserve our limited sense of being in bodily life, but through silence practice, we seek to place ourselves in the state that characterizes the sustaining presence of ultimate Being. This essential state is none other than joy or bliss. Fasting addresses food directly. Celibacy, though many argue it is about sex, helps us

[9] See Bharati's (2002) "Five Pillars of Sadhana," a chapter in his book *Night Birds*. See also Bharati's (2004) work, *The Song of Silence: Subtleties in Sadhana*.

detach from all the senses as well as the sensory activity of the mind (manas) that operates through them. Conquest of sleep addresses the fountain of sleep and is a practice that gradually, over some time, leads the mind into samādhi.

Tapas and Health

Many people approach tapas, the five pillar practices, as exercises in self-denial or mere endurance of suffering. They suppose that one must learn how to do without a particular fountain. This has its risks, since the fountains are the drives of the mind/body to sustain life and maintain normal functioning. In the case of sleep, for example, I knew someone who once decided that she would conquer sleep. Her guru was encouraging. She gradually set her alarm so that she slept a few minutes less each night. This continued for some weeks. One evening, as her guru was lecturing and she was writing notes for him on a whiteboard, she suddenly lost consciousness and fell over backwards, asleep. Her brain and nervous system had reached a point where they could no longer function adequately without the sleep they needed to reorganize themselves. She later learned that conquest of sleep happens through gradually deepening one's relaxation practice and concentration to the point where one can consciously enjoy sleep in the state of yoga-nidrā. Sleep is reduced by practicing in such a way that the need for it decreases because you enjoy it with directed attention. You begin by remaining aware during the process of falling asleep, taking your meditation into sleep with you, as it were. You also engage in relaxation practices, moment-to-moment breath awareness, and practices of yoga-nidrā that gradually deepen to the point where more of your nervous system can rest even when you are awake.

This healthy and natural process of overcoming sleep illustrates our approach to tapas. Taking charge of any of our instinctive drives involves not the arduous endurance of self-denial, but the nourishing enjoyment of concentration. All joy in human experience, and, one might say, all "en-joyment," derives from our ability to focus. Remember your deepest moments in meditation. Were they not joyful? Were you aware of aching joints at those moments, at that depth? Our most splendid joys come from our keenest absorptions. And as we'll see, joyful concentration does not simply overshadow pain; rather, our awareness is so powerful that joy replaces suffering, transforming the mind/body's actual perception to varying degrees.

A similar transformation can even occur when we are motivated to pursue an experience based on an instinctive drive. If we really concentrate on enjoying what we're doing, the joy that we feel satisfies the mind to such a degree that most of the time we need less of the initial experience. If you really taste your food with concentration, you tend to eat less. You consider taking a second helping of something you just tasted, and your mind says, "I have already tasted that. Do I really need more of it?" This is fasting! If you really enjoy your sexual life with concentrated, mindful awareness, you discover the way that it opens a pathway to escape the narrow confinement of ahaṁkāra. You find deep joy in the beauty of your partner and the connection to something higher than your psychological self, which satisfies the mind's craving. You will probably find yourself gradually needing sexual release less often. You will likely also begin to sense the light of a higher connection to consciousness shining all around you. The burning of tapas becomes not a burning up of the body, but a burning aspiration to maximize joy, to realize the ānanda of Brahman.

A wonderful traditional description of this process can be found in the ninth-century *Śiva-sūtra* of Vasugupta (III.38). The commentator, Kṣemarāja, quotes the *Vijñānabhairava Tantra* (69–72):

> The experience of joy which rises at the moment you are united with and are absolutely embracing your life partner is actually the joy of *brahman.* This joy can only be known by a trick. If, however, you do not know this trick, then it is just the

> union of two beasts. (69)
> O Devi, it is not only in the union of two partners where you will get entry into God consciousness but, if you possess the trick, then also at the time of remembering that sexual union you will gain entry into God consciousness. (70) . . .
> If at the time you experience the joy that arises in your consciousness when you eat a nicely prepared feast or taste a delicious drink you have the trick to attain the awareness of *Bhairava,* then you will enter into the bliss of God consciousness when you are eating or drinking. (72) (as cited in Lakshmanjoo, 2007, pp. 220–222)

Bhairava is one of the names of Śiva, the personified deity who represents the principle of divinity through which all things return to their origin. Recall from Chapter 1 that Śiva is also the principle of pure consciousness and the first Guru. We experience the sublime awareness of Bhairava through the trick of the depth of our own awareness and the acuity of our concentration. As is so often the case in Yoga, realization lies in the deep and persistent refinement of the fundamentals, not in advanced technique. Tapas invites us to refine our most basic Yoga skill—mindful awareness—in each moment, spectacularly transforming even our most ordinary, sensual activities. Through the final perfection of mindfulness, our senses return to their origin in pure consciousness, dissolving back into the mindfield through pratyāhāra.

In his 2011 book *Radical Healing,* Rudolph Ballentine, MD, also describes this process, emphasizing the role of deepening awareness in returning towards pure consciousness (pp. 447–453). Ballentine (2011) explains tapas as feeling an impulse driven by desire from one of the primary fountains and choosing not to express it until it finds a channel into a higher and more constructive articulation. The energy of the impulse builds and builds—the burning of tapas—until it finds the higher pathway, led, he says, by spanda, "your innermost spark of creativity" (Ballentine, 2011, p. 450). As he describes, mindful awareness plays the central role in this process:

> When you repress or deny, you simply shove the impulse out of your awareness. It keeps trying to express itself, and if you refuse to let it have its usual way, it will find another, more indirect way. That expression may look different on the surface, but it's really only a new version of the same old behavior. . . . The energy transmutation of tapas, on the other hand, demands *total awareness* [emphasis added]. . . . The energy it needs for expression is [thus] rescued from its [habitual] circular trap. You contain the building energy and allow it to move you only when your *sharpest discrimination* [emphasis added] senses that it is ready to burst forth into a course of action or thought that is not only authentic and fulfilling, but is also one that will propel you into a new way of being. (Ballentine, 2011, p. 450)

The consequence of growing into a new way of being, of our further development, of course, is joy. And as Ballentine (2011) suggests, what enables our growth is the discrimination of buddhi: mindful awareness, or tapas. The lovely thing about this way of thinking about tapas is that it gradually becomes your greatest joy in life. Once you begin to taste the joy of this attitude, it becomes easy to practice tapas all the time, not just on a special retreat or on designated days. There is a maxim in Yoga that says, "Eat *only* when you are fasting! Speak *only* from silence! Sleep *only* when you are aware! Make love *only* from celibacy!" These pillars of sādhanā are the antidotes to the primary fountains, and we can practice them all the time. But we must employ them from mindful awareness. Only from such a nonjudgmental space, in which we neither suppress nor react to our basic desires, can we witness their churnings until insight takes them into a new expression. This process feels joyful. It brings freedom.

Far from an exercise in self-denial, tapas is a healthy and joyous experience of refined awareness. It cannot be otherwise. Yoga would assert the following: 1. Growth into our fullest potential implies simultaneous progression in meditation; 2. We must be undistracted by the mental agitation of instinctive desire to meditate; and 3. We cannot both achieve deep absorption and try to subdue the primary fountains by depriving the mind/body of the very strength and health that absorption requires. (Recall the vi-kṣepas and antarāyas of Chapter 1.) Growth and mindfulness thus go hand in hand. Denial and mindfulness do not. The way to practice tapas is to use mindful awareness to transmute our basic desires into the joy that transcends them. For a similar perspective in the Christian tradition, see Sheldrake (2016).

Tapas and Affirmative Intention

There is another important reason for not approaching the practice of tapas as mere self-denial. If you want the mind not to focus on something, making a merely negative command requires that your mind remember and rehearse what it is not supposed to do in order not to do it. You deliberately create the saṁskāra you are trying to avoid! Try for a moment not to think about monkeys. As long as the focus of your attention is "monkey-not," all you have in your mind is monkeys! When we train the mind only by the practice of self-denial, we condition it to focus on the object of desire that is not there. Fasting becomes "food-not," and soon all you can think of is food. This focus invokes and intensifies the craving of the ever-present desire from the primary fountain of food, and suddenly all you can think is, "When is the next meal?" "When can I go get that ice cream?" Using negative commands is destined to fail because the mind never escapes the primary fountains. Using mere self-denial, you will eventually experience a binge.

The mind needs to be able to shift its focus of attention entirely. To succeed in uprooting desire, the mind must find a positive focus: the joy or the beauty of an experience. This is not a focus on the pleasure, on the satisfaction of the desire by its object, but on the experience of reaching something higher—a greater beauty—through the taste, led as Ballentine (2011) might say by spanda, spontaneous and creative intuition. Recall that *spanda* is a term from Kashmir Śaiva philosophy that refers to the spontaneous, creative power of divinity. The experience of receiving this intuitive impulse, this new way of experiencing an old instinct, is one of beauty and aesthetic rapture, which becomes a springboard to higher experience, to states of superconsciousness. The Tāntrik system refers to this transcendent beauty as *Śrī* and to the science of gaining access to it *Śrī-vidyā.*

Beauty, aesthetic rapture, is always a representation of divinity and its omnipresence all around us. So let the experience of the little food you eat be so deep and intense that the joy from that concentration replaces desire as the focus of the mind. Let your mind/body's hunger be satisfied by joy rather than by food. Only in this way can we truly master desire; otherwise, constantly seeking an end to desire by satisfying it with its objects is an endless pursuit.

One day I was with Swāmī Veda shopping for electronics. He was getting tired, so we stopped to get some fresh-squeezed orange juice. He sat opposite me, and with a knowing look that I had learned to pay attention to, he said, "Stoma, have you ever taken a sip of orange juice to go into samādhi?" He took a tiny sip and off he went for a few minutes. When he opened his eyes, he said, "No one knows how to taste!"

This approach to the process of tapas gradually fills your mind with joy. Furthermore, it is very difficult in such a state not to be generous and compassionate towards others. Tapas nurtures the growth of joyful-mindedness (*muditā*) in you, one of the characteristics of a clear and pleasant mind.

Tapas and the Transformation of Fear and Pain

You can see how this method of ascetic practice can help to reset your mind's balance in relationship to the primary fountains, by moving the mind in the direction of less dependence on them. We have already discussed how this works with food, sleep, and sex. What about self-preservation, rooted in fear? How does one enjoy fear (and pain) with concentration?! It sounds preposterous and contradictory. Still, the general principle holds.

Pain is another of those common experiences that has proven almost impossible to define scientifically in a way that everyone can agree upon. And yet everybody knows what pain is experientially. According to the Yoga perspective, all our fears stem from our belief that the life of our mind/body must continue. So the experience of pain in the body is primarily a fear reaction, fear that the body may not continue or fear that we may lose function in some way. Neurologists used to say that pain was the subjective experience of nerves signaling damage to the body. We now know that bodily damage is only a small part of the picture. For instance, it is relatively easy to modify the experience of pain in hypnosis and to even make it disappear. This is accomplished in several ways: by redirecting attention, by changing the cognitive context of the pain, or by changing its meaning. Redirecting attention changes how your nervous system integrates pain signals in your experience of pain. Changing the thoughts associated with pain alters its meaning in the flow of narrative that becomes your long-term memory. Changing the meaning of the pain involves redirecting how the nervous system understands the physical pain signal and therefore how that signal links to other parts of the brain and nervous system. As your attention shifts and your understanding changes, the experience of pain transforms.

At a training conference in clinical hypnosis, I once watched an unpublished video of a pediatrician undergoing surgery to remove bone spurs from his shoulder using only hypnosis (which is most likely a special case of yoga-nidrā) for both pain control (anesthesia) and control of bleeding (hemostasis). This kind of surgery is fairly heavy-duty carpentry, involving chiseling the bone spurs off with a hammer. The hypnosis technique applied was developed by

Alexander Levitan, MD, from the University of Minnesota Medical School, for use in surgery with those who are allergic to anesthetic agents. Prior to filming the video, the hypnotherapist had worked with the pediatrician, a student of hypnosis himself, and learned that he loved mountaineering. So in their trancework, the hypnotherapist suggested to the pediatrician that each time he felt the hammer in his shoulder during surgery, it could remind him of the feeling of pounding in pitons (this was back in the days when we still used pitons in climbing) to anchor his rope so that he could climb higher and enjoy a more beautiful ascent and a more breathtaking view.

The hypnotherapist essentially sent the pediatrician on a climb in his mind and used the sensations in the surgery to reinforce the positive experience of the imagined excursion in terms of its joy and beauty. The surgery was completed successfully, the wound was closed, and the pediatrician was reawakened from the trance. He rested for a brief period—about ten minutes—and then completed his morning rounds in the hospital with very little discomfort! (Although the neurophysiological mechanism of hypnotic anesthesia is not yet fully understood, Zeev-Wolf, Goldstein, Bonne, & Abramowitz, 2016, offer some promising leads. You can also get a feel for how clinical hypnotherapists work with patients by reading sample scripts and suggestions in Fredericks et al., 1990, pp. 85–108.)

The above example of pain transformation may seem dramatic. More commonplace for many people is the experience of back pain, which is extremely prevalent and carries high costs in terms of lost work and expensive medical care. John Sarno, MD, retired attending physician from the Rusk Institute of Rehabilitation Medicine at New York University, has asserted for years that almost all back pain is emotional, or psychosomatic, in nature. Thus almost all of it can be treated through psychoeducational means. According to Sarno (1981, 1998), physicians most often diagnose a ruptured disk that is pinching a nerve. If this were actually the case, the pinched nerve could produce acute pain for a few days before the nerve would die from loss of circulation. Nerves pinched in this way cannot cause chronic pain! He estimated that perhaps 1% of the cases at Rusk actually involved physically caused pain (Sarno, 1998, p. 43ff.).

Sarno began a program of treatment where patients had to disavow their primary physician's diagnosis, stop their pain medications, and participate in several lectures about the psychosomatic mechanism of pain production. In Sarno's (1998) theory, one's unconscious mind, to distract a person from emotional issues that seem too hard to face (because of fear), senses anomalies in the spine and selectively inhibits blood flow to nerves and muscles; this is the actual, physical cause of the pain. Patients learn to conduct a dialogue with their mind and to say, "Thank you for trying to protect me by providing this distraction. I no longer need your help with this. Please oxygenate the nerves and muscles immediately." It works much like hypnosis. If patients have truly convinced themselves of the psychosomatic hypothesis and have become aware of the emotional issues they need to face, the pain often disappears instantly. In one follow-up study of patients who used Sarno's (1998) method, all of whom had structural abnormalities in their spines (e.g., ruptured or herniated disks demonstrated by MRI or CAT scan), 88% of patients experienced cessation of their pain without recurrence on a second follow-up (p. 73). In Sarno's (2006) work, those who require further treatment are referred to outpatient psychotherapy, and only a tiny percentage are referred to orthopedic surgeons (pp. 129–183). Sarno's (2006) psychoeducational process, described in detail in his book *The Divided Mind: The Epidemic of Mindbody Disorders,* is so effective that at the time of that work's publication, it was the principal treatment employed for back pain at Rusk Rehabilitation, widely regarded for its innovative care and research as the world's oldest university-affiliated rehabilitation program.

I experienced the effectiveness of Sarno's method during my own adventure with back pain in 2008. After doing some yardwork that was not very taxing, I found myself lying on the floor of my living room by the end of the evening, howling in agony with extremely severe back pain and sensations of electrocution in my lower extremities. The pain persisted through the night, and sleep never came. The next morning, I went to the hospital emergency room. I was amazed when the doctor told me that he would give me a fairly large intravenous dose of morphine and the muscle relaxant Xanax. After he pushed the medication into the intravenous line, we waited. It took two-and-a-half hours to feel any effect! (For physical pain, intravenous medication should be effective almost immediately.) Over the next few days, the pain abated somewhat, but then it began gradually to creep back until, after a few weeks, at 57 years old, I walked like a person in his 80s or 90s. My left quadriceps muscle lost so much strength and muscle mass that on two occasions it would not hold my knee straight, and I toppled over from a relaxed standing posture!

At the same time, a therapy client introduced me to Sarno's work, and I was gradually convinced that his theory described the case in my own mind/body. At that point, after studying my back issue for some time and thoroughly persuading myself of the rationale behind Sarno's approach, I, too, was able to have a dialogue with my mind that would instantly terminate any pain that began to arise. I discovered that the pain was an effort to distract my attention from emotional issues left over after the death of my mother earlier in the year. My unconscious mind was capable of shifting patterns of circulation in my nerves and muscles to create a distracting pain—or to eliminate it. A willingness to face these issues, and the fears associated with them, freed me from the need for a distraction, and so my unconscious could end the discomfort. I experienced how quickly this kind of psychosomatic relief can occur once I reached the threshold of convincing myself of the model. And meaningfully, this experience brought me to a point of greater joy and peace in my relationship with my mother. (To work with your own pain and what it might have to teach you, try Exercise 3.9 in Appendix A.)

Facing our fear. One important and well-known principle in dealing with fears is to face them rather than avoid them. If you avoid a fear, it generally intensifies and begins to generalize to more and more things. It is often accompanied by a thought process full of "what-ifs," each what-if larger in scope and horror than the last. In extreme cases, people end up developing agoraphobia, a condition where they cannot step outside their homes. Sometimes they cannot even leave their beds. When you face a fear, it gets smaller. (Obviously, with fears that are emotionally overwhelming, the process is very gradual.) In work with therapy clients who are trying to decide on a course of action, I usually recommend that they survey their options, and wherever they feel the most fear (within a manageable range), that is usually the direction in which to move. If you follow this guideline and learn to face your fears, gradually this emotion becomes just the alarm system it is supposed to be. It keeps you mindful and thus keeps you out of danger appropriately. And as your ability to confront your fears deepens, you eventually have nothing to fear, not even death.

A dear friend of mine died not long ago. A few weeks before she died, she sent a message to all her friends in a singing group to which we both belonged. She said that her Parkinson's disease had finally become terminal, and she found out that she also had stage four liver cancer. She felt grateful that she would likely die before becoming debilitated and would not have to go to a nursing home:

> I am neither physically nor otherwise devastated . . . and I want you all to know that our singing has been one of the best things in an already rich life. I wouldn't have believed I would ever enjoy such a community. . . . I would really like to host . . . singings. (personal communication, 2013)

I wrote back offering some help from Yoga for the process of departing the body when the time came, and she was very interested. I will never forget our conversation. We had a wonderful session singing together with the rest of our friends in the group. After the singing, she began our conversation by saying, with a face full of joyful excitement, “Stephen, I am so excited! I can hardly wait to die! *What* an adventure!!” She died just a few days later, peaceful, joyful, and surrounded by the love of friends and family. Any fear that she had of death was dwarfed by the joy of the love around her and the adventure of transition from the body. I had no idea that I knew such an ascetic. May we all experience such a passing!

It is perhaps strange to think that one can actually enjoy the pain we encounter in life, even to the point of enjoying the process of moving towards death. As these examples illustrate, this is not a masochistic enjoyment, one where we derive pleasure and satisfaction from an experience of pain, as if it were something we deserved. Rather it means approaching everything that happens in our mind/body with a sense of wonder and curious interest, no matter what comes to us. This allows us to deepen our awareness of ourselves in ways that help us understand our mind/body and our emotions more deeply so that we can go beyond the pain. The result of the practice of tapas is that we gradually cease to fear altogether. If, as Yoga says, all our fears generate from abhiniveśa, the fear of losing our bodily dwelling, and if we can transcend even this, then what is there left to fear? Nothing. We can always transform our instinctive drives into an experience of higher Being through tapas. The full and joyful potential of Yoga practice is available to us in any moment; we have only to reach for it through mindful awareness and enjoyment through concentration. The same awareness that we cultivate in tapas we also apply to the practices of svādhyāya and īśvara-praṇidhāna, the second and third elements of Kriyā-yoga.

Svādhyāya

Svādhyāya, “self-study,” has several meanings in Yoga, all of which concern the application of mindful awareness. One of these is simple breath awareness. As we discussed in Chapter 1, Yoga and other meditative traditions equate breath awareness with the establishment of mindfulness because it leads to awareness of all of one's experiences. This means bringing your awareness to everything that you do. My morning routine was transformed at one point after reading a beautiful essay by the Vietnamese Buddhist monk Thich Nhat Hanh (1975) about washing the dishes mindfully (pp. 3–5). As I watched my breath, I began to attend much more closely to what I was doing. I started to enjoy the warmth of the water, the way the soap helped food slide off the plates, the light glistening through clean glassware, and, finally, the kitchen back in order. In this way, the simple activities of daily life become wonderful opportunities for practice. I now feel deprived if I leave the house without washing the dishes!

A second meaning of *svādhyāya* is the study of sacred texts. In the Yoga tradition, these are called *āgama,* literally, "that which has come" to us. This includes the teachings recorded in texts. However, āgama also includes the experience of the words and actions of a realized master, a living book. The practice of svādhyāya, whether through a written text or the text of a personal relationship with an enlightened being, is the way that we learn the hypotheses of the science of Yoga, which we test in our own experience to confirm. This is how we internalize the map of the territory that is uniquely ours to walk on our journey to spiritual realization. We then become our own living book as we learn to follow the Guru within.

There is also a process of contemplative reading of the textual sources, not simply for information, but to see more deeply into and even beyond their ideas and categories. We thus prepare the ground to transcend the limitations of our analysis. Our buddhi can then receive a flash of intuitive insight that gives us the meaning of the text for our particular mind/body. We receive that truth in a way that we simply know *(jñāna)* and need no further verification. (Although in the beginning some verification from an authoritative source helps us to calibrate our insight, to know when we are receiving insight and when we are fantasizing.) This is one aspect of *jñāna-yoga.*

According to Vyāsa's commentary on *Yoga-sūtra* II.1, the third traditional meaning of *svādhyāya* is the recitation of mantras in meditation *(japa)*. Through the gradual refinement of our awareness of the sounds in a mantra (going beyond even physical sound) we are led to deeper and deeper concentration and mindful awareness. For more on the practice of mantra, see Chapter 10.

Īśvara-praṇidhāna

The third component of Kriyā-yoga is īśvara-praṇidhāna. This is commonly translated as "surrender to divinity" or "religious devotion," but these are really preliminary forms to the meaning that Patañjali intends. In the commentary on YS I.23, Vyāsa makes it clear that the meaning of the term here is "practicing the presence of God" (Arya, 1986, pp. 278–279), meaning intentionally placing one's mind close to divinity at every moment. This kind of mindful attention to the common Being (known variously as Brahman, God, etc.) that we share with everything around us, even inanimate objects, attracts the graceful attention of divinity, and this grace eventually culminates in samādhi. In the preceding sūtras, Patañjali describes the prerequisites for samādhi, and then in this sūtra he says, "Or by īśvara-praṇidhāna," as if to indicate that this is a shortcut. In my own practice, I have sometimes asked myself, "At what level of Being are myself and this tree/rock/blossom the same? How can I see, feel, our common being?" I have found that contemplating these questions results in a very sweet sense of joyfulness in the mind/body. As we move deeper and deeper into the practice, it becomes as though divinity is playing hide and seek with us in the forms around us.

A friend of mine who is a professed solitary recalled reading a story in *The New Yorker* about a woman who went out into her family's garden just after breakfast one day and became fascinated with a particular blossom that just seemed to absorb her attention. The next thing she knew, she was being summoned back into the house for dinner many hours later! If we pause for a moment to take in this story, we feel the similarities between īśvara-praṇidhāna and the practices of svādhyāya and tapas. The woman in the garden illustrates so beautifully the absorption that we aim to experience in all three. It is only a matter of shifting the object of our attention. Whereas in tapas we attend mindfully to the urges of the primary fountains—and in svādhyāya we focus our attention on our breath and daily activities, sacred texts, or our relationship with a master—īśvara-praṇidhāna calls us directly to rest in the joy of ultimate Being.

Final Thoughts

The technique of Kriyā-yoga involves various ways of looking at the application of mindful attention to every facet of our life. In so doing, our whole relationship to our instinctive drives changes. Gradually we experience a deepening joy and beauty that satisfies the motivations of our desires. In other words, we add bright, harmonious, and peaceful *(sāttvik)* saṁskāras to our mindfield to thin out and rebalance our painful saṁskāras to the depths of our mind. This ultimately results in karmik propensities that create a future for us that is more and more conducive to deep concentration, meditation, and realization. We will discuss the theories of karma and saṁskāra in more detail in the next chapter. In the final chapter, we will examine how the practices of Kriyā-yoga bear fruit in the qualities of a clear and pleasant mind.

Chapter Five

Yama and Niyama: Yoga as Relationship

In the latter part of the *Yoga-sūtra*'s second chapter (II.29–55), Patañjali describes the eight limbs of Yoga that we know so well. They begin with the five yamas and then the five niyamas, all practices that help us lovingly and carefully to choose our behaviors and, with them, our personality propensities (saṁskāras) and karma. *Yama* may be translated as "ethical restraint." This is because the first of these attitudes is *ahiṁsā* (nonharm, nonviolence), and the other four yamas are extensions of that attitude. There must be someone or something towards which we practice the yamas, so they are intrinsically relational. The niyamas are, too. *Niyama* may be translated as "personal discipline." That list begins with *śauca* (purity), and the remaining four practices in the list extend and deepen that purity. These include the three practices of Kriyā-yoga from the previous chapter. Here again we deal in relationship, although niyama primarily addresses relationship to oneself.

Taking these two limbs together highlights the extent to which Yoga—and our karma—is relational. Whenever Patañjali makes a list in the sūtras, the order of the items on the list is significant. So it means something that he has placed the work with yama and niyama first and second in the process of working towards Self-realization. As if that were not enough, he explicitly highlights the importance of relationship in sūtra II.31. He states that the principles of the yamas apply "at all times, in all conditions, at all levels of practice and attainment." From beginning to end, Yoga is about relationship. It is very easy to become self-absorbed in our Yoga practice, making it all about "me" and "my enlightenment." But just as we share our life with others, we also share our practice and our realization with others, whether we recognize it or not. Both our joy and our pain, and others' joy and their pain, are somewhat functions of each other. Thus we will look at the yamas and the niyamas from a perspective that includes both the theory of karma and some salient concepts from interpersonal neurobiology. We will also emphasize the yamas and niyamas as fundamental expressions of our nature. Because our Being is inherently relational, when relationship is denied, our individual saṁskāras darken, and our "collective shadow" looms large.

Karma

To begin working with yourself in relationships, it is important to understand the functioning of your mind and emotions through the process of karma, which we alluded to in Chapter 1. *Karma* means "action." Once our pure Being has become (embodied), we begin to do, to act. Each action that we perform creates a mental impression in the depths of our minds (citta), a "seed," as it were, of future action. We carry in our little folded-over wave of the universal mindfield all the impressions (saṁskāras) from all our current and previous embodiments. Each of these impressions provides a quantum of emotional momentum, and the sum total of these creates a mental action (vṛtti) that impels us to act in a certain way from moment to moment throughout our lives. Most of the time we simply react to this momentum and act according to it. This creates a similar impression to the one that prompted the action in the first place; our newly created impression then deposits into the depths of our unconscious mind until it "ripens" and is ready to bear its fruit, again impelling our action. This amounts to recycling the same impressions, the same seeds or saṁskāras, over and over again. The process of change and growth involves becoming aware of our moment-to-moment emotional momentum and deciding whether to act according to it or do something different, to act rather than react. This is the essence of human free will and *karma-yoga.* So we reconstruct the reservoir of saṁskāras in our minds one action, one thought, one feeling at a time and, in this way, gradually reshape our karma.

Personal change, culminating in full psychological integration and samādhi, is a gradual process. It might seem overwhelmingly gradual, but remember that it took the Buddha 500 incarnations from the moment he intended to become enlightened to reach the point where he had cleansed his mind so thoroughly that enlightenment could dawn. The good news is that we have some time to work with ourselves. The other good news is that as we progress on this path, we grow from joy to joy. (There really isn't any bad news!) No matter how we may fall short from time to time, every good thing we do counts and must bear its fruit at some point. You can see, for example, how performing "random kindness and senseless acts of beauty" can help to shape a future that maximizes our momentum in the direction of enlightenment. Buddhists call this kind of mental momentum *bodhi-citta,* "enlightenment mind." (For more on this notion, consult *Bodhicāryavatāra* of Śāntideva, an eighth-century Buddhist text available in many English translations; see Shāntideva, 2011.)

Over the course of a lifetime, as you exhaust the karmik momentum of the saṁskāras that were ripe to bear their fruit in your current body and draw near the end of your life, a new set of seeds ripens to bear its fruit in the next bodily life. According to Patañjali, these ripening seeds of karmik momentum coalesce into a *karmāśaya* (reservoir of karma) that arises in our mind as we leave the current body; our karma then guides our subtle mind to birth circumstances that provide opportunities for these seeds to bear their fruits in the next body (YS II.12–14). This is how we find and "choose" our parents in the next life. The momentum of actions in our previous bodily life heavily determines these choices.

Interestingly, since we live in family groups that interact with each other in deeply patterned ways, we may often find ourselves living with the same beings life after life, gradually learning the lessons we have to receive from each other. In this way, families serve as "karmik pools." This is just as true for our biological families as it is for our families of choice, intimates we choose in life who are distinct from those given to us at birth. How many times have you encountered a person you have not previously met, and yet you recognized each other immediately and seemed to know each other in deep ways? So our intimate friends and lovers swim in this pool, as well. We might say that the process of karma-yoga is about learning to swim skillfully, beautifully, in the karmik waters of our relationships. This perspective adds another layer of meaning to Kṛṣṇa's teaching in the *Bhagavad-gītā* (II.20), *Yogaḥ karmasu kauśalam,* "Yoga is skill/beauty/wellness in action." We know whether we are acting skillfully in our lives based on our relationships with others, and the results of our actions are more far-reaching than we often realize.

Interpersonal Neurobiology: Relationship Maps and Mirror Neurons

In addition to this Yogic perspective on working with relationships, there is some very interesting neurobiology involved. Remember that the mind is a "relational and embodied process that regulates the flow of energy and information" (Siegel, 2010, p. 52). It is the relational aspect of the mind as it operates through the brain and nervous system that we will examine now.

Relationships certainly involve a "flow of energy and information" (Siegel, 2010, p. 52). This happens both consciously, in terms of what we intend to communicate, and unconsciously, in ways that may or may not be intentional. Some communication has more energy (e.g., pure expression of emotion), and some has more information (e.g., an explanation of the larger context of those emotions). How do our brains and nervous systems make sense of this?

The brain contains a particular kind of neuron called a *mirror neuron.* These are distributed throughout the brain and are activated when other people act in specific sequences that allow us both to perceive and to understand what they are doing and to create a model of that behavior in our own minds. This modeling ability helps us to imitate other's actions to "try on" a new behavior and see how it fits with the rest of the behavioral pattern that we call our (psychological) self. When we watch someone yawn and find ourselves yawning in response whether or not we are tired, our mirror neurons are active. When we learn to understand another's behavior and "wear" it as our own, a system of mirror neurons wires together. A model of ourselves is thus created; a "me-map" is born (Siegel, 2012b, section 42, p. 1).

As our brains develop in childhood, our mirror neurons also develop, and they wire into the system based on interactions with our parents. Babies are cute for a reason! Their cuteness attracts the big people so they get close to a baby's face, within the infant's range of focus, and begin responding to the baby's somewhat random emission of behaviors. These interactions stimulate the growth of the infant's mirror neurons and their wiring with each other and with other parts of the nervous system. Thus the child gradually makes a mental model of his or her parents' minds and consequently of him- or herself. As the child forms a "self-model," he or she makes all kinds of experiments with behavior, some of which the child keeps, and some of which he or she discards. So infants borrow the mirroring and modeling capability of their parents in the process of creating a psychological sense of self. Their cuteness initiates a pathway to jumpstart their processes of both intra- and interpersonal development. It is a process of direct transmission from parent to child, hence the Yoga tradition's dictum that parents are our first gurus: They teach by transmission! From the very beginning of life to the end, Yoga is about relationship.

This system of interpersonal modeling is carried out through what interpersonal neurobiologists call *resonance circuits*. These comprise the interconnections among the mirror neurons and various functions of the brain and nervous system. In seeking to understand others, we intentionally create models of their minds that we carry in our own minds. To the extent that our models are accurate, there is likely to be an experience of compassion, the ability to "[feel] with" the other person (Siegel, 2012b, section AI, p. 16). The same process applies as we try to understand ourselves. As we alluded to in Chapter 2, interpersonal neurobiologists call this ability to sense experience "attunement" (Siegel, 2012b, section 23, pp. 1–5). When attuned, we "resonate" to others' experiences, or to our own. Our skill in resonating with, or attuning to, others and to ourselves determines the accuracy of our internal models, our maps of "me," "you," and "we" (Siegel, 2012b, section 42, pp. 1–8). To the extent that others resonate with us accurately, we feel understood and often loved. When we attune accurately to ourselves, we're able to identify our thoughts, emotions, and motivations. If we struggle with internal attunement, we feel distant from our own inner life, and our experiences and motivations are somewhat unclear to us. Self-compassion is a matter of internal resonance with our "me-map"; compassion for others concerns the accuracy of the resonance of our "you-maps." Our maps are a vital part of the "circuits" along which we resonate with other people and ourselves.

As with the rest of the functioning of the nervous system, our resonance circuits seek integration, in response to which we feel joy as we grow. In other words, we are driven towards attunement: We yearn for relationship as a kind of natural urge. In spiritual terminology, humans are compelled to give and receive compassionate, integrated, resonant attunement. This is why, as the poet John Donne wrote, "No man is an island / entire of itself." We need relationships to grow and to develop. We need a community around us: a family, a family of choice, a tribe (which is an extended family), a community, a nation. It is fundamental and necessary to the growth and maturation of our nervous system. (To identify areas in your life where you might wish to enhance the quality or depth of your relationships, either with yourself or with others, see Appendix A, Exercise 3.10. A list of specific strategies for enriching your relationships can be found in the same appendix, Exercise 3.11.)

Our Need for Relationship and the Origin of Our Shadow

Our urge towards interpersonal integration—Self-realization—also involves the cultivation of all kinds of positive attitudes, or drives: compassion, love, friendship, understanding, and forgiveness, to name but a few that allow community to happen. These positive drives, of which Swāmī Veda speaks in his book *The Human Urge for Peace: What is Right with the World* (Bharati, 2013a), are all differentiations of the neurobiological drive towards both internal and relational integration: the deep, erotic human drives towards mindful awareness, attunement, and joy!

When we examine the relational practices of the yamas and niyamas, we will see how they contribute to the development and expression of these positive drives. It is these drives that support the progress of human evolution (as well as the progress of spiritual "evolution"). But just as our growth depends upon our developing the best of our nature, it also asks us to take responsibility for the "worst," the "shadow" side of our conditioning. We have established that we must not focus our attention on negative qualities by suppressing or indulging them (lest we create further similar saṁskāras). Yet we must also accept all the potentialities within us, "taking the good with the bad," as it were, so that we might find our own direction and emphasis in our individual pursuit of the yamas and niyamas. We will return to this subject in the next section.

In the meantime, let's establish why the yamas and niyamas are so critically important by discussing the positive drives and their shadow together. Here is another important relationship, as each plays its own role in human and spiritual evolution. Far from depending on "survival of the fittest" in a competitive world, the species that are most successful (ants, for example) are the ones that have the most functional and collaborative social organization. Humans, too, succeed as a species relative to our abilities to learn, adapt, and build social collaboration. Our ancestors banded together in tribes for physical protection against the elements and other animals. Eventually they settled in agrarian communities and divided the labor amongst themselves, allowing their minds more free time to explore and to innovate and their brains the opportunity to evolve as a result. Who we are today, the relative mental advancement that we enjoy as individuals, depends on the groups of other human beings, past and present, who have joined together to grow.

We have sustained social advancement through the ages with compassion, love, friendship, understanding, and forgiveness. But we know that human history and the modern era are sadly replete with devastating examples of humans imposing qualities opposite these on each other. This is our collective shadow. We might observe that our societies have evolved despite this shadow, and in cynicism we could ask how important the positive drives really are. We might think that perhaps our shadow, something like survival of the fittest, has provided us with the strength and the smarts to endure, or at least the opportunity to express the positive drives and to evolve as a result. (While the latter might seem true in a relative sense, pure joy is Self-existent and always has been. It does not depend on the shadow to evolve. In fact, *evolving towards joy* is a contradiction of terms because although we feel like we are evolving, we are actually uncovering something that has always lived within us, as us. We use these terms because they reflect our felt experience, but both human and spiritual evolution are "unfoldings" more than they are "evolvings.") When we think of the human species in terms of our evolution, we must emphasize that if strength comes from a will to survive, we accomplish this strength and our species' survival through loving relationship rather than through brutish competition.

In the animal world, survival of the fittest often implies fighting to the death and abandoning the sick and the lame. These competitive and short-sighted behaviors, when adopted by humans, create societies that are unjust and unstable and threatened by war, revolt, terrorism, and hate crimes. They tend not to endure. All these behaviors people commit because they feel a lack of relationship, a disconnection from or abandonment by their fellow human beings. Pick any atrocity in the news, and reflect on whether this theory might not somehow describe its underlying cause.

The intention of this discussion is not to discourage us, but to help us acknowledge reality as our senses perceive it, as well as to see where our Yoga practice fits within it. The shadow can be deeply painful. When we witness an insidious human rights violation, Yoga asks us to breathe into our observations and feel the unsettling anger and fear that arise from a simultaneous assault on all our primary fountains. The core of our being becomes fundamentally disturbed at even the thought of horrific behavior because it is so antithetical to who we are. Extreme emotions like horror, terror, and rage tell us when something is diametrically opposing both our basic nature as Self and our basic needs as the psychological self.

We must remember this when considering our fellows who commit horrific acts. As difficult as it may seem to accept, their truest nature is love and peace, just as ours is. But because of the veil of our human condition, when one's core love and peace are thwarted, humans, when not watchful, respond with angry acts of varying offense. We are all susceptible to our own *saṁskārik* emotional momentum, which can combine with traumatic injury, mental illness, or the unjust frustration of primary fountain needs. These can push us over the limit of our self-restraint (nonviolence), beyond which we commit violations against our essential Being. From the minor to the obscene, we and our fellows commit violent acts because our own being (which we know, deep in our bones, "should" be love and peace) has instead become disturbed. All our maps are "out of tune." Weary and frustrated, we avoid our pain by projecting it outwards, inflicting much the same experience on others that we ourselves eschew. In avoiding ourselves, we are not attuned to our me-map. In forcing our pain on others, we are not attuned to their needs, to our you-maps of them, or to the we-maps of our relationships. Whereas knowing the Self implies complete integration of all our maps, extreme violence is the manifestation of its opposite, "dis-integration." Do you see the shadow nature of this phenomenon? The worst human acts are the result of our deepest and best yearnings for the nature of Self, unfulfilled and consequently perverted, sometimes terribly.

Yet our most despairing and painful moments, when we acknowledge and accept them as such, can become an opportunity to move back towards ultimate love and compassion. Our breaking points, when we admit how broken we feel, facilitate our letting go of fear, judgement, and control and, most importantly, self-identification. They break open a space in our ego for Guru to enter in and put us back together. It's as if we each are a lightbulb covered in a layer of thick paint. The light of Guru is always with us, shining brightly, observing our activities with love and allowing Its consciousness to move through buddhi and all our layers of being to energize our lives. Enjoyable, soothing Yoga practices allow the light of Guru to become more visible as our practices gently chip away at the paint. But our pain can roar at us loudly, its intensity sometimes blasting the paint away and shocking us into abandoning our psychological self's facade of control. In its place, we can realize, sometimes abruptly, our reliance on Guru's love and presence. Take, for example, the experience of Christ's Apostle Paul, stuck down by the Guru's light on the road to Damascus as he single-mindedly plotted the persecution of Christians (Acts 9:3–9).

Mindfully, we can hold the causes and purposes of pain in our hearts and take care of our own shadow, whether it manifests as anger or some other emotion, soothing it as a mother would comfort her child. Without suppressing what arises, we can call on the Guru force to help us refrain from action until we remember the healing qualities of relationship, including desperately needed compassion and forgiveness. We can ask Guru to help us employ the preventive care—the yamas and niyamas—to which we must hold fast. These are also the salves without which recovery and continued social existence would be impossible. In this way, the collective shadow provides us as individuals with an opportunity to practice our intention to develop the positive drives. When many individuals within a society take up this work, humanity evolves, or rather, unfolds; when they turn away from it, society withers.

On June 12, 2016, a gunman killed 49 people and injured 53 at a gay nightclub in Orlando, Florida, the worst mass shooting in United States history. In its wake, a local radio station posted a quotation on its Facebook page by the late Mr. (Fred) Rogers. Disarmingly simple, the words of this much-loved expert in neighborly relations speak to our basic focus in spiritual practice:

> When I was a boy and I would see scary things in the news, my mother would say to me, "Look for the helpers. You will always find people who are helping." To this day, especially in times of disaster, I remember my mother's words, and I am always comforted by realizing that there are still so many helpers—so many caring people in this world. (K-LOVE Afternoon Show)

We demonstrate our own caring and grow towards its deepest expression by practicing the yamas and niyamas. Acknowledging shadow, we notice what needs to be done and we do it, focusing not on what is wrong, but on what is right. We help because we know that being in positive relationship, both with Guru and with each other, drives us forward as individuals and as a species. This applies both in the aftermath of great pain and in our hopeful reach towards our fullest potential.

Even our most searing pain points to the Self. All our drives, positive as well as negative, are ultimately the drive for the joy of unfoldment and Self-realization. The fulfillment of this work with ourselves and with each other is eventually to transcend even the duality of good and evil. It is not simply a matter of converting "bad" saṁskāras into good ones, although the process of thinning down our afflicted vṛttis does at first entail replacing darker saṁskāras with brighter ones. Then eventually even our bright saṁskāras are burned in the fire of knowledge in samādhi, resulting in our final liberation. In this way, the yamas and niyamas are not based in morality, although in our unliberated condition they are in truth the basis for morality.

The Yamas

Ahiṁsā, Nonviolence

The first of the yamas, ahiṁsā, develops through the growth of compassion, gradually extinguishing fear. We cultivate compassion and nonviolence in our lives not so much in any particular technique or practice, but in becoming deeply aware of our own suffering and, by doing so, becoming increasingly sensitive to the suffering of others. To the extent that we avoid our own pain and the things we fear in life, we become incapable of offering genuine compassion to other humans, much less to other creatures. The inability to feel someone else's pain is another way to say that we have disconnected from him or her. This person can now more easily become the object of the limits of our self-restraint. So whatever you dissociate from, whatever you run from in your life, is your path to nonviolence.

This can work itself out in many ways. For example, I grew up with a father who sold rifles and ammunition and was a great hunter and fisherman. When I accompanied him on his hunting and fishing adventures, it was great to be with my dad and to walk the harvested fields in the misty autumn dawn or to sit silently in a boat on a quiet lake in the glorious summer sunshine. But the death of the animals anguished me deeply, and I used to weep bitterly watching the captured fish slowly dying. My father didn't know what to make of this. He likely did not feel this pain within himself and so could not feel it in me. At first I did not know what to do with the pain either, and so in a sense, I ran from it. But, as is the case whenever we avoid something, this sensitivity didn't leave me, and so in my early adult years I decided to eat a vegetarian diet. In the same way, let your practice gradually follow your awareness and your sensitivities. The important practice here is to be aware of your own heart deeply and to respond to that awareness in shaping your behavior. It is helpful to practice intentionally reducing the violence of your relationships with other beings through practices that many texts describe, but your greatest obstacles and your greatest breakthroughs will always relate to your own deepest pain.

Some people approach ahiṁsā and the other limbs of the Yoga path as if they were rules. This approach ignores one's inner awareness and can lead to behavior that is violent towards ourselves or others. For example, there are certainly people who cannot tolerate a vegetarian diet and remain healthy. For them, vegetarianism is violence towards the body. They can find other ways to express the growth and deepening of their compassion.

As compassion develops within us, our presence changes in perceptible ways. Patañjali (YS II.35) describes how the establishment of nonviolence in people results in their presence becoming so benign that even wild animals lose their aggression near them. Swāmī Rāma recounts a story of walking in the jungle with his master when they encountered a large king cobra on the path, its head raised in an aggressive posture, about two meters (six feet!) off the ground. The master calmly approached the snake, gazed lovingly into its eyes, and began gently stroking the snake's head and hood, at which point the snake quietly lowered itself to the ground and moved away (Rama, 1978).

Swāmī Rāma's master had conquered the final fear, that of death.

As we discussed in the previous chapter, the primary fountain of self-preservation motivates this most deep seated of fears. So great was the master's compassion, and so deep was his understanding of the nature of life and death, that he learned to see his bodily life as no more important than that of any other being, even valuing others' lives above his own. This is a culminating result of bodhi-citta practice. He felt no fear with the snake or in any other moment because the primary fountain of self-preservation no longer trapped him. Nonviolence is the result of pacifying fear. The remaining yamas can also be understood as practices that moderate and ultimately extinguish fear, as they move us away from violence and towards compassion.

Satya, Truthfulness

The second yama, truthfulness, involves the accuracy of our mind's internal maps of ourselves, others, and our relationships. If we are truthful to ourselves, as the sayings from many cultures go, we cannot be false to anyone. If our behavior is true to our personality, then we are communicating honestly and congruently; our behavior matches our thoughts and feelings. This means that our actions are in harmony with our me-map. In terms of our behavior towards others, there is a balancing act where the question is always how accurately we resonate with the people around us. For example, we have all known people who resonate excessively with others' pain in ways that result in action that is also excessive. In this case, we might say that their you-map and their me-map are incongruent, not resonating accurately with each other, so that their we-map is also incoherent. These individuals are not really attuned to those around them, and they are not attuned to their own needs. As a result, their behavior is often too much, as in the case of codependency or caretaking beyond one's capacity, or too little, as in the case of emotional neglect.

We must always contextualize truthfulness by the principle of nonviolence, or, in positive terms, compassion and accurate resonance. In his commentary on the *Yoga-sūtra* defining *satya* (YS

II.30), Vyāsa states that truthful speech takes into consideration the benefit of all beings; otherwise, it is only a simulation of virtue. His interpretation reflects the often quoted principle that our speech should always be *hita,* beneficial; *mita,* measured; and *priya,* loving. Otherwise, partial truths easily become weapons in a heated exchange. A partial truth is no truth at all. Remember a time when you have used this type of ammunition against someone, and reflect on how you might have spoken differently.

When truthfulness is firmly established in us, the attunement of our me-map is perfectly accurate and aligned with the spiritual Self (ātman). Patañjali says in sūtra II.36 that we then "become the resort of all actions and the fruits thereof" (Bhāratī, 2001, p. 531). (The Sanskrit word *āśrayatvam* in the sūtra is a future participle of the verb meaning "resort to." So a person who has become truth itself is the source of all actions and their results.) Hence, according to Vyāsa, our "speech becomes unfailingly efficacious" (Bhāratī, 2001, p. 531). When our me-map attunes to Self, ultimate attunement of all three sets of maps (me, you, and we) can be said to occur because Self permeates all: When we experience Self directly in samādhi, our me-map that we usually ascribe to ahaṁkāra becomes no less than the map of the universe. This results in a situation where one will not speak untruth, and whatever one does say will "unfailingly" come true (Bhāratī, 2001, p. 531). Jesus said to his disciple Peter, "You will deny me three times" (Matthew 26:34, Mark 14:30, Luke 22:34). Peter protested with all his heart, but the master knew his heart better. He was more attuned to the highest reality, and when the time came, Peter gave in to his fear three times.

Asteya, Nonstealing

Following the principle of *asteya,* nonstealing, means using only that in life which is legitimately yours. In other words, your sense of possession is congruent with your self-identification. You do not misappropriate, which is violence towards some other. Your we-map is attuned to your me-map. As your self-identification with the internal spiritual Self (ātman) gradually increases, your self-identification with external objects slowly shrinks. There is less and less in the world that you feel to be yours, and whatever has seemed to be yours you become more willing to give to others. In the same way that the positive face of nonviolence is compassion, the positive face of nonstealing is selfless generosity. After renouncing the wealthy life of his father's family and literally stripping himself naked in front of his town, St. Francis of Assisi, seeing a beggar on the street whose clothes were more ragged than his own, would beg that person, joyfully and lovingly, to trade clothes with him. So the notion of asteya goes well beyond simple nonstealing and becomes compassionate generosity.

Of one whose mind and heart have grown in this way, Patañjali says in sūtra II.37, "all treasures attend upon him" (Bhāratī, 2001, p. 534). In one sense, this is an affirmation of divine providence, the ability of divinity to provide whatever one needs unasked. When one has reached the point of owning nothing because identification with the spiritual Self is complete, then the whole world becomes one's own. However, Patañjali implies an even deeper meaning here. The "treasures" he refers to are *siddha*s and *deva*s, celestial beings who attend to, or care for, one who is totally engaged in selfless service. When we realize that nothing we "own" is ours, divinity responds by giving us all that we need and more.

Brahmacarya, Single-Hearted Love

Brahmacarya, literally "moving or walking in Brahman," is often misunderstood. Many commonly discuss this attitude in negative terms as sexual abstinence and mislabel it as celibacy for its own sake, a rule to follow, when brahmacarya is more like a state to attain. Even Vyāsa defines it as "control of the secret organ" (Bhāratī, 2001, p. 534). Most interpreters of his commentary identify the "secret organ" as one's genital organ because it is kept private. In fact, the secret organ is the mind. It is secret because no one can see it. Although the mind is the field of "energy and information" (Siegel, 2010, p. 52) through which all our senses operate, we can only encounter it internally. So brahmacarya is not control of one's sexuality, but control of one's mind.

One reason many tend to focus on brahmacarya only as control of sexuality is that our enjoyment of sex involves all the senses—active as well as cognitive, and the whole of the mindfield—bringing the mind to a truly one-pointed concentration (integration) that results in a brief moment of ecstatic joy. In Yoga, intentionally one-pointed (joyful) concentration leads to withdrawal of the senses, and sensory withdrawal prepares one's buddhi for Self-realization (YS II.41). In the moment of sexual orgasm, we glimpse that ultimately attuned state for a split second, in a relatively uncontrolled way; we haven't yet established it in our Being with consistency. So we latch on to the thought that harnessing the sexual energies will bring the mind to the one-pointedness required to initiate the remainder of this process.

While this is possible, it requires enormous discipline. Our approach cannot skip ahead to sensory control, sexual abstinence for its own sake, trying to hold our sexuality still, as it were. The difficulty of this effort often takes the mind away from the very one-pointedness that mindful sensory withdrawal requires. To attain concentration first, we must learn to work with all our energies, sexual and otherwise, in a gradual process of awareness that involves much more than sex or abstinence. We must "walk with Brahman" all the time and in many ways, not just in relationship to our sexuality. Rather than thinking of brahmacarya as a rule to follow, then, it is more accurate to understand it as a description of a realized state. Brahmacarya is the experience of a mind established in ultimate attunement with the Self, ātman. (To be out of that ultimate attunement can be considered violence towards the Self.)

What would it be like to live in the state of Self-attunement all the time? It is hard to imagine one's nervous system being able to tolerate such unrelenting ecstasy. And yet that is the self-report of advanced Yogis. Brahmacarya is the experience of the bliss (ānanda) of *ātman-Brahman,* the joy of our individual Self's union with God, in the same way that a guru joyfully aligns to the primordial Guru. Yogananda (1971) described it in his account of his first experience of samādhi as "oceanic joy . . . exhaustless bliss . . . a swelling glory!" (p. 149). "From joy I came, for joy I live, in sacred joy I melt!" (Yogananda, 1971, p. 152). If one were capable of such a life, who would trade that for only a few seconds of ecstasy in the physical release of sex?! An advanced Yogi capable of controlling the secret organ of the mind, far from suppressing sexuality, simply has lost the need for or the interest in it.

The word *celibacy* in English derives from the Latin *caelibatus,* "unmarried," and hence "single." This Latin term relates to the Sanskrit *kevala*, meaning "solo" or "solitary." The term for liberation in the Yoga system is *kaivalya* (an abstract form of the word *kevala*), the state of being ultimately solitary. A good English translation from the Christian literature on spiritual practice would be "ultimate interior solitude." (See, for example, the works of St. Teresa of Avila, especially *The Interior Castle,* in Peers, 1946/2007.) To many this might sound lonely, but in a state of ultimate attunement, where one experiences "exhaustless bliss" (Yogananda, 1971, p. 152), there is no loneliness possible. Divinity is ever present.

As in Yoga, the Judeo–Christian traditions cite celibacy as a first principle of single-hearted love, a solitary inner state in which one is "unwed" to anyone or anything other than God. In Hebrew this principle is called *sh'ma*: "You shall love the Lord your God with all your heart and with all your soul and with all your mind" (Deuteronomy 6:4–9). It is given in the Torah, it is one of the chief mantras of meditative Judaism, and Jesus restates it in the New Testament of the Christian Bible. He calls it "the first and greatest commandment" (Mark 12:29–30).

In an ultimately attuned mind, where external behavior is

congruent with internal attunement, one simply does not trade the great joy for a partial joy, in the same way that one would not trade the great truth for a partial truth. Brahmacarya means walking in this awareness at all times. In this state of being, all the senses resonate with the ultimate attunement of the mind and heart, and so sexuality is not repressed, but nor are its energies expressed in the usual way. An ultimately attuned person, according to Patañjali (YS II.38), attains *vīrya,* "capacity," "mastery." Vyāsa interprets, "One intensifies and advances unhinderable good qualities, and having become an adept [*siddha*], he becomes capable of placing knowledge into the disciples" (Bhāratī, 2001, p. 536).[10] This word *vīrya* relates to the English *virile* and refers not to sexual power, but rather to the power to initiate states of higher consciousness in others.

If we think back to our earlier discussion of tapas, it becomes clear that one does not learn to be celibate by simply avoiding sex. It begins from learning to enjoy one's sexuality with concentration and from training the mind to perceive the presence of divinity everywhere (*ātma-tattva-avalokanam,* "looking for the essence of Self, which is God"). In Christian terms, this is the practice of the presence of God. As one's attunement with that divine presence grows, the tendency to be satisfied with smaller pleasures gradually and joyfully decreases. Brahmacarya is never a process of mere self-denial.

Aparigraha, Nongrasping

Finally among the yamas we have *aparigraha,* "nongrasping." The Sanskrit verb root √*grah* is cognate with the English words *grab* and *grasp*. The prefix *pari-* is the same as the Latin *peri-*, "around." So *aparigraha* is literally "not grabbing around." Vyāsa clarifies that this attitude develops out of realizing the violence and suffering that result from attachment to owning and guarding possessions and objects of desire. It also develops when we feel the pain that accompanies their loss. When we understand this, greed and

[10] The insertion is Swāmī Veda's.

attachment of all kinds gradually cease.

Related to asteya, nonstealing, the attitude of nongrasping also concerns the way in which the greed to possess (even knowledge) decreases as we increasingly become attuned to the spiritual Self (ātman or puruṣa). As we cease to identify with external things—objects, people, or even our physical bodies and our mindfields—we become less concerned with exerting the power and control that come with ownership. As a result, a fullness of realization comes to us of "the how and why of incarnations" (YS I.39, Bhāratī, 2001, p. 539). This is related to the knowledge described in sūtras I.48–49 and IV.29. The knowledge that comes is the *ṛtam-bharā-prājñā,* "truth bearing wisdom"—not knowledge in a general sense, but the particular knowledge of all things—or, in Chapter 4, the *dharma-megha-samādhi,* meditative experience of the "raincloud of virtues"—omniscience that floods the mind, filling every space like a monsoon storm.

We often think of aparigraha as a simple decrease in materialism. It also implies, in our relationships, a decrease in our envy ("I should have that") and a decrease in our jealousy (seeing an object that is not ours and believing, "That is mine!"). This is a fine attunement of our we-maps. We can enjoy our relationships without possessing or controlling others. If we have no expectations of others, then we can never be disappointed. Every success becomes something to be celebrated, and every failure becomes an understandable event, the learning from which success may result the next time.

There is also a decrease in spiritual materialism. How often have we measured our spiritual progress in terms of how much or how long or how deeply we can do a certain practice? Our practice can become a kind of object we possess, rather than an act of selfless love that we celebrate and enjoy. We begin to have a subtle interest in power and control, which is the beginning of attachment. Christian solitary Maggie Ross (2007b) has written, "Presumptuous control, beyond the capacity of the creature, is the sin of the Garden." That is why the knowledge described above only dawns when we have become so dispassionate (*parā-vairāgya,* supreme dispassion) that we lose even the attachment to liberation. (For an excellent read on this subject, consult Chögyam Trungpa's 2002 book, *Cutting Through Spiritual Materialism.*) Only then do we become genuinely innocent, *Adama* in Aramaic, and re-enter the Garden (of Eden).

Patañjali describes the yamas as "the universal [unconditional] great vows, to be practiced at all levels of *yoga*" (YS II.31, Bhāratī, 2001, p. 486). They form the behavioral picture of a spiritual attitude in practice, and their attainment forms the portrait of a siddha, one who has accomplished Yoga. The secret in the practice of these attitudes is not so much in following a set of rules, but in gradually, through awareness, improving the attunement of your me-map to the spiritual Self; this results in the greater accuracy of your you-maps, which gives you greater compassion, and in the attunement of your we-maps, which increases your understanding and your generosity of heart in relationships.

The Niyamas

We now come to the niyamas, practices for our internal sense of self-relationship that enable us to make the behavioral changes implied in the yamas. Vyāsa's commentary describes these as practices that help to eliminate *vitarka*s, which Swāmī Veda often referred to as "misratiocinations"[11]: logical errors, cognitive distortions that result in suffering. The Alcoholics Anonymous program would characterize these distortions as "stinkin' thinkin.'" In the language of interpersonal neurobiology, these are errors in attunement to ourselves caused by modeling ourselves and others based on a lack of awareness, based on ignorance *(avidyā)*.

In a word, all vitarkas, distorted ideas and thought processes, are

[11]As a scholar of both Sanskrit and other classical, revealed languages, Swāmī Veda would often use Greek and Latin roots to coin a word to arrive at a more precise translation of all the levels of meaning in the Sanskrit. The results are sometimes a little cumbersome.

the result of *violence*. In sūtra II.34, Patañjali details all the different kinds of direct and indirect involvements we may have with violence, their causes in painful emotions (based on desires), and their varying intensities. He then goes on to describe how we can increase the purity of the mindfield by "cultivating the opposite wing," *prati-pakṣa-bhāvanā,* that is, by cultivating the opposite attitude of the vitarkas. This supports our relational attunement and our internal integration and is precisely the process of tapas discussed earlier. We replace pleasure—the fulfillment of desire by its objects (food, sleep, sex, and self-preservation)—with joy, an aesthetic rapture generated by enjoyment through concentration.

Śauca, Purity

The first niyama, śauca, includes both external and internal purity. External purity refers to physical cleanliness and to the maintenance of the physical body through a healthy diet, as well as to internal cleansing practices that make it possible for the body to remain relaxed and the mind to be undistracted. Internal purity refers to the process of citta-prasādana or *bhāva-śuddhi,* emotional purification, the principal subject of this book. Our lack of attunement to the care of the physical body and to emotions in the mindfield results in distraction in the form of a lack of concentration and physical discomfort at best, or disease resulting from "dis-ease" at worst. These are the *vi-kṣepa*s (another term for *kleśa,* painful modification of the mind) from Chapter 1 and Patañjali's YS I.30. It's interesting to note that even in our body-bound habit of mind, we are still not accurately attuned to the bodies to which we are so attached!

Almost every spiritual tradition has some notion of spiritual or ritual purity. And almost every tradition has some kind of rulebook about how to behave to maintain and deepen that sense of purity. In Christianity and Judaism, there are the law books of the Torah, in particular the Levitical Code. In Islam, there is Sharī'ah. In Hinduism, the *Dharma-śāstra.* But we cannot grow spiritually or develop spiritual purity merely by rule. Such an approach quickly becomes an exercise where the rules of purity become more important than "the first and greatest commandment" (Mark 12:29–30) to love divinity with all your heart and mind. The principles in the books are guidelines, but the real measure of your efforts at greater purity, as with nonviolence, are your sensitivities and mindful awareness and how they guide your behavior. Otherwise śauca becomes a sort of obsessive-compulsive disorder where obedience to rules overshadows the love of God.

As awareness and attunement increase, as purity becomes established in a person's mind and heart, Patañjali (YS II.41) describes how the mind becomes (in this order) clear, good-minded, one-pointed, and in control of the senses, and one's buddhi becomes qualified for the direct realization of the spiritual Self (ātman). This sense of clarity also implies stability of the mindfield and stillness of the mind/body.

Saṁtoṣa, Contentment

Saṁtoṣa means being satisfied with whatever comes to you. It is related to nonstealing (asteya) and nongrasping (aparigraha). When there is an ultimate attunement to the spiritual Self, one is always satisfied, and there is no desire to take any more of anything than is absolutely needed. When Swāmī Rāma's master would appear to help people, they would usually offer food or sweets, but he never accepted anything so that people understood "his" actions as pure grace. Yogananda's master showed extreme patience with his pupil's restlessness for an experience of samādhi, which took him away from his duties at the *āśram* (ashram). The master explained, as we discussed with aparigraha above, that if he had no desirous expectations of anyone, including Yogananda, how could he be disappointed by Yogananda's behavior (Yogananda, 1971, p. 147)? This is the psychological experience of contentment.

There is also a physiological experience of contentment in the processes of relaxation. This is not confined to exercises done lying on our back in *śavāsana*, the corpse posture. Even in moment-to-moment, day-to-day life, the moment one begins to observe the breath, the central nervous system initiates the relaxation response, and the body physically relaxes. Because there is no essential difference between body and mind, the mind also calms down, and disturbing, "violent," desire-based emotions begin to subside. As we've discussed, this creates a slightly more objective space from which to observe one's arising emotions and a bit more time to decide how to respond to them rather than merely react. The relaxation of the mind/body thus creates a softening of our attachments to our reactions, which is an experience of relative contentment. As we become more and more skilled at doing this in a moment-to-moment way throughout our day, we can eventually learn to remain perfectly relaxed at all times. This is the real perfection of śavāsana, the corpse posture! So the less attuned we are to our mind and body, the more tension we carry, the more violent emotional reactions we experience, the more illness we suffer, and the less we feel content. But the more we can attune to our mind/body, and ultimately to the Self, the more content we become.

The Final Three Niyamas

The last three niyamas—tapas, svādhyāya, and īśvara-praṇidhāna—comprise the process of Kriyā-yoga described in the previous chapter and prescribed by Patañjali for the middle category of Yoga practitioners. These practices are especially useful to aspirants who have created a medium level of karmik momentum on their spiritual path and whose minds can usually be characterized as disturbed but beginning to see moments of concentration (vi-kṣiptam; see Chapter 1). As you recall from the previous chapter, Kriyā-yoga "thins down" *(tanu-karaṇa)* the painful operations of the mind (kleśa) (YS II.2). So in our practice of the final three niyamas, we emphasize the thinning down of pain, which gradually results both in the greater attunement of our mind/body to the spiritual Self and in the reduction of ignorant nonattunement. In Chapter 4, we examined these niyamas as practices of mindful awareness. Let's focus briefly in this chapter on their application to the notions of relational attunement and resonance.

Tapas, enjoyment through concentration. Patañjali describes tapas as withstanding the pain that comes from the experience of pairs of opposites, like heat and cold, standing and sitting, and so forth (YS II.32). The *vibhūti* (natural development) that comes from the establishment of tapas is mastery of the body and senses. In terms of relational attunement, tapas helps us attune to our perception of bodily life. As we described earlier, the process of tapas, gently and joyfully, helps us to lessen our dependence on the instinctive drives and the energies they provide to support our physical existence. Because tapas shifts our balance in relationship to the four primary fountains of desire, it reduces the emotional pain generated by contact with either too much or too little of the fountains. Mastery over the body and senses then emerges as a natural development, a vibhūti.

As Vyāsa clarifies, the process of tapas "destroys the macula of the veil of impurities" (Bhāratī, 2001, pp. 556–557) that obscures our natural abilities. The veil of impurities is our dependence on the primary fountains, in other words a lack of attunement to our own bodies and senses out of a failure of awareness, or ignorance (avidyā). The macula that Bhāratī (2001) describes refers to the impurity of our mindfields, as contrasted with the purity of the immaculate Self. The word *macula* derives from the Latin *maculatus,* the past participle of a verb meaning "to stain;" *macula* also means "marked with spots" (read saṁskāras), so tapas removes the spots (*saṁskāra*s) on our veil of impurities (primary fountain dependence). Tapas "unsticks" our "sticking points," which would otherwise reinforce the veil (false viewpoint) that separates us from the Self and that causes us to need the primary fountains for our sustenance rather than to know and depend on our wholeness as Self to sustain us. This veil remains with us until final liberation removes it, along with all our spotty sticking points: our "good" and "bad" saṁskāras, the light and shadow sides of our being.

In the meantime, the veil prevents us from realizing all that is within our realm of possibility, including both the seemingly ordinary ability to calm our emotions and the seemingly extraordinary ability to perform feats typically understood as miraculous. When we lift the veil, astonishing capacities known as *siddhi*s reveal themselves. Thus we can understand the siddhis of Yoga also as vibhūtis.

It may seem astounding to think that the siddhis are innate to humans, but Radin (2013) very clearly demonstrates this in his book *Supernormal: Science, Yoga, and the Evidence for Extraordinary Psychic Abilities.* Rather than studying the siddhis of Yoga through examining highly accomplished practitioners, Radin set out to see to what extent these abilities exist in ordinary people who practice no Yoga or meditation. In rigorously designed experiments testing a range of psychic phenomena such as telepathy, precognition, and clairvoyance, Radin showed that these capacities are present at low but measurable levels in *everyone*—with a degree of certainty that means it is not possible that these were just random results. (Radin's experiments were meta-analytical—they grouped together a large number of studies to enhance the statistical power of the results and to vastly reduce the likelihood that the results were random.) Radin also showed just as clearly that these abilities increase with increasing meditation practice. So the siddhis are not just a point in theory; they are a demonstrable phenomenon.

Attunement to our body and mind-born senses, forged through mindful awareness, eases the pain of our existence and removes the veil of ignorance so that in a renewed and genuine innocence we may re-enter the Garden of Eden, the place of the natural, spiritually attuned human, Adama. Bhāratī (2001) clarifies the mechanism of this process and the One who makes it possible:

> The *siddhi*s obtained through *tapas* . . . are not additions to or attainments by a personality. It is only that impediments that were obstructing the natural manifestation of certain ever-existent realities and forces have been eliminated. When a black cloth is removed from one's eyes, it is not that the sun has been created at that moment. (p. 560)

The siddhis are available to us always—as realities we attune to rather than attain, access (not own), through tapas.

Svādhyāya, self-study. The previous chapter defined *svādhyāya* as having three meanings according to the *Yoga-sūtra:* mindful awareness, study of texts, and mantra recitation (japa). We might also add the Vedāntin practice of self-inquiry, *ātma-vicāra.* These are all contemplative efforts to reach out with our mind and heart to attune ourselves to ultimate Being in the spiritual Self (ātman) and its macrocosmic correlative, Brahman. (Again, we could refer to *Śūnya, God, God-not, YHWH,* or any other culturally conditioned term for the ultimate ground of Being.) Patañjali (YS II.44) describes the consequences of firm establishment in svādhyāya as "concert with one's chosen deity" (Bhāratī, 2001, p. 558). Vyāsa clarifies that this refers not only to deities *(deva*s*)*, but also to sages *(ṛṣi*s*)* and adepts *(siddha*s*)*, all of whom show themselves to the aspirant and "remain occupied in performing his [or her] works" (Bhāratī, 2001, p. 558). In other words, when one is successfully attuned to this higher Being, in a movement of providence, spiritual beings take care of the circumstances of life to allow the aspirant to make more time for practice and selfless service born of compassion.

Again, this may seem miraculous, but it occurs in smaller ways as well when *sādhaka*s (spiritual aspirants) make a firm intention (saṁkalpa) to complete an important practice. For example, I had visited India with Swāmī Rāma and Swāmī Veda in 1974 but had not been back since. In 1995 I knew that they had both been very ill, so I made an intention to visit them the year after I had completed my doctoral studies in psychology. On the day of my commencement ceremony, as I was leaving the house to collect my diploma, I decided to call Swāmī Veda to let him know that I would be coming in a year. The budget for the trip was to be about $10,000 by my best estimate, and I had no idea where the money would come from.

About a week after making the call, a woman came into my office whom I had seen for psychotherapy at a very low rate because, by herself, she had very little money, although she came from a wealthy family. She had just received an inheritance and wanted to pay me the full fee for those sessions, so she wrote me a check for $10,000! I came to learn later that I only thought it was my decision to make that trip; I realized that it had been the intention of Swāmī Veda and Swāmī Rāma all along, although a harmonious intention on my part was also required. There are many similar stories of providence making a way for those who have made a serious commitment to their practice.

Īśvara-praṇidhāna, ultimate attunement to Great Being (Brahman). The final niyama, establishment of īśvara-praṇidhāna, results in samādhi as the aspirant's *dhyāna* (meditation) attracts the Guru's *abhi-dhyāna* (responsive meditation as a flow of grace). The aspirant's "faculty of wisdom," Vyāsa says, "fully knows reality as it really is. That's it!" (Bhāratī, 2001, p. 561).

Yoga and Cognitive Behavioral Therapy

After listing the yamas and niyamas in YS II.30–32, Patañjali recommends in sūtra II.33, "when . . . deviant thoughts present themselves [one should counter these by] cultivating and impressing upon oneself the opposite principles" (Bhāratī, 2001, p. 505).[12] Contemporary psychotherapy would call this approach *cognitive behavioral therapy (CBT).* This technique recognizes that distortions in a person's thinking result in emotional pain, and it corrects these either at the level of thought (equivalent to saṁskāras and vṛttis) or at the level of deeply ingrained habits of personality, so-called

[12] The brackets are Bhāratī's.

cognitive schemas, roughly equivalent to *vāsanā* in the terminology of Yoga. The sūtra described above explains the origins of these deviant thoughts as varieties of violence born of ignorance, in other words the lack of accurate attunement to spiritual reality. To counter these thoughts, and to balance the karmik books, as it were, one cultivates the opposite principles, based on compassion and truth. This produces bright saṁskāras that modify the impact of the painful ones (kleśas). How do we accomplish this?

Chapter 8 on journaling and Chapter 9 on therapy will delve into this subject in more detail, but before we get to these, let's look at an important foundational term from Patañjali, *bhāvanā.* This is a difficult word to translate into English. In his first volume on the *Yoga-sūtra,* Swāmī Veda translates *bhāvanā* as "cultivated concentration; cultivating and absorbing a meaning; an internal process of impressing an object of concentration *(bhāvya)* onto the mind" (Arya, 1986, p. 450). It is more than mere thinking or mere feeling. The word *bhāvanā* derives from the Sanskrit root √*bhu,* "become." The word *vibhūti* is from the same root. As the subject of the third chapter of the *Yoga-sūtra,* vibhūti represents the ultimate natural development of sāttvik (pure and clear) bhāvanā. To achieve this, one so steeps one's heart in an attitude that the attitude is what one becomes. It is very much like the injunction in the Judeo–Christian sh'ma to assume a mindset "with all your heart and with all your soul and with all your mind" (Deuteronomy 6:4–9). For example, when you observe yourself feeling jealous or angry towards someone, you deliberately cultivate thoughts of behaving towards him or her in a generous and loving way. Moving beyond thinking to contemplation, you hold these thoughts in your heart, knowing and feeling them with your whole being so that your new behaviors reflect these. Essentially, you replace violence with compassion.

Final Thoughts

As we practice the yamas and niyamas in a spirit of bhāvanā, we go beyond the thinking mind, replacing thoughts born of ignorance (nonattunement to ātman) with contemplations and behaviors that are sāttvik, pure and clear. Our suffering gradually decreases, the impact of our saṁskāras on the mindfield becomes more sāttvik, and the mindfield itself becomes progressively more clear *(prasāda)* and settled *(sthita)*. Drawing closer to ātman, we witness deep-seated changes taking place in the personality as the mind and senses resonate with higher Being. When the veil of ignorance dissolves, both through our own efforts and through grace, natural abilities (vibhūtis) emerge, and sāttvik qualities in the personality shine forth as natural developments. These are the brahma-vihāras (*maitri,* friendliness; *karuṇā,* compassion; *muditā,* joyful mindedness; and *upekṣā,* "overlooking," nonreaction), which are, in part, the subject of the final chapter of this book. We can say that these qualities are the fruits of our efforts with the yamas and niyamas. Notice that, as we might expect, each of these is a relationship skill. From beginning to end, Yoga is about relationship.

Growth and relationship feel so good that they draw us towards them. But we must also remember that even our shadow—and perhaps especially our shadow—the painful aspects of ourselves that we avoid—also leads us towards our growth. It points to areas that we have not yet integrated and shows us which opposite actions to cultivate. Because of awareness of our shadow, we step into the light. This highly intuitive process requires all of our being and involves our intention to shift our karma. Because our physical body houses our karma by storing our saṁskāras, our emotional patterning, we turn next to āsana, the physical postures of Patañjali's Rāja-yoga.

Chapter Six

Āsana:
What Is Your Posture in Life?

In the preceding chapter, we saw how the momentum of a person's saṁskāras determines the nature of that person's incarnation, and we introduced the concept of karmāśaya. As you depart your body, the saṁskāras that are becoming ripe to bear the fruits of their action in the next life coalesce into the subtle karmāśaya pattern, which guides the subtle body through the transitional stage between bodies (*bardo* in Tibetan) and into the circumstances of your next life. The Tibetan text *Bardo Thödöl, The Tibetan Book of the Dead* (Padmasambhava, trans. 1993) describes how those who are destined for reincarnation, towards the end of this transitional period, begin to have visions of various couples making love and gradually come to see the people with whom they have the optimal chance to live out the karmik pattern of their karmāśaya. If the match is good, conception occurs. So for Yogis, it takes three people to make a baby! (It has become clear to me working in therapy with people who are planning to adopt that the same karmik processes appear to guide the choice among parents and children.)

So the mind/body with which you are born is the physical expression of the saṁskāras you brought into this life. Your current body is a physical manifestation of your previous emotional habits! It is, in this sense, a continuation of the patterns of relationship in your previous mind/body. Your posture is much more than just the position of your physical body. It is your overall posture in life.

One meaning of the word *habit* in English is the body. The closest word in Sanskrit to the English *habit* is *vāsanā,* which literally means "dwelling." The body is the physical structure within which your habits dwell and are lived out. And that is the subject of the third aṅga of Yoga, āsana. How do you stand? Do you stand like a mountain—solid, balanced, aligned, relaxed—so that there is no fatigue? Or do you lock your knees in tension? Do you sink your chest downward so that your shoulders seem to carry the weight of the world, throwing your lower back out of alignment and causing your head to droop forward and the muscles in the neck to become tight enough to give you headaches? In this chapter, we will look at how your relationship with your mind/body carries emotions physically and stores them in the tissues of your physical body. We will examine how mindful awareness and a deeper attunement to your mind/body can help you make contact with these hidden emotions and in the process contribute to clarifying your mindfield in your physical being.

Here again we return to Siegel's (2010) definition of mind: "a relational and embodied process that regulates the flow of energy and information" (p. 52). In this chapter, we will emphasize the embodied aspect of mind. Remember that we previously discussed the interesting recent realization that your brain is not limited to your central nervous system and the grey matter inside your head. In fact, your whole body is brain from head to toe. Every tissue and system in your body contributes to how you know things, even to the formation of intuition. They all contribute to a "sixth sense" called interoception, perception of that which is interior. The interoceptive structures in the brain—the lamina of the spinal cord, vagus nerve, and the insula (especially the right anterior insula) of the middle prefrontal cortex (the integrative structure behind your forehead)—all collect information from the body and connect it to various parts of the cortex. This is how we get "gut feelings," how we come to know things "in our bones," or become "heartsick" in response to others' suffering.

So interoception is how we sense emotions within the physical body and how we often sense intuition. How often have you had a feeling in your stomach that something just is not right no matter how much your mind may review the information and insist that everything is fine? How often have you had an interaction with someone that left you feeling a little sick to your stomach or tense in your neck and shoulders? These sensations reflect the enormous amount of information that your cognitive senses gather unconsciously, which comes to you as a feeling state with an anatomical point of reference. For this reason, it is essential that you attend to what your body may be telling you whenever you work with your emotions (see Appendix A, Exercise 3.1).

How the Body Stores Emotion

How do emotions come to be stored in our tissues? One route is the psychosomatic pathway described in our discussion of pain in Chapter 4. The unconscious mind may create discomfort in the nerves and muscles by changing the circulatory patterns in those tissues. Another pathway is trauma, introduced in Chapter 2. When we are traumatized physically or psychologically, the structures in the midbrain, principally the amygdala and hippocampus, take a traumatic snapshot, which may include physical sensations, images, cognitions, and emotions. This traumatic snapshot remains permanent. If various regions of the cortex do not modify it by forging integrative connections, thus weaving it into the narrative structure that is our explicit memory, trauma can recur as an unintegrated implicit memory or "flashback" (Siegel, 2012b, section AI, pp. 33, 38). This flashback may entail sensations in body parts that were affected in the traumatic incident. Stimulating these sensations can trigger flashbacks.

I once worked with a man in therapy who came to me because he was afraid he would beat his two sons. After some initial work on emotional awareness, we began to work on a system of parenting that involves giving your children developmentally appropriate verbal affirmations. At the age of his sons, two and five years, one of these affirmations was "I'm glad you're a boy!" (Males seldom hear this after the moment of their birth, and my client had never heard it at all.) My client could not get the words past his throat. Whenever he tried to articulate this affirmation, a lump of pain in his throat made him freeze. When I asked him to wonder about it with a sense of curious interest, he began to remember having been orally sexually abused by his father. He carried a tissue memory of this in his throat, and so whenever he felt himself wanting to cry, as the lump gathered, he felt as if he were about to be abused again. This triggered a panic state and made him freeze emotionally and physically.

Another client had been brutally abused physically, emotionally, and sexually early in life by his stepfather. In his fifties, he was in the hospital and suddenly began to experience severe pain in his hip, which, at first, had no medical explanation. In hypnosis, we learned that his stepfather had once twisted that leg so hard that the hip joint fractured, and he was never taken to a hospital to have it properly treated. An x-ray later confirmed his raggedly healed fracture. In this way, our bodies can literally remember past trauma in our bones and other tissues, often as part of the traumatic snapshot of sensation registered by the amygdala in implicit memory.

The same principle holds with muscles and the fascia that enclose them. If we have had to brace our body against trauma or repeatedly had to defend ourselves against an attack, the patterns of muscle tension that were involved often persist. For this reason, recent advances in the treatment of trauma have demonstrated that effective therapies always include the body somehow (Emerson & Hopper, 2011; Levine, 2010; B. van der Kolk, 2014). The body plays an intrinsic role in less extreme cases as well. Think of someone in your life with whom you have had a difficult relationship. Imagine the gestures and tones of voice that set off your emotional reactions to him or her. Notice what happens in your body as you recall these triggers. What do you feel in your neck, your shoulders, your lower back, your stomach, your heart? What changes do you perceive in your breath? These are the bodily expressions of your emotional posture. These can become chronic habits in the relationship between your nervous system and musculature. Many forms of bodywork try to create awareness of this kind of "body armor" and help you to learn new habits. You learn to dwell (vāsanā) in the body in a different way.

Thinking of our bodies in this way gives a whole new meaning to the practice of āsana. We are not simply trying to get into some challenging looking position depicted in a book or get better abs or increase our basal metabolic rate. Āsana is really about exploring in a very deep way the fleshen fabric of our lives. We use the central skill of Yoga, the application of mindful awareness, to conduct this exploration and, in so doing, integrate every aspect of our nervous system, including our emotional experience: sensation, cognition, motivation, and saṁskāra. The result of this integration is, again, joy!

Sthira and Sukha: Steadiness and Comfort in Āsana and in Life

Patañjali defines āsana (YS II.46) as that which is "steady (*sthira*) and comfortable (*sukha*)." If we look to the traditional commentaries on the term *sthira*, their remarks are straightforward. Some commentators talk about showing no trembling of the limbs. Many people interpret this in their practice as a suggestion to hold still. This is not exactly correct. It is not a process of holding the body still, as this requires effort and tension. Rather, it is the quieting of the mind/body relationship to the point where the mind/body loses its desire to move altogether. Instead of holding still, one becomes stillness itself in mind and body. Feeling this kind of stillness is often a revelation to Yoga students. Suddenly they find themselves in that stillness one day thinking, "I could move my body if I wanted to—but I don't want to!!"

A secondary meaning of *sthira* is found in Vyāsa's commentary: "*sama-saṁsthāna,*" "balanced configuration," which refers to maintaining the alignment of the head, neck, and trunk in meditative awareness. The trunk is the primary part of the body for purposes of meditation, and all the postural practices of āsana prepare the mind/body to meditate. This refers not just to sitting meditation, as we shall see shortly, but also to every posture the body assumes. People who have mastery of the mind/body through āsana sit and move with a sense of impeccable balance and grace, in part because their head, neck, and trunk calibrate themselves freely in a coordinated, adaptable relationship with each other. Their movement is more of a dance than just moving the body around. For these people, their motion is just as meditative as their still sitting. Their balance and stability (sthira) result in comfort and ease (sukha) that we can see. Thus, *samatvam Yoga ucyate,* "balance [in all things, including the body] is called Yoga!" (BhG II.48).

In terms of principles of behavior change, there is also a good reason that Patañjali places stability first. Stability and change are always engaged in an intricate dance in human beings. We tend to think of them as opposites when, in fact, they are two sides of the same coin. They complement each other. Biologically, this is an important principle. All biological (and therefore behavioral) systems rely on homeostasis as their built-in stability factor. Homeostatic mechanisms try to keep things the same to preserve the integrity of the system. In therapy with people, if I try too hard to get them to change some behavior, guess what happens? They "resist." Historically, psychotherapists in many disciplines have blamed clients for their resistance. But I learned after some years that their resistance to my efforts almost always represents a response to my lack of respect for their stability needs. A person needs to feel a certain stability to feel safe enough to undertake the risk to change. Often in therapy, the best way to help people change is to support the status quo!

Even in the practice of āsana, establishing an initial stability is a critical part of helping individuals to deepen their experiences of their physical and subtle bodies into unknown territory, where change can happen. In adjusting students, it is advisable for teachers first to meet them with a stabilizing touch to announce their presence, warmth, and willingness to help them. Then, once a student is stable, a teacher can adjust. After adjusting, the instructor should also remain for a moment until the person restabilizes him- or herself in the new expression of the posture before moving on to the next person (see Parker & Sharma, 2013).

Stability also plays a role in the stubbornness of our emotional habits as they exist in the body. We are accustomed to feeling our bodies in a certain way, and changing a habit may at first feel uncomfortable and risky. We want to return to what we are comfortable with. So the first thing is to really feel how things are, not just in the usual casual and habitual way, but to deeply feel all the rest of our habit, the physical and emotional parts that we usually leave unconscious. Once this awareness is established, some initial effort and some initial discomfort will likely be required to establish a change. In this process, it helps greatly to hold the new posture (whether it is an āsana or a way that we tend to carry ourselves day to day) for some time (30 seconds at a minimum). During that time, we must remain aware of how the change feels. If it brings discomfort, we can explore dropping into the underlying sensation of awareness, which itself feels good. As we enjoy the new posture mindfully, our middle prefrontal cortex is rewiring our nervous system into a new configuration. Gradually, as the new habit is learned, the mind/body can relax around it and allow it to become our "new normal."

Relaxing into Endlessness

The next sūtra (II.47) takes the explanation of āsana a step further: "[The posture is perfected, made steady and comfortable] through relaxing the effort and coalescence [of awareness] with the endless or with endlessness" (Bhāratī, 2001, p. 576).[13] Here again there are two important terms: *prayatna-śaithilya* and *ānanta-samāpatti or ānantya-samāpatti.*

Prayatna-śaithilya is relaxation of *all* effort. Only by such relaxation can one obtain genuine stillness of the mind/body. One of the secrets of haṭha-yoga is that subtle energy, prāṇa, does not flow where there is muscle tension (see Arya, 1985, *Philosophy of Hatha Yoga*). Yet does it not require some muscle tension to hold an āsana? Initially perhaps, especially as we learn a new physical habit. But in the refinement of āsana, eventually we eliminate even that tension. Remember from our discussion of yama and niyama how, as the impurities of body and mind are gradually removed, the veil of our ignorance—our struggle to maintain attuned, mindful awareness—is gradually thinned away so that the natural sāttvik qualities of the mind/body can come forward. In the same way, when we completely relax a posture, physically and mentally, the flow of subtle energy can naturally hold the body without muscular tension.

This may seem an extravagant claim. Yet here is an illustration. In the AHYMSIN Himalayan Yoga Tradition Teacher Training Program in which I teach, Swāmī Veda was once lecturing in a segment on biofeedback, a technique pioneered by his master, Swāmī Rāma. (In biofeedback, a person trains him- or herself to regulate bodily processes that are otherwise involuntary: muscle tension, heart rate, blood pressure, and even skin temperature.) For the sake of illustration during the lecture, we had connected an electromyograph (EMG), a device that measures muscle tension, to Swāmījī. Throughout the lecture, he was standing and writing on the whiteboard as one of our faculty, a physician named John, monitored the readings on the instrument. John began to chuckle, and after a few minutes, Swāmījī asked what was so funny. The doctor said in astonishment, "Swāmījī, this is impossible! There is not enough tension in your body for you to be standing up! We would only

[13] In his translation, Swāmī Veda completes a grammatical connection implied in Patañjali's word choice. The brackets are Bhāratī's.

expect to see these kinds of readings in a corpse!" This is an instance of the perfection of śavāsana, the corpse posture: remaining totally relaxed even when standing and moving about. We saw earlier that Swāmījī did not require deep sleep to express the delta brain waves that ordinarily typify only that state. Similarly, one does not need muscular tension to support the body. When the body is completely relaxed, prāṇa can flow unobstructed to sustain it, and the advanced practices of haṭha-yoga become possible, even spontaneous.

The second important term in sūtra II.47 is either *ānanta-samāpatti* or *ānantya-samāpatti,* "coalescence with Ananta, the endless" or "coalescence with endlessness," respectively. Both readings of the text are correct ways to describe the same experience, though they have slightly different meanings, the subtleties of which are beyond the scope of this chapter. The word *samāpatti* is the same term that Patañjali uses in the first chapter of the *Yoga-sūtra* to describe the mental concentrations in the various levels of the lower states of spiritual realization, or saṁprajñāta-samādhis. Swāmī Veda explains,

> When the mindfield is coalesced into endlessness (*ānantya*), such as that of space, and reaches uninterrupted identification, then, its identity (*ahaṁ-kāra*) with the body configuration ceasing, the posture no longer causes discomfort. The correct techniques for this mental practice are suggested in the *dahara-vidyā* passages of the *Upaniṣad*s [*Chāndogya Up.* VIII.1.1ff.]. (Bhāratī, 2001, p. 582)[14]

Both coalescence into ānantya and into Ananta make a mythological reference to Ananta, the King of the *Nāga*s (serpent beings), also known as *Śeṣa-nāga,* of whom Patañjali is said to be an incarnation. In Hindu mythology, Ananta is the great serpent upon whose back the deity Viṣṇu sleeps in his yoga-nidrā after the dissolution of the manifest universe. He is described as the stable

[14] Swāmī Veda provided the information in brackets and parenthesis.

support of all the universes within universes within universes. Included within these is our own body:

> By the well-known dictum, "what is in the universe, that also is in the body," these images of vastness are then assimilated into an interior cosmology of the meditator. . . . Coalescence then means the state in which projection into cosmic form and assimilation into interior awareness become indistinct. . . . *Śeṣa* . . . is seen in the tradition as the snake of the eternal *kuṇḍalinī.* (Bhāratī, 2001, pp. 583–584)

For the interested reader, the scholarly details of the inner meditative meanings of the mythological figure of Ananta are well worth reading (Bhāratī, 2001, pp. 580–584), though they are also a bit beyond the scope of this chapter. The bottom line here is that the practice of āsana is a meditative practice culminating in the deepest meditation, samādhi.

We summarize here Bhāratī's (2001) detailed account of this process of samāpatti (pp. 585–586). In the first phase, practitioners purify their minds and emotions, "abandoning unsettled modes of life and cravings" (p. 585). Then they explore relaxation exercises, carrying the exercises into the practice of physical postures, which become steady and comfortable. At this point, they undertake the inner, mental practices whereby they eliminate their identification with the limited sense of the mind/body through a stabilizing focus on *kūrma-nāḍī* between the heart center and the throat center (YS III.31). Through this concentration, practitioners expand their identification into identification with all of space and the endlessness of the physical body of the universe (*virāṭ*). This includes the energies of Kuṇḍalinī, the power of consciousness (*cit-śakti*) through which the body is created and maintained. Sustaining the āsana in this way, without disturbance, makes it possible to merge into samādhi.

Above, the important phrase is *without disturbance*. The

disturbances (vi-kṣepa), their accompaniments, and how to eliminate them are, of course, the subject of this book. Sūtra II.48 describes the vibhūti, the naturally occurring accomplishment, of one who has perfected āsana: "Thereby one is no longer impeded by pairs of opposites" (Bhāratī, 2001, p. 587). To be unimpeded by pairs of opposites is to move beyond all dichotomies and paradoxes and to become emotionally nonreactive. This does not mean emotionless, simply acting rather than reacting. It includes transcending the primary fountain needs (for example, for self-preservation in terms of moderate temperature that is neither too hot nor too cold). It also means going beyond dualistic, either/or thinking (for example, manas's judgment of experience as either "good" or "bad"). Cultivating this way of being is the intention of haṭha-yoga, which merges the opposite solar (*ha-*) and lunar (*-ṭha*) aspects of the subtle body. This in turn opens the suṣumnā channel (see Chapter 7) in meditation so that the practitioner can enter the deeper states and attain the final goal of haṭha-yoga, samādhi. The perfection of āsana without disturbance is one doorway among others into enlightenment. In sūtra II.48, Vyāsa explains that the contemplative phases of āsana described above bring practitioners to a state of nonreaction to sensation, which makes them stable and still in every sense. He notes that the practice of āsana eliminates unsteadiness of the mind/body (aṅgamejayatva), while the practices of yama and niyama eliminate pain (duḥkha) and ill-mindedness (daurmanasya). In the next chapter, we shall examine how breathing techniques and subtle energy practices (prāṇāyāma) eliminate disturbances in the breath and make complete withdrawal of the senses (pratyāhāra) possible.

Endlessness and Interpersonal Neurobiology

How can we put the process described above into more practical terms? Translating into the contemporary language of interpersonal neurobiology, we might say that we use the focusing power of mindful awareness as interoception first to become much more sensitive to the body itself (anna-maya-koṣa) and then to sense the part of the mind that is not in the physical body (our other four koṣas) and finally ātman-Brahman; we thus separate the physical body from our me-map. This expands our me-map to a much larger frame (because, in reality, the physical body is contained within the subtler koṣas). The distinction between body as microcosmos and macrocosmos thus begins to disappear. We are changing the conditioning of our mind, which perceives the limitation of the physical body, and beginning to sense the truth of Patañjali's assertion in YS IV.5 that there is only one mindfield in which our apparently individual mind/bodies are simply waves in a great oceanic awareness. This is the true and final stability (sthira). (To develop your own interoception, I highly recommend the relaxation exercises taught by Swāmī Veda and Swāmī Rāma; see Appendix A, Section 1.)

The true and final comfort (sukha) also involves the use of our interoception, this time to explore how emotions are stored in the tissues of the body. Learning to relax those tissues helps us to let go of self-limiting thoughts and behavior tendencies and reidentify our minds with the universal mindfield. One can imagine the degree of joy that might accompany growth of that magnitude!

Once I was practicing in an āsana class where we were intentionally doing long holds of a very deep expression of the pigeon posture, *kapoṭāsana.* As I eased into the depth of the posture over some minutes, I became aware of intense waves of nausea that were clearly emotional in origin. There were no images or memories that came with these sensations to give me a sense of their source, but it was clear that I was storing a lot of emotional vulnerability in the muscles of my thighs. This is not uncommon among North American and Northern European males whose cultures tend to train us to overcontrol our emotions and sexual impulses. I simply observed the arising of these emotions with an open mind and heart, and eventually they quieted down and did not trouble me again.

In another example, a therapy client whom I had not seen for several years returned to me complaining of severe depression. Symptomatically, he did have a severe major depressive episode. He happened to mention that he had recently started taking Yoga classes and was really enjoying them. I strongly supported his continuing these classes. For several weeks, every time he reached a certain point in the fixed sequence of postures, he would burst into tears and sob for five or ten minutes. He experienced these reactions with a great sense of relief. In retrospect, it became clear that he was releasing from his body stored sadness over alienation from his family of origin, which was very important to him.

When images and memories come to you as the result of a deeply relaxed, mindful, exploratory practice, the reattunement of your relationship to your mind/body involves the incorporation of "implicit" sensations and images into the flow of your self-narrative, your explicit, autobiographical memory (Siegel, 2012b, section 36, pp. 23–30). Memory consists of sensation and image plus language, which helps us to give a meaning, a place, and a sequence to our experiences. For those who have been traumatized, or who have experienced great emotional difficulty as in the case above, connecting these is the real work of healing. The narrative that emerges is a new sense of our psychological self. Once these sensations and images have been incorporated into memory and slip firmly into the past, we can let go into a new sense of self, even physically. This happens again and again until eventually, by exploring the parts of our mind that are not in the body, we gradually grow into an ultimate attunement with our spiritual Self.

If one is to take the practice of āsana to this depth and to the relaxation described in sūtras II.47 and II.48, it requires a technique in the performance of postures that is rather different from the norm in contemporary practice in much of the world. One *must* remain constantly aware of the flow of the breath. The process of moving into the posture must begin from stillness (sthira), move through inner stillness, and return to stillness. There are six steps to this process:

centering, moving into the posture, stabilizing the posture, deepening the posture, moving out of the posture, and recentering. Awareness at every stage is critical. One needs to use just the minimum muscle tension to establish the posture at first. Muscles in the rest of the body should be kept *completely* relaxed. Mindful awareness should help you to explore the depth of your relationship to your mind/body and to experience a sense of joy in feeling the body's capacity to expand without having to hurt yourself. Then the deeper mental contemplations in the deepening process can take you to the place where even the above tension relaxes, and prāṇa alone holds the posture. Getting to this depth means using your skill at mindful awareness to sense any tension representing somaticized emotion and allowing it to release, watching all the while for images or memories that may give you a clue about the origin of the tension. You hold the posture in such a way that the breath continues to flow at all times. Any pause in the breath means that you are creating tension and blocking the flow of prāṇa by pushing your limits. You are going too far too fast, trying to "hold still" rather than becoming stillness itself.

If you follow this procedure, your limits will gradually and joyfully expand ahead of your efforts, and you will keep yourself safe from injury. Practicing in this way, you may well come to the end of a session of postures—even a very active and challenging one—and find yourself so relaxed and energized that you feel no need for any relaxation in śavāsana! In fact, you will have already been meditating in motion.

Final Thoughts

We began this chapter by characterizing our physical body as the concrete form of our emotional habits, a physical "story" of ourselves, life after life. To further study this way of working with your mind/body, you might enjoy Swami Sivananda Radha's (2006) excellent book, *Hatha Yoga, The Hidden Language: Symbols, Secrets & Metaphor.* You might also try Exercise 3.3 in Appendix A. As we work in this way with our posture in life, the fabric of that story (our body), and our āsana, we gradually build ourselves a new dwelling: one that is more in attunement with our deeper spiritual Self, one that is more available to give and receive the gifts of love and selfless service. In the next chapter, we will examine how practice with breath and prāṇa helps us to untie emotional knots in our energy body (prāṇa-maya-koṣa) and bring us to a natural transition where the senses dissolve back into the mindfield (pratyāhāra), and we enter the inner limbs of Yoga practice.

Chapter Seven

Prāṇāyāma and Pratyāhāra: Unkinking Your Nāḍīs, Expanding Your Energy, and Turning the Mind Inward

The fourth and fifth limbs of Yoga, prāṇāyāma and pratyāhāra, go together. This is one of the secrets (*rahasya*) of Yoga, secret not because the masters of Yoga seek to hide information, but because practitioners only discover the connection when they have a certain meditative experience. In one sense, all the limbs of Yoga go together all the time, continuously reinforcing each other. In another sense, they feel sequential. As practitioners, we can first observe and work with our relationships to others, yama, as a foundation for approaching ourselves in the second and third limbs, niyama and āsana. (Remember that relationship to others enables us to form a sense of psychological self in the first place and contributes to shaping our saṁskāras.) By becoming aware of how our relationships have influenced our development, we are empowered and directed in our work with ourselves. Conversely, our work in niyama and āsana should improve the quality of our relationships. In this way, the limbs are both sequential and recursive. These three practices—yama, niyama, and āsana—help us to refine our emotions so that they no longer create warps and knots in our energy field, a development greatly assisted by the breathing and subtle energy practices of the fourth limb, prāṇāyāma. Prāṇāyāma especially promotes emotional stability and is most effective when combined with our work in the limbs above.

In general, we move from grosser to subtler practices, yet these are not discreet stages. They are truly tools that we continue to use as each brings life and movement to the other. Each Yogic limb supports the others, but prāṇāyāma and pratyāhāra share a special relationship. To understand it, first let's turn our attention to prāṇāyāma, the interface between our gross and subtle layers of embodiment.

Prāṇāyāma: The Science of Prāṇa

Prāṇāyāma is the science of both the physical breath and its accompanying flows of subtle energy (prāṇa). Here we find the vital connection between the complementary members of our mind/body. Just as our mental and emotional states influence our body, in one way through the quality of our breath (we've all experienced shallow breathing when we feel nervous, for example), we can also regulate the condition of the body, using the breath to calm mind and heart. (Sometimes we might feel nervous *because* our breathing is shallow, and regardless of the cause of our anxiety, we can reduce it by slowing and smoothing our breathing.) So the breath—and Yoga would say the prāṇa carried within our breath—becomes our bridge between the mind and the body when we approach prāṇāyāma as a physical exercise. Even in this gross application, we serve our intention of emotional purification and thus our larger goal of Self-realization. Through prāṇāyāma we also find many of the gateways into the subtle, deep states of meditation. For this reason, prāṇāyāma is very detailed in the Yoga tradition and could lead the investigation of these topics in current empirical research, if modern scientists are wise enough to follow the ancient ones. (See Bharati's 2006 book *Yogi in the Lab: Future Directions of Scientific Research in Meditation* and "Defining Yoga-Nidra: Traditional Accounts, Physiological Research, and Future Directions" by Parker, Bharati, & Fernandez, 2013.)

Although we cannot measure prāṇa in a direct way physically because it is nonphysical, we can measure its physical correlates, for example brain wave patterns or other physiological processes whose absence indicates when prāṇa alone is supporting the life of the body. These include movement without muscle tension, life without breathing, and conscious activity without the beta brain waves of waking consciousness. Contemporary research is only just beginning to describe prāṇāyāma in physiological terms (e.g., Telles, Singh, & Balkrishna, 2014), extending the early work of Swāmī Kuvalayānanda and his collaborators at the Kaivalyadhama Yoga Institute, founded in 1924. Until recently, no one had used an electroencephalogram (EEG) to study the electrical activity of the brain during common prāṇāyāma practices or to observe the interaction of prāṇāyāma with the brain and nervous system in the short and long term. The Meditation Research Institute at Swāmī Rāma Sādhaka Grāma has just begun to design protocols to study the EEG changes that occur during basic prāṇāyāma practices. We may not be able to study prāṇa directly because it is intangible, but through increasingly more sensitive methods of investigation, there is much we *can* learn about even the physical effects of prāṇa.

Svara-Yoga: The Study of Rhythms in Prāṇa from a Dhyāna-Yoga Perspective

It is interesting to note that in Freud's early years of practice, he was investigating with his colleague, Wilhelm Fliess, the nature of what physiological studies have come to call the *nasal cycle*. This cycle describes the alternation of activity in the right and left nostrils, long known and observed in the Yoga tradition. Freud and Fliess had also identified a relationship between the erectile tissue of the nasal turbinates and the erectile tissues of the genitals, among other organ systems (Ballentine, 2011, p. 178). Unfortunately, Freud was not in a position to take this research very far at the time he was working. Along came World War I, as well as his interest in hypnosis and its potential for communication with the unconscious, and he was off and running in a different direction, more productive for the time.

According to Ballentine (2011), however, German scientists were able to map connections between regions of the interior of the nose and other organ systems throughout the body (p. 178), providing evidence of the holographic nature of the mind/body, each part a reflection of the pattern of the whole organism.[15] The furthest that more recent neurophysiological investigations have gone into this phenomenon is to identify alternating nostril activity as a sign of the alternating activity of the right and left cerebral hemispheres of the brain (Micozzi, 2015, pp. 337–338). But just what links the functioning of our nasal passages to that of our brain hemispheres and other organ systems? A master of *svara-yoga* would say that it is prāṇa.

Svara-yoga is the science of breath and prāṇik rhythms that are accessed through meditation, *dhyāna-yoga.* This science might have provided the key to unlocking the mystery of the nasal cycle, but in Freud's time the knowledgebase did not exist to connect this cycle to brain activity. It is also unlikely that Freud was aware of svara at all. In any case, we can imagine how differently psychotherapy might have developed had he had a master of svara-yoga to guide him!

Like so many of the subdisciplines of Yoga, svara is a vast science by itself with very few written texts available. One of them, *Svara-svarodayam*, is accessible and has been translated in a very good introductory book titled *Swara Yoga: The Tantric Science of Brain Breathing* by Swami Muktibodhananda (1999) of the Bihar School of Yoga. Swami Rama (1988), who was a master of this science, provides more detail in his book *Path of Fire and Light: Volume One* (pp. 65–94). The svara system uses awareness of rhythms in the subtle body to help us understand when our mindfield is suited to particular activities. It can help us make our actions more effective and efficient. It also places human beings in a holographic context, following with considerable detail the holism between the macrocosmic universe "out there" and the microcosmic universe that we each are.

---

[15] For example, reflexology makes a similar assertion, correlating all mind/body functions to specific regions of the feet, hands, and ears; the part (foot) contains instructions for the whole (mind/body).

Just as the human mind/body displays holographic features—for example, the quality of our breath reflects our overall degree of calmness or agitation—we can understand individuals as holograms of both matter and Spirit. Recall from Chapter 2 that human beings undergo all of life's evolutionary stages as we develop in the womb. Remember also that our brains include structures from each significant era in the evolution of consciousness, from the reptilian brainstem through the neocortex. In these ways, human beings can be seen as storehouses for evolutionary advances in conscious life on earth. Our mind/bodies are biological microcosms for life itself, at least on our planet. In a similar way, recall one of the traditional meanings of svādhyāya, self-study. At the subtlest level of being, the individual spiritual Self (puruṣa, ātman) is said to be the microcosmic equivalent of Brahman, the ground of Being, Spirit, or God. Thus, the holographic nature of Being-in-existence appears at both the subtle level of Spirit and the gross level of matter. The part/microcosm contains the whole/macrocosm. A master of svara-yoga is in touch with these patterns and can write out your entire horoscope including your significant past life experiences, karmik issues, and future direction based on observing the parameters of your breath. So svara-yoga's meditative approach to prāṇa is somewhat different from the practices of prāṇāyāma to which we are accustomed. Svara-yoga will assist us later in mindfully and sensitively observing the behavior of our breath in relation to the internal experience of our mind.

Prāṇāyāma: The Study of Prāṇa from a Haṭha-Yoga Perspective

These are the practices with which most of us are familiar. Some people assume that haṭha-yoga concerns only the practice of āsana. But recall that haṭha-yoga is not limited to physical postures. It includes any activity that unites *ha-* and *-ṭha*, the nāḍīs *iḍā* and *piṅgalā* into *suṣumnā*, explored later in this chapter. So one of the chief practices of haṭha-yoga is prāṇāyāma.

Prāṇāyāma is a compound of two words, *prāṇa* and *āyāma*. First, let's take a closer look at *prāṇa*, which refers to the subtle energy that is the life force of all. The word has many levels of meaning, from *Mahāprāṇa,* a synonym for *Kuṇḍalinī,* the creative energy of consciousness in the entire cosmos, to *prāṇa-vāyu*, the flow of subtle energy in an individual mind/body, to nāḍīs and *cakra*s, which describe specific currents of energy within the mind/body. Early writers in the West tended to confuse prāṇa with physical breath and even sometimes translated the word as "oxygen"! The physical breath is a vehicle for the energy of prāṇa, as is food.

Āyāma can be translated as "control," although this word implies the kind of effort that tends to disrupt subtler processes. A careful reading of *Yoga-sūtra*s I.34 and II.50 demonstrates that this sense of effort in these practices is to maintain and deepen mindful observation, not to huff and puff and struggle to hold the breath. *Āyāma* also can mean expansion, both in the sense of increasing the quantity of prāṇa and in the sense of expanding the gross experience of prāṇa into one that is subtler. In a technical sense, *āyāma* as control can also mean contraction, when the purpose of a deeply subtle exercise is to use our awareness to maintain the flow of prāṇa between two points or to contract this expanded subtler prāṇa into a point-limit, or *bindu*, in meditation (Bhāratī, 2001, pp. 592–593).

So in its grosser form, prāṇāyāma comprises the breathing exercises of haṭha-yoga, and in its subtler, expansive form, it includes Patañjali's exercises of subtle prāṇāyāma (*sūkṣma-prāṇāyāma*) and the awareness of svara. Through these, one learns the spontaneous retention of prāṇa in order to increase it or make it subtler, as well as learns how to direct its movement, initially through exercises done in the corpse posture, śavāsana. In these ways, prāṇāyāma prepares our nervous system to receive prāṇa in greater quantities, adapting our mind/body for pratyāhāra and the remaining inner limbs.

More on Prāṇa: The Prāṇa-Maya-Koṣa, Prāṇa-Vāyus, Nāḍī System, and Cakras

Just as we can understand prāṇāyāma from multiple vantages and at varying depths, prāṇa itself works in many capacities. Understanding these—the prāṇa-vāyus, nāḍī system, and cakras—as well as the part of our mind/body that is made of prāṇa, the prāṇa-maya-koṣa—will help us appreciate all that goes on "behind the scenes" as we purify our emotions. The functions of prāṇa can also "take the stage" when we experience them directly and come to know them intimately. When this happens, we have laid the groundwork for pratyāhāra to emerge.

The discussion and exercises of this book are intended to help us clear our path, and all the limbs of Patañjali's Rāja-yoga assist us. If the limbs acquaint us with our inner world, our own unique terrain, then the knowledge and experience of prāṇa brings this landscape into sharper relief. Knowing how to access prāṇa, understanding the various conceptual frameworks that describe it, and appreciating how our thoughts and emotions affect the subtle body all inspire us to work at the subtle body level to cleanse our mindfield.

The prāṇa-maya-koṣa. As we alluded to in Chapter 1, part of the mind/body is comprised of prāṇa: the energy sheath, or prāṇa-maya-koṣa. (The Yoga system refers to this layer as the grossest part of the subtle body, ṣūkṣma-śarīra.) Like prāṇa itself, the prāṇa-maya-koṣa is not very amenable to direct empirical investigation due to its nonphysical nature. We can only study it through its correlated effects. For example, you may sometimes have felt a subtle pull between your thumb and forefinger when you have been deeply relaxed in śavāsana. The sensation is one of not knowing whether the fingers are touching as the energy moves to close a natural circuit. Or in the practice of an āsana, you might have felt a subtle, nonphysical tingling sensation, "like the one created by the movement of an ant (over the body)" (Singh, 1979, p. 64, verse 67), perhaps accompanied by heat. These are often people's first direct experiences of prāṇa and its currents in the subtle body.

The prāṇa-vāyus. Just as we can identify the sensation of prāṇa and experience its "geographical" locations in the mind/body, we can also speak of prāṇa in terms of currents (*vāyu*s, "winds") that sustain the functioning of a specific physical body. There are five principal currents, detailed in Table 7.1, and a number of subsidiary ones. They are described by the general bodily regions that they energize and in terms of how we sense them as a flow in meditation.

Other currents include *kṛkara*, which induces sneezing, hunger, and thirst; *kūrma*, which energizes expansion and contraction, such as opening and closing the eyes; *nāga*, which induces belching and promotes clarity of mind; *devadatta*, which induces yawning; *dhanaṁjaya*, which induces hiccups and actually remains in the physical body after death; and *mahāvāyu*, which concerns the functioning of the brain (Rama, 1988, p. 72).

One can sometimes sense the five principal flows of prāṇa when doing postures or at other times. For example, we all experience the strong downward push of apāna-vāyu when we feel the urge to defecate or urinate. Conversely, to feel the inward and upward pull of prāṇa-vāyu, lie on a firm surface on your back with a thin cushion under your head. Close your eyes, and systematically relax the muscles in your body. If any are especially tight, send your awareness inside the middle of the tension gently and lovingly until you feel the muscle let go. When your body is quite comfortable, observe your exhaling breath, and rather than take an inhalation, just prolong the exhalation until an inhalation begins spontaneously. Let it be as complete as it wants to be, and notice what you feel inside.

Just as the currents of prāṇa energize the above physical processes of cleansing and nourishing, they do the same at the subtle, energetic level. Some of the relaxation exercises we do, particularly point-to-point breathing (Appendix A, Exercise 1.4), make use of awareness of the movements of prāṇa; in that technique, following the movement of the breath down and up the physical body helps us become aware of our subtle body and gradually begin to use our

Table 7.1

Prāṇa-Vāyus: Their Locations, Functions, and Elements

Name	Location/Sense of Flow	Physical Function	Mental/Emotional Function	Element
Prāṇa-vāyu	Larynx to base of heart/flows inward and upward.	Nourishing: swallowing and inhalation. Energizes the heart and lungs.	Assimilation of information through the cognitive senses.	Air
Apāna-vāyu	Navel to anus/ flows outward and downward.	Cleansing and elimination: urination, defecation, ejaculation, and childbirth. Energizes the kidneys, bladder, colon, and genitals.	Ability to let go of that which we no longer need.	Earth
Samāna-vāyu	Heart to navel/ flows around navel area.	Digestion: assimilation of nourishment. Energizes the stomach, intestines, liver, and pancreas.	Ability to separate desirable from undesirable thoughts and emotions. Ability to receive love and care.	Fire
Udāna-vāyu	Larynx upward/ flows upward and outward.	Expression: exhalation, coughing, vomiting, sneezing, speaking, singing, and exiting the body at death. Energizes the tongue, vocal apparatus, eyes, and facial muscles.	Expression of thoughts and emotions.	Space
Vyāna-vāyu	Whole body (*deha*)/ flow is centripetal and rotation is centrifugal.	Coherence and integration: horripilation (getting goosebumps) and perspiration. Energizes the skin and musculoskeletal, nervous, and circulatory systems.	Coherence and integration of a sense of self.	Water

mind to move the energy currents where we want them to go.

The nāḍī system. Our subtle body gives rise to the currents (vāyus) above and is arrayed like a magnetic field. Many people in school have done an experiment where they place a magnet under a piece of paper and sprinkle iron filings over the paper. The filings take the shape of the lines of force in the magnetic field. In the same way, the gross matter of the physical body is arranged around currents of energy, which are called *nāḍīs* (literally, "tubes"). Different texts give different accounts of the number of nāḍīs in the human body, ranging from 72,000 to 350,000 or more, depending on the degree of resolution in one's ability to sense them. The totality of the subtle body is said to extend beyond the physical body to a distance of twelve finger breadths in all directions (Bhāratī, 2001, p. 593). This would seem to account for the Western preference to keep approximately this distance between bodies in polite social interaction. Have you ever encountered someone whose physical presence seemed "electric" when you stood or sat close to him or her? It is likely that you sensed the force of that person's subtle body.

Nāḍīs are of many different sizes, some major and some minor. Where two of them intersect, there is a conjunction, a *sandhi*; where there are five, there is a *marma*, a vital point where the subtle and physical bodies tie together. These marma points figure in Āyurvedic therapy, the ancient medical science of India, the "science of [long] life" (Bharati, 2013b, p. 6). Though the correspondences are not exact, they also play a role in martial arts and the techniques of Traditional Chinese Medicine, such as acupuncture. Where four nāḍīs intersect, there is a *cakra*, literally a "circle" or "wheel." The subtle body contains thousands of cakras. For example, each joint in the body is a minor cakra. In the popular understanding of Yoga today, most of the attention is devoted to the six major cakras, which parallel the spine and correlate with certain plexuses of the nervous system. These are vortices of subtle energy that have many different functions and are the major "transformers" that convert subtle energy into its physical manifestations and drive the relationship between aspects of body and mind. We will explore the cakras in more detail shortly.

Although we might distinguish the prāṇa-maya-koṣa as the home of nāḍīs and cakras in the mind/body, the nāḍīs and cakras as systems are not limited only to the energy body. In fact, both systems operate in at least three of the bodily sheaths, or koṣas: the physical body (anna-maya-koṣa), the energy body (prāṇa-maya-koṣa), and the gross mental body (mano-maya-koṣa). In Āyurveda, there are three types of nāḍīs: 1. *Mano-vaha* ("mind vehicle") nāḍīs channel the flow of the sensory mind (manas); 2. *Prāṇa-vaha* ("prāṇa vehicle") nāḍīs channel the flow of subtle energy; and 3. *Sroto-vaha* ("fluid-vehicle") nāḍīs channel the flow of physical fluids. These grosser nāḍīs correspond to our blood, lymphatic vessels, and nerves. The subtler nāḍīs control the grosser nāḍīs, and so disturbances in one's emotions and thoughts easily become warps and kinks in the prāṇa system and eventually physical disturbances in the body (Bharati, 2013b, p. 6). One way of looking at the task of emotional purification from the perspective of the prāṇa body is the unkinking and smoothing out of the warps of energy in the nāḍīs and cakras along with their connection to both the mind and the body in preparation for the great energetic enhancement of spiritual awakening.

The flow of subtle energy in the process of spiritual awakening is called *Kuṇḍalinī*, "the serpent power" referred to in the title of Sir John Woodroffe's (1865–1936) great work on the subject (see Woodroffe, 1972). It is symbolized as a serpent and, as such, this notion of the energy of the subtle body exists in similar forms in many cultures. For an excellent survey of these, see Campbell (1981, pp. 281–301). Just as Āyurveda's marma points overlap with certain bodily junctures in martial arts and Traditional Chinese Medicine (TCM), the energy body concepts of Taoism and TCM strongly parallel the Yoga description. Of note are those that concern the functional channels of energy in Taoist Yoga and the central and governor vessel meridians in Traditional Chinese Medicine. Both energy channels are felt along the center of the body, just as we sense Kuṇḍalinī rising along the spine. Certain acupuncture meridians also trace some of Yoga's specific nāḍīs. Many, including this writer, have experienced how acupuncture treatments can propel one into a very deep state of relaxation. There are many other cross-cultural examples that identify the flow of subtle energy in the mind/body, and especially its central sensation along the spine. (In truth, however, the subtle body exists both within and outside the three dimensions we usually perceive. Thus we can sense the subtle body "in" our physical body, and we can observe remarkably consistent physical correlates across cultures. Yet the subtle body, for all its tangible sensations, is not limited to these.)

The three principal nāḍīs. Of all the nāḍīs in the subtle body, three are primary. They are called *iḍā, piṅgalā,* and *suṣumnā* in haṭha-yoga or, in the svara science, *lunar (candra) svara, solar (sūrya) svara,* and *void (śūnya) svara.* (As with the cakras, a number of other nāḍīs are named, but these are beyond the scope of this book. For an explanation of these, see Daniélou, 1973.) In the subtle body, these nāḍīs originate just above the lowest cakra, which we sense physically at the perineum and the base of the spine. They intersect each of the major cakras on their way upward. Iḍā and piṅgalā terminate at the nostrils, while suṣumnā continues upward into sahasrāra at the crown of the head and beyond. (Not a cakra in the usual sense, the sahasrāra is where a Yogi's consciousness rests in the highest samādhi.) The principal nāḍīs, or svaras, are easily identifiable through their association with the alternating activity of physical breath in the nostrils.

Piṅgalā-nāḍī/sūrya svara. When the right nostril is active, piṅgalā-nāḍī, the solar svara, is flowing. At this time, your body likes to be active and warm, and your mind is inclined towards the logical operations of the left brain. This is the time to do aerobic exercise or work in the garden or balance your checkbook.

Iḍā-nāḍī/candra svara. When the left nostril is active, iḍā-nāḍī, the lunar svara, is flowing. During this period, your body likes to be cool and relaxed, and your mind inclines towards the metaphorical and creative thinking of the right brain. Whenever I have a writing project to do, I wait until the left nostril is flowing because then the writing simply flows. If I try to write when the right nostril is active, it becomes a complicated struggle. These energies alternate in activity approximately every 100–110 minutes, somewhat less than every two hours.

Suṣumnā-nāḍī/śūnya svara. During the time when your nostril activity is changing, you will find for a brief time that both nostrils are flowing equally. This is the activity of suṣumnā-nāḍī, or śūnya (void) svara. When suṣumnā flows, if you observe carefully, you may notice that your mind feels a spontaneous sense of joyfulness that has no outward cause, and you also feel a natural tendency to turn your attention inward in meditation. There are only two activities suited to this svara: meditation and exit from the body. Yogis have learned over the centuries how to catch the flow of this svara and prolong it to make their meditation continuous, easy, and natural. For those interested in more detail, the *Svara-svarodayam* (Muktibodhananda, 1999) mentioned earlier contains long lists of which activities fit with which svara.

The cakras. Just as the nāḍīs serve multiple, multilevel functions, and the marmas link together our subtle and physical bodies, the cakras tie together the various layers of our embodiment and their associated activities. The second cakra, for example, has physical functions involved in reproduction and elimination as well as energetic functions in terms of all that flows (the element water). As the seat of vyāna-vāyu, it determines the shape of your subtle and physical body. The mental and emotional functions of the second cakra include generating both the urge to merge with another for purposes of reproduction and the motivation to commit to relationships and goals. Table 7.2 summarizes some of the activities of each cakra, which I often include in lectures. (Note that the

Table 7.2

Cakras: Their Locations, Functions, Primary Fountains, and Elements

Cakra	Approximate Anatomical Focus (*Kṣetra*)	Physical Function	Energetic Function	Mental/Emotional Function	Primary Fountain	Element (*Mahābhuta*)
Mūlādhāra ("root support")	Perineum (between anus and genitals)	Elimination Through Defecation, Physical Foundation	Cleansing and stabilizing. Seat of apāna-vāyu.	Survival, Security, Groundedness	Self-Preservation (Fear)	Earth: Solidity
Svādhiṣṭhāna ("her own abode")	Genitals	Reproduction, Elimination Through Urination, Ejaculation, Childbirth	Connection with another's energy body, coherence of bodily shape. Seat of vyāna-vāyu.	Merger and Commitment	Sexuality	Water: Liquidity
Maṇipūra ("city or region of gems")	Navel	Digestion, Balance (center of gravity of the body)	Intake of food, separation of prāṇa from its food vehicle, and assimilation of prāṇa. Seat of samāna-vāyu. Interconnection point of all nāḍīs.	Control of Emotions and Relationships	Food	Fire: Transformation. Energy
Anāhata ("unstruck [sound]")	Center of Chest (at terminus of sternum)	Intake of Breath, Maintenance of Heartbeat	Separation of prāṇa from its breath vehicle and assimilation of prāṇa. Seat of prāṇa-vāyu.	Compassion, Nurture, Selfless Love	Deep Sleep	Air: Gaseousness
Viśuddha ("purified")	Pit of Throat	Speech, Upward Cleansing (cough, etc.)	Outward expression of energy, bodily exit at death. Seat of udāna-vāyu.	Creativity, Expression/ Silence, Control of Hunger and Thirst	Dream Sleep	Space: Matrix of Manifestation
Ājñā ("command")	Between Eyebrows	Integration of All Physical and Mental Function	Absorption of prāṇa into mindfield and beyond.	Intuition, Discrimination	Joy, Discrimination	---

sahasrāra, sometimes referred to as the seventh cakra, is not included on this list because, as mentioned above, it is not a cakra in the same sense as the lower six. It is typically only accessible meditatively to very advanced practitioners.) For a detailed discussion, I recommend Chapter 10 of Ballentine's (2011) *Radical Healing.*

Sense your cakras. You can learn to sense the area of activity (*kṣetra*, "field") of the cakras in your own body. They are often associated with anatomical landmarks in the physical body, but the actual location may be somewhat different for you. In my body, for example, the third cakra is located about two inches above my navel. That is where I have sometimes felt the subtle tingling of energy movement in that cakra. To learn where the cakras operate in your body, and which are most active in you, practice Exercises 2.2 and 2.3 in Appendix A.

If you consider what is happening emotionally in your mind at any given moment in terms of the activity of your cakras, you may uncover some clues about which psychological issues are involved in an emotion and where the motivation for a given emotion is coming from in the four primary fountains. This is an exercise of svara-yoga. It can be very helpful to record these rhythms in a journal over some time to get an idea of the flow of these energies and the corresponding emotions in your mind (see Appendix A, Exercise 3.2).

Mindful Breathing

For purposes of emotional purification, the physical process of breathing becomes very important. Our breath is simultaneously one of the subtlest mind/body functions we can access without any training,[16] and the awareness of it helps the mind to moderate the still subtler nāḍī system, which remains mostly out of direct reach to all but the most adept practitioners. For this reason, as we attempt a more profound stillness in our practice, our awareness of breath

[16] I do not mean to imply that we can practice in any old way. Our breathing instructions *are* important; rather, I mean to emphasize that, with rare exceptions, we all come into this world equipped with the ability to moderate our breathing. In finding a teacher and studying texts, we learn how to apply this innate ability skillfully.

becomes both our inner guidepost and our companion, a passageway to our own uncharted territory. The role of breath awareness in inducing the relaxation response also serves to pacify our emotions and thereby purify our nāḍīs. Gradually, as the physical breath becomes subtler and more still, we can begin to feel the gentle, nonphysical sensation of prāṇa described above.

Breathe with Your Diaphragm

If you have ever watched infants breathe, you notice that they have a natural diaphragmatic breath. Their abdomens rise and fall as their chests remain mostly still. As we grow up, we gradually lose this natural method of breathing, probably under the influence of a lot of modeling by parents and teachers and the accumulation of tension and emotional knots. The teacher at the head of the class says, "Okay, kids, take a deep breath!" and then models an exaggerated chest breath using the intercostal muscles. These muscles have little ability to move air in and out of the lungs, and making this effort intrudes upon the natural process of breathing with which we are born. As the habit of chest breathing develops, carbon dioxide levels in the blood increase, contributing significantly to anxiety.

One way to greatly reduce anxiety is simply to retrain your breath. An easy way to do this is to practice a Yoga posture called *makarāsana*, the crocodile posture. Just about everyone can do this, and I hope you will give it a try. To practice makarāsana, lie on your belly, fold your arms overhead, and rest your head on your forearms. This positioning encourages diaphragmatic breathing because it prevents your chest muscles from moving your chest, compelling you to breathe with your diaphragm, abdominal muscles, and the muscles of your lower, floating ribs. (See Appendix A, Exercise 1.5, for additional instruction, including how to perform this posture safely and when to avoid it.) Alternatively, another somewhat more challenging way to learn diaphragmatic breathing is to hold the shoulderstand, *sarvāṅagāsana.* This is a much more advanced practice. This posture reverses the diaphragm's usual relationship with gravity, making it easier to breathe from the correct muscles. You will feel it immediately. The effects of makarāsana can typically be felt within about 10 minutes. For an optimal result, the usual recommendation for sarvāṅagāsana if using it for this purpose is to hold it for at least 30 minutes. Only do this if you are well experienced with the posture and can maintain it completely relaxed and without overextending the neck. If this approach interests you, I recommend receiving feedback on your alignment from a qualified instructor and working with him or her to establish a schedule that gradually increases your holding time. For such a long holding time, be sure to use a blanket under your shoulders to protect your neck. If you can do this, the habit of diaphragmatic breathing should establish itself relatively quickly.

Attend to the Quality of Your Breath

Yet another aspect of the physical breath rhythm is very important: the smoothness of the flow of breath. Mind tends to flow in parallel with the breath. When there is a gap in your breath, there is a corresponding gap in the continuity of your attention. It is through these gaps that miscellaneous thoughts and emotions enter the flow of your meditation, indicating the scatter-brained condition practitioners know as "monkey mind." The smoother and more continuous your breath, the smoother and more continuous you'll find your concentration to be. (The traditional description of meditation is like a continuously flowing stream of oil.) When you notice miscellaneous thoughts in your meditation, re-engage your awareness by looking for tension in the body. Your awareness will help you to relax it; then bring your awareness to the breath. This will smooth it, and you should be able to resume your meditation.

Lengthen the breath. The length of your breath also matters. Yoga practitioners count one breath from pause to pause, so if you maintain a perfectly smooth and pauseless cycle of breathing, no matter how many exhalations and inhalations there are, it is all one breath. For the Yogi, the lifespan of a mind/body consists not in the number of years it has to live, but in the number of breaths allotted to it. According to the Tantra tradition (and this is in accord with modern medicine's understanding), the average person breathes about 15 times per minute, 21,600 times per day. If you can simply slow and lengthen your breath, Yogis would maintain that this is the easiest way to enable yourself to live longer. If you cut that average rate by half on a steady-state basis, this might add as many as 18–20 years to your lifespan. In deep meditation, it would not be uncommon to take one to two breaths per minute. So this is a powerful tool for improving your health and longevity that requires only the awareness to change your moment-to-moment habit of breathing!

Smooth the pause between breaths. Most important of all is the nature of the pause between exhalation and inhalation. You may recall from Chapter 1 that Patañjali counts ordinary, unconscious exhalation and inhalation (pra-śvāsa and śvāsa, respectively) among the maladies (antarāyas, YS I.31) that accompany mental disturbances (vi-kṣepas, YS I.30). He is basically saying that ordinary, unconscious breathing is a mental illness, an illness caused by emotional disturbance! When we get lost in agitation, we focus not on our breath, but on our suffering, and so breathe unconsciously; we then default to a pathological pause in our breath, shortening its length and ultimately shortening our lifespan. Only the application of mindfulness to our breath smooths and lengthens it, transforming our breath into the conscious exhalation and inhalation of prāṇāyāma (bāhya and abhyantara, or recaka and pūraka; see YS II.49 in Bhāratī, 2001, pp. 595–596). Mindful awareness itself gradually smooths over the pauses after the exhalation and after the inhalation so that the breath flows continuously. A positive side effect of this mindful breathing, and perhaps a built-in purpose for it, is the longer lifetime we gain in which to pursue Self-realization and to serve others.

I once heard a story about a master Yogi who was about to leave his body. He had called his disciples together, as is the tradition, except for one person who was having trouble with transportation. That person would not be able to arrive for two days. When the master was informed, he wrote to the other disciples, "That should be fine; I still have two breaths left."

This point can be controversial among teachers of meditation. Many of them, especially in the Buddhist traditions, actually teach one to focus on that pause. I once had an energetic discussion with a very senior teacher in the Tibetan tradition at a psychology conference. When I raised the point about eliminating the pause, he said, "Don't do that! Buddhist psychologists have discovered that this causes a type of psychosis called meditation psychosis." We went back and forth about it several times, and as the exchange was becoming heated, we decided it best to move on. I was quite confused because my masters have all been very clear and emphatic on this point. As I contemplated the question through the afternoon, I suddenly realized that the difference is between forcing the elimination of the pause and allowing it to relax away in a natural process of evolution. It is no different than with a posture: To force a posture always risks exceeding one's limits and getting injured. The point, as we noted previously, is the relaxation of all effort in order to find the posture in your body. Similarly, struggling to force the pause away creates effort that disrupts the flow of prāṇa. Seek to become stillness itself; then the breath will be continuous, and prāṇa will flow.

Rather than pushing through the pause in the breath, use your awareness to *follow* the flow of the exhaling breath. Let the exhalation extend as you continue to relax your mind/body, and as you did in the prāṇa-vāyu exercise, hold your awareness steady through the transition, until the inhalation begins spontaneously. Do the same with the inhaling phase of the breath. Gradually the pause will begin to close naturally. You may notice an increase in the sense of energy that you feel. This is because a positive feedback loop seems to exist between our awareness, the quality of our breath, and the refinement of our awareness. The loop begins with mindful awareness of breath. This results in a change to the physical quality of our breathing as it inclines towards pauselessness. The mind becomes more still (as reflected in the smoothing of the pause), and the mind continues to refine its attention. This again results in the pauseless breath, and the mind refines its attention once more. The cycle repeats, building upon itself and increasing the ability of our prāṇa to flow.

Yet the feedback loop only seems to be between the pauseless breath and our awareness. In reality, it's all consciousness clarifying and pacifying itself. The pauseless breath, though part of the process, is always only a result or a byproduct of it, never a cause. Even though we practice in a certain way, it is awareness, not the breathing technique itself, which encourages pauseless breath and meditation to unfold. We'll return to this idea shortly. For now, let's remember that from the Yoga perspective, physical exercises only appear to be the cause of physical results. Our mind/body has no consciousness of its own but relies on spanda, the spontaneous pulsation of consciousness from the Self (ātman, puruṣa), which dances on the two-way mirror of buddhi. The Self's (Śiva's) counterpart, Śakti, as the creator and sustainer of all manifest universes, is the source of all activity. Through intuition in buddhi, the Self intends our breath to become pauseless. The Self witnesses our experience of pauseless breathing and responds by again intending the further smoothing of the breath, through buddhi and through all our koṣas. When you can maintain the continuity of the pauseless breath in your meditation (or, rather, when you can observe Śakti maintaining the pauseless breath), you will find that there will be no breaks in your concentration. So long as the breath is continuous, you are receiving indication that Śakti is sustaining your practice in a refined way. The focus of the mind will not shift.

All Yoga exercises, from any layer of embodiment, affect all the other layers through the Self's intention. In a physical breath exercise, we may feel like we can slow our breathing to slow the heart rate and calm the mind, but we don't actually work "up" the layers of our embodiment this way. Rather, the Self (through buddhi) meets us at the layer we can access, the physical body, or deha, for example, and then Śakti flows from buddhi to manas to calm the mind, to prāṇa to cleanse the nāḍīs, and to the body to slow the heart rate and breath. The breath itself is not responsible for mental changes that Śakti initiates. The tail never wags the dog.

In the same way, though the brain and nervous system play the major role in sustaining changes once they are wired in, the energy source that ultimately powers them both is Śakti. Figure 7.1 illustrates the pathway of emotional purification through the mind/body. That Śakti meets us at any layer of embodiment and then works through all the layers of our being to help us affect personal change implies Her use of multiple methods. In addition to pauseless breathing described above, She may initiate relaxation using other physical and subtle body practices and various meditation techniques. The relaxation that results from any of these might be measured in whether and how clearly pauseless breathing manifests. Perhaps even in our relationship to the primary fountains, a dedicated practice of enjoyment through concentration could induce pauselessness. The practice matters less than the attention given to it. Each practice is simply a tool, an object with which to occupy manas so that buddhi can be revealed. Yet Patañjali (YS I.30–34) champions the pauseless breathing method as one of our sharpest tools for this job.

In Chapter 1 we discussed sūtras I.30–31, Patañjali's account of the nature of mental and emotional disturbances and the illnesses that accompany them. These represent the condition of the mind in the absence of Self-intended mindfulness. In I.32–34, Patañjali recommends various mindfulness practices, inspired by the Self, as the way to stabilize the mindfield. Sūtra I.32 includes the practice

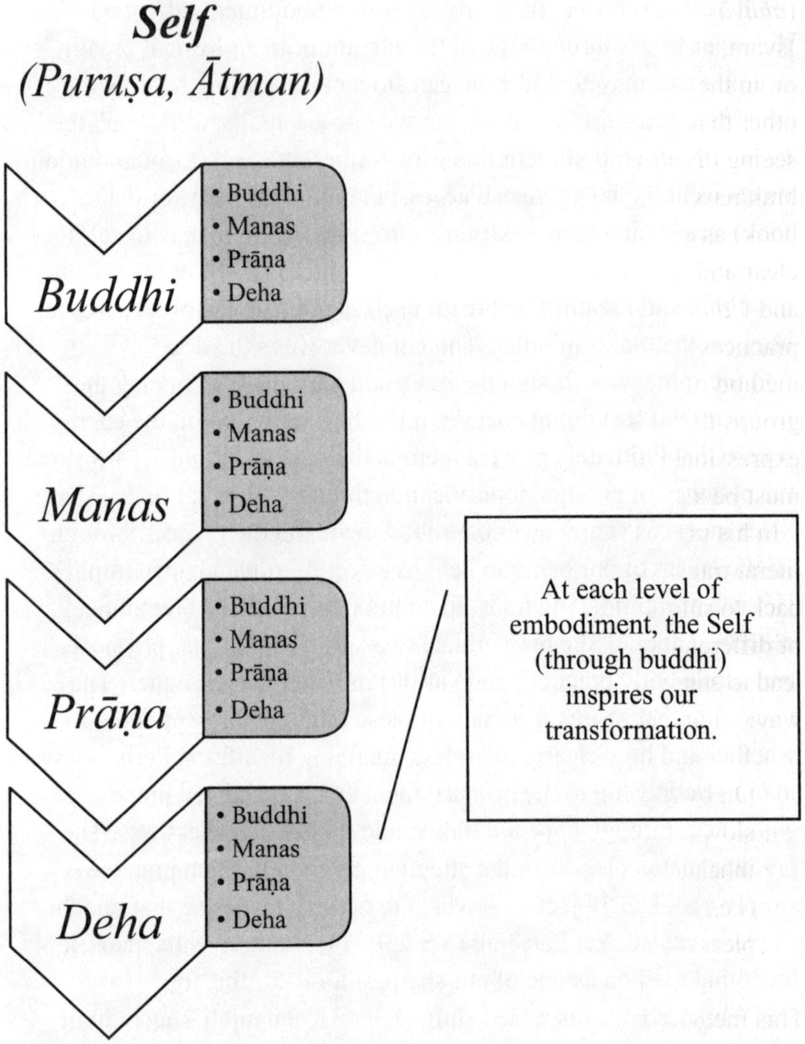

Figure 7.1. The Path of Emotional Purification Through the Mind/Body. We approach Yoga practice from the layer of embodiment we can access (e.g., the physical body, deha), but the pure consciousness of the Self ultimately inspires Śakti to work through buddhi and all our layers of embodiment to initiate emotional clarification.

(*abhyāsa*) of a single reality or truth, *eka-tattva*. The single reality is Īśvara, as in *īśvara-praṇidhāna*, the practice of the presence of God, or, in the terminology of Vedānta, *ātma-tattva-avalokanam*, none other than the extension of mindful awareness to its ultimate depth, seeing divinity everywhere you look. In I.33, Patañjali describes the brahma-vihāras (which we will explore in the final chapter of this book) as attitudes to practice mindfully to attain *citta-prasādana*, a clear and pleasant mindfield. In I.34, he recommends *pracchārdana* and *vidhāraṇā*, mindful ways to follow the breath. Each of these practices—īśvara-praṇidhāna, the brahma-vihāras, and Patañjali's method of prāṇāyāma—relies on mindfulness. Because Patañjali groups these practices together, and because the first two are expressions of mindfulness, we know that the third, on prāṇāyāma, must be also.

In his most recent translation of sūtra I.34, Bhāratī (2014) uses the literal translation from Vyāsa, which begins with the word *or*, to refer back to sūtras I.32–33 and demonstrate that Patañjali is making a list of different, specific expressions of mindful awareness practices that lead to samādhi. Patañjali recommends observing the breath in this way:

> Or, by making the breath and *prāṇa* light and tenuous through slow exhalation (pracchārdana) and carefully controlled inhalation (vidhāraṇā) together with concentration on the same (i.e., both parts of the breath) [the mindfield is purified, made pleasant, and its stability is established]. (Bhāratī, 2014, p. 346)[17]

This method of breath instruction, when considered in light of mindful awareness, calls us to let go of self to open to Self, and in this space, to witness the breath as it becomes pauseless.

Traditional commentators here seem to misunderstand Patañjali's intent. Most interpret pracchārdana and vidhāraṇā to refer to

[17] The brackets in this translation are Bhāratī's. I have inserted the material in parenthesis.

exhalation and inhalation, and, by extension, retention of breath to stabilize the mindfield and enter samādhi. Swami Veda's commentary (Arya, 1986), however, clarifies that Patañjali discusses those retention techniques in the second chapter of the *Yoga-sūtra* (and nowhere in the text does Patañjali repeat himself; this is axiomatic of the *Yoga-sūtra*, though many commentators seem to ignore this). It follows that here Patañjali must be describing a different process. In fact, he is describing how to move, through mindfulness, more and more deeply into the subtlety of the flow of pauseless breath (Arya, 1986, pp. 347–348), as we have been discussing.

Working with awareness of breath is so vital to the process of emotional purification that Patañjali includes it with his "short-cut" practice of īśvara-praṇidhāna and with the ever-important brahma-vihāras, practices which both the traditions of Yoga and Buddhism recognize for their essential role in spiritual growth. Many practices, including these, feel as if they assist us in our concentration, and we often discuss them in ways that suggest they do. It is not the Yoga practices alone, however, but also the Guru-śakti's facilitation of the practices, which causes Patañjali's mindfulness methods to develop our concentration and to smooth out the knots in our nāḍīs.

Wait for spontaneous breath suspension. When your mindfulness practice has sufficiently unknotted the nāḍīs and established in you the habit of diaphragmatic, smooth, pauseless, relaxed breathing, a moment will come in your meditation when the breath becomes so long and subtle that you have trouble knowing whether you are breathing or not. You may soon notice for certain that the breath has ceased, without any anxiety or urgency to continue breathing and perhaps with even a positive sense of joy and additional inwardness (YS II.50).

This cessation of breath is called *kevala-* ("solo-") or *sahaja-* ("spontaneous-") *kumbhaka*, or suspension of breath. (It is not retention, which would imply an effort to hold the breath.) This is an important sign of progress in your meditation and an entry point into the deeper states. It signals not only a deepening of your breath awareness but also your readiness to use the practices of breath retention.

Like the pauseless breath, kumbhaka is also a controversial issue among Yoga teachers. Today, many often teach retention almost from the beginning. According to Swāmī Rāma, this could present problems in the long run. Both he and Swāmī Veda were always very clear that from a meditative and karmik perspective, practicing breath retention with effort before it occurs spontaneously in sahaja-kumbhaka strengthens all of one's saṁskāras across the board, painful as well as pleasant, so that one is then guaranteed a more painful and difficult process of emotional purification. Even the *Haṭha-yoga-pradīpikā* (HYP II.4–5) warns the practitioner not to practice retaining the breath (*sahita-kumbhaka*) until the nāḍīs are sufficiently purified. The text provides some external signs of sufficient nāḍī purification, including slimness of the body (HYP II.19), a glow of good health (HYP II.19), and an increase in digestive function (HYP II.20). It also mentions one internal sign, the appearance in the mind of nāda, subtle nonphysical sound (HYP II.20). One additional sign of readiness for intentional retention of breath (sahita-kumbhaka) that the *Haṭha-yoga-pradīpikā* does not mention is the spontaneous occurrence of *kevala-kumbhaka* (S. V. Bhāratī, personal communication, 2005).

In considering our own readiness to practice breath retention, it is important to remember that awareness (and not the object of awareness) drives nāḍī purification. Practitioners sometimes wonder how, then, a method that focuses on the pause in the breath can be problematic. Should it not matter what we focus our attention on, as long as we're focusing it? Furthermore, if prematurely lengthening the pause in the breath strengthens our saṁskāras, is this not an example of the "tail wagging the dog," to refer back to our earlier discussion? If so, this would illustrate a physical practice working upwards through the layers of our being to influence the subtle and causal bodies, a phenomenon that contradicts the Yoga view. If the tail wags the dog here, then our logic crumbles, and, with it, the practical advice of the masters.

To reconcile these discrepancies, we must consider this apparent paradox: Practicing certain breathing methods will strengthen or weaken our saṁskāras, but no breathing method can strengthen or weaken our saṁskāras. Remember that it is our awareness that makes all the practices of Yoga effective. The awareness of Self inspires Śakti to animate the practices. It is Śakti who cleanses our nāḍīs and refines our awareness (or doesn't). The difference is that in pauseless breathing, Śakti relaxes all our bodies—causal, subtle, and physical (in that order)—and thereby moves manas out of the way so that She can do Her work. When we choose to focus on the pause prematurely, however, our ego identifies with the effort ("I am holding my breath"), disturbing Śakti's flow as prāṇa and creating tension. Manas then *gets in the way*, obstructing the clarifying work that Śakti would otherwise do. The energy of Śakti then becomes tangled in the warps and knots of our energy field, further strengthening both our positive and negative saṁskāras.

Remember that we are always in samādhi. But how we relate to this fact—how we direct our attention—makes all the difference in whether we realize it in a given moment. Many texts in both the Buddhist and Kashmir Śaiva traditions recommend focusing on the pause in the breath, but the experiential secret (rahasya) is that it is spontaneous kumbhaka, not the pathological pause, on which we should concentrate. Spontaneous breath retention implies no effort at all. In this way, it is similar to pauseless breathing. In each, Śakti relaxes manas out of the way, allowing the awareness of buddhi to break our self-identification with our saṁskāras. Losing their momentum, they are replaced with brighter counterparts. The pain of the mindfield thus reduces overall, until a-saṁprajñāta-samādhi eventually dissolves all our saṁskāras, leading us to final liberation.

Somewhat counterintuitively, the process that encourages

spontaneous kumbhaka is the one in which we keep our mindful awareness stable through the transition in the breath. It is this pauseless breath that eventually invites spontaneous suspension. So if we want to experience the pause, we should first become comfortable with the pauseless. The relaxation of our effort reduces the pause without our interfering with it or forcing it away. Concentrating on the ordinary pause right away, however, will likely strengthen and lengthen it in the pathological sense, resulting in more mental disturbance. On the other hand, concentrating on the spontaneous kumbhaka once it has already occurred strengthens the positive saṁskāra for the spontaneous kumbhaka to happen again in the future. From here, we can safely explore the breath retention techniques of Patañjali's second chapter.[18] It is a fine distinction but a very important one.

Practice Channel Purification

Since we ought to practice breath retention only once it has occurred naturally, and such spontaneity only happens when our nāḍīs are sufficiently pure, we work to cleanse our nāḍīs. In general, all the efforts we make to lengthen and smooth the breath and to work through our emotional issues through yama, niyama, and āsana contribute to the smoothing of the nāḍī system. The prāṇāyāma exercise that most specifically addresses this need is the channel purification (*nāḍī-śodhana*), or alternate nostril (*anuloma-viloma*), exercise. In this practice, we alternately open and close the nostrils as we exhale and inhale. (A detailed description appears in Appendix A, Exercise 2.1.) The attention to the quality of breath in this exercise switches on the parasympathetic nervous system, which, in turn,

---

[18] The *Yoga-sūtra*'s first chapter, which contains directions for encouraging spontaneous breath retention, is for the most advanced Yoga students, who can enter samādhi from the start of their practice. For these disciples, spontaneous retention comes quickly. The first half of the second chapter is for disciples with some karmik momentum for spiritual practice, who are qualified to use retention practices once the spontaneous suspension of breath has already occurred. The second half of the second chapter, describing the entire scope of Rāja-yoga, is for beginners with the mildest momentum. Patañjali's choice to place retention in the second chapter, while omitting the necessity that spontaneous suspension precede it, indicates his leaving the practical teaching to the oral tradition.

calms and relaxes the mind/body. The alternating stimulation of the cerebral hemispheres of the brain increases communication across the corpus callosum, the large cable in the brain that connects and integrates the two hemispheres. This helps to balance the activity of the nervous system and can aid in opening the suṣumnā channel. Over a long period of time, this balancing of the hemispheres appears to modulate the activity of the limbic system so that one becomes less emotionally reactive overall.

This phenomenon is similar to the hypothesized explanations for the effectiveness of trauma therapies like eye movement desensitization and reprocessing (EMDR). In EMDR, clients are asked to bring a traumatic experience to mind for brief periods while focusing on an external stimulus such as lateral eye movements, hand-tapping, or audio stimulation. Like anuloma-viloma, EMDR alternately activates both brain hemispheres, which helps the limbic system to create new connections with the cerebral cortex and, in this way, to recontextualize traumatic snapshots in the amygdala (implicit memory), as described in Chapters 2 and 6. Activating both hemispheres enables the hippocampus to consolidate those reframed experiences into actual, explicit, narrative memory. Traumatic memories finally then slip into the past rather than cause individuals to feel like their trauma is always about to happen in the next second.

Preeminent trauma researcher Bessel van der Kolk, MD, was once the featured presenter at a hypnosis conference I attended. I had often wondered whether he thought alternate nostril breathing from Yoga might be an effective therapy for trauma, especially for those people for whom EMDR is too intense. The difference is that EMDR therapy asks the client to hold a specific traumatic experience in his or her mind in terms of images, cognitions, and emotions. For people with histories of multiple trauma, working on one traumatic experience can begin, by association with its emotions, cognitions, or images, to chain into other traumatic experiences, one after another, until a person is emotionally overwhelmed and in a panic state. This is not therapeutic; it merely causes people to become traumatized all over again. Alternate nostril breathing has no specific focus on trauma, so its effect is a more gradual, gentle, and generalized reduction in emotional reactivity. When I asked van der Kolk whether he thought nāḍī-śodhana would be an effective trauma intervention, not only did he respond that he thought so, but he also shared that he often refers clients to Yoga teachers (B. van der Kolk, personal communication, June 2009).

Final Thoughts

When we revisit the concepts from this and previous chapters, we find that the prāṇāyāma practices of Yoga do several important things to support and promote the process of emotional purification. These ancient techniques are excitingly consistent with the perspective of modern interpersonal neurobiology:

1. Focusing awareness on the breath activates all the integrative functions of the middle prefrontal cortex. This allows individuals a more objective space from which to be aware of emotions as they arise and to decide how to respond rather than simply react.
2. Yoga asserts that relaxing through the pause in the breath helps the mind to maintain its attention and concentration on a single object. And the more we practice, the more proficient we become. Thanks to our brain's ability to reshape itself, we thus grow in our ability to experience an ever more continuous flow of mindful awareness. From this space, we watch our emotions and our conscious responses to those emotions arise and pass away, again and again. More and more each time, we train ourselves to respond constructively, both to ourselves and to others. As a result, according to interpersonal neurobiology, our emotional stability increases over time. Yoga would add that through this process, we are also purifying our nāḍīs.
3. Breath awareness, and especially focused attention on the

exhalation phase of the breath, activates the parasympathetic relaxation response. The resultant release of oxytocin into the blood stream alleviates mood problems and counters stress, as well as promotes human bonding and healing, all of which contribute to our emotional health.

4. Respiratory physiology tells us that diaphragmatic breathing improves gas exchange in the lungs, lowering CO2 levels and thereby reducing anxiety. With our anxiety in check, our me-, you-, and we-maps as identified by interpersonal neurobiology are likely to become much more accurate.
5. Alternate nostril breathing reduces overall emotional reactivity and helps in the gradual resolution of traumatic flashbacks.

We have discussed the occurrence of spontaneous breath retention (sahaja- or kevala-kumbhaka) as one sign of progress in the elimination of emotional warps in the prāṇa sheath. When this process of allowing prāṇa to flow smoothly progresses further, and the practice of prāṇāyāma has become quite subtle, the mind undergoes a natural evolution towards deeply focused concentration (YS II.53). In other words, pratyāhāra simply happens! In the same sense that the vibhūtis of the yamas and niyamas naturally evolve once these practices are well established, pratyāhāra naturally occurs when the breath has become sufficiently subtle and has finalized the stabilization of the mindfield (YS II.52).

Pratyāhāra is thus much subtler than some modern practitioners realize. Some people define this term to mean simply an intentional inward turning of ordinary attention, as we do in the relaxation exercises performed in śavāsana. As a result, they mistake these as exercises in pratyāhāra. It is actually much more profound than this. Those practices are preliminaries to pratyāhāra that prepare the mindfield (citta) to entirely reabsorb the senses and the sensory, disputative mind (manas). So pratyāhāra refers to a *total* disconnection of the senses and manas from their objects; it also refers to their dissolution into the nature of the pacified and stabilized mindfield. This disconnection of the senses is so absolute that one could fire a 45-caliber pistol next to your ear, and you would neither hear nor feel anything. (For a detailed discussion of this process, see Bhāratī, 2001, pp. 636–644, 744–779.) The mindfield full of silence at this point, citta easily obtains a focus and begins natural entry into the process of saṁyama: the seamless, gradual progression through concentration (dhāraṇā), meditation (dhyāna), and superconscious meditation (samādhi), which constitute the inner limbs of the practice of Yoga.

Chapter Eight

Making a Friend of Your Mind: Self-Dialogue and Journaling

Is your mind your friend? That may seem like an odd question, but after 35 years as a psychotherapist, I certainly have encountered many people who are not on particularly friendly terms with their minds. (And I don't refer simply to psychotherapy clients!) How can you practice friendliness (maitri) towards others if you can't be friendly towards yourself? And if you take a semiconscious, often hostile or critical dialogue into your meditation with you, what happens? It takes over, and soon your meditation is nothing but a painful session of self-punishment or criticisms of others.

There is already a dialogue in progress within your mind whether you are aware of it or not. We continuously talk to ourselves about the events that concern our lives, and most of this dialogue goes on at an unconscious or preconscious level. In this chapter, we will work with both. The unconscious stores deeply held beliefs and habit patterns that shape our personality. It is home to our me-, you-, and we-maps and to our saṁskāras, one of the four components of emotion. (The other three components of emotion—sensation, motivation, and cognition—live primarily in the preconscious and conscious minds.) The unconscious mind contains important components of the core of our psychological self, and we often cannot recall the formative childhood memories and past life experiences that comprise it. Yet these can influence the quality of our meditations. Through practicing the exercises in this chapter (e.g., dream work at the end) and perhaps by participating in therapy (the subject of the next chapter), we can sometimes move unconscious memories into the preconscious mind, where we can more easily gain access to them to improve our meditations. One can retrieve information from the preconscious (i.e., subconscious) mind fairly easily just by attending to it. Journaling about our sensations, motivations, and cognitions and engaging in self-dialogue prove quite useful in bringing the preconscious to light.

Swāmī Rāma often said that next to meditation itself, intentional self-dialogue is the most powerful assistance one can find for deepening meditation. For this reason, we follow our Chapter 7 discussion of pratyāhāra and the process of saṁyama with an exploration of the distinctly cognitive exercises of self-dialogue and journaling. Just as during mindfulness practice, buddhi engages manas in watching the breath so that buddhi can be revealed, journaling and self-dialogue engage manas constructively—reasoning with it, comforting it, calming it, and clearing it—so that we can later enjoy meditation. Journaling and self-dialogue uncover the agitations of manas, enabling us to know what might be bothering us and what we must therefore set aside (temporarily) as we sit. It can be as simple as a brief conversation with your mind before beginning to meditate, so that lingering concerns and issues don't take over your meditation time. If you ask your mind whether there is anything you need to deal with before you meditate together, you may be surprised when your mind answers you back! Then you have the option to identify any action items for the immediate future and to tell your mind that you will consciously entertain longer term issues when your meditation is completed. (As with any friend, be sure to keep your promise.) Your mind is then free to concentrate on your practice.

This is an important method for cultivating the power of intention (saṁkalpa). Creating saṁkalpas helps you learn to make clear commitments to yourself about what you will do and then follow through on those promises. This becomes especially important in the advanced stages of practice, where you may face very deep states of meditation that are pleasurable beyond anything you can currently imagine. It can be very seductive to remain in these pleasurable states rather than to progress towards liberation. One needs a firm power of intention in these moments and often the additional help of a guru.

Cultivating saṁkalpa will also help you build a trusting relationship with your mind, just as you would with a friend. Trust is built, in part, on the experience of making—and especially of keeping—your commitments to each other. Gradually, as the friendship becomes more intimate, and as the trust grows, your friend can reveal more of him- or herself to you. This is a psychological way of talking about the process of self-inquiry, or ātma-vicāra, in the Vedānta philosophy. Swāmī Rāma often said that as your relationship with your mind deepens, your mind will reveal all its secrets.

Meet Your (Psychological) Self

As you begin to explore the nature of your self-dialogue, you may first need to simply become aware of it. As an exercise, first pay attention to what you are feeling at a given moment. Next, ask yourself what the feeling is. Many people have difficulty identifying and naming what they feel. If this is the case for you, take some time with this. Part of learning to name emotions is just having the vocabulary. In the twelve-step recovery program, people often begin with whether the emotion is mad, sad, glad, scared, or ashamed. From there your emotional vocabulary can grow as your awareness of emotions grows. Then ask yourself how you are thinking about your life and how your thinking helps you to feel that way. Simply listen, and observe with mindful (breath) awareness. Soon you will probably detect a flow of thoughts that are giving meaning to your experience. Once you are aware of this inner voice, you can begin to inquire into the nature of its thoughts. If you choose to journal the flow of thought over time, you will likely become aware of certain habits of interpretation that this voice may have, which shape how you experience emotions.

Common Anxious Thought Patterns

For example, when you are worrying or feeling anxious, you may notice a pattern where you repeatedly ask yourself, "What if *x* happens?—And then what if *y* happens?!—And what about *z*?!!" At each step in the process, the fearful consequences escalate into a bigger and bigger problem, and soon panic overwhelms you. If you follow this paradigm mechanically, you can actually give yourself a panic attack. Once you have observed this pattern with awareness, there is a bit of objective space from which you can ask whether your interpretation of events is realistic, whether it makes sense. For example, you might say to your mind, "Now wait a minute! How much of all this is really likely to come true in your experience?" It might be, perhaps, 10%. Then you can ask your mind what you could realistically do to deal with that 10% in the next day or week or month. Once you have those intentions in mind, you can commit to yourself, "Okay, I'll do these things and just drop the rest."

Another anxious thought pattern involves the interpretation of events as terrible, horrible, awful, disastrous, or catastrophic. If you believe that you are in a disaster, things are, by definition, beyond your control. You have no power or choice about them except to remain a victim, feeling terror and horror. As you observe this flow of thought, you can ask yourself whether it is realistic. Does your characterization of the event make sense? Is it really a disaster? Most likely the circumstances are actually only painful, difficult, or challenging. Painful, difficult, or challenging are all situations where you have the power to apply your ability to cope and to deal with events. These words give you back your sense of capability and choice in difficult circumstances. Simply reframing the language of your interpretation here makes the difference between terror and simply fearful uncertainty, which is manageable and can even become a positively stressful, motivating challenge. By contrast, if you are realistically in a true disaster, you can choose to empower yourself by letting go of what you cannot change.

Common Depressive Thought Patterns

People who feel depressed much of the time may often find themselves using the word *should* frequently in their self-dialogue. The great cognitive psychologist, Albert Ellis (1913–2007), used to call this "shoulding on yourself." If all you have are "shoulds" for yourself, you are never just okay. Another depressive thought pattern is the formula, "If only I would do *x*, then I would be okay." Again, in this situation, you always interpret your efforts as inadequate. Who wouldn't feel depressed?!

The Voice in Your Head Isn't You

Once you are aware of a dialogue in progress, you might ask yourself in whose voice you hear your mind participating. Very often people will notice a parental voice, usually of the parent with whom they had the greatest struggle or of the parent who was the most critical. This can be a valuable clue to understanding what unfinished emotional business you may have brought with you into the present from your upbringing. Remember how parents help to create a child's sense of self by lending the infant their resonance circuits and interacting with the child through these circuits; this helps the child to gradually create an internal map of me in addition to maps of you and we. As this process continues in our own development, we internalize images of our parents' circuits; these become you-maps and we-maps that we carry in our minds. These maps often affect the way we respond to others, and they even become the voices of our self-dialogue. The things that we criticize in other people are very often irritating to us because they mirror our own unfinished growth.

Psychotherapy calls this type of distortion of relationships *transference* because you transfer onto another person the unfinished aspects of your own development. Psychotherapy makes use of this phenomenon and helps you to transfer onto the therapist the relationship you had with a parent when you were younger. This enables your mind to revivify and complete unfinished parts of your personality development. Of course, because transference is a distortion, the work of therapy is to gradually understand the nature of this misrepresentation in order to arrive at a realistic sense of relationship in the present. In this way, you use a therapist's resonance circuits to revise the you-maps you carry of your parents and to complete the process of developing a healthy psychological sense of self.

In spiritual practice, most of the problems that people have with spiritual teachers have this quality of transference. An ability to recognize this in your dialogue with your mind may help you to better use spiritual guidance. In my experience with my own teachers, it took me many years to untangle what were my transference reactions (e.g., "S/he is the father/mother I never had!") from my genuine spiritual issues and needs for further growth and development. Moving beyond this very important phenomenon is quite challenging, and a practice of internal dialogue with your mind can strongly assist you in doing so.

Practice Self-Dialogue: Learn to Comfort Your Inner Child and Open to Grace

Sometimes people visualize the me-map of their younger self as a child who exists inside their minds and hearts. Interacting with this inner child image can provide an opportunity for the adult self to use its experience in life and its loving intention to heal emotional wounds that the child part of us carries.

Mark was a man who worked with me in therapy for ten years on difficult personality issues. Many of these revolved around the death of his father when Mark was just four years old. The critical moment of therapy came one day when he said that he had found two pictures of himself from his school years. The picture from when he was five years old looked like a younger version of his current face. The previous year's picture was very different and obviously came from a time before his personality problems developed. We did a relaxation exercise in a seated position, and I asked him to hold a crayon in his nondominant hand and rest it on a sheet of paper. After the relaxation, I asked him to hold the earlier of the pictures in mind and let any message from that younger part of himself just come into his hand and move the crayon. After a moment, the crayon began to move, and then after a while, it stopped. I asked him to gently open his eyes and look at what he had written. He was astonished to see his name, printed as if by a four-year-old, and the words, "I'm here." My client was quite a skeptic, but his skepticism flew out the window when he saw these words because he had no awareness of writing anything.

Then I asked Mark to go inside again, calling to mind the same image. I asked his deeper mind to just say, "I'm here. How can I help?" As he did so, his face flushed a bit, and I began to see moisture gathering beneath his eyelids. Mark had very carefully prevented anyone from seeing him cry all his life—not even once. After a few minutes, he opened his eyes, dumbstruck, and as tears began to fall, he said that the child was there and had said to him, "I've been waiting for you for so long, and I'm so lonely." In this moment of self-compassion, he began to sob as if he had never cried in his life. (And he really hadn't!) From this critical moment, he rapidly began to change and to complete the therapeutic process.

In Mark's case, it took him ten years of talking with me to make the relational space of therapy safe enough to face the fear he felt about the pain and grief in that child part of himself. He needed emotional safety to allow himself to be sufficiently open and vulnerable, so that he could be touched through our relationship with healing compassion. Then he was able to extend the same healing touch to his grieving younger self. Previously, he had channeled the energy of that grief into rage, contempt, and then the anesthesia of substance abuse. Here, he had channeled that energy into love and healing, into making himself whole.

It is little different in the critical moments of spiritual growth, when we need to make a leap into the unknown territory of greater Being. Our relationship with our preceptor needs to be solid and safe enough for us to become, as Jesus would say, like a little child who can receive a gift of spiritual breakthrough ("grace," prasāda). So often we think of ourselves in sādhanā, our spiritual practice, as approaching the moment when we will be uplifted as a powerful, strong being. The truth of the situation is exactly the opposite; we must work through the blocks that our ego places in our way, exhausting our own imperfect efforts, until there is a moment of spiritual crisis. Only then is there an opening in our illusory self-identification for grace to enter and raise us up.

Journal About Your Conscious (and Preconscious) Mind

A journal can help us identify the blocks of our ego, the negative thought patterns whose energies we can rechannel into healing until grace fills us. Each exercise below is intended to provide you with a useful form of mental dialogue to help you inquire into the cognitive aspect of your emotions. Remember that some discomfort in this process in natural, and the relaxation exercises of Yoga are always available to you as a support, especially to calm manas, which can become stirred up as we journal (see Appendix A, Section 1). If you feel that some thought patterns are too frightening or too difficult to address on your own, please see the following chapter for recommendations on when and how to consult a mental health care professional.

Witness How Your Thoughts Influence Your Emotions

A very useful journaling exercise is to look for thought patterns that shape your emotions. The process is as we described it above: First, identify the feeling. Note it down. Then ask yourself what the feeling refers to. When your mind responds, note this, too. Then ask yourself what you think or believe that helps you to feel this way. Record the results. Finally, you can ask yourself whether that belief is realistic in that situation. This should enable you to decide how to respond to the feeling skillfully rather than to simply react. Over time, you may notice patterns, and you will grow in your ability to anticipate similar thoughts and choose more constructive responses. When these have positive consequences, let yourself dwell on the good feelings that come to you for 30 seconds or so to allow your nervous system time to rewire the new pattern into your neural networks.

For example, you might notice yourself feeling angry. Ask yourself what that feeling is about. To what does it refer? You become aware that the feelings are about a certain person. Next, ask yourself what you believe about that person or the situation you are in with him or her that causes you to feel anger. As you observe the flow of your self-dialogue, you may notice yourself thinking that the person should behave in a certain way. Now you can ask yourself whether this belief makes sense in the situation and whether acting angry will be skillful. If so, then proceed to act assertively. If not, then you can ask your mind what would be more helpful, and you can make a different decision. When similar situations arise with this person in the future, you will already have a measure of awareness and some strategies for responding. Just be careful not to project previous circumstances onto a new situation. Throughout this process of mindfully observing your self-dialogue, you have your emotions rather than your emotions having you. As we have said before, modern psychology calls this cognitive behavioral therapy, but this is nothing new—Yogis have been practicing it for millennia (YS II.33).

Observe How the Primary Fountains Affect Your Emotions

You can also examine the motivation for an emotion in light of the four primary fountains. Again, ask yourself what you feel. Note this down. Then ask yourself to which desire the feeling might refer. (Remember the wisdom of Alcoholics Anonymous about how addictive behavior tends to happen when we are hungry, angry, lonely, or tired: HALT. This often helps to identify the relevant fountain.) In what way is that desire either expressed or frustrated? Are there other feelings that enter into the situation? How might you transform your desire into a joyful challenge through the process of tapas? For example, in the case of anger, you might begin by just observing it with a sense of wonder: "What is all this anger? What is it about? Where does it come from?" As above, ask yourself who the target of the anger is. Now consider which fountain of desire is being frustrated. Then your mind is open either to find a more compassionate way to meet whatever legitimate need you may have or, if there is no true need, to enjoy the feeling of emptiness when the object of your desire is absent. For example, fasting entails not only deeply enjoying the beauty of the food you eat but also enjoying the sense of emptiness, cleanness, and freedom that accompany the choice to abstain from eating.

When you practice this exercise over time, you will become more skilled at identifying some of the same issues that repeatedly surface. A particular fountain might dominate many different situations, or perhaps any fountain may become agitated given a certain situation, type of interaction, or particular person. These patterns are your ego's sticking points, and emotional purification is all about getting unstuck.

Practice Self-Affirmation

Another useful practice with the cognitive side of emotions is to offer yourself realistic affirmations that support your mood and your growth. You can track these in a journal or simply practice affirmation throughout your day. Many of us grow up in families where the aesthetic of child rearing is to help children grow by making them aware of where they are having problems and by trying to solve those problems. If you solve them all, so the thinking goes, everything will develop as it should. This idea is problematic for a couple of reasons.

One of them is the corollary belief that if we offer kids positive feedback, they will become spoiled or entitled. (Certainly, if that is all you offer your child, without including appropriate limits and boundaries, that might happen.) However, far from this, one of the ways that we build a healthy me-map is through receiving positive feedback for behavior that we are trying out. The lack of this positive reinforcement can leave holes, as it were, in our self-models as children, and we can carry these with us into adulthood.

For example, I have worked in therapy with many gay men who grew up thinking they could never be athletes based on a lack of positive reinforcement from parents or the reactions of their peers. Later on, in their adult life, they began to run or swim and discovered not only that they had skill but that, "Hey, this feels good!!" The ability to affirm ourselves makes a difference in our evolving self-modeling. So don't be afraid to say to yourself, when it's appropriate, "Good job! You did that well!" You will probably experience an immediate, positive jump in your mood. And since our nervous systems habitually respond more rapidly to painful rather than to positive experience, feel free to linger in your awareness with that positive mood and self-affirmation for 30 seconds or so. Again, this will wire it into your neural networks and allow it to become a resource in response to such moments in the future.

Affirm Others

A second problem with the above method of child rearing is that it amounts to training children's minds only to criticize themselves and others, creating in them a belief that if they correct all the criticisms, they will be okay. The trouble with this is that people become such talented critics that they actually lose the ability to see what is good in themselves or in the life around them. We have all experienced this in some form or another and can help each other and ourselves to move beyond it. The key to this practice is to realize that, at a deep level, we are all already okay—and we can affirm this truth for each other.

Get out of your own ruminating thoughts by expressing your gratitude to others for what they have done well and for the ways that they have helped you. Offer encouraging support when they seem to need it and genuine, positive acknowledgement even when they don't. In this way, you will enhance your relationships with others, experience the healing benefits of relationship from our second chapter, and likely receive some of the same support you offer to other people. You will intentionally sow some bright seeds of future action (saṁskāra) into the depths of your mind. This practice will make you feel good in the short term and promote altruism that will make you feel even better in the long term. By looking for the good in those around you, you may even be more likely to see it in yourself.

Just as we need others to develop our own psychological self as children, we continue to need other people throughout our lifetimes. Our interactions with others teach us about our own mind, and the way back home to ourselves can often be through traveling outward to others. Though relationships can cause us harm, as in some of the examples in this book, relating to others also heals us and keeps us well. How does your mood improve when you focus on affirming someone else? What positive aspects of another person draw you towards him or her? These are likely attributes that the Self is suggesting you develop for your own growth. A bonus of this exercise is that by offering happiness to others, you train your mind to believe that you already have enough of it to go around. As above, you can try logging this experiment in a journal to see how it shifts your mood and changes how others respond to you over time. But most importantly, make it a point to practice this throughout your day. Remember that Patañjali begins with the yamas—Yoga is all about relationship!

Keep a Daily Journal of Beauty, Joy, and Wonder

Swāmī Veda once gave everyone in our worldwide *sangha* (spiritual family) an assignment to keep a journal in which each day you record at least one thing that gave you a sense of beauty, joy, or wonder.

Most of us didn't take the assignment very seriously at first. One day he arrived in a city to give some lectures, and a disciple called him up to ask him to lunch. He accepted the invitation. At lunch, after some initial pleasantries, the man produced a large package, beautifully gift-wrapped. Swāmījī unwrapped the package and saw there a stack of journals representing two years of this work. The man told Swāmījī that the practice had completely changed the quality of his mind, and he was continuing to do it. Before the practice, he had tended towards a pessimistic outlook and a depressed mood. The journals were a treasured gift of self-transformation.

Keeping a journal of beauty, joy, and wonder can help you retrain your mind to see what is good in yourself and in your life and to see the beauty around you. As a daily practice, this can enhance your sense of well-being. As a therapeutic measure, it will help you when you seem surrounded by nothing but problems and moving towards a hopeless corner in life. When you need help not believing all the thoughts in your mind, your journal will be there for you, a place where you, yourself, have affirmed the goodness in and around you. Most importantly, when a person becomes suicidal, with thinking so distorted that it appears there is no beauty in the world and nothing worth living for, the journal becomes a reminder of the evidence to the contrary. As you deal with the inevitable struggles life presents, this practice will help you avert the trap of an overly critical mind and support your resilience.

Maintain a Practice Log

A journal can also be a helpful tool in which you log your Yoga practices, assess your progress, and identify patterns. For example, you might ask yourself when you tend to break your Yoga practice and for what reasons? What influences seem to support your practice, and which inhibit it? What are the belief systems that you use to either maintain or undermine your practice? You can record various experiments. For example, take one month to focus on each yama and niyama (see Appendix A, Exercise 3.11). Write about how that attitude affects your life and how you encounter obstacles. You might look at each one as it relates to nonviolence, which is the foundation of them all.

You might also use a journal to do research on yourself. Spend a month or more tracking the rhythms in your breath. You could track nostril activity and its relationship to your various pursuits and compare these to the lists in the svara texts. Or you could use the mirror experiment described in Appendix A, Exercise 2.3, to chart the flow of the activity of elemental energies in your breath and note how these relate to your thoughts, feelings, and actions. You might also track how the postures in your daily practice affect your awareness of the cakras or the flow of your thoughts and feelings (see Appendix A, Exercise 3.3).

Byron Katie: Do "the Work"

Another interesting journaling approach has been popularized by the contemporary spiritual teacher Byron Katie. She had a life full of serious problems but one morning awoke in a high spiritual state that seemed to resolve all her difficulties. When she thought about how to pass this along to people, she began doing a process she called "the work" with them (Katie). She asks each person to write out the belief associated with his or her emotion. Then she has them ask themselves four questions, which she has made freely available on her website (http://thework.com/en/do-work):

1. Is it true? (Yes or no. If no, move to 3.)
2. Can you absolutely know that it's true? (Yes or no.) [A much harder test!]
3. How do you react, what happens, when you believe that thought?
4. Who would you be without the thought? [An invitation to envision a different way to believe and feel.] (Katie)[19]

[19] The parenthetical insertions are Katie's. I inserted the material in brackets.

Next she asks people to do what she calls a "turnaround" (Katie), also described online. To experience this, turn what you believe around 180 degrees, and see how that fits. Often, you'll experience some revelation from thinking outside the box of your current self-identification (ego).

In Chapter 6, I described a male client who was depressed and who broke down in sobs at the same point in a sequence of āsanas in every class. This man had had a difficult time with his family of origin since our previous therapy session, and they had stopped communicating. This was extremely painful to my client because family was very important to him. His son's wedding was approaching, and he was deeply concerned that his conflict with his parents would wreck the celebration. I described Katie's process to him, and he was intrigued. He went home, downloaded the worksheets from her website, and filled them out. At the top of the page, he wrote this belief: "They don't love me unconditionally." He responded to her questions as follows:

1. Is it true? "Yes—that's why we are not speaking."
2. Can I absolutely know that it's true? "Well, I suppose it's possible I might be wrong."
3. How do I react, what happens, when I believe that thought? "Depressed."
4. Who would I be without the thought? "I wonder . . ."

Then for his turnaround he wrote, "I don't love *them* unconditionally." This gave him pause. As he reviewed his behavior, he had to admit that this was true. He saw how *he* could change the situation by changing his behavior rather than trying to get them to change theirs. He was able to focus on the part of the problem that he had the power to change.

My client returned a few weeks later after the wedding. He said that he had hoped that therapy would help him to be neutral and cordial towards his parents and extended family. In fact, he was warm, loving, and welcoming to them. Then, as you might imagine, they began talking to him again. Their differences were still there, but they had restarted the conversation, and everyone felt more hopeful. We all share this capacity to bring clarity, insight, and responsibility to our own role in a situation and to our sometimes distorted thinking, which, when modified, can lead to skillful behavior. To learn more about the work and to get a feel for how you can apply it, I highly recommend Katie's (2002) book, *Loving What Is: Four Questions That Can Change Your Life.*

These are several examples of how you can journal about your emotions and learn a great deal about their origins and their dynamics. With awareness of your emotions and patterns—and therefore with a wider range of choices in how you can respond to yourself and others—you can gradually change your karma, one action at a time.

Journal About Your Unconscious Mind: Learn from Your Dreams

Another useful journal project is to record your dreams. Freud called dreams "the royal road to the unconscious." Dream analysis is a valuable intervention in psychotherapy, where we often undertake a detailed interpretation of dream content. Even without this kind of intensive interpretive effort, however, a dream journal often helps to identify important issues that tend to stay in the unconscious or preconscious background.

Walk the Royal Road

To capture dream material, it is important to keep a journal or digital voice recorder at your bedside. As soon as you awake in the morning, record everything you can recall about the night's dreams. This material remains in your awareness for only about three to four minutes after you awake unless the dream is extraordinary. Refrain from reaching for interpretations of any kind, and just record as many details as possible, including obvious references to the activities of the previous day. The text may seem crazy to you. Often the more bizarre a dream symbol is, the more important and interesting the message. And the stranger the symbolic encoding of the message, the more psychologically defended your ego is to receiving it.

Once you have recorded all that you can remember, return to the task of making sense of the dream at a different time. Then you can think about what the dream referred to, who or what the characters represented, and what the narrative of the dream was saying. Let associations to the symbols in the dream come to your mind, and use your heart to sense which meanings are right for you. What is your relationship to each symbol? What are the relationships of each character or symbol to the others? Use your feeling intuition rather than just your rational mind to explore these questions. How do the symbols in the dream create a story? You may find that as you work on the narrative of a dream, other dreams may come to you over time to extend and enrich that narrative.

During my own personal psychotherapy, I kept a dream journal for some years. One day I was preparing for a therapy session and didn't feel that I had much to talk about. I paged through the journal to see whether there was anything there that would give me a clue. I turned the page to a dream I had recorded several weeks earlier. It seemed quite ordinary at the time. As I looked at it again, I was amazed to see that it was an existential map for the remainder of my life! We spent the next several sessions working with that dream. The dream acquired a life of its own, its meaning changing and developing each time we worked with it. Dreams are not static entities. They are living, ongoing communication with the unconscious part of our mind, and they reveal new insights the deeper we look into them.

This process helps us to establish a relationship with our unconscious mind. The unconscious is the largest part of our ordinary mental functioning. It operates our whole body without our having to try. If we choose to exercise some control, most of the time we have only to ask. This is the domain of hypnosis as well as certain Yoga practices (see below). Communication with this part of the mind is always elliptical, indirect, and usually in the form of symbols. It also tests us to see whether we are paying attention. The more we do attend, and the more awareness we apply, the more information we will likely receive, and the more direct the communication can become. If you would like to try a walk down Freud's proverbial royal road, two excellent little books on working with dream material (though from a Jungian methodology) are clear and engaging and meant to enable readers to work with dreams themselves. These are Robert Bosnak's (1998) *A Little Course in Dreams* and Robert A. Johnson's (1986/2009) *Inner Work*, both listed in this work's References.

Practice Yogic Dreaming

There is a Yogic discipline of dream work as well. The textual evidence of this is mostly in the Tibetan tradition (Rinpoche, 1998). These practices relate to the larger practice of yoga-nidrā, where one seeks to consciously enter deep, dreamless sleep through a concentration at the heart cakra. You can do something similar with your dream sleep. Access your dreams by focusing at the throat cakra as you fall asleep. This cakra is the seat of the dream state in Indian Yoga, Tibetan Yoga, and Taoist Yoga. You can also facilitate the activity of your dreams by intensive practice of the lion posture, *siṁhāsana*, which stimulates the activity of the viśuddha-cakra at the throat. One friend of mine experimented with doing the lion 35 times each day and said, "My dreams went wild!"

Final Thoughts

Once you have opened a conscious inner dialogue with your mind, your inner world can really open up to you. With greater awareness of your interior mental and emotional life, you become a better friend to yourself, you have more attention to give to your meditations, and you have more to offer others. You can track your growth and development and identify patterns in your life that are holding you back. For those who are interested in pursuing this further, consider looking into the writing of Ira Progoff (1977/1980/1992), who has advocated the use of journaling for self-development for many years.

Chapter Nine

What About Therapy?

Sometimes our own efforts to deal with an emotional problem are just not enough. We may have exhausted our resources in working with a problem. We may experience emotional reactions that are far out of proportion to the facts of a situation. We may feel too afraid to face something without the support of a companion on the journey. Or our mood or thinking may create such obstacles that we can't think clearly enough to sort ourselves out or even function day to day. In this chapter, we will explore questions about when psychotherapy, medication, and/or complimentary therapies may be useful in the process of emotional purification. We'll also discuss some guidelines for how to find a therapist and what to expect in psychotherapy. As a psychologist, psychotherapist, and Yoga teacher for many years, I have observed how often people intend to deal with the pain in their lives but try to do so in ways that attempt to step over or around their suffering rather than face it. Sometimes people take up Yoga in hopes that by doing so they won't need to consult a mental health professional. This problem is growing more pervasive now that therapy and Yoga are beginning to merge in the modern interpretation of Yoga.

There certainly are some Yoga teachers who are perfectly good counselors and therapists, some of them mental health professionals themselves. However, there is nothing in any Yoga teacher training that really prepares instructors with the skills to do this work with their students. Conversely, trainings in Yoga for mental health professionals too often focus only on practices and techniques (e.g., Weintraub, 2012) rather than on the fundamental attitudes that make the practices of Yoga work, for example training in the process of spiritual formation or in the relational use of healing to offer spiritual guidance. (*Spiritual formation* is a term for cultivating spiritual growth in others. *Relational healing* is using relationship as a healing tool—not just the psychological aspects of a relationship, but the spiritual ones as well.)

Practicing Yoga with someone is as much a matter of direct transmission of a state of consciousness as it is about what the spiritual guide or therapist "does" with a student or client. Unfortunately, many therapists tend to focus on technique as the solution rather than on the relationship with the client. This approach, which prioritizes technique over relationship and/or experience, encourages therapists to use Yoga practices out of context, without having their own regular practice of meditation and the other aspects of Yoga. In such a situation, a therapist's effectiveness is likely to be limited, and in a few cases even harmful. This is important to keep in mind when finding a therapist. Or, when pursuing our own Yoga practice without one, we must ask ourselves whether we are attempting to use Yoga out of context to side-step a problem. Could we also benefit from working with a therapist?

Determining When to Seek Psychotherapy

When do we need psychotherapy? The simple answer suggested above is when our own efforts have been insufficient, when our personal resources have not succeeded in solving a problem, or when something is just too threatening to face alone. Certainly, if you have become so despairing that you are having thoughts of suicide or self-harm, that is a time to reach out for professional help without delay.

Finding a Therapist with the Right Skill Set

How do you find a good therapist? First, think about what kinds of services you may need. If you are feeling suicidal or inclined to hurt yourself or others, you can reach out to emergency services immediately, usually in the form of a hospital emergency department, telephone hotlines, or walk-in mental health clinics. If you don't know where to turn, you could also call your physician for referrals to emergency services. At these times, knowledge of Yoga is helpful, but stabilizing the situation is the priority.

If you require medication, you probably want to look for a psychiatrist or prescribing psychologist, like a psychiatric nurse practitioner or the rare psychologist with expertise in medication management. Additionally, some psychologists (in the United States) have licensure to prescribe through military training. If you need some testing and refined diagnostic assessment, you might think about finding a psychologist. If you have a chronic illness and require coordination of many services, a social worker with some experience in case management might be the right person. Almost all the mental health disciplines practice some form of psychotherapy, so part of your decision will rest on the skills and disciplinary training of available practitioners. This you can easily assess based on a practitioner's resume or website.

Assessing a Therapist's Integrity, Training, and Experience

Once you have an idea of which skillset you are looking for, the harder task of assessing the personal qualities of a psychotherapist begins. One avenue to explore is to ask your family and friends who know you well whether they have had good experiences with anyone. From the therapists's side of the desk, I can tell you that the best referrals usually come by word of mouth from personal experience. If you don't have any leads from family and friends, don't be afraid to ask a prospective therapist for a resume or an exploratory conversation. This does not have to be a full-hour session. If a therapist is unwilling to do this, then run in the other direction. It may mean that he or she is overcommitted to making money or lacks the sensitivity to understand the importance of a first impression in deciding from whom to receive such a deeply personal service.

Give some attention to the person's training and professional experience. Again, don't be afraid to ask for that resume. The information can be useful, and the therapist's response to the question can give you a clue about how secure the person is about his or her own skills and integrity. If the therapist has written books or articles, these writings may give you a sense of how he or she approaches the work of therapy and his or her relationships with clients. Clients seldom do this, but you would certainly ask for references if someone were going to remodel your house! This can also tell you whether a therapist has any connection with Yoga. In the US, he or she might be a registered Yoga teacher (RYT) with the Yoga Alliance (https://www.yogaalliance.org) or a member of the International Association of Yoga Therapists (http://www.iayt.org). The latter organization has recently begun certifying yoga therapists (CYT). Many countries also have their own registries and certifying bodies. A registry is simply a list of people who have graduated from a training program with certain characteristics. It is not a certification of competence. Remember that the degrees and licenses and specialty certifications on the wall or on a resume only certify a certain minimum level of proficiency.

Choosing a Therapist Who Is a Good Fit for You

The most important consideration in choosing a professional to work with is the degree to which you feel a connection with the person. In terms of interpersonal neurobiology, this is the amount of resonance you experience with him or her. Does the therapist seem to understand who you are as a person in addition to understanding the problem? Does the therapist allow you to talk, or does he or she interrupt with interpretations and advice all the time? Are his or her remarks mostly intellectual, or do they seem to come from the heart? Does the therapist seem to be compassionate enough to feel your emotions *with* you? Is he or she willing to say things to you that you may not want to hear and do so in a compassionate way? What does he or she know of Yoga and meditation? How open might the therapist be to including Yoga practices in the therapy process?

In addition to answering these questions, pay attention to how the person feels to you. How does the encounter feel in your stomach and heart? These are where the process of intuition registers all the data that your senses gather from outside of your conscious awareness, and these are where your inner voice begins to formulate questions or reservations. This kind of intuitive first impression is usually pretty accurate. In addition to following your first instincts, check in with them over time. It is just fine to agree to meet for a certain number of sessions and then assess how the therapy is going before you commit to a long process.

Resonance circuits and the therapy relationship. In Chapter 5, we discussed the role that mirror neurons and resonance circuits play in helping people to develop a sense of themselves and others. Parents essentially lend a child their highly developed resonance circuits to initiate the child's development, and in the process, they continue to grow and change, as well. What happens neurologically in psychotherapy is quite similar. The sense of personal connection that you feel with a therapist is the sign that there is good contact between the therapist's resonance circuits and your own. This allows any of your unfinished processes of growth and development to restart themselves in therapy. So the therapist becomes a kind of quasiparental figure, at least for a while. This process of mutual resonance then begins the transference of qualities of your parental relationship onto the therapy relationship, as we discussed in the previous chapter. It is as if the internalized versions of your parents—which you carry in your mind and heart and which likely have not changed much since you were four or five years old—come out into the therapy relationship and come alive again. Sorting out the ways in which this transference distorts the relationship with your therapist (and, by extension, with others in your life) is much of the work of therapy. Learning to distinguish between who the therapist is and who you perceive the therapist to be based on your own projections helps you to become aware of those habitual projections. You can then see where else in your life you might be engaging in similar thought patterns (perhaps with your spiritual teachers?), and you can generally complete any unfinished development.

The phenomenon of transference occurs in every therapy relationship, regardless of its theoretical foundation, because therapy is based in the interpersonal neurobiology of resonance circuits. Yet different styles of therapy have different emphases in how they work. A psychoanalytic or psychodynamic therapist will focus primarily on the therapy relationship and how it resonates with developmentally important relationships. A cognitive-behavioral therapist will focus on a client's own relationship between cognition and emotion. Gestalt therapy and many of the other humanistic therapies (e.g., existential therapy, person-centered therapy, and transpersonal psychology) focus on deepening awareness of emotions and all their components (sensation, cognition, motivation, and saṁskāra). Though each of these therapies does not necessarily name the components as such, they do work with them, assisting individuals with taking responsibility for their emotions and for their choices in how they respond to events in their lives. Many of the above therapies are rapidly adopting meditation and mindfulness to facilitate awareness, which is the key ingredient in all of them. Other therapists include family therapists, who work with a relationship system rather than focus on individuals within that system, and hypnotherapists, who work with the unconscious part of the mind, with its vast and efficient creative and healing abilities. Regardless of the theoretical label a psychotherapist may use, almost all therapists combine these approaches to some degree—hence the importance of choosing a therapist based on the sense of connection that you feel.

The importance of the quality of this connection is something that I cannot stress enough. When I think back over my own personal psychotherapy, I do not recall a lot of the specific things my therapist said to me. What I will never forget is the way he sat across the room weeping with me as I described painful aspects of an experience. He felt my experience as I felt it and genuinely understood me. Over time, as you come to know each other and particularly as the therapist comes to know you well, a moment will come when you can face the fearful aspects of what you are there to work on. You will feel some fear, but that fear will be manageable when there is someone to accompany you. At that moment, you will feel sufficiently safe to be vulnerable enough to allow the raw nature of problematic thoughts and emotions to arise, and you will feel comfortable enough to be held in your therapist's loving attention. If you can get to this point, often you will feel empowered to reach more deeply into your mind and heart (and, sometimes, especially with trauma, into the body) and find a new solution that you had never considered before.

On one occasion in my own therapy, a psychologist whom I greatly admired committed suicide. I recall opening the newspaper one morning and feeling traumatized to read the headline news of his death. Immediately I descended into a deep depression that I did not understand. My whole conscious acquaintance with this person consisted of a five-minute phone call! My therapist was a close friend of this man. Thankfully, it was not hard to arrive at the awareness that, actually, I was furious at him for having done this, and I was internalizing the rage and taking it out on myself, hence my depression. After that, I felt more comfortable expressing my rage and anger about what he had done. Working with another therapist about a year later, someone who was also a close friend of the deceased psychologist, I began to rant about what had happened, and in the middle of it, the therapist said the most shocking thing:

"Stephen, this rage of yours is really odious and disrespectful!" I was completely stunned, stopped in my tracks. I knew that this man loved me, and he was still holding me lovingly in his attention. As I sat in my confusion for a few moments, all of a sudden, as if from out of my cells, intense raw pain and grief came pouring into my voice, and I howled and wept like a banshee for a full ten minutes. From within this experience, I couldn't believe what was happening. When I had calmed down and gotten my emotional balance again, we looked at each other with some surprise and began to process what had just occurred.

We learned that my unconscious mind actually had a very deep relationship and love for the psychologist, despite how little real time we had shared with each other. That part of my mind had followed him very closely (from a distance) for several years, constructing an age-progression model for my professional life and development, a me-map for the future. When the course of that model ended in suicide, it was little wonder that I was deeply wounded and, at the same time, offended by it. Because other factors in my upbringing had made this intense grief too fearful to face by myself, I externalized it in the form of rage. This was my effort to try to understand and somehow cope with it by putting it outside myself. When my therapist contained this externalization, or "acting out" of the emotion, suddenly I could experience it directly, with mindful awareness, and that opened the way for my own self-compassion to do the real work of healing. I might have done this on my own after many years, but therapy sped up the resolution of this problem and helped me with several other issues in my life, as well.

This is characteristic of therapy done well. Not only does it heal the problem at hand, but also it usually gives you the inner resources to resolve other issues that you have postponed because of it. This healing also reaches out across generations. In families, it helps to prevent the generational transmission of painful behavioral inheritances. The whole relational system of the family gets healed.

If your heart becomes more compassionate and more capable of self-healing, you also pass this along through interpersonal resonance circuits to everyone you love and feel connected to. It becomes a gift to everyone around you. I would argue that your ability to heal yourself with a therapist-companion also helps you to heal the sources of those inheritances in generations past. Even if people are no longer in the body, we now know from the ideas of quantum physics that quantum effects are both nonlocal and nontemporal (Radin, 2013). So the effects of this healing ripple out in all directions in space and time.

Determining When to Use Medication

In addition to asking about when and how to find a therapist, people often raise the question of taking medications for mental health problems. There are many instances where a course of medication can help to reduce symptoms that are impacting a person's ability to function, especially in the short term. Many people struggle with sleep, appetite, and clarity of thought and can become so confused and exhausted that they can hardly function, much less work out a serious personal problem. (Recall Vyāsa's description in Chapter 1 of the mūḍha mindfield, stupefied by intoxication or mental or physical illness.) If this describes your experience, medication can allow you to rest, nourish yourself, and clarify your thinking so that you can participate in useful therapy. If you have been diagnosed with a major mental illness like bipolar disorder or schizophrenia, your healthcare provider will know what course of treatment to recommend to you as an individual, but generally people with major mental illnesses will require some degree of medication over an extended period, including, possibly, for life. However, it is important to understand that even in the case of mental illnesses whose cause is mostly biological, medication is almost never a cure. It is a support. Much about our progress in dealing with an emotional problem or a mental illness depends on what we are able to accomplish in modifying our lifestyle and in how much we can enter into a process of therapy.

Many people feel conflicted about the use of medicine in dealing with emotional problems, and these conflicted feelings are not without justification. Psychopharmacology is still a relatively blunt instrument. Even though knowledge about neuroscience has exploded in the last few years, we are still only at the beginning of our ability to understand the enormous complexity of the brain and nervous system. We are only a little more than half a century past the first discoveries of psychiatric medicines that worked in any way, and there has been almost no research about the long-term implications of any medication. The effectiveness of medication also remains dubious in some common cases. For example, one of Western medicine's premiere journals *JAMA (Journal of the American Medical Association)* published a patient-level meta-analysis of six studies and 718 patients who were diagnosed with major or minor depressive disorder. Fournier et al. (2010) found that the effectiveness of antidepressant medication increases with symptom severity, and although medication substantially benefits individuals with major depression, people with mild or moderate symptoms, on average, experience minimal or no benefit beyond the placebo effect.

Let's look at another example: The discovery of the role of neurotransmitter systems in mood disorders opened the door to medication strategies that greatly improved people's quality of life, at least for a while. These antidepressant medications, many of which are still in use, seek to correct imbalances in our brain's chemical transmitters (neurotransmitters), which carry information across synapses, the connections between nerve cells (neurons). Most of these medications act to increase the amount of neurotransmitter in the synapse by blocking the process of its removal. As a static intervention, this works just fine. However, biological systems are not static. They are cybernetic; they receive feedback from their environment and change their behavior accordingly. As the quantity of a neurotransmitter builds up in the synapse, the brain begins to produce less of that chemical substance. As a result, almost all of these medications "wear out" over time in terms of their therapeutic effect. So it is important to do what you can to make lifestyle choices to help the brain and nervous system maintain themselves in a more sustainable fashion (Emmons, 2006, 2010, 2012).

We know, for example, that in uncomplicated major depression or in common types of anxiety disorders, aerobic exercise, at least 30 minutes a day four or five times per week, will often moderate depression and anxiety to the point where no medication is needed. When I am working with people who have these diagnoses, we almost always spend some time figuring out what kind of aerobic exercise will help them in this way. It need not be anything defined officially as "exercise" requiring a gym membership or a trip through a locker room. Social dancing is a fine aerobic workout, as are roller blading, cross-country skiing, swimming, and many other activities that don't involve lifting weights or enduring the boredom many people experience on exercise machines.

Meditation and psychotherapy also improve the balance of neurotransmitters, depending on the mental illness, to a degree comparable to psychotropic medication (Imel, Malterer, McKay, & Wampold, 2008; Goyal et al., 2014). In this regard, I recommend moment-to-moment mindfulness and the relaxation practices that Swāmī Veda and Swāmī Rāma taught, detailed in Appendix A. And as we previously discussed in Chapters 6 and 7, the helpfulness of āsana and prāṇāyāma in the treatment of psychological trauma is clear. Yet the literature on outcomes in the majority of mental health problems consistently shows that the most effective treatment is medication in combination with psychotherapy. It is important to consider all the tools at our disposal. Indeed, each illness presents its own treatment protocol, and increasingly, psychotherapists are including the whole mind/body in their approach. (For more on this, see Emmons, 2012, *The Chemistry of Joy Workbook: Overcoming*

Depression Using the Best of Brain Science, Nutrition, and the Psychology of Mindfulness.)

Including Complementary and Alternative Medicine in Your Treatment Plan

As Emmons (2012) and many other mental health professionals are finding, therapies that work in concert with psychotherapy and allopathic medication can support the health of the brain and nervous system to promote emotional well-being. For example, homeopathy provides remedies that operate at the level of subtle energy, just as the lifestyle and dietary recommendations of Āyurveda impact our prāṇa. In each system, physicians assess a person holistically and recommend treatments based on an individual's unique presentation of physical, mental, and emotional symptoms.

Homeopathy

The homeopathic system bases its theory not on categories of disease, but on the specific *symptom picture* a person presents. Major depressive disorder does not exist in the homeopathic system, but there is a remedy for low energy that is worse in the morning, accompanied by a loss of appetite for food and sex and persistent negative thoughts about oneself and one's life. Ballentine (2011) describes homeopathic medication as working like a software patch in a computer's operating system. A process of successive dilutions and agitations (*succussion*) imprints an energy pattern on a solution of water and alcohol, which ill people ingest as a remedy or apply as a topical ointment. Homeopathy traditionally investigated remedies by giving them to healthy people and noting the symptoms that appeared. By exposing people to something that initially increased their symptoms, homeopathy discovered how to mobilize and strengthen the mind/body's own ability to resist illness, sometimes with amazing speed.

In my own case, I once arrived at our āśram in India with a

head cold that I had picked up in Holland. I had the cold for about three days at that point, and if it behaved as it had for my Dutch hosts, I knew I was in for a week or two of continuously worsening symptoms. Previously, the homeopathic remedy *Gelsemium Sempervirens* had worked for me, so I took a dose. My nose, which had been running through the whole plane trip, and my stuffy head cleared in about one minute, and the symptoms did not return. Not every remedy works this well or this quickly, but generally the better the match between the symptom picture and the remedy's symptom picture, the swifter and more effective the remedy.

As homeopathy does not distinguish between physical and mental illness, most of the symptom portraits of homeopathic remedies include mental and emotional symptoms. It stands to reason that this would be an interesting modality for psychology and psychiatry to explore, but despite both anecdotal and empirical evidence for its effectiveness, homeopathy tends to be held back (Caulfield & Debow, 2005). The modern allopathic medical model, limited by data it gathers from the sensory world, cannot find the mechanism for how homeopathy works—because it is looking in the wrong place. Homeopathy's primary method, succussion, results in no measurable amount of the original substance remaining; the only remnant of the original is its energetic imprint. So this modality works at the mind/body level of subtle energy, or prāṇa, in the prāṇa-maya-koṣa. "How" homeopathy is effective is not to be found at the level of contemporary Western medicine in the anna-maya-koṣa (the mind/body sheath literally made of food), but on the next most subtle level, in the realm of quantum physics. And we are just beginning to enter the era of quantum medicine (see Goswami, 2004/2011, *The Quantum Doctor: A Quantum Physicist Explains the Healing Power of Integral Medicine*). If you wish to experience homeopathy's effectiveness for yourself, Ballentine's (2011) *Radical Healing* provides a guide for making your own experiments.

Āyurveda

Recall from Chapter 7 that Āyurveda is a science of long life. It is based on health practices that are largely preventative and, like homeopathy, it is based on a notion of wellness rather than illness. Āyurveda is very similar to ancient systems of medicine in the classical Western cultures. Its physicians tend to give interventions in terms of lifestyle and dietary recommendations, including herbal remedies and cleansing practices that are designed to improve function in critical organs, like the liver. They prescribe herbs not so much by their physically active ingredients, as would be the case in allopathic medicine, but rather by the energetic properties of an herb and its whole ecology. Herbs, for example, are typically harvested only in a certain season, at a particular phase of the moon, and at a specific time of day so that they capture certain energetic qualities.

The energy of an Āyurvedic remedy interacts with the energy of an individual's mind/body. Āyurveda classifies people by constitutional types based on three observed qualities of matter (*guṇa*s*: sattva, rajas,* and *tamas*), which are similar to the four humors of traditional Greek medicine. These qualities of matter—purity or balance (sattva), passion or movement (rajas), and ignorance or lethargy (tamas)—interact to create the three *doṣa*s, or energetic qualities said to be the building blocks of personality and body type. There are three doṣas (*kapha, pitta,* and *vata*), and most of us can be described primarily by one. Some of us have a nearly equal presentation of two, while fewer individuals experience a balance of all three. Kapha people have large-framed bodies and are sedentary, have low energy, and may be prone to lethargy, respiratory ailments, and depression. Pitta types have a fiery disposition, are easily angered, and have thinner bodies, a high energy level, and a tendency towards inflammation. Vata people have minds that are blown around like the wind; they struggle with consistency and tend towards digestive problems and anxiety. Āyurvedic prescriptions are based on which activities and foods tend to either aggravate or pacify one's constitutional type. Rather than offer more details here, I would refer the reader to Ballentine's (2011) *Radical Healing* and Chopra's (1990) *Perfect Health.*

Final Thoughts

Psychotherapy—perhaps with adjunctive allopathic, Āyurvedic, or homeopathic treatments and lifestyle modifications—can play a significantly positive role in emotional purification. It often speeds up the process by clearing emotional blocks of which we may not even be aware. Psychotherapy can help to resolve unfinished emotional business with our parents and our upbringing that we often project onto significant others in our lives, including, possibly, our spiritual teachers. Sorting out our projections, we liberate our further growth and development to continue their unfoldment. The process of emotional healing also deepens our compassion and develops our ability to be helpful to others in their suffering. As we work with ourselves, our own efforts create healing ripples that carry into our relationships, past and present.

PART III

Working with the Mindfield:
Expand Your Awareness to Citta and Beyond

Chapter Ten

Mantra and Emotional Purification

In this chapter, we will discuss the use of both ordinary and personal mantras and so-called *special mantras* in the process of emotional purification. It is common these days in modern, Westernized Yoga to use mantras gathered from books as if they were a collection of magic words. Simply speaking or even thinking their gross syllables has some effect, though it is negligible. Certainly, when chanted from the heart in devotional *kīrtana*, literally "singing," mantras do harness and direct our emotional energies to a certain extent, and this does contribute to the purification of those emotions. But the science of mantra is an exceedingly deep and detailed study and practice that has much in common with contemporary quantum physics. One could in fact argue, as Swāmī Veda often did in conversation with physicists, that this science and its associated meditative science of Śrī-vidyā constitute the long-sought unified field theory.

Mantra just might reconcile the seeming contradictions of all that we currently know about how the universe works through relativity and quantum mechanics. Quantum theory would hold that consciousness initiates the manifestation of energy and matter (Goswami, 2004/2011) and thereby produces changes in the mind and eventually even in the body of the practitioner. A detailed examination of how this occurs is beyond the scope of this book. As with neuroscience, the ultimate answers lie in meditative experience that is well beyond what we can measure empirically, although Radin

(2013) has demonstrated nonlocal quantum causation through mental means. Other exciting discoveries, or rather, affirmations, are likely to follow. It is exciting to contemplate the future ability of science to test the role of consciousness in the workings of the universe. But we need look no further than the countless Yogis and Buddhas who have known it for themselves. You, too, can know for yourself, through your own direct, personal experience, that mantra, used in the proper manner and over time, can substantially reconstruct, purify, and pacify the universe that is your personal mindfield.

What Is Mantra?

Let's begin by discussing the simplest explanation of mantra as a sound we use to focus our concentration in meditation and mindfulness practices. Some might say it is a word or words, but there are many mantras that are sounds, which have no dictionary meaning at all. In fact, in understanding the impact of a mantra on the mind/body, the lexical meaning of the words is almost irrelevant.

It is somewhat more accurate to say that a mantra is a sound body of specific aspects of the energy of consciousness. These energies interact with and modify our individual mindfields in the mental koṣas of the mind/body (vijñāna-maya-koṣa and mano-maya-koṣa). The mindfield then alters the flow of subtle energy, or prāṇa, in the energy body (prāṇa-maya-koṣa), and those subtle currents gradually reshape the physical part of our mind/body (anna-maya-koṣa). In this way, mantra plays an important role in unraveling the knots and kinks in our mindfield and energy system, clearing a path for the eventual awakening of the full energy of consciousness, Kuṇḍalinī. Since mantra operates in the realm of the intangible parts of the mind, there is little that current neurobiological research can contribute, at least directly, to understanding how mantra works. Indirectly, however, we can study mantra by noticing its effects on the brain, defined as animating the whole body from feet to crown.

Mantra and Karma

To understand the practical function of a mantra, we can observe its karmik effect on the mindfield and, by extension, its physical effects on the grey matter in our heads, the function of our nervous systems, and even the habitual carriage of our bodies in space. Because our muscles develop according to their use, we can also say that over time, the positive influence of a mantra on the mindfield alters even the body's physical structure. As mantra practice clears our mindfield of emotional knots, we feel better about ourselves and our lives, and we in turn carry ourselves more upright, with greater ease and grace. Our more functionally balanced use of the body results in physical musculature that is the same. This is how mantra influences most layers of our being, from the vijñāna-maya-koṣa down to the anna-maya-koṣa.

More specifically, as we discussed in Chapter 5, every thought, feeling, and action we make leaves a trace, an impression on the mindfield called, in Yoga, saṁskāra. And as we discussed in Chapter 6, the body is the physical representation of our mindfields' subtle impressions, our habits. Our saṁskāras accumulate to create our bodies and our personalities and to impel us towards similar future action. If, however, in the throes of a saṁskāra's momentum (and in the brain et al.'s strong propensity to repeat a familiar action), we insert into an ordinary flow of thought and emotion a relatively peaceful and pure thought and emotion in the form of a mantra, we may be more likely to take a more compassionate action. The resulting saṁskāra will then leave its own mark on the mind/body and create a purer potential momentum the next time around; it will be easier for us to make a new and better choice. In this way, mantra assists in restructuring the mindfield, brain, and body, action by action.

Mantra and Sphoṭa

Another way to think of the impact of mantra on the mind/body is to consider how we understand language. The process is not an analytical one. We don't analyze letters and individual sounds to understand the meaning of what someone has said. When we hear someone call our name, we don't deduce who is being addressed by linguistic analysis; we hear a holistic, gestalt meaning and know in a flash (*sphoṭa*) what or who is meant. We don't even have to know the same language. If I walk up to a stranger in a foreign country and say, "Thud!" or "lull," he or she will have an experience of the intended meaning even without speaking the language I used (Bharati, 2002, pp. 34–35). Mantra works in the same way. Its meaning is a gestalt flash of subtle energy.

Mantra and Energy

A mantra embodies specific spiritual energies. These energies may strengthen constructive aspects of someone's personality or might provide a certain energy that is insufficiently present. For example, individuals who are depressed might receive the seed (*bīja*) mantra *hrīṁ*, which embodies the *rājasik*, fiery cosmic energy of the Divine Mother. Gradually this will help them to energize their personalities to counter the lethargy and inertia of their depression. As we often see in psychotherapy, as people begin to recover from their depression, they may initially feel more anger and irritability, which is actually a good sign that their energy is returning. Someone who is very physically and emotionally unstable might receive the seed (bīja) mantra *klīṁ*, which embodies the energy of cosmic tamas, stability. Over time that person would gradually cultivate a greater stillness of body and steadiness of heart.

In the Hindu tradition, these energies carry the faces and forms of deities, devas, "the shining ones." (Mantra energy is also sometimes experienced primarily as light rather than sound.) These "deities" are not the same as God is understood in an Abrahamic, Western sense; they are all rays from the same sun, aspects of the same singular Being and Reality. In other traditions, the forms may vary somewhat, but these energies appear to be archetypal in the sense that they are shared widely across cultures. For example, *aiṁ* is the seed (bīja) mantra of the energy of wisdom, inspiration, creativity, and spiritual awakening and is the seed (bīja) mantra for the deity Sarasvatī in the Hindu tradition. *Aiṁ* also embodies Mañjuśri Buddha, the Wisdom Buddha in Mahāyāna Buddhism; Dolma in Tibetan Buddhism; Kwan Yin in East Asian Buddhism; Athena in the ancient Greek tradition; and Sophia, the wisdom principle in the Judeo–Christian tradition. The same kind of mantra science that we find in the texts of Kashmir Śaivism can also be found in Kabbalah, the texts of mystic Judaism. And many of the energies of the Hebrew alphabet's phonemes are described in ways that resemble the explanations of basic sounds in the Yoga tradition. This is one of the ways that Yoga can function across many different religious traditions as a science of spiritual practice.

How to Practice Mantra

As we noted at the beginning of this chapter, there is a difference between simply using a mantra you have found in a book and using a mantra in the traditional Yogic manner. The difference is in receiving a mantra whose energies have been fully awakened by the meditation of a master of mantra meditation, in an authentic lineage (*paramparā*) through the process of initiation (*dīkṣā*). A lineage is said to be authentic if the transmission of the experience of a mantra's energy has been passed down from teacher-initiators to disciples in an unbroken succession. The term *paramparā,* literally "one after another," refers to the person-to-person transmission of meditative experience through the ages.

When you take initiation, you receive a personal mantra that is uniquely suited to you. A drop of the energy of the Guru force enters your mind/body as the teacher chants a mantra into your right ear. This quantum of energy gives the mantra power of its own within your mindfield as the presence of the Guru there. It will do its work in the depths of your mind/body whether you attend to it or not.

Of course, the more effort you contribute, the stronger the result. I have met people who received a mantra in the 1970s when it was a trendy thing to do and did nothing with it until several decades later. They returned to our meditation center saying, “I paid no attention to this mantra all these years, and now I can’t get it out of my mind!” Sooner or later the initiated mantra will bring you back to some kind of practice.

Swāmī Rāma would often describe mantra as the greatest friend of your mind, one that comes forward in moments of disturbance or danger to lead your mind in a clear and balanced way. When one is preparing to leave one’s current body, the mantra emerges to guide the transition from one body to the next. So this is one thing you *can* take with you when you die! (See, for example, Rama, 1996, p. 113, or Bharati, 2002, p. 43.)

For those who lack access to initiation or who have decided to forego being initiated, there is a natural mantra in the daily rhythm of your breath that works in much the same way. In Yoga the sound of the breath is described as *so 'ham* (*so aham* = “I am that”), *'ham* accompanying the exhalation and *so* accompanying the inhalation. (There are some traditions of mantra that reverse this order.) This mantra repeats in our minds with each breath, on average 21,600 times per day. That is why it is often referred to as “unrecited recitation,” *ajapājapa*. This mantra has many subtleties to it, and a number of *Upaniṣad* texts describe these subtleties (e.g., *Yoga-cuḍāmaṇi-upaniṣad, Yoga-śikha-upaniṣad*, and *Haṁsa-upaniṣad*, ca. 100 BCE–300 CE).

The simplest practice for infusing your mind with the energy of a mantra, whether *so 'ham* or a personal mantra received through initiation, is simply to repeat it (or, more properly, to listen to it repeating itself) as you pay attention to your breath. Do this as much as you can during the day. Inevitably your attention will move to other things, but whenever it does so and you become aware of it, simply bring your attention back to the breath and to the mantra.

With initiation, the mantra has its own energy to bring itself to your mind over and over. With *so 'ham* and without initiation, this depends more on your own efforts. Using mantra in your meditation is a similar process, in which you listen within for *so 'ham* or your personal mantra. You allow the mantra to flow with your breath and your mind, leading your mind inward towards an experience of the silent presence of the mantra. (For more detailed practice instructions, see Appendix A, Exercise 2.4.) This is the same method used by Orthodox Christian practitioners of *hesychasm* with the prayer, "Lord Jesus Christ have mercy upon me a sinner." It is described in the nineteenth-century Russian spiritual classic *Way of a Pilgrim* (Harvey, 2001), which documents the spiritual education of an unknown pilgrim in his search for an ever deeper experience of God.

Receiving a Personal Mantra Through Initiation

Mantra initiation is a simple, intuitive, and meditative process in which one receives a personal mantra from a qualified preceptor, or initiator. The request for this gift should come from your heart, your sense that this is a right step for you. It is a step that links your mind to the Guru mind in a way that goes beyond the life of the body, so there is some measure of spiritual commitment to it. It is not necessary to renounce your religious path to take this step. It should be an addition and assistance to deepening whatever religious commitment you may have. You also needn't think of yourself as Hindu to receive a mantra. In the Himalayan tradition, we strive to guide people from within their own religious traditions, and mantras are given from within those same traditions.

Once you have decided to receive a mantra, you are usually asked to arrive for your initiation at a specific time and place, having kept your mind quiet and energetic for the preceding day or two. For that purpose, it is a good idea to maintain a formal practice of silence or at least refrain from much of your usual thought and communication, keep a light stomach, and abstain from sexual release in order for the subtle energies to build in your mind/body. You usually bring some fruits or flowers or both as symbols of the fruits of your actions that are surrendered to the Guru lineage. You may also be asked to make some financial commitment within your means, which is then dedicated to the work of the Guru's spirit in the world. (For Christians, read "the work of the Holy Spirit." Our lineage, for example, uses these funds to provide medical care for swāmīs and for sādhus, mendicant spiritual seekers.)

When you enter the room, you sit with the preceptor, usually at a right angle to him or her, so that your right ear faces the initiator. The initiator then performs a meditation that creates a common mindfield for the two of you, and he or she enters an inner mental space of intuition in the presence of the Guru force. The initiator mentally makes a gentle request for a mantra, and then you both wait in silence. When the mantra given by Guru is clear in the mind of the initiator, he or she chants the mantra in your ear a number of times. You then sit together in meditation, and any special instructions can be given for the use of the mantra in your meditation. This first mantra is called your *root mantra (mūla-mantra),* or *guru-mantra,* and is usually kept for life. Sometimes a preceptor may be moved to change your guru-mantra, but this is not a common occurrence. Your guru-mantra can be used at any time with any activity along with the awareness of your breath. Since it is the presence of the Guru force in your mindfield, allow the mantra to lead your meditation where it will.

Additional Initiations

As a disciple's meditation deepens and progresses over the years, there are successively higher levels of initiation as well. Once the ground is prepared by the process of purification, the Guru raises the disciple's mind to a higher level through the power of the Guru's own mind. (This is called *śakti-pāta*, the descent of energy.) This necessarily entails increasing the flow of energy through the mind/body, so eliminating the resistance posed by emotional conflicts is essential in avoiding injury. These higher initiations may range from a gentle and gradual increase in the depth of meditative experience to a sudden experience of light as described in Chapter 11 of the *Bhagavad-gītā* or the Biblical stories of the transfiguration of Jesus (Matthew 17:1–9, Mark 9:2–8, Luke 9:28–36) or the conversion of Saul of Damascus (Acts 9:3–9, Acts 9:13–19, Acts 22:6–21). Such forceful initiations bring the aspirant very close to a full spiritual realization. These may be given with or without a mantra and can be conveyed in many different ways. For those who are interested in this topic, it is described in the *Kulārṇava-tantra*, translated by Arthur Avalon (2007, i.e., Sir John Woodroffe), and in *Mantra and Meditation* by Swāmī Veda (Arya, 1981, pp. 147–159, 161–176).

Japa and the Evolution of Your Mantra Practice

Your experience of mantra will change over time as it becomes woven into the fabric of your mind. It will likely become subtler, the mantra gradually losing its gross body of syllables and becoming just a feeling, a pulsation, a vibration, and eventually a sort of hum at the background of all your thought processes. Mantra repetition is called *japa* and exists at many levels (Arya, 1981, pp. 202–204). Because japa is one of the ways the inner Guru guides your deepening knowledge of your Self, it is one of the traditional definitions of *svādhyāya* (one of the niyamas, YS II.32) and one of the constituents of Kriyā-yoga (YS II.1).

The most superficial level of japa is written japa, or *likhita-japa*. Here the mantra is written out over and over, often with specific colors of ink on particular paper. The great master Neem Karoli Baba would sit every day and write the mantra *Rāma* in a notebook. (*Rāma* is the name of the incarnation of the concept of dharma. His story is recounted in the epic *Rāmāyana*.) One day towards the end of his life, Mahārājjī, at work doing his likhita-japa, stopped writing, turned the notebook around, and pushed it across the table to his disciple Siddhi Mā, saying, "Now you write!" In this way, he passed along his *śakti*, his power as a teacher, to his successor. A short time later he left his body.

Slightly more subtle than written japa is spoken, or *vācika*, japa (as well as the sung form, kīrtana), using the vocal organs. The next subtler is *upāṁśu* (whispered) japa, where the lips are sealed, though the tongue moves as the mind observes the mantra's process of arising as a thought and entering the vocal organs. In *mānasa* (mental) japa, the vocal organs are completely relaxed, and one repeats the mantra only mentally. Here a process begins in which the mantra moves back through the stages of its manifestation to subtler and subtler layers. From gross speech (*vaikhari*, "the braying of an ass"), we move to mental japa in the *madhyama*, or middle levels of the mind up to buddhi. Here the feeling of the mantra continues, and the syllables that are its gross body drop away. This is often an anxious moment for an inexperienced meditator who begins to feel he or she is cheating on his or her commitment to perform the japa. (When this happens in my meditation, I simply ask my mind, "Is it all there?" and I generally get a straightforward answer.) Gradually the concentration gathers the mantra vibration into a singularity, or point-limit (bindu). Bursting through this point, a process that takes most people a very long time to manage, the mind enters the first stages of samādhi (saṁprajñāta-samādhi), sending the meditator into the *paśyanti* level. This is the level of revelation at which the spiritual texts of the world are given to the one-pointed mind of a seer-sage. The final level, *parā*, an experience of pure silent presence, carries one into the highest, a-saṁprajñāta-samādhi.

We might say that a mantra functions like a ball of string that the original seer of the mantra unraveled for us. He or she left the depths of the cave of meditative silence and moved towards the experience of the external world so that we might retrace the process of the mantra's manifestation back to the original meditative state. Once we have done so, we have attained siddhi (accomplishment) of the mantra.

Special Mantras for Healing and Cultivating the Mindfield

Just as personal mantras are tailored to individuals, often to balance the personality and to assist progress on the path, special mantras establish particular qualities in the mindfield. They also deal with specific difficulties. Whereas a personal mantra remains part of an individual's core practice, often over many years, a special mantra is a shorter term intervention, practiced in addition to one's personal mantra or, in rare cases, temporarily in place of it. Thousands of mantras can be used for this purpose. They range from a single syllable to hundreds of verses. The entire text of the *Devī-mahātmyam*, for example, is a special mantra in the Himalayan tradition. It is roughly the same length as the *Bhagavad-gītā*, 700 verses. The Vedic *Gāyatrī* mantra, on the other hand, is said to embody the entire Veda in a single verse. It is often used to catalyze the process of emotional purification, among other objectives. There are twenty-four different Gāyatrī mantras that call forth the energy of specific devas. Another common special mantra practice is to use the *Mahāmṛtyuñjaya* mantra for healing or to cope with the fear of death.

Mantras like these can be used in a gentle and general manner, for example doing one *mālā* (108 repetitions) per day, or in a more intensive practice called *puraścaraṇa* (literally, "moving forward"), where a certain large number of repetitions is performed in a specific time frame. (A mālā, or *japa-mālā*, is a set of 108 beads used to count repetitions of mantras for such special practices.) Undertaking a special mantra practice or a puraścaraṇa of any mantra should be done carefully under the guidance of a preceptor and may be done with or without initiation. Specifically, it is not recommended to begin these practices on your own. Individuals who undertake practices that are too intense risk precipitating mental or physical illnesses if the mantra is inappropriate or if the pace of practice is too intense. (For more information, see the chapter on special mantras in Bharati, 2002, pp. 85–101.)

Final Thoughts

A comprehensive explanation of the use of mantra in meditation and spiritual practice is a very large subject, well beyond the scope of this book. Especially if you are interested in considering an initiation into a personal mantra practice, this material is worthy of further study. *Mantra and Meditation* by Swāmī Veda (Arya, 1981) mentioned above is an extraordinarily comprehensive treatment of both the theory and the practice of mantra. He draws from his own deep experience and from Sanskrit sources unavailable to those who are not Sanskrit scholars. David Frawley's (2010) book *Mantra Yoga and Primal Sound: Secrets of Seed (Bija) Mantras* is a wonderful complement to this volume, as are Swāmī Veda's booklets *Mantra What and Why, Mantra After Initiation,* and *Special Mantras*, each a chapter in *Night Birds* (Bharati, 2002).

In mantra practice one begins with a word repeated verbally or mentally in the process of meditation or moment-to-moment mindfulness. Gradually the experience of that sound is refined, made subtle and deep in the practices of meditation, taking us beyond where our rational mind can go in understanding the world. We journey to the end of language, then to the end of thought itself, and into the depth of silent contemplation. In the open-hearted gaze of beholding, we are drawn into a point-singularity (bindu) and through that point into superconsciousness, where our words cannot follow.

Chapter Eleven

Behold the Silence

The practice of silence is a cornerstone in nearly all spiritual traditions. Among Yoga's five pillars of sādhanā (silence, stillness, fasting, celibacy, and conquest of sleep), silence is the one practice that contains all the others because it deals with the entire mindfield. Silence of the body is stillness. Silence of the primary fountain of food is fasting. Silence of the outward expression of sexuality is celibacy. Yoga-nidrā is the silence of sleep. Replacing our fears through tapas is the silence of self-preservation. Silence is tapas, par excellence.

Silence does not imply a simple absence of speech, but an ultimate completeness, a paradoxical fullness/absence, Brahman/Śūnya, at the core of the mindfield. It is accompanied by an exquisite joy. The mindfield has a multitude of layers, each deeper layer more silent, more joyful, and vibrating at a higher frequency. Practicing silence allows us to still the superficial layers of the mindfield to enter its depths and to eventually allow those depths to surface in our day-to-day practice of mindful awareness, even when not engaged in formal silence practice. The ultimate fullness of the depth of the mindfield makes mucking around in the shallows a relatively restrictive and painful experience by comparison.

When one's inner silence can come forward from within, then we can speak and yet remain in silence, eat while fasting, make love while remaining celibate, sleep while conscious, and move from stillness with the grace, economy, beauty, and presence of a dancer. Our entire life can be transformed in place. We may speak the same words, but they have a different impact on and reception by the hearer. We may do the same tasks, but we do them without attachment to their results, and we cease to be bound by the inevitability of karma. As the Zen saying goes, "Before enlightenment, chop wood; carry water. After enlightenment, chop wood; carry water."

Silence Speaks in All Spiritual Traditions

Since the practice of silence involves the entire mindfield, it touches every genuine spiritual path. One of the ancient Vedic words for a Yogi is *muni,* "a silent one." This is also the meaning of the English word, *monk*. In the Psalms of David, divinity whispers, "Be still, and know that I am God" (46:10). Jesus spent forty silent days of ascetic practice (tapas) in the desert as he began his public ministry. There are many Christian orders that center their practice on silence, among them the Carthusians, the Trappist Cistercians, and the Camaldolese Benedictines. The Sufi practitioners of Islam undergo a forty day *chilla*, a period of tapas performed in silence. The Buddhist traditions practice many different kinds of silent retreats, from the Vipassanā retreats of the Theravāda tradition to the exacting meditation retreats of the Tibetan tradition, where one spends, at a minimum, three months in a space of one cubic meter, where one can neither lie down nor stand. The only choice is to sit and meditate in silence.

There is a similar variety of practices among indigenous traditions. When Swāmī Veda went to visit the lineage holders of Voodoo in Benin in French West Africa, they asked him to wait for ten days since they felt they needed to fast in silence to be sufficiently pure to properly receive such a guest (S. V. Bhāratī, personal communication, September 2012). In her fictional book *The Mutant Message Down Under*, author and nurse-practitioner Marlo Morgan (1994) relates what she has learned of Aboriginal practice; she is told by her guide that "civilized" people cannot communicate telepathically like the Aborigines because we have private thoughts. In other words, though fictional, Morgan's book makes a very real point: Our involvement with a separate sense of selfhood, and the mental noise this generates in the superficial layers of the mind, blocks our access to the deeper, more silent layers of the mindfield, which all the universe shares.

These deeper layers of the mind point to the one reality. The practice of silence extends the "practice of one reality" (*eka-tattva-abhyāsa*, YS I.32), cultivating our ability to deepen our awareness into every activity of life. This contemplative effort is called by many names in different traditions: by dhyāna-yogis, *īśvara-praṇidhāna* (placing one's mind close to divinity at every moment); by Vedāntins, *ātma-tattva-avalokanam* (looking around for the essence of Self everywhere); by karma-yogis, *karma-yoga* (action without attachment to results); by Buddhists, saṭṭi-patthāṇa (mindfulness); and by Christians, *practice of the presence of God* (Lawrence, 1982). Silence creates a frame of experience within which we become ever more deeply aware. Once we are aware of what we do and how we do it, as we have said throughout this book, we have a choice to feel and act differently.

Silence Communicates Practical Benefits

In practical terms within the Yoga tradition, we tend to look at silent practice as a matter of conserving the energy of the mindfield. Try a simple experiment, and remain silent for half a day or even a full day, if you can manage. This will make you aware of how much energy you spend just in talking! You may notice at the end of the period that you feel a little less tired, are a little more focused, and have more energy. It may be easier for you to maintain mindful awareness of your breath, your thoughts, and your feelings. If you practice meditation with a mantra, you may notice that the repetitions become faster and subtler.

As the superficial layers of the mind quiet down, emotions and issues that you have banished to the periphery of your awareness or even into your unconscious have an opportunity to arise. This is why during silent retreats people will sometimes say after a few days, "I have to get out of here! I'm having all these thoughts and feelings I don't like." Contrary to being an indication that the practice isn't working, it is a clear sign that the cleansing process is proceeding nicely. I usually encourage people at this point to persist, to allow issues to arise while maintaining a sense of awareness, wonder, and curious interest, and to inquire into their sources and their operation. In this way, practitioners can gradually understand and transform their troubling thoughts and emotions.

Immerse Yourself in Silence:
Take a Silent Retreat (or Create Your Own)

Often people think of a silent retreat as a big commitment. It needn't be. Like most things in Yoga, it's important to start simply, well within your capacity. So consider perhaps taking a couple of hours or a half-day to begin. Take this retreat on a day when you can remain in solitude. In addition to silencing your speech, practice *indriya-gupti*, "protection of the senses," by being a bit mentally withdrawn and more physically still, freeing your mind from distracting noise: computer screens, mobile phones, radio, television. When you walk, rather than looking around, keep your attention focused about a meter ahead of your feet. When you move, move with awareness, feeling your whole body from inside, head to toe. Practice āsana the whole time; perform all your movements as if you were doing formal āsana practice. When you eat, really taste your food with concentration. This is the time to chew your food purposefully and with attention—30, 50, 100 times—whatever the folk wisdom says. You will probably eat a little less. On retreat you can also practice the things that you never seem to have time for, like relaxations and other subtle body practices. Most of all, focus on doing sitting meditation and on repeating your mantra. Consider keeping a diary of your experience to help you assess your progress over time.

If you absolutely need to communicate with someone, you can always write a note. Mahatma Gandhi used to keep silence one day a week, and he would continue his work, communicating with notes as necessary. (One must be careful, however, of the temptation to chatter away in notes!) During silent retreat, we realize how much is communicated with a subtle gesture. Over time, you will learn to communicate in silence with or without external signs. While his master, Bengali Baba, was still in the body, Swāmī Rāma used to return to India during part of the year to spend time with him. They would usually spend several months together communicating without a word being spoken.

As you develop a sense of comfort and positive anticipation for these shorter periods of silence, feel free to lengthen them. In our Himalayan system of practice, we usually suggest that people advance their practice according to their capacity from half-days to a full day, then to three days, five days, ten days, and beyond these to 40 and 90 days, one year, five years, and so forth. There is a monk named Candraswāmī in Uttarākhand, India, who once decided to do a 10-day silent retreat. During this time, he fell so in love with the practice that he decided to keep going a day at a time. That was more than 27 years ago. His āśram today is a wonderful place to experience the beauty of silent practice.

Practices for Silent Retreat

There are several other practices that one might consider during these periods of silent retreat. The three below are easily carried into day-to-day life. As you grow in the practice of silence, there are many techniques that you can add to these, but these are a good beginning. (For more about the practice of silence, see Bharati, 2002; Ross, 2013, 2014b.)

Relax your forehead. Simply keep your forehead constantly relaxed. It is very difficult to behave badly or even to feel angry when you do this. Relaxing your forehead can also serve as an anchor to remind you to relax the rest of your mind/body. It doesn't take long for many people to maintain this relaxation in their normal day-to-day activities, where this is a surprisingly powerful method of cultivating mindful awareness.

Roll your tongue. Another practice is to keep your tongue rolled up into your palate (*jihva-mudrā*). Just place the tip of your tongue behind your upper teeth, and slide it back along the hard palate. This is practically useful because if you have a desire to speak, you have to unfold your tongue first, which gives you a moment to think about what you want to say and how to say it, or whether to speak at all. Both the Yoga and Qi Gong traditions also recognize that this *mudrā*, or gesture, closes an energy circuit in your subtle body, which helps your attention to follow the spine without pause as you breathe in meditation. In addition, jihva-mudrā makes the sublimation of sexual energy in particular easier to manage.

Practice the root lock. A complementary gesture is the root lock, or *mūla-bandha*, where you gently pull up on the pubococcygeal, or PC muscle, in your perineum. (The PC muscle is located at the base of the abdomen between your anus and genitals. It is the muscle you relax to urinate.) This *bandha* ("lock") seals the lower circuit of the spinal passage, creating effects similar to those above. In the beginning, it requires some conscious effort; eventually the bandha becomes spontaneous.

If She Can Do It, You Can Do It

I had an elder friend at our āśram in India who lived in Singapore. She was a very worldly person with a silent sage hidden inside. The first time she decided to try a longer 40-day period of silence, she invited me to lunch and said, "Oh, Stoma, I'm no swāmī! I'm just doing this because Swāmī Veda told me I should. I don't want to disappoint him!" About a week later, I encountered her out on her afternoon walk. Ordinarily our meetings were jolly occasions. This time she kept her gaze to the ground and simply signaled by a wave of her hand that I should not disturb her. The lower half of her face had already undergone a deep and thorough relaxation that subtly changed her appearance, and it was clear, by the beauty in her face, that she was enjoying the experience deeply already. After that retreat was finished, she returned every year to do another one, always for 40 days. After several years of this, she came to do a 90-day retreat, and about 60 days along, she experienced a stroke and left her body. It was clear to everyone that as much sadness as we felt in losing her company, she had ended her life exactly as she had hoped to, in the joyful embrace of the practice of silence.

The Mental Cleanse Is Worth the Challenge

Of course, the cleansing process of silence can be a challenge, and as we discussed above, we must become aware of the issues that we try to avoid. On retreat, we need to deliberately allow those issues to present themselves so that we can come face to face with ourselves in the mirror of the silent mind. The longer the practice, the deeper this cleansing can go into the mindfield.

In particular, we can encounter interesting differences between practicing in solitude and practicing in a group. In solitude, we experience our difficulties in self-relationship. Often there is a confrontation with the mind and its self-critical chatter. This is a ground for experiments with niyama in our relationship with ourselves. To the extent that we empty our sense of self-identification, we often feel a deep kinship with our surrounding environment. Ross (1990) provides a beautiful literary account of such a silent retreat in *Seasons of Death and Life: A Wilderness Memoir.*

In a group practice, the presence of other people is likely to bring forward issues in our relationships with others. This is a fascinating laboratory because the usual process of talking things through is not available. The presence of others seems to intensify the process of cleansing and forces us to rely on inner guidance. In 2008 several friends and I completed a 90-day retreat together. As the retreat progressed, we could feel the increasing speed and agility of our minds. But as I sat one morning doing japa, which consumed six-and-a-half to eight hours per day, I painfully noticed my mind making critical observations of all my fellow retreatants, my beloved friends. My mind was most unkind in these observations, and I felt at a loss to understand where this was coming from. I struggled and struggled for several days and finally failed in my self-examination. I had to simply give up (surrender my ego's efforts at controlling knowledge), go within, and ask the Guru for help.

Early the next morning, as we sat in the cold doing our practice with fire offerings, I peered up into the dark tent and mentally saw the word *unlovable* in flames. Immediately I understood that my perfectionism towards myself and my friends was a fearful and defensive compensation for having felt unloved early in life. If only I could be right, do it right, do it perfectly, then I would be worthy of the love I felt I lacked. Was this true now? Absolutely not! It was a crazy thought in the context of my current life, but old habits of the mind die hard, sometimes very hard. Hadn't I dealt with this in ten years of therapy? Apparently not completely. Immediately I felt tears of release from that emotional trap and a sense of joy at having understood enough to be freed a bit more. In the next session of sitting meditation, the Guru sent an inner sign that this was a correct understanding, and after that moment, I fell back even further into the joyful presence of Mother Silence.

Silence Teaches Us to Empty Ourselves and Allow Grace to Fill Us

Let's revisit Psalm 46:10 in the English translation of the Bible: "Be still, and know that I am God." The Hebrew translation of "be still" is from the verb *raphah*, meaning to be weak or vulnerable, to let go, to release. It is an injunction not only to be quiet but also to let go of our self-identifications, of the psychological self's fearful and defensive efforts to control and know as an exercise of power. It asks us to release our grasp on being right so that there is space for the grace of the Guru to enter this process and raise us up through love. As it does, we feel a sense of inward opening into divinity, what M. Ross calls the experience of "ever-increasing inviolable vulnerability" (personal communication, 1992). To experience such a state requires the mindfield to be purified of its fearful obsession with preserving our psychological self. Once again, it is in our vulnerability, not in our power, that our spiritual growth is nurtured and realized.

This phrase from the psalm actually makes a lovely contemplative exercise, repeated starting with the injunction "Be still" and adding a word with each iteration: "Be still" / "Be still, and know" / "Be still, and know That" (Brahman, God/God-not) / "Be still, and know that I" (I that is the true Self rather than the psychological self) / "Be still, and know that I am" (Realize the meaning of the haṁsa mantra, *so 'ham*, "I am that I am," Exodus 3:14) / "Be still, and know that I am God."

As you open into the space of what Christian practitioners refer to as *kenosis*, self-emptying, it becomes possible for grace to fill us, to show us a different and more loving way. We enter into a greater fullness and a sense of wonder and joy, usually at the price of some tears, captured in the Biblical word *behold*. Divine, shining beings—angels, when they appear to humans in the Bible—tend to say two things (which are actually synonymous): "Fear not!" and "Behold!" When we are suddenly confronted with a deeper experience of Spirit, we are always afraid. Our limited egos resist the need to relax away a little more (the psychological meaning of death) so that we can move deeper into the unknown. So the angels ask us to move through our fear. How? By beholding, by holding in mindful awareness the fullness of everything before us. Ross (2013) describes this beautifully in a Christian context. The brackets are my own in order to connect her insights to the terms of Yoga:

> This living beneath the level of personality . . . brings us in our entirety, warts and all, to fullness. To behold God in everything [in Yoga, īśvara-praṇidhāna, or in Vedānta, ātma-tattva-avalokanam] is the antidote to frenetic activity, to stress and busyness. It enables us to live from and continually return to and dwell in the depth of silent communion with God. And as this is something that God [or Guru] does in us, we have only to allow it, to cease our striving and behold. . . . "Behold" is the marker word throughout the Bible. It signals shifting perspective, the holding together . . . of radically different points of view. It indicates when the language of belief is silenced by the exaltation of faith as these paradoxical perspectives are brought together and generate, as it were, an explosion of silence and light. This silence holds us in thrall, in complete self-forgetfulness. Our settled accounting of ordinary matters is shattered and falls into nothing as the light breaks upon us. (Ross, 2013, pp. 22–24)

Final Thoughts

As we discussed in Chapter 3, much has been made of Freud's tortured theorizing of a "death instinct," or thanatos, which he set as the countervailing force to eros, the drive for growth and development. In so doing, he missed a vital spiritual point. It is not death or the physical mother's womb that we seek in our struggle with desire. It is the depth of silent (divine) presence and joy that is the ultimate fulfillment of our instinctive urge to grow. We do not hunger for an experience of death, but for an ultimate experience of silence that is the death of death, the dissolution of limited egoity, and the end of small mindedness, called *āṇava*, literally, "atomic-ness," in the Kashmir Śaiva philosophy. Each time we cultivate silence—whether during formal silent retreat or on a retreat of our own making, and whether for a moment, an hour, or many days—we draw closer to the womb of Mother Silence. In awe, we behold Her as the matrix in which all things exist and to which all things return.

Chapter Twelve

Am I Making Progress?
The Nature of a Clear and Pleasant Mind

From time to time, we all wonder whether we are making any progress on the path of spiritual realization. We tend especially to wonder about this when our efforts seem to have reached a plateau, and we question whether we are somehow stuck. When this thought arises, we may also want to ask ourselves where it comes from. Why do we feel it necessary to prove that we are progressing? Do we need to bolster our self-esteem at a moment when we are demoralized, despairing, or feeling worthless? That may call for some adjustment in how we are treating ourselves within our own mind/body. Or are we trying to reassure ourselves that we are better off in our spiritual life than others? Why?

We often attempt to evaluate our progress through measurements: "I can sit in meditation for an hour!" "I can do a handstand!" "I can retain my breath for four minutes!" "I only sleep three hours a night!" "I can do a mālā of the Gāyatrī mantra in five minutes!" As you read these statements, I suspect they may inspire images of a child balancing on a bike for the first time: "Look, Mom!!" It can be a joyful celebration of competence, but it also often conceals a subtle, ego-driven interest in power. This is one of the greatest and most subtle seductions for the ego on the spiritual path. We often imagine ourselves at our spiritual best with great powers of one kind or another. *Power has no place whatsoever in the assessment of spiritual progress.* When the masters use power, they are quite clear that it is not theirs and does not come from them even though it may come through them.

In *Autobiography of a Yogi*, Yogananda (1971) tells such a story about his master, Śrī Yukteśvara (pp. 296–299). While still a boy, Yukteśvara's best friend, Rāma, fell ill with Asiatic cholera, which often kills within hours. When Yukteśvara expressed his alarm to his guru, Lahiri Mahāśaya (also known as Śhyāma Caran Lahiri), Mahāśaya stated confidently that doctors were with Rāma, and the boy would be fine. During Yukteśvara's vigil at his friend's bedside, Rāma died. After weeping for some hours, Yukteśvara went to his guru full of rage and reproach. The master urged him to calm down and sit in meditation, but Yukteśvara remained disturbed. The next morning, Mahāśaya told Yukteśvara to pour some castor oil into a container, go to Rāma's house, and drip seven drops into Rāma's mouth. Yukteśvara remarked that he didn't think it would do much good since his friend had been dead almost a day, but he had also learned to take his guru at his word. When the seventh drop of oil passed his friend's lips, the body gasped a breath in, and his friend suddenly awoke and excitedly related the story of seeing the master in a blaze of light. This made it clear that the healing came through the power of the Guru lineage, not through Mahāśaya's mindfield or personality.

Swāmī Rāma told a story from his youth when he discovered a sādhu who could make fire appear from his mouth. He was very impressed by this. He returned to his master and told him that he didn't think his master was much of a Yogi because he had found someone who could breathe fire. The master quietly asked the sādhu's name. When Swāmījī said the name and took his master to the sādhu, the master said, "A match will produce fire in a second; if you wish to spend twenty years to produce fire from your mouth, you are a fool. My child, that is not wisdom" (Rama, 1978, pp. 105–106).

Love: Our Greatest Measure of Spiritual Growth

The quality that matters most in terms of assessing spiritual progress is selfless love. Have you become a more loving person towards yourself as well as others? People often asked Swāmī Veda whether they were making progress. His answer was usually, "Are your relationships better?" Sometimes, because we are not always the best judge of our loving qualities, he would say, "Ask your mother-in-law!" In other words, ask someone with whom you are not always in agreement. The real test is when your adversary experiences you as more loving.

This does not mean merely being nice. There are times when the loving thing in a relationship is to share your angry feelings or to confront someone who is misbehaving. Even your vehemence can be a form of love in the right circumstances. Swāmī Rāma's love could be very intense in this way, but he would never waste his energy if a person was not ready to benefit from his angry discipline. And he would let go of his anger once it had served its purpose. He had a certain disciple whom he loved deeply and whom he treated as a daughter. Sometimes he would try to be angry with her, and she would just give him a look that said, "I know what you are doing!" and they would just burst out in laughter. She had gotten the point.

A Clear and Pleasant Mind: Steady Wisdom in the *Bhagavad-Gītā*

Our relationships are our litmus test for the quality of our mind. And as the title of this book suggests, we can measure our spiritual progress in terms of our mind's qualities. To what degree has it become clear, pleasant, and stable? A clear and pleasant mind, with many paradoxical qualities, exhibits strength that is both gentle and flexible. It is like water that yields to everything and yet wears away everything.

A portion of the second chapter of the *Bhagavad-gītā* (II.54–72) describes the person of steady wisdom (*sthita-prajñā*). Arjuna first asks Kṛṣṇa what such a person is like: "How does a person of stable wisdom speak forth? How does he sit? How does he walk?" (Rama, 1984b, p. 100, BhG II.54). Kṛṣṇa answers that such a person, having abandoned the desires of the mind/body (through the process of tapas described previously), is "satisfied within the Self by the Self" (Rama, 1984b, p. 104, BhG II.55). He or she is established in a state of ultimate joy. This person has no pain and no attraction to pleasure, and fear and anger have disappeared from his or her mindfield (BhG II.56). "Like a tortoise withdrawing his limbs" (Rama, 1984b, p. 106, BhG II.58), a person of steady wisdom has removed his or her senses from their objects—pratyāhāra. The *Bhagavad-gītā* describes how the four primary fountains drive ordinary people to pursue the objects of the senses, generating all emotional disturbances to the detriment of mindful awareness and buddhi's discriminating faculty (II.62–63). By working through the process of tapas, however, the person of steady wisdom obtains a clear and pleasant mindfield in which suffering ceases (BhG II.64–65).

It is said, "That which is night to the ordinary human being is day to the wise, and that in which the ordinary human being remains awake is night to the wise one who sees" (Rama, 1984b, p. 115, BhG II.69). In other words, the clarified mindfield maintains its mindful awareness even in the midst of deep sleep. In the light of such awareness, the ordinary waking state is so peaceful that it seems like sleep.

Put another way, "As water enters the ocean, which is totally full yet whose basin and boundaries remain stable, he whom all the desires enter similarly attains peace, and not one who desires the desires" (Rama, 1984b, p. 117, BhG II.70). To desire a desire is to be subject to the motivations of the four primary fountains. A mind attached to the primary fountains (and therefore unfulfilled) will lose its peace in the presence of these objects because it cannot yet observe them without feeling desire. A stable mindfield, however, is like the ocean, full and fulfilled with desireless joy. When objects of desire enter this mind, it remains undisturbed because people with this mind can enjoy and maintain their peace, regardless of the objects that come and go. The mindfield that is full of greater joy (ānanda) remains undistracted by smaller desires. Undisturbed, clear, pleasant, and stable, it naturally and spontaneously moves between all the layers of the mindfield, easily turning inward through pratyāhāra to the process of saṁyama (the continuous progression through dhāraṇā, dhyāna, and samādhi) towards superconscious meditation. Such a mind, tuned to the superconscious, perfects its capacity for compassion and becomes suffused with loving kindness.

The Weaker (*Vyutthāna*) and Stronger (*Samādhāna*) Mindfield

Another way to describe a clear and pleasant mindfield is in terms of the characteristics of a weaker versus a stronger mindfield. Patañjali describes two trends in a person's mindfield in the *Yoga-sūtra*. The weaker mindfield of an ordinary person is vyutthāna: restless, disturbed, and inclined to leave the meditation seat. The stronger meditative mindfield is samādhāna, inclined towards samādhi. It is still, clear, and able to harmonize all dichotomies and paradoxes. When you ask someone with a samādhāna mindfield whether something is one way or another, the likely answer is, "Yes!" And the explanation that follows will show how the two opposite qualities are complementary to each other.

This is why the masters of so many spiritual traditions use riddles of various kinds, for example the *koans* of the Japanese, Chinese, and Korean Zen traditions. Specifically, riddles are applied

1.) To find the positive concealed in the negative.
2.) To free the mind of the habit of being in conflict, by learning to resolve the conflict.
3.) To de-condition the mind of its conditionings, to lift it from habit patterns, to free it from running in set grooves, and thereby
4.) To develop fresh insights of [a] positive nature into

relationships, communication and events, as well as philosophical realities and truths, and

5.) To liberate the mind and consciousness from what *Vedānta* calls *upādhi*s, conditioning produced by our involvement in *māyā*. (Bharati, 2013c, p. 77)

By design, such riddles jolt us out of the conditionings of the mindfield in terms of the ideas, concepts, and categories through which our mindfield filters all our knowledge in the process of perceiving. Until we reach the state of superconscious meditation, we never see things as they are, in their Being. We only see an aggregate of categorical concepts. I look at my best friend and see that he is human; I notice his gender, ethnicity, appearance, name, physical characteristics, vocation, and so forth—but I do not see his Being (because I do not see my own Being!). So the samādhāna mindfield is one that gradually becomes concentrated enough to punch through all these conditionings to the Being at the core of everything.

The chart below characterizes the contrast between the qualities of the weaker (vyutthāna) and the stronger (samādhāna) mindfield. I compiled it, with some additions, from a series of talks by Swāmī Veda (Bharati, 2013d).These qualities provide a sketch of a stronger mindfield and can be the start of a checklist, one that you might keep in a journal to assess the stronger and weaker parts of your own mindfield. You can use this list to appreciate your stronger areas and to think about how you might address the weaker ones (see Appendix A, Exercise 3.8).

The Brahma-Vihāras: Natural Developments of a Samādhāna Mindfield

As you work out the emotional knots and warps in your mind/body and prāṇa system—as the mindfield becomes purified, clarified, and steady—certain qualities of personality gradually begin to manifest. These are the brahma-vihāras, referred to as such in the literature of both Yoga and Buddhism. Sometimes in Buddhist literature, they are also called the *four great treasures* or the *four indispensables*. Both traditions consider them vibhūtis, natural developments of human potential that appear when the emotional disturbances that block their emergence are cleared. (In fact, Patañjali refers to the brahma-vihāras directly as vibhūtis in sūtra III.24.) The process is very similar to that discussed in Chapter 5, when vibhūtis develop as the attitudes of yama and niyama become established in one's personality.

Patañjali discusses the brahma-vihāras in another light, as practices, in Yoga-sūtra I.33. This, too, parallels the Buddhist tradition. The translation below names each brahma-vihāra. I have inserted the Sanskrit:

> By cultivating and impressing into oneself the sentiments of amity and love [maitri], compassion [karuṇā], gladness [muditā] and indifference [upekṣā] with regard to those comfortable, those suffering, the virtuous, and the non-virtuous (respectively), the mind is purified and made pleasant. (Arya, 1986, p. 340, YS I.33)

Vyāsa, in his commentary on this sūtra, says,

> One should cultivate amity towards all living beings who are endowed with comforts and pleasures, compassion towards those who are suffering, gladness towards those of a virtuous nature, and indifference towards (those of) non-virtuous disposition. As one cultivates himself thus, his white [*sāttvik*] nature increases, grows. Then the mind is purified and becomes pleasant. Purified and pleasant, it attains the state of one-pointed stability. (Arya, 1986, p. 341)[20]

The brahma-vihāras, as the four indispensables, are also discussed as practices in considerable detail in Chapter 9 of the great Buddhist

[20] The parenthetical and bracketed insertions are Ārya's (Swāmī Veda's).

Table 11.1
Characteristics of a Weaker Versus a Stronger Mindfield

Weaker (Vyutthāna) Mindfield	**Stronger (Samādhāna) Mindfield**
Interested in difference and distinction	Interested in commonality and complementarity
Sees parts	Sees the whole as interconnected
Jokes about others and their faults	Jokes about him- or herself and his or her own struggles
Tends to be rigid in belief and behavior, lacks resilience	Has flexibility of thoughts and emotions, is resilient and compassionate
Remembers injuries from others, forgets injuring others	Remembers injuring others, forgets injuries from others
Forgets good and kind acts received from others, remembers kindnesses done for others	Forgets kindnesses done for others, remembers kindnesses received from others
Uses the first-person pronoun constantly	Avoids the first-person pronoun
Justifies his or her actions	Apologizes for his or her actions
Is feared by others: People do not say no to this person because they fear him or her.	Is loved by others: People do not say no to this person because they love him or her.
Holds a grudge	Forgives and moves on
Seeks to criticize weakness in others	Seeks to understand weakness in others
Sees others' faults	Sees his or her own faults
Blames self and others	Takes responsibility, is accountable
Hurt by others' anger	Seeks to understand the pain behind others' anger and to do something to alleviate it
Easily fatigued	Regenerates quickly
Makes the body's illnesses into a mind condition	Uses the mind to heal the body
Suspicious	Trusting
Complacent	Contented (saṁtoṣa)
Lives and acts from fear	Reassures others by his or her presence

Table 11.1

Characteristics of a Weaker Versus a Stronger Mindfield (cont.)

Weaker (Vyutthāna) Mindfield	**Stronger (Samādhāna) Mindfield**
Demands	Gives
Judges	Accepts
Seeks his or her own pleasure	Takes joy in the pleasure of others
Feels continually empty and unsatisfied and therefore overindulges	Feels a sense of inner fullness and contentment and enjoys more with less
Chatters, speaks loudly to be heard	Speaks softly, from inner silence, and is understood through presence
Moves randomly	Moves with grace and economy, as in a dance
Gobbles his or her food mindlessly out of a sense of emptiness	Tastes the beauty in food and the love with which it was made and so eats less
Easily distracted	Focused and concentrated
When alone, feels lonely. (If there is nobody else present, nobody is home.)	When alone, feels solitary—by oneself with oneself
Seeks others' criticism as self-punishment	Seeks others' criticism for self-improvement and to know aspects of him- or herself that are hard to look at

Note. This table, with some additions, is based on a series of talks by Swāmī Veda. (See Bharati, 2013d, *The Signs of Spiritual Progress in Meditation*, Swāmījī's last recorded lecture before he entered silence, which he held until his passing in July 2015.)

meditation manual *Visuddimagga* (Sanskrit, *Viśuddhi-marga), Path of Purification* (Buddhaghosa, trans. 2011).

It is interesting that the qualities of the brahma-vihāras and of the weaker and the stronger mindfields described above are consistent with findings of the emotional development research conducted over the last 35 years by Richard Davidson, PhD, and his team at the University of Wisconsin–Madison. In their work, Davidson (2012) and his colleagues identify and name the brain pathways that underlie six dimensions of emotional style, each of which can be increased or decreased through mental training:

1. *Resilience*, one's ability to adapt to and recover from emotional challenges;
2. *Social Intuition*, one's ability to read others' emotions;
3. *Outlook*, one's tendency towards a positive or negative attitude or somewhere in between;
4. *Sensitivity to Context*, one's ability to understand cues in his or her social environment and to act accordingly;
5. *Self-Awareness*, one's ability to recognize his or her own thoughts, feelings, and body sensations; and
6. *Attention*, one's ability to concentrate, ranging from being focused to unfocused.

Davidson (2012) places each element on a spectrum and observes that individuals demonstrate each capacity in varying degrees. In a similar way, we might experience each of the brahma-vihāras as more or less evident within us. If we compare Davidson's (2012) emotional style elements to the brahma-vihāras, it is not hard to see the parallels:

- Maitri (friendliness, amity): high social intuition with a positive outlook;
- Karuṇā (compassion): high self-awareness, high social

intuition, and high sensitivity to context;
- Muditā (joyful mindedness): positive outlook with considerable resilience;
- Upekṣā ("overlooking," even-mindedness): sensitivity to context with a positive outlook.

Although we may engage the brahma-vihāras or Davidson's elements of emotional style as practices to train the mind and heart, let us stress that these qualities also appear naturally in the personality of someone whose mindfield is becoming purified.

Maitri. One who embodies maitri becomes a friend to all. With this sense of universal friendship, one considers even adversaries to be friends. Ultimately there remain no enemies of any intensity, within or without. One has made peace with oneself and in his or her interactions with other beings. Maitri is very similar to the establishment of nonviolence in one's character, whereupon other people and even animals lose their hostility and enmity in that person's presence. This quality is the basis of the well-known Buddhist practice of metta (maitri) meditation, described briefly in Appendix A, Exercise 2.5.

Karuṇā. Friendship towards all creatures rests on a foundation of compassion (karuṇā), the ability to feel others' suffering as if it were one's own. The more we work through the particulars of our own suffering in life, the more acutely we can sense the suffering of others and the more motivated we become to try to relieve it. We might even begin to feel others' physical injuries as if they were happening in our own mind/body because our awareness is becoming less bound to a limited sense of ourselves.

Muditā. As one realizes the primary fountain of joy through tapas, the mindfield naturally becomes more joyful (muditā) overall. One is less bound by the painful emotions (kleśas, viparyayas) that are the consequence of the limited pleasures of the other four fountains.

Upekṣā. The last of these qualities, upekṣā, is often translated as "indifference." It literally means "overlooking." Another better translation is "nonreactivity." Out of a sense of compassion towards the realization that everyone is struggling with some kind of suffering, you become less likely to get caught up in struggles that only make the painful propensities in other people stronger. Swāmī Rāma used to advise his disciples in conflict with each other to look beyond one another's current behavior to the people they knew they could become. Taking this long view of others' struggles and their growth and development helps one acquire the patience and even-mindedness to find a loving way to help other people and oneself deal with the suffering that is at the root of troublesome behavior.

As these qualities—the pure, ripe fruits of lifetimes of endeavor—develop in one's personality, the mindfield becomes stable and inclines towards deeper and deeper meditation. The disturbances of the mindfield quieted, the mind/body settles into an ultimate stillness that gradually becomes imperturbable. The breath, no longer buffeted by the twin emotional currents of pain and pleasure, can become long and subtle and gradually cease in the ultimate peace of kevala-kumbhaka, where prāṇa alone sustains the life of the body. The mindfield in this silent state is then free to turn entirely away from external objects and find an intensifying focus in the process of saṁyama, deepening towards superconscious meditation in samādhi.

Final Thoughts

From the perspective of neurobiology, we might consider samādhi to be not only the ultimate integration of the brain and central nervous system, but also the ultimate integration of the mindfield, which organizes all our neurological systems (and more). Of course, in this very deep state of superconsciousness, we are moving into the realm of the intangible, which will always be difficult for empirical science to measure. Before we experience it ourselves, the only evidence of this state is the peace and silence we feel in the presence of a person who has attained it. We know we are on our way when our relationships improve, when we embody the qualities of the samādhāna mind and the brahma-vihāras, and especially when the brahma-vihāras emerge in us as vibhūtis. Then with our attainment of ultimate integration comes the interior experience of ultimate joy, the ānanda of Brahman, the only thing that permanently satisfies the restlessness of the desires of the four primary fountains through the perfection of the fifth. This is the joy of ultimate Self-realization.

May you slip the chains of desire you have forged over lifetimes
in the mindfield through ever more joyful tapas!
May you float in ecstatic peace on That silent ocean
of consciousness!
May your glance, your touch, the field of your pacific presence
dissolve the suffering of anyone who crosses your path
or touches your mind!
Oṁ tat sat brahmārpaṇam astu! Oṁ Śāntih! Śāntih! Śāntih!
(Oṁ That alone is true, real, existent! May this be an offering to
[That] Brahman!
Oṁ Peace! Peace! Peace!)

References

As the bibliographic material for this book gradually accumulated, I decided to divide it into three lists. The first contains self-help resources, the second comprises scholarly works on the philosophy and practice of Yoga and meditation, and the third consists of scientific articles and books. Many of these titles are annotated. I hope that this division and these notes will assist you in finding what you are looking for.

Self-Help Resources

Ballentine, R. (2011). *Radical healing* (2nd ed.). Honesdale, PA: Himalayan Institute Press.
This is a masterful work by one of the leaders of the contemporary holistic health movement. Ballentine is particularly well attuned to the mental and emotional dimensions of health problems, having been trained originally as a psychiatrist. His book is both interesting theoretically and useful practically, giving detailed instructions on practices in many different domains of holistic health, including nutrition, fasting for cleansing, Āyurveda, and homeopathy. I highly recommend it to anyone interested in the whole mind/body.

Benson, H. (with Klipper, M. Z.). (2000). *The relaxation response* (Rev. ed.). San Francisco, CA: HarperTorch.
This was the first popular book to describe the relaxation system in the brain and is a pioneering work in our understanding of the neurobiology of meditation. It first came out at the peak of the meditation craze in the mid-1970s and began to give us a scientific way to understand the impact of meditation and Yoga. Since then, the Benson-Henry Institute for Mind Body Medicine at Massachusetts General Hospital (affiliated with Harvard Medical School) has continued its work investigating the neurobiology of relaxation and its effects on health and wellness.

Benson-Henry Institute for Mind Body Medicine. (n.d.). *Mission and History.* Retrieved from http://www.bensonhenryinstitute.org/about/mission-and-history

Bosnak, R. (1998). *A little course in dreams* (M. H. Kohn, R. Bosnak, & Shambhala Publications, Trans.). Boston, MA: Shambhala.
This little book is a very readable and practical guide to working with dreams written by a Jungian analyst and using a Jungian method. I often recommend it to clients as a way to understand how dreams operate and how we can work with them. Bosnak makes good, practical suggestions for how to do this as a lay person. For serious problems or dreams that seem to defy understanding, one should seek the help of a professional.

Cameron, J. (2002). *The artist's way: A spiritual path to higher creativity* (10th Anniversary ed.). New York, NY: Tarcher/Putnam.
Many people have found this book to be a useful guide to enhancing their spirituality using their creative side (right hemisphere of the brain). It is quite consistent with the Yoga path.

Chia, M. [Mantak]. (2008). *Healing light of the Tao: Foundational practices to awaken chi energy.* Rochester, VT: Destiny Books. (Original work published 1993 as *Awaken healing light of the Tao*)
Chia offers a very good and very readable general introduction to Taoist meditation practices and their relationship to Taoist philosophy. He makes it easy to see the many connections between Taoism and Yoga, particularly in terms of the flow of energy in meditation along the spine and the parallels between the major energy centers (*dan tiens*) of Taoism and the cakra system of Yoga. The differences are illuminating. For example, when scanning the body in Qi Gong, one attends to the internal organs rather than the muscles. Chia's psychosomatic focus might be very helpful to people with various illnesses in those organ systems. This book is also very positive in its approach to sexual energy as an important contributor to the overall energy of the human organism. This approach would be very healing to anyone who has felt alienated from his or her sexuality or felt that in some way it was an obstacle rather than a part of the path.

Chia, M. [Mantak] (with Chia, Maneewan). (1986). F. Morrow, V. Meszaros, & J. Chilton (Eds.). *Healing love through the Tao: Cultivating female sexual energy* (1st ed.). Huntington, NY: Healing Tao Books.

Chia, M. [Mantak]. (with Winn, M.). (1984). *Taoist secrets of love: Cultivating male sexual energy*. Huntington, NY: Healing Tao Books.
This book and the one immediately above are written for men and women

respectively and go into some detail about how one's sexuality fits into his or her overall scheme of spiritual energy. The books also describe the contribution of sexuality to the life of the mind/body. In particular, they offer specific exercises for nurturing that energy—not by indulgence, but by learning to rechannel it into higher centers in the body. Books on Yoga often talk about learning to make these energies flow "upwards" (*ūrdhva-retas*), but they are very short on ways to help this rechanneling occur. These books are solidly based on Taoist tradition and teaching and manage to avoid the sensationalism of many other books on the subject. They also do not limit their discussions of sexuality to heterosexual people and are helpful for those who feel alienated from their sexuality. For example, it was a rude awakening for me when I discovered in my thirties that I was still living by the notion common in much of Christianity that one can be a spiritual person or a sexual person but not both. I have practiced these methods and found them effective. (See also Sovatsky, 1994/1999, below.)

Chopra, D. (1990). *Perfect health: The complete mind/body guide* (1st ed.). New York, NY: Harmony Books.

Many have called this book a very complete adaptation of Āyurveda to the culture and science of the West. It is a very good introduction to the basic ideas of Āyurveda, including descriptions of the constitutional types and dietary and herbal remedies for imbalances in them. Chopra provides some simple tools for assessing your type and designing strategies to work with it. He links the traditional approach of Āyurveda to medical science (he is a board-certified internal medicine physician) and to quantum ideas along the lines of Amit Goswami's (2011) *The Quantum Doctor*, below. For a good annotated bibliography of traditional books on the subject, see Ballentine (2011).

Davidson, R. J. (with Begley, S.). (2012). *The emotional life of your brain: How its unique patterns affect the way you think, feel, and live—and how you can change them.* New York, NY: Hudson Street Press.

This is a highly readable account of the sweep of the extensive work of Richard Davidson and his research team over the years on the neurophysiology of emotional development and how meditation affects it. The book includes a self-assessment scale that is an interesting indicator of one's emotional style. This potentially gives the reader another way to assess progress in the process of emotional purification, as these domains of emotional style tend to parallel the brahma-vihāras fairly closely.

Emmons, H. (2010). *The chemistry of calm: A powerful drug-free plan to quiet your fears and overcome your anxiety*. New York, NY: Touchstone.
Henry Emmons is a holistic psychiatrist who approaches the treatment of mental illness by integrating traditional allopathic approaches with lifestyle changes, nutrition, and alternative systems of healing. He provides lucid explanations of the role of neurochemistry in anxiety and depression and the relationship of neurochemistry to lifestyle interventions. His books, including two others listed below, have been very useful to many of my clients, and I highly recommend them to people who would like to minimize their reliance on conventional medications.

Emmons, H. (with Bourgerie, S., Denton, C., & Kacher, S.). (2012). *The chemistry of joy workbook: Overcoming depression using the best of brain science, nutrition, and the psychology of mindfulness*. Oakland, CA: New Harbinger Publications.

Emmons, H. (with Kranz, R.). (2006). *The chemistry of joy: A three-step program for overcoming depression through Western science and Eastern wisdom*. New York, NY: Fireside.

Hunter, M. (2011). *Back to the source: The spiritual principles of Jesus*. CreateSpace.
Hunter, a licensed psychologist and marriage and family therapist, has attempted to go back to the spiritual principles of Jesus in a way that cuts through many religious misinterpretations of Jesus's spiritual teachings to try to discern what he actually taught to his disciples. Hunter applies his findings to many contemporary issues and problems. He also seeks to understand how these principles are harmonious with and in support of twelve-step recovery efforts. His book is very well done and reflects his efforts as a sincere seeker who, through his own spiritual practice, is helping others.

Hunter, M. (2012). *Conscious contact: The twelve steps as prayer*. CreateSpace.
This is Hunter's further effort to help twelve-step practitioners find practices of prayer that support their spirituality. I recommend this work for people in addiction recovery.

Johnson, R. A. (2009). *Inner work: Using dreams and active imagination for personal growth*. New York, NY: Harper & Row. (Original work published 1986)

Johnson is an outstandingly humane and lucid writer and Jungian analyst whose work on Jungian themes is very readable and opens the door to a relationship with the unconscious for the lay reader. This is another book in addition to Bosnak (1998) above that can help the reader understand how the unconscious works and how it communicates with the rest of the mind through dream and symbol. I would also recommend any of his other books that appeal to you. You won't be disappointed.

Kabat-Zinn, J. (2005). *Wherever you go, there you are: Mindfulness meditation in everyday life* (10th Anniversary ed.). New York, NY: Hachette Book Group.

Jon Kabat-Zinn, PhD, is widely regarded as one of our times' leading popular mindfulness teachers, especially for his role in helping to bring mindfulness meditation into mainstream culture through his Mindfulness-Based Stress Reduction (MBSR) Program. In this best-selling volume, he offers a straightforward account of mindfulness that is both poetic and down to earth. It is accessible to beginning and experienced practitioners, and although the influence of Buddhism on his work is clear, he espouses no particular belief system. Instead he describes the methods and mindsets that put us in touch with the fullness of our being. Though not in these words, Kabat-Zinn portrays the desireless joy of tapas that we explored throughout this book and how to understand the essence of observation through buddhi. He includes both the necessity of taking responsibility for one's shadow side and the joy of living in the light. This book offers a practical and inspiring example of how one can integrate mindfulness into one's daily life, mindset, and being.

Katie, B. (n.d.). *The work of Byron Katie: Do the work.* Retrieved from http://thework.com/en/do-work

Katie, B. (with Mitchell, S.). (2002). *Loving what is: Four questions that can change your life*. New York, NY: Three Rivers Press.

This book is a very helpful introduction to "the work," a form of cognitive therapy that Katie has used with people ever since she awoke one morning from a life full of serious problems into a world of clarity. She teaches people to work skillfully with the relationship between thinking and feeling in the process of healing emotional conflicts. I have used this book with therapy clients and have found it particularly useful for those with an obsessive and self-critical turn of mind.

K-LOVE Afternoon Show. (2016, June 13). With today being MakeaDifference# Monday . . . Let's look for ways to be 'helpers.' [Facebook post]. Retrieved from https://www.facebook.com/kloveafternoons/photos/a.142637813988.143495.22225443988/10154926840983989/?type=3&theater

Lawrence, B. (1982). *The practice of the presence of God.* New Kensington, PA: Whitaker House.
This spiritual classic, compiled from sayings of the French Carmelite monk Brother Lawrence after his death in 1691, helps the reader to understand what it means to practice the presence of divinity from a Christian perspective. Swāmī Veda often described this book as the best ever written on īśvara-praṇidhāna, the mindfulness practice of intentionally placing one's awareness in proximity to divinity at every moment.

Levine, P. (2010). *In an unspoken voice: How the body releases trauma and restores goodness*. Berkeley, CA: North Atlantic Books.
This book represents a breakthrough in understanding the way that traumatic emotional experience is stored in the body and how to work with the body therapeutically to become aware of and modify those emotions.

May, R. (1996). *The meaning of anxiety* (Rev. ed.). New York, NY: Norton.
Originally published in 1950, in its day May's book was a thoughtful exploration of the existential meaning of the escalating anxiety of the modern world and how to deal with it. It is even more relevant today given the atmosphere of fear in which much of the world lives.

Morgan, M. (1994). *Mutant message down under* (1st ed.). New York, NY: Harper Perennial.
This fascinating account of an encounter between a Western-trained nurse and a company of Aboriginals in Australia offers many interesting tales and raises serious questions about the impact of civilization on human lives. After the book was published, Morgan stated that it was fictionalized, perhaps to protect her informants.

Nelson, J. W. (2012). *Running on empty: Transcending the economic culture's seduction of our youth.* Minneapolis, MN: Beavers Pond Press.
Nelson's book is an excellent account of how contemporary society creates problems for adolescents and young adults by exploiting their relationship with the primary fountains. In his more than 30-year career as a school psychologist, Nelson has deftly used Yoga to counter scattered attention, overeating, and problems with handling emotions and sexuality.

Peers, E. A. (Ed. & Trans.). (2007). *Interior castle: St. Teresa of Avila.* New York, NY: Dover Thrift Editions. (Original work published 1946)
This spiritual classic, written by St. Teresa of Avila in 1577, beautifully describes the experience of interior solitude. When Swāmī Veda visited her monastic cell, he said that he had never encountered such strong vibrations of spiritual silence.

Progoff, I. (1992). *At a journal workshop: Writing to access the power of the unconscious and evoke creative ability.* New York, NY: Tarcher/Putnam. (Original work published in two volumes, *At a journal workshop,* 1977, and *The practice of process meditation*, 1980)
Progoff (1921–1998) spent his entire career writing about the use of journals in doing inner work with oneself psychologically and spiritually. An extensive background on his journaling method and its application in many fields is available online (http://www.intensivejournal.org).

Robinson, M. (2009). *Cupid's poisoned arrow: From habit to harmony in sexual relationships*. Berkeley, CA: North Atlantic Books.
Robinson gives an excellent scientific account of the neurophysiology of sexual response. She also offers a searching personal quest to find a pathway into higher experience through a disciplined approach to living one's sexuality. This personal approach is very engaging and can help the reader to shift his or her sexual interaction from excitement-based sex, centered on the brain's dopamine system, to affection-based sex, based on the attachment hormone oxytocin. Among other things, this can be a pathway to healing for those who are sexually addicted or who are addicted to internet pornography. It is also very useful for long-term couples (of any orientation) whose sexual life has become more a matter of habit and conditioning than breakthrough and personal discovery.

Ross, M. (1990). *Seasons of death and life: A wilderness memoir.* San Francisco, CA: HarperCollins.
Ross is a professed Cistercian solitary also trained in psychoanalysis. She is keenly aware of the psycho–spiritual dimensions of healing and is an incisive critic of the ways Christian religion can hinder authentic spiritual practice. She is also a tireless advocate for the practice of silence and solitude. In my personal experience, Ross is the Christian monastic in whose presence I feel the deepest meditative presence. She lives and writes in Europe and the US, having spent many years in solitary meditation practice in "caves" of her own making and in various monastic settings. In this book, she recounts her experience of a year in silence and emotional healing on the California coast, where she befriended a wounded raven whom she nursed back to health and who still comes to her call. She narrates her struggles with emotional purification in the crucible of solitude and also the way that solitude informs her loving care, during the latter part of her year in the wilderness, for her friend, Muskrat, who is dying. Her writing is simply beautiful.

Ross, M. (2007a). *Pillars of flame: Power, priesthood, and spiritual maturity.* New York, NY: Seabury Books. (Original work published 1988)

Ross, M. (2007b, June 28). V The human experience of God at turning points: A theological expose of spiritual counterfeits [Web log post]. Retrieved from http://ravenwilderness.blogspot.co.at/2007_06_01_archive.html

Ross, M. (2013). *Writing the icon of the heart: In silence beholding.* Eugene, OR: Cascade Books.

Ross, M. (2014a). *The fountain and the furnace: The way of tears and fire.* Eugene, OR: Wipf and Stock. (Original work published 1987)
This is a wonderful work on spiritual healing, based on the "path of tears" of the early Syrian monastics of the fourth century. It is based on Ross's scholarship in that Aramaic tradition and is informed by her analytical training. It demonstrates beautifully that we heal through and by way of our wounds rather than despite them. In this way, Ross shows how Christianity can become a genuine path to spiritual healing.

Ross, M. (2014b). *Silence, a user's guide—Vol. I: Process.* London, UK: Darton, Longman & Todd.
This is probably the best work of its type on the practice of silence in the West (a hefty claim, I realize, but Ross is a very deep practitioner and a wonderfully articulate writer). In it, she gives a very clear historical and theological explanation of how the Church became so hostile to silence and solitude even though these are, in reality, core practices of Christian spirituality.

Sheldrake, P. (2016). *Befriending our desires* (3rd ed.). Collegeville, MN: Liturgical Press.
Sheldrake describes a relationship to desire that is similar to our discussion of the practices of tapas in relationship to the four primary fountains. He uses the writings of Christian mystics—Meister Eckhart, Catherine of Siena, and others—to re-establish the importance of eros as the energy that drives spiritual growth and development.

Tagore, R. (2011). *Gitanjali, song offerings*. New Delhi, India: Prakash Books. (Original work published 1912)
Tagore (1861–1941) is a Nobel Prize-winning poet of Indian literature. A deeply spiritual figure, he founded his famous school at Shantiniketan in Bengal as an effort to provide a spiritually based education. (Swāmī Rāma spent part of his high school education there, where he developed his skills as a painter.) This English translation of *Gitanjali* won Tagore the Nobel Prize in 1913. It includes a whole-hearted and reverential introduction by the Irish poet William Butler Yeats (1865–1939). In both this work and the original (published in Bengali in 1910), Tagore offers a rich and beautiful garland of spiritual insights. Tagore is another beautiful writer, and I would recommend any of his titles that appeal to you.

van der Kolk, B. (2014). *The body keeps the score: Brain, mind, and body in the healing of trauma.* New York, NY: Penguin.
This recent book is another contribution to the growing body of literature that is making it clear that in healing trauma one cannot leave the body out, given the way that the entire body is part of the brain and nervous system. For those working with trauma, this is a very important read.

Yoga Philosophy and Practice Resources

Alighieri, D. (2007). *Paradiso* (R. Hollander & J. Hollander, Trans.). New York, NY: Anchor Books.

Swāmī Veda often argued that the traditional Western cultures of the Greek, Latin, and Aramaic worlds were nearly identical to the ancient culture of India. Dante's (1265–1321) *Paradiso* is not only a wonderful metaphor; it is a catalog of actual meditative states, according to Swāmī Veda, who said that through his meditative experience he could teach Śrī-vidyā using this text.

Arya, U. (1981). *Mantra and meditation*. Honesdale, PA: Himalayan Institute Press.

This book, published under Swāmī Veda Bhāratī's premonastic name, Uṣarbudh Ārya, is a very important, comprehensive, and readable work on the science and practice of mantra in meditation by a master of that practical tradition. It includes aspects of mantra from the science of grammar from various philosophical schools, particularly the Mīmāṁsā school and, most importantly, the Kashmir Śaiva philosophy. Beyond the content, Bhāratī's experience comes from having been initiated in the inner tradition of mantra to the fullest extent by his master, Swāmī Rāma of the Himalayas.

Arya, U. (1985). *Philosophy of hatha yoga* (2nd ed.). Honesdale, PA: Himalayan Institute Press.

This little book is a unique exposition of the meditative subtleties of haṭha-yoga practice and how they contribute to the deepening of meditation. As above, it was published under Swāmī Veda Bhāratī's premonastic name. There is much here about the relationship between the subtle and physical bodies that one will not find in any other book on haṭha-yoga. For example, Bhāratī discusses the natural tendency of energy circuits in the nāḍīs to close as the source of the spontaneous (sahaja) experience of mudrā and bandha. He also discusses the practice of āsana as worship. In the last chapter, he reveals a new set of sūtras on the subtle practice of haṭha-yoga.

Arya, U. (1986). *Yoga-sūtras of Patañjali with the exposition of Vyāsa: A translation and commentary. Vol. I: Samādhi-pāda*. Honesdale, PA: Himalayan Institute Press.

As mentioned above, Uṣarbudh Ārya is the given name of Swāmī Veda Bhāratī of Rishikesh, India. His translation project took place during the

1980s at the request of his guru, Swāmī Rāma. Bhāratī's translation and commentary comprise a formidable work, but it is probably the definitive translation of our time. His dense and Latinate renderings of the sūtras are an attempt to capture the many levels of meaning in the original Sanskrit. (English and Sanskrit are not only different languages; they are different types of languages.) It would help readers greatly to first begin studying the sūtras with a less dense translation, like the ones by Georg Feuerstein or Christopher Chapple.

Bhāratī has the unique qualifications of being both a consummate scholar, having been raised speaking Sanskrit as his first language, and of being an adept Yoga practitioner with the experiential ability to reconcile conflicts among the commentators and bring out subtleties they have sometimes missed. His work is a lovely example of a samādhāna mind in action. A revised edition of this volume (Bhāratī, 2014, below) is expected to be published around 2020 and will more than double the size of the existing volume with extensive explanatory essays and appendices and a wonderful exposition on the life and work of Patañjali.

Atreya, B. L. (2005). *The vision and the way of Vasiṣṭha: Compiled with a detailed introduction by B. L. Atreya and translated by Samvid* (Samvid, Trans.). Chennai, India: Samata Books.

Though Atreya wrote in the 1930s, he remains the predominant scholar of the *Yoga-vāsiṣṭha*, one of the most vibrant and beautiful of all the texts in the Yoga tradition. The *Yoga-vāsiṣṭha* is a vast, highly literary epic poem designed to teach Vedānta through stories and through the heart rather than through the intellect, including within it the whole or partial texts of many Yoga *Upaniṣad*s and systematic texts of Vedānta philosophy. This large work spans six sections, hundreds of chapters, and approximately 28,000 verses, making it the fourth longest epic poem in Sanskrit. In *The Vision and the Way of Vasiṣṭha*, Atreya provides the reader with 2500 of these verses, distilling the major themes of the text. The *Yoga-vāsiṣṭha* is my favorite text in Sanskrit.

Bhāratī, S. V. (2001). *Yoga-sūtras of Patañjali with the exposition of Vyāsa: A translation and commentary. Vol. II: Sādhana-pāda*. Delhi, India: Motilal Banarsidass.

This is the second volume of the translation begun by Arya in 1986, listed above. (As that entry mentions, Uṣarbudh Ārya was Swāmī Veda Bhāratī's premonastic name.) This volume has a number of detailed and interesting appendices, including an essentially complete listing of all the textual accounts of the aṅgas (limbs) of Yoga; all the lists of yamas and niyamas across Hindu, Buddhist, and Jain texts on Yoga; an appendix on the oral tradition of Yoga; and appendices on aspects of ordinary and subtle prāṇāyāma and pratyāhāra. This is a definitive scholarly translation and so is most appropriate as a reference or for the experienced reader in the field.

Bharati, S. V. (2002). *Night birds*. Rishikesh, India: AHYMSIN.

Bharati, S. V. (2004). *The song of silence: Subtleties in sadhana*. Minneapolis, MN: The Meditation Center.

This book and *Night Birds* above are compilations of booklets on aspects of spiritual practice that Bhāratī wrote over a number of years. They are practical and helpful guides. The titles include *Mantra: What and Why, Mantra After Initiation, Five Pillars of Sadhana, Daily Schedule of a Sadhaka, Silence*, and many more.

Bharati, S. V. (2006). *Yogi in the lab: Future directions of scientific research in meditation*. Rishikesh, India: AHYMSIN.

In this book, Bhāratī discusses his critique of scientific inquiries into meditation and Yoga and suggests a number of qualitative additions to methodology that would greatly enhance the value of such research. He also reports on some of his own early experiments in the laboratory at Swāmī Rāma Sādhaka Grāma in Rishikesh, India, and at the Institute of Noetic Sciences in Petaluma, CA. In the preparation for one of these experiments, the investigator, Dean Radin, PhD, noticed that even when apparently awake, talking, and moving about, Bhāratī's brain never seemed to deviate from producing the delta waves of deep sleep. Bhāratī wrote this book to be an adjunct to empirical research, using it to explain the technique in which the finer layers of buddhi observe the activity of the rest of the mind.

Bharati, S. V. (2009). *Wanam: Africa and India, a spiritual dialogue*. Rishikesh, India: AHYMSIN.

This little book describes Bhāratī's discoveries about the commonalities between the spirituality of the Yoga tradition and the indigenous religions of Africa. He primarily draws from his visits to Burkina Faso and Benin as well as from his encounter in Benin with the lineage holders of the voodoo tradition. He also discusses his conversations with the great Zulu shaman Credo Mutwa.

Bharati, S. V. (2013a). *The human urge for peace: What is right with the world*. Minneapolis, MN: Ahymsa.
Bhāratī produced this work in the process of a teaching collaboration with the Peace Studies program at the University of Innsbruck, the official training program for United Nations peacekeepers. During this exchange, Bhāratī conducted seminars on meditation as a pathway to inner peacekeeping.

Bharati, S. V. (2013b). *Kundalini: Stilled or stirred?* Delhi, India: DK Printworld.
This book offers a welcome antidote to the flood of speculative writing on cakras and Kuṇḍalinī in the marketplace. Bhāratī writes from firsthand experience about many current misconceptions and provides a useful experiential (and poetic) insight into what the process of awakening these subtle energies entails.

Bharati, S. V. (2013c). *Sadhana in applied spirituality*. Rishikesh, India: AHYMSIN.
This book contains a number of essays on the application of spirituality to relationships, both at home and in the workplace.

Bharati, S. V. (2013d). *The signs of progress in spirituality and in meditation* [Audio recording]. Rishikesh, India: AHYMSIN.
This was one of Swāmī Veda's last published lectures before he left the body in July 2015. He actually gave several lectures on this topic, trying to help people understand the nature of a strong and spiritually evolved mindfield.

Bhāratī, S. V. (2014). *Yoga-sūtras of Patañjali with the exposition of Vyāsa: A translation and commentary. Vol. I: Samādhi-pāda* (Rev. ed.). Unpublished manuscript.
This is the revised edition of Arya's (1986) work above. It more than doubles the size of the existing volume with extensive explanatory essays and appendices and a wonderful exposition on the life and work of Patañjali. Its release is anticipated around 2020.

Bharati, S. V. (2015). *Whole hearted: Applied spirituality for everyday life*. Minneapolis, MN: Dhyana Mandiram.
This exceptionally personal and plainspoken book gives very practical guidance for how to bring the gifts of meditation into your day-to-day life

in business or with your family. It is especially helpful for those who are new to meditation or considering how meditation might be helpful to them. *Whole Hearted* wonderfully complements and amplifies the main points detailed in this volume.

Buddhaghosa, B. (2011). *Visuddhimagga, the path of purification: The classic manual of Buddhist doctrine and meditation* [Rev. 3rd ed. e-book version]. (B. Ñāṇamoli, Trans.). Retrieved from http://www.accesstoinsight.org/lib/authors/nanamoli/PathofPurification2011.pdf
This is the standard translation of the classic Buddhist meditation manual from ca. 430 CE, produced by the Buddhist Publication Society. Chapter 9 focuses on the practice of the brahma-vihāras. It is available online as a free PDF download (see above).

Bühler, G. (Ed. & Trans.). (1969). *The laws of Manu: Translated with extracts from seven commentaries*. New York, NY: Dover Books. (Original work published 1886)
This is an old and esteemed English translation of the most important of the *Dharma-śāstra*s, or law books on right behavior in the Hindu tradition.

Campbell, J. (Ed.). (1971). *The portable Jung* (R. F. C. Hull, Trans.). New York, NY: Viking Penguin.
This is a fine little compendium of Jung's writing for those interested in gaining a sense of Jung from his original writings.

Campbell, J. (1981). *The mythic image*. Princeton, NJ: Princeton University Press.
This work, by perhaps the greatest twentieth-century scholar of myth writing in English, does a beautiful job of describing the continuity of mythic forms across cultures. Campbell covers not only the cultures of "major" civilizations but also the myths of indigenous traditions. He presents a strong argument for Jung's hypothesis that within the collective unconscious (what a Yoga practitioner might call the transpersonal mindfield), myths operate as patterns of energy that take on different forms, languages, and so forth from culture to culture. Alain Daniélou (1984/1992), for example, has a lovely book about the existence of Śiva in Western culture within the figure and cult of Dionysus (see below). These patterns of energy can also be called mantra.

Daniélou, A. (1973). *Yoga: The method of reintegration.* New York, NY: University Books.

Daniélou was a self-taught scholar who moved to India from France in the 1930s and lived there until the Partition of India in 1947. He learned Hindi and Sanskrit and became an accomplished *vīna* (veena) player. After his return to Europe, he became the first head of UNESCO's music organization and was one of the founders of the world music genre. He was also deeply involved in the study and practice of Yoga. As a disciple of the well-known guru Karpātri Swāmī (mentioned in *Autobiography of a Yogi* by Yogananda, 1971, below), Daniélou was the first Westerner initiated as a brahmin in the Lingāyat tradition of Śaivism.

This book is a jewel. First published in 1949 with American editions following in 1955 and 1973, it is very much in need of reprinting. It is an excellent compendium of quotations about many aspects of the Yoga tradition from original sources, many of which are hard to find in translation. Daniélou's translations are clear and readable. At a time when Yoga is often misrepresented for commercial reasons, this work is highly recommended for serious students of the tradition.

Daniélou, A. (1987). *The way to the labyrinth: Memories of east and west* (M.C. Cournand, Trans.). New York, NY: New Directions Books.

Daniélou's autobiography is a fascinating read. He knew so many of the great figures across the arts in the mid-twentieth century, conducted Igor Stravinsky's funeral, and lived peacefully as one partner in a gay couple in the most conservative city in Northern India throughout his time there—in a home of a mahārāja on the river to which the viceroy used to send guests to see what a traditional Indian house looked like! Though Daniélou's book does not address the subject of emotional purification directly, it reveals his scholarship to be informed by the inner tradition to an extraordinary degree. His brief essay on the flaws in the intellectual life of the West at the end of the book is well worth the price of this text.

Daniélou, A. (1992). *Gods of love and ecstasy: The traditions of Shiva and Dionysus* (East-West Publications, Trans.). Rochester, VT: Inner Traditions International. (Original work published 1984 as *Shiva and Dionysus*)

This book was a revelation to me. In it, Daniélou details the astonishing parallels between the religious and spiritual traditions of Śiva and Dionysus, thus helping the Western practitioner identify the presence of the spiritual energy of Śiva in the Greek pantheon.

Digambarji, S., & Kokaje, R. S. (Eds. & Trans.). (1998). *Haṭhapradīpikā of Svātmarāma* (2nd ed.). Pune, India: Kaivalyadhama S.M.Y.M. Samiti.
This critical edition of the *Haṭhapradīpikā* (HYP) was completed through the careful work of the scholars at Kaivalyadhama, the oldest and most comprehensive of the modern Yoga institutes in the world, in Lonavla, India. Dating from the fifteenth century, the HYP synthesizes the Yoga path from the perspective of the text tradition of haṭha-yoga. The edition cited here is probably the most complete version of this text. Most translations are prepared from a single manuscript, and this edition has the benefit of a range of manuscripts. For the scholar, there are useful appendices in the back identifying, among other things, verses quoted in other texts as belonging to HYP but not listed in the extant versions. This would seem to point towards undiscovered manuscripts. Some of this material was later published in a 2001 translation edited by Gharote and Devnath and published by the Lonavla Yoga Institute.

Emerson, D., & Hopper, E. (2011). *Overcoming trauma through yoga: Reclaiming your body*. Berkeley, CA: North Atlantic Books.
This is a very thoughtful account of the use of Yoga with people who have experienced trauma. Even though it proposes a special method of using Yoga, I find it to be a good description of general Yoga practice if one's goals are to understand the subtlety of mind/body relationship and to deepen one's meditation. The authors' sense of caution about the use of touch is laudable, but if a teacher is well trained in working with trauma and knows the client, there is a strong argument to be made that not using touch denies the client the prime mover of human growth and development.

Feuerstein, G. (2013). *The psychology of Yoga: Integrating Eastern and Western approaches for understanding the mind.* Boston, MA: Shambhala.
This is an interesting book that compares Western psychology with Yoga psychology from a scholarly perspective. It is primarily a theoretical text rather than a book about the practice of spirituality or psychotherapy.

Forbes, B. (2011). *Yoga for emotional balance: Simple practices to help relieve anxiety and depression*. Boston, MA: Shambhala.
In this book, clinical psychologist and Yoga teacher Bo Forbes provides tools to help people manage stress and heal from anxiety and depression.

(She emphasizes using Yoga to address the latter in conjunction with psychotherapy and medication, not to replace necessary medical care.) Her discussions on self-compassion, patience in establishing foundational skills, regularity in practice, and learning from pain apply to us all. This book is unique in that Forbes wrote it as a response to her observation that talk therapy, when it does not incorporate body awareness, can too easily allow clients to "rehearse" their negative emotions and thereby agitate their nervous systems, reinforcing habitual thought and behavior patterns. She argues that long-held restorative Yoga postures (performed lying on the floor and supported with props like pillows and blankets), accompanied by mindful breathing, can allow the nervous system to relax and to process stored emotions, often at levels partially or entirely below conscious awareness. This can help people to engage more constructively in cognitive therapeutic approaches and allow them to make strides in therapy much more quickly than with either approach alone. Forbes works gently and progressively with the breath and, unlike many contemporary teachers, omits breath retention practices that are often premature and in some cases even harmful. She includes useful practice routines, strategies for modifying poses to suit one's own body, and ideas for how to replace Yoga props with common household items. This is a thorough and yet simple-to-use guidebook that can teach you how to develop awareness of your whole mind/body over time.

Frawley, D. (2010). *Mantra yoga and primal sound: Secrets of seed (bija) mantras*. Twin Lakes, WI: Lotus Press.
This book is an excellent companion to Swāmī Veda Bhāratī's book *Mantra and Meditation* (Arya, 1981) above. Frawley gives detailed information about the nature of the vibratory energies of the sounds of the Sanskrit alphabet as well as thorough practical advice about mantra-sādhanā that complements Bhāratī's work. The two men were great friends, and Bhāratī even assisted Frawley (2014) with his book, *Vedic Yoga: The Path of the Rishi*, towards the end of Bhāratī's embodied life.

Goswami, S. S. (1999). *Layayoga: The definitive guide to the chakras and Kundalini*. Rochester, VT: Inner Traditions International.
This is a very detailed explication of the cakras and Kuṇḍalinī based on traditional sources.

Hanh, T. N. (1975). *The miracle of mindfulness* (1st ed.; M. Ho, Trans.). Boston, MA: Beacon Press.
This is a classic text by one of the great Buddhist teachers of recent times, as enjoyable as it is instructive. In it, Hanh describes the everyday cultivation of mindful awareness. This is the basis for the self-observation we need in order to engage in the process of emotional purification. It was here that I found his beautiful comments on washing the dishes mindfully.

Harvey, A. (Ed.). (2001). *The way of a pilgrim, annotated and explained* (G. Pokrovsky, Trans. & Annotation). Woodstock, VT: SkyLight Paths.
This little book is a beautiful and engaging story of a simple Russian peasant seeking to follow the injunction in Orthodox Christian practice to "pray without ceasing," with every breath, using the Jesus prayer (see Appendix A, Exercise 2.4). Like a wandering swāmī, he travels from place to place and encounters a number of spiritual adventures on the way. The author makes frequent reference to *Philokalia*, a collection of writings in Greek from the deep meditative traditions of the Orthodox Church (e.g., by Saint Simeon the New Theologian). *Philokalia* is available in English translation.

Kulārṇava tantra (A. Avalon, Trans.). (2007). Delhi, India: Motilal Banarsidass.
This text, translated by Arthur Avalon (i.e., Sir John Woodroffe) is an important text of Tantra that explains, among many other things, modalities of initiation into Yoga. Woodroffe was both a scholar of Sanskrit and a dedicated sādhaka whose work remains among the very best on Tantra after a century.

Lakshmanjoo, S. (2007). *Shiva sutras: The supreme awakening* (2nd ed.). J. Hughes (Ed.). New Delhi, India: Munshiram Manoharlal.
This translation and commentary, by the last publicly known master of the Kashmir Śaiva tradition, is a good starting place for those interested in this school of Tāntrik philosophy. Lakshmanjoo's (1907–1991) explanations are relatively plain spoken and easy to grasp compared to the more scholarly works; this shows the depth of his personal sādhanā. In his explanation, he follows the commentary of Kṣemarāja. For those with some Sanskrit, the original *Śiva-sūtra* text, thought to be composed by the ninth-century sage Vasugupta, is included.

Muktibodhananda, S. (1999). *Swara yoga* (Rev. 2nd ed.). Munger, India: Bihar School of Yoga.

Swāmī Muktibodhānanda offers a very good introduction to the science of svara and includes a translation of *Śiva-svarodaya*, one of the only texts that exists outside the oral tradition of Yoga. That text includes extensive lists of pursuits that fit with the cyclical activity of the cardinal energy channels, as well as ways to investigate the relationship between these energy flows and the elemental energies in the cakras, and much more.

Nityamuktananda, S. (2007). *The five great elements rediscovered: A comprehensive guide to the expression of life* (Rev. 3rd ed.). Lonavla, India: Kaivalyadhama Ashram.

Swāmī Nityamuktānanda has written the definitive transcultural explanation of the five great elements (*mahābhūta*s—earth, water, fire, air, and space). She looks at them from a broad perspective, taking into account how both Eastern and Western cultures conceptualize them (although in this case, the more relevant distinction is probably between traditional and modern cultures). Her focus is on what is shared, not on the differences, which means that she is likely to be closer to the truth. In addition to explaining the role of these energy states in the composition of the matter of the universe, Swāmījī also discusses their psychological importance and has devised a self-assessment system based on her work that could probably be standardized as a personality assessment instrument.

Padmasambhava. (1993). *The Tibetan book of the dead: First complete translation* (R. Thurman, Trans.). New York, NY: Viking Penguin.

This fourteenth-century text is a Tibetan account of the process of leaving the body at death. It details the stages through which one passes in the transition either into enlightenment or towards birth in a new body. A very interesting work, *The Tibetan Book of the Dead* shares some similarities with the same type of text in Egyptian traditions and with Hindu accounts in the *Liṅga*- and *Garuḍa-purāṇa*s.

Parker, S., & Sharma, A. (2013). The use of touch in yoga teaching and therapy: Principles and guidelines for effective practice. *International Journal of Yoga Therapy*, 23, 69–70. Retrieved from http://www.iayt.org

In this article, we have articulated some of the important considerations in touching students during the process of adjustment in teaching Yoga. In the context of the debate, stimulated by liability issues, about whether or not to touch Yoga students or Yoga therapy clients, we make the argument that the central role of touch in driving human development would make it unethical not to touch students, and we detail thought processes and techniques concerning when and how to do so.

Radha, S. S. (2006). *Hatha yoga, the hidden language: Symbols, secrets & metaphor* (Rev. ed.). Kootenay Bay, Canada: Timeless Books.
This is an excellent book for beginning to explore the spiritual depths of the postures of Yoga. It works at many different levels with Swāmī Sivānanda Rādha's (1911–1995) penetrating insight and her keen ability to design exercises for self-exploration, typical of all her books and, formerly, of her teaching in person.

Rama, S. (1977). *Joints and glands exercises* (1st ed.). Honesdale, PA: Himalayan Institute Press.
Swāmī Rāma taught what he called *joints and glands exercises* to limber the body, stimulate the endocrine system, and mindfully move prāṇa through the body in a systematic way in preparation for āsana or subtle body practices. This is the original publication and, more so than other editions, closely reflects what Swāmī Rāma actually taught.

Rama, S. (1978). *Living with the Himalayan masters: Spiritual experiences of Swami Rama* (1st ed.). Honesdale, PA: Himalayan Institute Press.
This is Swāmī Rāma's autobiography. He structures it as a collection of anecdotes rather than as a chronological narrative. As a teacher, I have often heard magical and delightful stories about people's experience with this book, including several instances where the book literally fell into their hands while they were walking through a bookstore. As with the autobiographies of many great teachers, it is inspiring and gives a sense of the author's mission in the world. (I find that the biographies and autobiographies of their close disciples often give a better sense of what they were like to be with day to day.) This book has been an important inspiration to many, many seekers. The short chapters are very nice to use in a process of contemplative reading, as in the Benedictine tradition of *lectio divina.*

Rama, S. (1984a). *Exercise* without *movement, manual one: As taught by Sri Swami Rama of the Himalayas*. Honesdale, PA: Himalayan Institute Press.
This book explains a series of practices that use mindful attention and

relaxation to exercise the physical and subtle bodies without a lot of physical activity. It includes his versions of the tension relaxation exercise, 61 points, and śithali-karaṇa. (Instructions for each can also be found in this work's Appendix A.)

Rama, S. (1984b). *Perennial psychology of the Bhagavad Gita* (U. Arya, Trans.). Honesdale, PA: Himalayan Institute Press.
Swāmī Rāma provides an excellent contemporary commentary on this most read of all Indian texts. The *Bhagavad-gītā*, sometimes referred to affectionately as simply the *Gītā*, is an extraordinarily syncretic presentation of meditative philosophy that harmonizes many of the disparate schools of Indian philosophy, including Buddhism and Jainism. Themes of the philosophy of action (karma) make it a critical text on ethics. Its promulgation of the principle of nonviolence occurs in the midst of the story of a great battle, the crux of the larger work in which the *Gītā* finds itself, the epic *Mahābhārata*. So important is the *Gītā* in the Vedānta tradition that it holds the status of an *Upaniṣad* (revealed wisdom, *śruti*, as opposed to philosophical or historical thought, *smṛti*, found in the rest of the *Mahābhārata*). Because the *Bhagavad-gītā* is one of the cardinal texts of the Vedānta tradition, philosophers arguing for a particular school of Vedānta interpretation must provide a commentary on it. Swāmī Rāma's commentary is psychologically oriented; the clear and precise translation is by Swāmī Veda Bhāratī.

Rama, S. (1988). *Path of fire and light: Vol. one, advanced practices of yoga.* Honesdale, PA: Himalayan Institute Press.
This book is edited from a lecture series of the same title given at the Himalayan Institute in Honesdale, PA. Swāmī Rāma sought to describe some of the more advanced practices of Yoga after many requests from students and disciples. Among other practices, he describes extremely advanced practices of prāṇāyāma and several subtle body practices, such as his version of yoga-nidrā.

Rama, S. (1989). *The art of joyful living*. Honesdale, PA: Himalayan Institute Press.
This is probably the book by Swāmī Rāma that is most devoted to working with oneself in the process of sādhanā, personal spiritual practice. I have read and reread this many times; I hope you will, too.

Rama, S. (1996). *Sacred journey: Living purposefully and dying gracefully* (1st ed.). New Delhi, India: Himalayan International Institute of Yoga Science and Philosophy.
Swāmī Rāma wrote this book during the last year of his life as he was preparing to leave the body. It is an unusually clear and plainspoken book about the nature of death and reincarnation. It is largely based on the *Kaṭha-upaniṣad* story of Naciketas, a seeker who confronts Yama, the Lord of Death, and asks to be taught the secret of what happens at the death of the body. It is as much about how to live one's life as it is about how to prepare for death.

Rama, S. (2002). *Conscious living: A guidebook for spiritual transformation.* Dehradun, India: Himalayan Institute Hospital Trust. (Original work published 2002 as *A personal philosophy of life*)
In this work, Swāmī Rāma seeks to assist the reader in deciding on a personal philosophy of life, which can guide him or her in the process of spiritual development.

Rinpoche, T. W. (1998). *The Tibetan yogas of dream and sleep.* Ithaca, NY: Snow Lion.

Shāntideva. (2006). *The way of the bodhisattva* (Rev. 2nd ed.; Padmakara Translation Group, Trans.). Boston, MA: Shambhala.
This is a revised translation of the great Buddhist text *Bodhicāryavatāra* (700 CE) with several commentaries. It is the main Mahāyāna Buddhist text on the cultivation of *bodhi-citta* ("enlightenment-mind") and the philosophy of the *bodhisattva.* A bodhisattva is a being who renounces even the desire for liberation and, out of compassion, is moved to be reborn repeatedly to assist other beings in their development towards liberation. The *Bodhicāryavatāra* is the text from which the Dalai Lama usually teaches. The version cited here is freely available online (http://promienie.net/images/dharma/books/shantideva_way-of-bodhisattva.pdf).

Singh, J. (Ed. & Trans.). (1979). *Vijñānabhairava or divine consciousness: A treasury of 112 types of yoga.* Delhi, India: Motilal Banarsidass.
Singh was one of the close disciples of Lakshmanjoo and, as a scholar, first produced English translations of the works of Kashmir Śaivism. Because Singh's works are scholarly, they are perhaps most useful to the general reader in combination with Lakshmanjoo's more plain-spoken commentaries.

Sovatsky, S. (1999). *Eros, consciousness, and Kundalini: Deepening sensuality through tantric celibacy and spiritual intimacy*. Rochester, VT: Inner Traditions. (Originally published 1994 as *Passions of innocence*)
This is a wonderful book for those interested in living a celibate life in a sex-positive way. It takes the Tāntrik perspective that what binds you is also what liberates you. Many people try to practice celibacy by merely trying to ignore or, worse, to suppress the instinctive drive of sexual desire. This approach can have disastrous results. Sovatsky has distilled his work as a Yoga practitioner and psychologist over a couple decades of psychotherapy helping couples and individuals cultivate a humane and joyful practice of celibacy. He has also contributed a theory of human development based on the unfolding of the *Kuṇḍalinī-Śakti*, the power of the Divine Feminine.

Trungpa, C. (2002). *Cutting through spiritual materialism.* J. Baker & M. Casper (Eds.). Boston, MA: Shambhala.
Trungpa's book, first published in 1973, has become a classic on keeping one's meditation and spiritual practice effective. This book is particularly good for practitioners from Western cultures, as it addresses the distortions that can occur when spiritual practices from other cultural backgrounds are brought into the West without a sense of their original context.

Vivekananda, R. (2005). *Practical yoga psychology*. Munger, India: Yoga Publications Trust.

Weintraub, A. (2012). *Yoga skills for therapists: Effective practices for mood management*. New York, NY: Norton.
This book gives a sense of how one might use many of the practices of Yoga in psychotherapy, especially the relaxation and breath practices that don't involve retention of breath. It is important in teaching such practices to clients that one is grounded in a personal practice of Yoga. To simply use these as techniques misses the point of the larger processes of self-transformation involved in the practice from start to finish and runs the risk of insufficient attention to how these practices may fit with other practices or other elements of therapy. Weintraub's book also lacks the traditional cautions about premature breath retention described in Chapter 7 above on prāṇāyāma, and these are important for psychotherapy. Premature use of retention, before the natural advent of spontaneous retention, or sahaja-kumbhaka, intensifies one's painful as well as pleasant saṁskāras and makes psychotherapy or other efforts at emotional purification more

difficult. In this sense, the premature therapeutic use of breath retention must be considered iatrogenic.

Woodroffe, J. G. (1972). *The serpent power, being the Ṣaṭ-cakra-nirūpaṇa and Pādukā-Pañcaka: Two works on laya-yoga. Translated from the Sanskrit, with introduction and commentary* (8th. ed.). Chennai, India: Ganesh.

This very thorough and scholarly work, first published in 1918, is still the best extant book on the phenomenon of Kuṇḍalinī. Woodroffe was not only a fine scholar and translator; he was also an advanced practitioner of the disciplines he wrote about. He served as a judge on the same Calcutta high court as Bengali Baba, the guru of Swāmī Rāma, before Bengali Baba renounced the position. I have been unable so far to find evidence of any spiritual connection between them.

Woodroffe, J. G. (2004). *Introduction to Tantra Śāstra*. Chennai, India: Ganesh. (Original work published 1952)

This little book is a great place to begin learning the basic ideas and terminology of the overall tradition of Tantra. It was first published in 1913 as *Introduction to Mahānirvāṇa Tantra* ("Tantra of the Great Liberation") and then retitled and republished as above in 1952. Of all of Woodroffe's works, this is probably the clearest and most approachable.

Yogananda, P. (1971). *Autobiography of a yogi* (11th ed.). Kolkata, India: Yogoda Satsanga.

How many of us got our start in Yoga in the 1970s through this book?! First published in 1946, it has been reprinted many times over, across the globe. With its stories of great Yogis and gurus, it is classic, informative, and highly inspiring.

Zambito, S. (2010). *The Yoga-Sūtra Sanskrit-English dictionary*. Sequim, WA: Yoga Sūtras Institute.

This is a wonderful resource for the serious student of the *Yoga-sūtra* who is not a Sanskritist. Much of the juice and many of the fine points of the text Patañjali has built into the structure of the words and sentences. Zambito has taken each term down to its source in the verb roots, which gives a much richer understanding. It is a great companion volume to his book *The Unadorned Thread of Yoga: The Yoga-Sutra of Patañjali in English* (1992). For that title, he has obtained permission from twelve (i.e., most) of the publishers of the English translations of Patañjali, and he has listed the translation of each sūtra from those different publications. This, too, is helpful to the non-Sanskritist in getting a sense of the depth of the original text.

Scientific Resources

Aimone, J. B., Li, Y., Lee, S. W., Clemenson, G. D., Deng, W., & Gage, F. H. (2014). Regulation and function of adult neurogenesis: From genes to cognition. *Physiological Reviews, 94,* 991–1026. doi:10.1152/physrev.00004.2014
This article provides a thorough review of research on adult neurogenesis and its relationship to cognition through gene expression.

Aimone, J. B., Wiles, J., & Gage, F. H. (2006). Potential role for adult neurogenesis in the encoding of time in new memories. *Nature Neuroscience, 9*, 723–727. doi:10.1038/nn1707

Altman, J. (1962). Are new neurons formed in the brains of adult mammals? *Science, 135,* 1127–1128. (PMID:13860748)
This was the first research article to wonder whether there is neurogenesis in mammal species.

Arias-Carrión, O., Freundlieb, N., Oertel, W. H., & Höglinger, G. U. (2007). Adult neurogenesis and Parkinson's disease. *CNS & Neurological Disorders - Drug Targets, 6*, 326–335. doi:10.2174/187152707783220875

Binder, D. K., & Scharfman, H. E. (2004). Brain-derived neurotrophic factor. *Growth Factors, 22,* 123–131. doi:10.1080/08977190410001723308

Broad, W. J. (2012). *The science of yoga: The risks and the rewards*. New York, NY: Simon & Schuster.
This is a good account of recent empirical research on Yoga and its implications for contemporary Western-inspired Yoga practice, especially its health benefits in terms of relaxation and stress reduction, as well as cautions about injury, for example vertebral artery strokes. One would have hoped for a better sense of the larger Yoga tradition in someone who has practiced since 1970, however. Broad's grasp of this appears confined to the limits of academic expositions that in turn limit his understanding. The physical practices of Yoga do not originate with Gorakṣa (tenth

century), as Broad reports, but are evident in the *Vedas* (ca. 5000–1500 BCE), *Upaniṣads* (1500 BCE to the present), and the *Yoga-sūtra* (second century BCE), often under the rubric of tapas rather than the term *haṭha-yoga*. His statement that we should not be surprised that today's Yoga teachers have sexual relationships with their students because haṭha-yoga is based on Tantra and Tantra is all about better sex makes as much sense as characterizing the Christian Eucharist as merely an exercise in cannibalism. Tantra is, among many other things, a science of celibacy that does not simply try to suppress or ignore sexuality, but that trains the practitioner in how to raise sexual energy into the higher cakras. The fact that Tantra doesn't shy away from sexuality does not mean that indulgence is its intention (see Sovatsky, 1994/1999, above).

Cahn, B. R., & Polich, J. (2006). Meditation states and traits: EEG, ERP, and neuroimaging studies. *Psychological Bulletin, 132,* 180–211. doi:10.1037/0033-2909.132.2.180

This is an excellent review article on the use of electroencephalography to study meditation.

Calabrese, F., Molteni, R., Racagni, G., & Riva, M. A. (2009). Neuronal plasticity: A link between stress and mood disorders. *Psychoneuroendocrinology, 34,* Suppl. 1, S208–216. doi:10.1016/j.psyneuen.2009.05.014

Carmichael, M. S., Humbert, R., Dixen, J., Palmisano, G., Greenleaf, W., & Davidson, J. M. (1987). Plasma oxytocin increases in the human sexual response. *The Journal of Clinical Endocrinology & Metabolism, 64,* 27–31. doi:10.1210/jcem-64-1-27

Caulfield, T., & DeBow, S. (2005). A systematic review of how homeopathy is represented in conventional and CAM peer reviewed journals. *BMC Complementary and Alternative Medicine*, *5*(12). doi:10.1186/1472-6882-5-12

Cortical Homunculus. (2016, December 29). In *Wikipedia*. Retrieved from https://en.wikipedia.org/wiki/Cortical_homunculus

Davidson, R. J., Kabat-Zinn, J., Schumacher, J., Rosenkranz, M., Muller, D., Santorelli, S.F., . . . Sheridan, J. F. (2003). Alterations in brain and immune function produced by mindfulness meditation. *Psychosomatic Medicine, 65,* 564–570. doi:10.1097/01.PSY.0000077505.67574.E3

Dickson, A. (Ed.). (1991). *On metapsychology, the theory of psychoanalysis: "Beyond the pleasure principle", "ego and the id"* and other works. New York, NY: Penguin.

Dor-Ziderman, Y., Berkovich-Ohana, A., Glicksohn, J., & Goldstein, A. (2013). Mindfulness-induced selflessness: A MEG neurophenomenological study. *Frontiers in Human Neuroscience*, *7*(582), 1–17. doi:10.3389/fnhum.2013.00582
This is a fascinating neurophenomenological case study of an advanced meditator who entered a subjectively reported state of selflessness. It was simultaneously investigated empirically with magnetoencephalography.

Eriksson, P. S., Perfilieva, E., Björk-Eriksson, T., Alborn, A. M., Nordborg, C., Peterson D. A., & Gage, F. H. (1998). Neurogenesis in the adult human hippocampus. *Nature Medicine*, *4,* 1313–1317. doi:10.1038/3305

Foster, P. P., Rosenblatt, K. P., & Kuljiš, R. O. (2011). Exercise-induced cognitive plasticity, implications for mild cognitive impairment and Alzheimer's disease. *Frontiers in Neurology*, *6*(2), 28. doi:10.3389/fneur.2011.00028

Fournier, J. C., DeRubeis, R. J., Hollon, S. D., Dimidjian, S., Amsterdam, J. D., Shelton, R. C., & Fawcett, J. (2010). Antidepressant drug effects and depression severity: A patient-level meta-analysis. *JAMA, the Journal of the American Medical Association, 303,* 47–53. doi:10.1001/jama.2009.1943

Fredericks, L. E., Rodger, B. P., Corley, J. B., Rossi, E. L., Cheek, D. B., Barber, J., . . . Kroger, W. S. (1990). Hypnoanesthesia and preparation for surgery. In D. C. Hammond (Ed.), *Handbook of hypnotic suggestions and metaphors* (pp. 85–108). New York, NY: Norton.
This is a chapter on the use of hypnosis for surgical anesthesia in a standard text on hypnosis. Among the authors is David Cheek, one of the originators of clinical hypnosis.

Freud, S. (1966). *The complete introductory lectures on psychoanalysis* (J. Strachey, Ed. & Trans.). New York, NY: Norton.

Freud, S. (1989). *The ego and the id, the standard edition: With a biographical introduction by Peter Gay* (J. Riviere, Trans.). J. Strachey (Ed.). New York, NY: Norton.

Freud, S. (2009). *Beyond the pleasure principle.* Eastford, CT: Martino Fine Books. (Original work published 1922)

Freud, S. (2010). *The interpretation of dreams: The complete and definitive text* (J. Strachey, Ed. & Trans.). New York, NY: Basic Books. (Original work published 1955)

Freud wrote this work in 1900, and the official translation by Strachey was published in 1955. It is the most complete articulation of Freud's theory of dream interpretation and remains a classic to this day.

Galbally, M., Lewis, A. J., Ijzendoorn, M. V., & Permezel, M. (2011). The role of oxytocin in mother-infant relations: A systematic review of human studies. *Harvard Review of Psychiatry, 1,* 1–14. doi:10.3109/10673229.2011.549771

Goldman, S. A., & Nottebohm, F. (1983). Neuronal production, migration, and differentiation in a vocal control nucleus of the adult female canary brain. *Proceedings of the National Academy of Sciences of the United States of America, 80,* 2390–2394. doi:10.1073/pnas.80.8.2390

Goswami, A. (2011). *The quantum doctor: A quantum physicist explains the healing power of integral medicine.* Charlottesville, VA: Hampton Roads. (Original work published 2004)

This excellent and very readable theoretical book uses quantum physical ideas to create a framework within which all the systems of medicine—in particular, allopathic, homeopathic, and Āyurvedic—can work collaboratively.

Gouin, J. P., Carter, C. S., Pournajafi-Nazarloo, H., Glaser, R., Malarkey, W. B., Loving, T. J., . . . Kiecolt-Glaser, J. K. (2010). Marital behavior, oxytocin, vasopressin, and wound healing. *Psychoneuroendocrinology, 35,* 1082–1090. doi:10.1016/j.psyneuen.2010.01.009

Goyal, M., Singh, S., Sibinga, E. M. S., Gould, N. F., Rowland-Seymour, A., Sharma, R., . . . Haythornthwaite, J. A. (2014). Meditation programs for psychological stress and well-being: A systematic review and meta-analysis. *JAMA Internal Medicine, 174,* 357–368. doi:10.1001/jamainternmed.2013.13018

Green, E., & Green, A. (1977). *Beyond biofeedback.* San Francisco, CA: Delacorte Press.
This is the Greens' account of their early research into voluntary nervous system control at the Menninger Foundation. It includes discussions of many of their experiments with Swāmī Rāma, for example his first demonstration of yoga-nidrā done under electroencephalography, his ability to stop the movement of blood through his heart, and his controlled demonstration of telekinesis.

Guastella, A. J., Mitchell, P. B., & Dadds, M. R. (2008). Oxytocin increases gaze to the eye region of human faces. *Biological Psychiatry, 63*, 3–5. doi:10.1016/j.biopsych.2007.06.026

Han, K. S., Kim, L., & Shim, I. (2012). Stress and sleep disorder. *Experimental Neurobiology, 21*(4), 141–150. doi:10.5607/en2012.21.4.141

Heinrichs, M., Baumgartner, T., Kirschbaum, C., & Ehlert, U. (2003). Social support and oxytocin interact to suppress cortisol and subjective responses to psychosocial stress. *Biological Psychiatry, 54*, 1389–1398. doi:10.1016/S0006-3223(03)00465-7

Honigberger, J. M. (1852). *Thirty-five years in the East: Adventures, discoveries, experiments, and historical sketches relating to the Punjab and Cashmere; In connection with medicine, botany, pharmacy, & together with an original materia medica and a medical vocabulary, in four European and five Eastern languages*. London, England: Baillière.
Honigberger was a British physician from nineteenth-century India. His text is one of the first accounts of medical observations of Yogis' extraordinary abilities.

Imayoshi, I., Sakamoto, M., Ohtsuka, T., Takao, K., Miyakawa, T., Yamaguchi, M., . . . Kageyama, R. (2008). Roles of continuous neurogenesis in the structural and functional integrity of the adult forebrain. *Nature Neuroscience, 11*, 1153–1161. doi:10.1038/nn.2185

Imel, Z. E., Malterer, M. B., McKay, K. M., & Wampold, B. E. (2008). A meta-analysis of psychotherapy and medication in unipolar depression and dysthymia. *Journal of Affective Disorders, 110*, 197–206. doi:10.1016/j.jad.2008.03.018

James, W. (1890). *The principles of psychology.* New York, NY: Henry Holt. doi:10.1037/11059-000

This is one of the seminal works of the great American psychologist who is well known for his writing about the psychology of religion and spirituality. Some of his ideas, like the difference between our experiences of I and me, are finding new empirical currency in neurophenomenological research.

Khalsa, S. B. S., Cohen, L., McCall, T., & Telles, S. (Eds.). (2016). *Principles and practice of yoga in health care*. Pencaitland, UK: Handspring.

This relatively comprehensive medical textbook on the use of Yoga in medicine and other healthcare disciplines became available as we prepared to go to press. The project was spearheaded by Sat Bir Singh Khalsa, PhD, an American-born researcher and assistant professor of medicine at Harvard Medical School. Also the director of research for the Kundalini Research Institute, research director for the Kripalu Center for Yoga & Health, and research associate at the Benson-Henry Institute for Mind Body Medicine, Khalsa is one of the most published researchers in his field. One of his primary collaborators, Shirley Telles, MBBS, PhD, is the most published researcher on Yoga. The book discusses clinical applications of Yoga but also provides very useful reviews of the research literature across a wide range of conditions, including mental health conditions. It is highly recommended for Yoga therapists, medical professionals, and other healthcare providers.

Khalsa, S. B. S. (with Gould, J.). (2012). *Your brain on yoga: A Harvard Medical School guide*. Boston, MA: Harvard University. (Electronic edition published 2012 by RosettaBooks, New York, NY)

Kosfeld, M., Heinrichs, M., Zak, P. J., Fischbacher, U., & Fehr, E. (2005). Oxytocin increases trust in humans. *Nature, 435*, 673–676. doi:10.1038/nature03701

Kovács, G. L., Sarnyai, Z., & Szabó, G. (1998). Oxytocin and addiction: A review. *Psychoneuroendocrinology, 23*, 945–962. doi:10.1016/S0306-4530(98)00064-X}

Lee, H. J., Macbeth, A. H., Pagani, J. H., & Young, W. S. (2009). Oxytocin: The great facilitator of life. *Progress in Neurobiology, 88*, 127–151. doi:10.1016/j.pneurobio.2009.04.001

Marazziti, D., Dell'Osso, B., Baroni, S., Mungai, F., Catena, M., Rucci, P., . . . Dell'Osso, L. (2006). A relationship between oxytocin and anxiety of romantic attachment. *Clinical Practice and Epidemiology in Mental Health, 2*(28). doi:10.1186/1745-0179-2-28

Marsh, A. A., Yu, H. H., Pine, D. S., & Blair, R. J. (2010). Oxytocin improves specific recognition of positive facial expressions. *Psychopharmacology, 209*, 225–232. doi:10.1007/s00213-010-1780-4

Micozzi, M. S. (Ed.). (2015). *Fundamentals of complementary and alternative medicine* (5th ed.). St. Louis, MO: Saunders.

Miller, E. K., & Cohen, J. D. (2001). An integrative theory of prefrontal cortex function. *Annual Review of Neuroscience, 24*, 167–202. doi:10.1146/annurev.neuro.24.1.167

Mu, Y., & Gage, F. H. (2011). Adult hippocampal neurogenesis and its role in Alzheimer's disease. *Molecular Neurodegeneration, 6*(85). doi:10.1186/1750-1326-6-85

Murphy, M., & Donovan, S. (1997). *The physical and psychological effects of meditation* (2nd ed.). E. Taylor (Ed.). Petaluma, CA: Institute of Noetic Sciences.
This comprehensive bibliography maintained by the Institute of Noetic Sciences (IONS) in California is continuously updated and has periodically appeared in print form. There is also an introductory online version (http://biblio.noetic.org).

Murphy, M. R., Seckl, J. R., Burton, S., Checkley, S. A., & Lightman, S. L. (1987). Changes in oxytocin and vasopressin secretion during sexual activity in men. *The Journal of Clinical Endocrinology and Metabolism, 65*, 738–741. doi:10.1210/jcem-65-4-738

Parker, S., Bharati, S. V., & Fernandez, M. (2013). Defining yoga-nidra: Traditional accounts, physiological research, and future directions. *International Journal of Yoga Therapy, 23*, 11–16. Retrieved from http://www.iayt.org

This article addresses research issues in the investigation of yoga-nidrā, arguing that the traditional textual definitions of yoga-nidrā imply measurable hypotheses for empirical investigation. It also gives a definition of levels of yoga-nidrā, which are based on Swāmī Veda Bhāratī's Yoga practice. These are measured by electroencephalogram (EEG) and are based on the instruction given to Bhāratī by his guru, Swāmī Rāma, who first demonstrated the state of yoga-nidrā under EEG measurement at the Menninger Foundation laboratory (see Green & Green, 1977, above).

Penfield, W., & Boldrey, E. (1937). Somatic motor and sensory representation in the cerebral cortex of man as studied by electrical stimulation. *Brain, 60*, 389–443. doi:10.1093/brain/60.4.389

This is the first graphic representation in the scientific literature of the sensory and motor functions of the cerebral cortex. Drawn according to the organs each function serves, it is a wonderful way to visualize how significant each function is relative to the others.

Radin, D. (2013). *Supernormal: Science, yoga, and the evidence for extraordinary psychic abilities*. New York, NY: Random House.

Radin presents a very interesting summary of empirical research, specifically on the vibhūtis discussed in the third chapter of the *Yoga-sūtra*. He approaches the topic not by seeking to study extraordinary practitioners, but by looking at the extent to which psychic potentials are present in ordinary people. The evidence is positive, strong, and solid. Radin is also able to demonstrate that these potentials become more evident with increasing practice in meditation. In addition to this, he reports some interesting experiments that support the notion of nonlocal quantum causality.

Raichle, M. E., MacLeod, A. M., Snyder, A. Z., Powers, W. J., Gusnard, D. A., & Shulman, G. L. (2001). A default mode of brain function. *Proceedings of the National Academy of Sciences of the United States of America, 98,* 676–682. doi:10.1073/pnas.98.2.676

Raichle, M. E., & Snyder, A. Z. (2007). A default mode of brain function: A brief history of an evolving idea. *NeuroImage, 37*, 1083–1090. doi:10.1016/j.neuroimage.2007.02.041
This article describes the origins of a line of neurophysiological inquiry into the parts of the brain that become quiet when the brain is doing an activity. This is a different direction than most of the field, which looks at the parts of the brain that are activated during an activity. This may have implications for identifying the neurological correlates of self-observation.

Reif, A., Schmitt, A., Fritzen, S., & Lesch, K.-P. (2007). Neurogenesis and schizophrenia: Dividing neurons in a divided mind? *European Archives of Psychiatry and Clinical Neuroscience, 257*, 290–299. doi:10.1007/s00406-007-0733-3

Reynolds, B. A., & Weiss, S. (1992). Generation of neurons and astrocytes from isolated cells of the adult mammalian central nervous system. *Science, 255*, 1707–1710. doi:10.1126/science.1553558

Rimmele, U., Hediger, K., Heinrichs, M., & Klaver, P. (2009). Oxytocin makes a face in memory familiar. *Journal of Neuroscience, 29*, 38–42. doi:10.1523/JNEUROSCI.4260-08.2009

Roazen, P. (1974). *Freud and his followers*. New York, NY: Knopf.

Sarno, J. E. (1981). Etiology of neck and back pain: An autonomic myoneuralgia? *The Journal of Nervous and Mental Disease, 169*, 55–59. Retrieved from http://journals.lww.com/jonmd/Pages/default.aspx

Sarno, J. E. (1998). *The mindbody prescription: Healing the body, healing the pain*. New York, NY: Hachette Book Group.
Based on his years as a physical medicine physician at New York University, Sarno was "banging the drum" about the psychosomatic nature of the majority of back pain complaints long before people cared much about mind/body medicine, and he has now been proven right by the evidence.

This book, introduced to me by a therapy client with a pain complaint, was instrumental in curing my own intense episode of back pain in 2008.

Sarno, J. E. (2006). *The divided mind: The epidemic of mindbody disorders.* New York, NY: HarperCollins.

This book by Sarno presents a detailed and research-based investigation of the psychosomatic formation of medical conditions.

Schlitz, M., & Braud, W. (1997). Distant intentionality and healing: Assessing the evidence. *Alternative Therapies in Health and Medicine, 3*(6), 62–73.

This study is a classic in quantum healing, demonstrating the measurability of positive nonlocal effects of various types of distant intentionality on healing, growth, and development, from praying for patients to simply thinking about grass seedlings growing in a laboratory.

Schmolesky, M. T., Webb, D. L., & Hansen, R. A. (2013). The effects of aerobic exercise intensity and duration on levels of brain-derived neurotrophic factor in healthy men. *Journal of Sports Science and Medicine, 12*, 502–511. Retrieved from http://www.jssm.org/

Selye, H. (1974). *Stress without distress: How to use stress as a positive force to achieve a rewarding lifestyle.* New York, NY: Signet.

Selye, H. (1978). *The stress of life: The famous classic—completely revised, expanded, and updated with new research findings* (Rev. ed.). New York, NY: McGraw Hill.

This title and the one above by Selye are the seminal treatises on the notion of stress and its effects on both physical and mental health.

Shapiro, F. (2001). *Eye movement desensitization and reprocessing (EMDR): Basic principles, protocols, and procedures* (2nd ed.). New York, NY: Guilford Press.

Siegel, D. J. (2007). *The mindful brain: Reflection and attunement in the cultivation of well-being* (1st ed.). New York, NY: Norton.

Siegel, D. (2010). *Mindsight.* New York, NY: Bantam Books.
This is an excellent and highly readable introduction to contemporary ideas about neuroplasticity and their applications in therapy. Siegel is plain spoken without sacrificing the level of detail necessary to convey these concepts and how they work. His developmental perspective is especially useful for those who work in the healing professions.

Siegel, D. (2012a). *The developing mind: How relationships and the brain interact to shape who we are* (2nd ed.). New York, NY: Guilford Press.
This is the latest edition of Siegel's text on brain development and its relationship to mind development. For those interested in the research details concerning interpersonal neurobiology, this is a great place to start.

Siegel, D. (2012b). *Pocket guide to interpersonal neurobiology: An integrative handbook of the mind.* New York, NY: Norton.
This book serves as a kind of dictionary of interpersonal neurobiology and as a guide to the details of the concept. It was instrumental in the writing of this book, and I also use it in my psychotherapy practice.

Sovik, R. (2000). The science of breathing—The yogic view. *Progress in Brain Research, 122*, 491–505. (PMID: 10737079)

Syvitski, J. P. M. (2012, March). Anthropocene: An epoch of our making. *Global Change Magazine, 78*. Retrieved from http://www.igbp.net

Telles, S., Singh, N., & Balkrishna, A. (2014). Role of respiration in mind-body practices: Concepts from contemporary science and traditional yoga texts. *Frontiers in Psychiatry, 5*, 167–168. doi:10.3389/fpsyt.2014.00167
This brief article begins to sketch the parameters of prāṇāyāma investigation, relating it to traditional textual sources. It is accompanied by many other studies that Telles has undertaken, mostly from the perspective of physiology. It does not investigate the electroencephalographic aspects of common prāṇāyāma practices, however. The Meditation Research Institute at Swāmī Rāma Sādhaka Grāma has just begun to design protocols for that exploration.

van Praag, H., Jacobs, B., & Gage, F. (2000). Depression and the birth and death of brain cells. *American Scientist, 88*, 340–345. doi:10.1511/2000.4.340

Walsh, R., & Shapiro, S. L. (2006). The meeting of meditative disciplines and western psychology: A mutually enriching dialogue. *American Psychologist, 61*, 227–239. doi:10.1037/0003-066X.61.3.227
This is an excellent review of the wide sweep of research on meditation, especially recent work.

Weiss, M., Baer, S., Allan, B., Saran, K., & Schibuk, H. (2011). The screen culture: Impact on ADHD. *Attention Deficit Hyperactivity Disorder, 3*, 327–334. doi:10.1007/s12402-011-0065-z
This is a literature review that, among other findings, describes the use of computer screens in the increasing incidence of ADHD and internet addiction.

Zeev-Wolf, M., Goldstein, A., Bonne, O., & Abramowitz, E. G. (2016). Hypnotically induced somatosensory alterations: Toward a neurophysiological understanding of hypnotic anesthesia. *Neuropsychologia, 87*, 182–191. doi:10.1016/j.neuropsychologia.2016.05.020
This article gives the reader an idea of how hypnoanesthesia works in terms of neurophysiology. Since hypnosis may be a specialized case of yoga-nidrā, this might also provide some clues about the neurophysiological correlates of the lighter stages of yoga-nidrā.

Appendix A

Exercises

The following exercises are organized into three sections: 1. for relaxing your mind/body and for accessing and cultivating your subtle body, 2. for deepening your awareness of your nāḍīs, cakras, and the transpersonal mindfield, and 3. for observing yourself and your relationships through journaling. The first two sections are provided in a summarized narrative form to teach the logic of the exercises' progression. With a bit of inference, you may expand these scripts to make a recording in your own voice to use in your practice. The material presented in Exercises 1.1, 1.3, and 1.4 is also available online by MP3 download as part of a recorded yoga-nidrā practice (http://www.cdbaby.com/cd/drstephenparkerstoma).

Section 1: Relaxation and Subtle Body Exercises

These relaxation exercises are part of a very detailed science in Yoga that is seldom written about in texts. It was preserved in the oral tradition of Yoga because the exercises were usually customized to the needs of individual students. These general forms are only examples of a vast number of practices that help in gaining awareness of the physical, prāṇik, and mental bodies and in gradually letting go of them, both in the sense of relaxation as well as in the sense of eventual disidentification with them. In these ways, they are also preparations for the practice of conscious deep sleep (yoga-nidrā) and the art of departing the body consciously.

Exercise 1.1 Basic Progressive Muscle Relaxation

This beginning exercise is a practice for relaxing the physical body. It is best practiced several hours after a meal. You might begin practicing in a quiet space, although as you get more skillful, you will gradually be able to relax anywhere. Some people use this for assistance in sleeping. If you are a person who experiences a lot of tension, this will work initially, but you may find with practice that this exercise actually leaves you feeling more awake at the end.

Lie on your back in *śavāsana,* "corpse posture" (see Figure A1.1 for modifications). Let your arms be separate from the body with the palms facing up. Your legs should be comfortably apart so that your hips can relax completely. Keep a thin pillow under your head, and feel free to cover your body with a light blanket or shawl. If you have problems with your knees or lower back, feel free to use a rolled blanket under your knees.

Systematically relax the muscles in your body from head to toe by feeling into the middle of any tightness you notice in the muscles until the muscles just let go. Begin with the top of your head and your forehead. As these muscles release and relax, feel into the muscles around your eyes and eyebrows. As your eyes and eyebrows relax, feel down into your cheeks and the corners of your mouth. As these let go, feel into the muscles at the corners of your jaw. Relax your neck, and feel down into your shoulders. Let them go. Feel down into your upper arms, then into your forearms, hands, fingers, and fingertips. Feel as if the breath is moving between the crown of your head and your fingertips for several breaths. Observe the flow of breath and prāṇa. Relax your fingertips, then your fingers, your hands, forearms, upper arms, and shoulders. Now feel down from your shoulders into the muscles in your chest. Release the tightness in your upper back and ribs, and feel down into your heart center in the center of your chest beneath the breastbone. Observe your breath flowing freely and deeply from the heart center for several breaths. Then feel into your navel region, observing the gentle rise and fall of your belly muscles, moving with the flow of breath and prāṇa. Feel down into your hip joints, and then down into your gluteal muscles, your thighs, your lower legs, feet, and toes.

Feel your whole body from head to toe, and breathe as if your whole body is breathing from head to toe for several breaths. Now, relax your toes, and feel back into your feet. Release your feet, and feel back into your lower legs. Relax your lower legs, and feel back into your thighs. Let your thighs go, and feel back into your gluteal muscles. Relax your gluteal muscles, and feel back into your hip joints. Continue to feel tension release in your body, moving back up the body: navel area, heart center, your whole chest, shoulders, shoulders down to your fingertips and back again, neck, jaw, cheeks, eyes and eyebrows, forehead, and the top of your head. When you are completely relaxed, let your breath flow from head to toe as you exhale, and from your toes to your head as you inhale. For a few minutes, feel the sweeping flow of cleansing and nourishing energy in the ceaseless ebb and flow of the wave of breath and prāṇa.

You can intensify the relaxation by deepening your awareness of exhalation and lengthening it, and by increasing the number of points of concentration. For example, you might include joints in addition to the muscles.

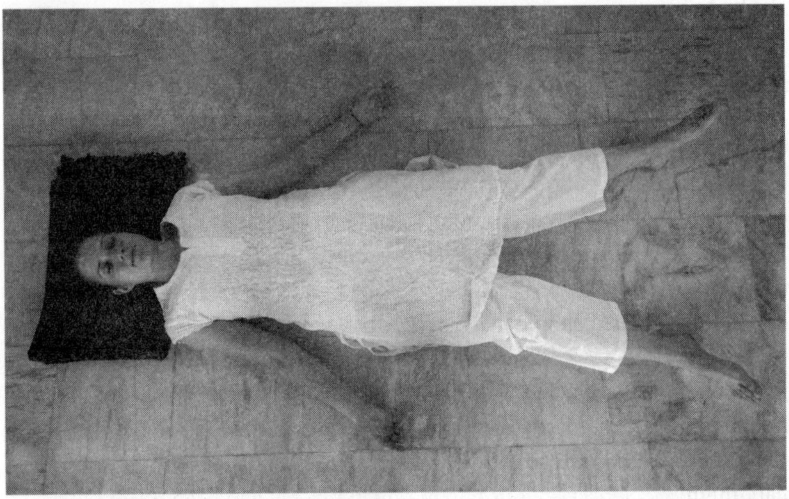

Figure A1.1. Śavāsana, the Corpse Posture. Let your arms be separate from the body with the palms facing up. Let your shoulders relax. Your legs should be comfortably apart so that your hips can relax completely. Keep a thin pillow under your head, and feel free to cover your body with a light blanket or shawl. If you have problems with your knees or lower back, try using a rolled blanket under your knees. If you are an expectant mother in your second or third trimester, you can modify this posture by lying on your left side with a pillow or folded blanket between the legs. Side-lying is also an option if lying on your back is uncomfortable for other reasons. If you are unable to lie on your back or side, feel free to prop yourself up with pillows or to rest in a comfortable chair.

Exercise 1.2 Tension Relaxation

This exercise is often thought of as an introductory practice for people who have trouble knowing how to relax a muscle. It does help with that, but it is also an advanced exercise for learning to differentiate one part of the subtle body from the rest for the purpose of learning to direct the movement of prāṇa. It is also part of the "exercise without movement" series that Swami Rama (1984a) taught. This exercise asks you to tense and relax the legs, the right and left sides of the body, the arms, and then the whole body. Throughout the exercise, keep the breath smooth, deep, and quiet. If the breath becomes disturbed or if your muscles begin to quiver, you are trying too hard and need to relax. Tension and relaxation should be applied slowly and gradually.

Make yourself comfortable in śavāsana (Figure A1.1), including covering the body if you like, using a thin pillow under your head and a folded blanket under your knees if you have knee or lower back problems. Withdraw your mind from all the space around you, and feel just the space your body occupies. Bring your mind back from all other time: back from the past in memory and back from anticipation for the future. Just feel the flow and the touch of your breath in your nostrils here and now. Then feel as if the breath is sweeping through the whole body, from head to toe and back.

Become aware of your right leg. Begin applying tension systematically from the toes, through the foot (pointing your toes), then into the ankle, calf, thigh, and gluteal muscles, adding tension in each muscle group intentionally. Hold the tension in the right leg (also feeling the relaxation on the left) for about 30 seconds. (It takes about 30 seconds for your nervous system to mindfully wire a positive feeling into your neural networks.) Then systematically relax the muscles in the same order in which you tensed them: toes, foot, ankle, calf, thigh, and gluteal muscles. Relax the right leg, and feel as if breath is moving through it, again for approximately 30 seconds. Now repeat the same process with the left leg. When you complete the tension–relaxation of the left leg, feel as if the breath is flowing through the entire leg for 30 seconds. Then repeat the entire exercise again on the right and then on the left. Finally, do the same exercise applying tension in both legs simultaneously and relaxing them together. Repeat this, too. When you finish, again feel as if the breath is moving through both legs, again for 30 seconds.

Now become aware of the right side of the body. Begin to apply tension simultaneously up the length of your right leg (as before) and your right arm. Let the back of the right hand rest on the mat with fingers extended as they tense. Gradually let the tension move up your body from your toes and fingers to your foot and hand, ankle and wrist, calf and forearm, thigh/gluteal muscles and upper arm/shoulder. When the whole right side is tensed (and the left side is completely relaxed), feel this for 30 seconds or so, and then gradually relax the tension in the same order as you applied it:

toes and fingers, foot and hand, ankle and wrist, calf and forearm, thigh/gluteal muscles and upper arm/shoulder. When you have completely relaxed the right side, feel the breath as if it is moving through the right side smoothly. Then repeat this process on the left side of the body. Take a few sweeping breaths as before, and repeat on each side of the body.

In the same way you did with your legs and feet, systematically tense and relax your arms on each side of the body. Starting with the right arm, keep the back of your hand on the mat, and extend your fingers as you tense your right hand. Let the tension creep gradually towards the shoulder. When the right side is completely tensed (and the left side is completely relaxed), feel this for about 30 seconds and then release. Do a few sweeping breaths, and then repeat on the opposite side. Repeat this exercise again on each side.

Finally, do the exercise with the whole body, tensing fingers and toes and gradually applying tension towards the core of the body. When your limbs are tensed, let the tension come into the body core, and finally tense all your facial muscles towards the tip of your nose. Hold the tension for about 30 seconds. Then systematically relax the body again, part by part. You can repeat the full body relaxation if you like. When you have finished, feel the breath sweeping through the body ten times before you exit the exercise.

There are a number of variations of this exercise that Swāmī Rāma taught to his disciples. To read how he taught this form, see Rama (1984a), *Exercise* Without *Movement, Manual One*, included in References.

Exercise 1.3 *Śava-Yātra,* "Journey of the Corpse":
31- or 61-Point Relaxation

This practice is traditionally performed to help one become more aware of the prāṇa-maya-koṣa, the body made of subtle energy, and the mano-maya-koṣa, the sheath of the sensory mind. It also enhances concentration. In this exercise, you will visualize a point of white light, like a star, at 31 or 61 points in your body. (The 31-point variation uses just the first 31 points in Table A1.3.) Try to move through the body at an even pace, pausing for a few seconds at each point. You can also move through the body by the numbers of the points if you prefer.

Begin by lying on your back in śavāsana, corpse posture (Figure A1.1). Relax your physical body using Exercise 1.1 above, Basic Progressive Muscle Relaxation. Feel the weight and solidity of the physical body against the floor,

Table A1.3
61 Points to Relax

1. Center of your forehead
2. Throat center (pit of your throat)
3. Right shoulder joint
4. Right elbow
5. Right wrist
6. Tip of your right thumb
7. Tip of your right index finger
8. Tip of your right middle finger
9. Tip of your right ring finger
10. Tip of your right small finger
11. Right wrist
12. Right elbow
13. Right shoulder joint
14. Throat center
15. Left shoulder joint
16. Left elbow
17. Left wrist
18. Tip of your left thumb
19. Tip of your left index finger
20. Tip of your left middle finger
21. Tip of your left ring finger
22. Tip of your left small finger
23. Left wrist
24. Left elbow
25. Left shoulder joint
26. Throat center
27. Heart center (between your breasts in the center of your chest)
28. Tip of your right nipple
29. Heart center
30. Tip of your left nipple
31. Heart center
32. Navel center
33. Perineum (halfway between your anus and your genitals)
34. Right hip joint
35. Right knee
36. Right ankle
37. Right small toe
38. Right fourth toe
39. Right middle toe
40. Right second toe
41. Right big toe
42. Right ankle
43. Right knee
44. Right hip joint
45. Perineum
46. Left hip joint
47. Left knee
48. Left ankle
49. Left small toe
50. Left fourth toe
51. Left middle toe
52. Left second toe
53. Left big toe
54. Left ankle
55. Left knee
56. Left hip joint
57. Perineum
58. Navel center
59. Heart center
60. Throat center
61. Center of your forehead

and feel the body sinking into the floor. Feel the breath flowing from head to toe for a few moments. Begin by bringing your attention to the center of your forehead and visualizing a point of white light, like a star. Then visualize a point of light in your throat center in the pit of your throat. Follow through the rest of the body in this way, using the order presented in Table A1.3.

Now feel all 61 points of light. Visualize yourself exhaling light through these points and inhaling light through these points. Experience yourself as a creature of light, exhaling and inhaling light. Enjoy this for as long as you like, keeping an intention to remain aware. Then begin again to feel the physical breath as a wave of breath and prāṇa flowing from head to toe through the entire body. Begin again to feel the weight and solidity of the physical body against the floor. Gently awaken the body as you would awaken your sleeping child, by softly moving your fingers and toes, moving your head from side to side. Feel free to give your body a nice stretch if you like.

Exercise 1.4 *Śithali-Karaṇa*, Point-to-Point Breathing

This exercise relaxes the subtle energy body (prāṇa-maya-koṣa), so it is best done after a preliminary progressive muscle relaxation (Exercise 1.1), which relaxes the physical body (anna-maya-koṣa). The intention of this exercise is to develop a mental habit of very deep conscious relaxation, so you don't want the mind to fall prey to its habit of lapsing into unconscious deep sleep. It is recommended that you not practice this exercise before sleep for that reason. Sometimes people experience a loss of contact with their surroundings, though they remain inwardly aware in deep concentration. If this happens to you and you lose outside contact, you may think you are sleeping. More likely, if your relaxation is sufficiently deep, you have experienced pratyāhāra, the sudden inward turning of the mindfield.

Lie on your back in śavāsana, "corpse posture" (Figure A1.1). Let your physical body be completely relaxed, and feel your body from inside, from head to toe. Feel the breath as if it is flowing from head to toe, exhaling from the crown of your head and inhaling from your toes for ten breaths. Now feel the flow of breath and prāṇa exhaling from the crown, inhaling from your ankles for ten breaths. Now feel the flow of breath and prāṇa exhaling from the crown, inhaling from your knees for ten breaths.

Now feel the flow of breath and prāṇa exhaling from the crown, inhaling from your perineum (halfway between your anus and your genitals) for five breaths. Now feel the flow of breath and prāṇa exhaling from the crown, inhaling from your navel center for five breaths. Now feel the flow of breath and prāṇa exhaling from the crown, inhaling from your heart center (between your breasts, beneath the breastbone) for five breaths. Now feel the flow of breath and prāṇa exhaling from the crown, inhaling from your throat center (in the pit of your throat) for five breaths.

Now feel the flow of breath and prāṇa exhaling from the center between your eyebrows and inhaling from the spot where your nose bridge meets your upper lip (*nāsāgra*) for five breaths.

Now feel the flow of breath and prāṇa exhaling from the crown, inhaling from your eyebrow center for five breaths. Now feel the flow of breath and prāṇa exhaling from the crown, inhaling from your throat center (in the pit of your throat) for five breaths. Now feel the flow of breath and prāṇa exhaling from the crown, inhaling from your heart center (between your breasts, beneath the breastbone) for five breaths. Now feel the flow of breath and prāṇa exhaling from the crown, inhaling from your navel center for five breaths. Now feel the flow of breath and prāṇa exhaling from the crown, inhaling from your perineum (halfway between your anus and your genitals) for five breaths.

Now feel the flow of breath and prāṇa exhaling from the crown, inhaling from your knees for ten breaths. Now feel the flow of breath and prāṇa exhaling from the crown, inhaling from your ankles for ten breaths. Now feel the flow of breath and prāṇa exhaling from the crown, inhaling from your toes for ten breaths.

Feel free to rest consciously in this exercise for as long as you like, but keep an intention not to fall asleep. Rather than simply opening your eyes, awaken the body gradually by moving fingers and toes, moving your head from side to side, and perhaps giving the body a nice stretch before you open your eyes.

Here is a summary of the exercise:

- Breathe, exhaling from the crown, inhaling from your toes ten times.
- Breathe, exhaling from the crown, inhaling from your ankles ten times.
- Breathe, exhaling from the crown, inhaling from your knees ten times.
- Breathe, exhaling from the crown, inhaling from your perineum five times.
- Breathe, exhaling from the crown, inhaling from your navel center five times.
- Breathe, exhaling from the crown, inhaling from your heart center five times.
- Breathe, exhaling from the crown, inhaling from your throat center five times.
- Breathe, exhaling from your eyebrow center, inhaling from the spot where your nose bridge meets your upper lip five times.
- Breathe, exhaling from the crown, inhaling from your eyebrow center five times.
- Breathe, exhaling from the crown, inhaling from your throat center five times.

- Breathe, exhaling from the crown, inhaling from your heart center five times.
- Breathe, exhaling from the crown, inhaling from your navel center five times.
- Breathe, exhaling from the crown, inhaling from your perineum five times.
- Breathe, exhaling from the crown, inhaling from your knees ten times.
- Breathe, exhaling from the crown, inhaling from your ankles ten times.
- Breathe, exhaling from the crown, inhaling from your toes ten times.
- Rather than simply opening your eyes, awaken the body gradually by moving fingers and toes, moving your head from side to side, and perhaps giving the body a nice stretch before you open your eyes.

Exercise 1.5 *Makarāsana,* the Crocodile Posture

Elevated levels of CO2 in our bloodstream contribute to feelings of anxiousness. One way to reduce anxiety significantly is simply to retrain your breath. An easy way to do this is a Yoga posture called *makarāsana*, the crocodile pose (Figure A1.5). This posture induces diaphragmatic breathing, which relieves anxiety by improving gas exchange in the lungs. Most people can practice this posture safely. However, do not practice the crocodile if you are more than three months pregnant, as soon as you are "showing," or if you have recently had abdominal surgery. Consult your health care provider before practicing this posture if you have an abdominal hernia or if you have any other concerns about its safety for your own mind/body.

In this posture, lie on the floor on your stomach with your legs apart, your hands resting on each upper arm, and your forehead resting on your (preferably, right) forearm. Your feet can be turned in or out depending on what is more comfortable for your body. You should be able to relax your shoulders, hips, and the rest of your body completely. Feel the pressure of your abdominal muscles on the floor and the rising and falling of the small of your back as you breathe. In this posture, with your elbows raised above your shoulders, your chest muscles cannot move your chest, and so you have no choice but to breathe with your diaphragm, abdominal muscles, and the muscles of your lower, floating ribs. There is no need to make an effort to breathe correctly in this posture. Simply observe your body breathing in this position for ten to fifteen minutes. If you have problems with severe anxiety and panic, the physical structure of this posture forces you to breathe correctly and can sometimes be a powerful physiological intervention. If used for this purpose, extend the time as long as you need to in order to feel the panic receding. If you feel claustrophobic with your head resting on your forearms, feel free to use your fists one over the other to raise your face a bit further from the floor.

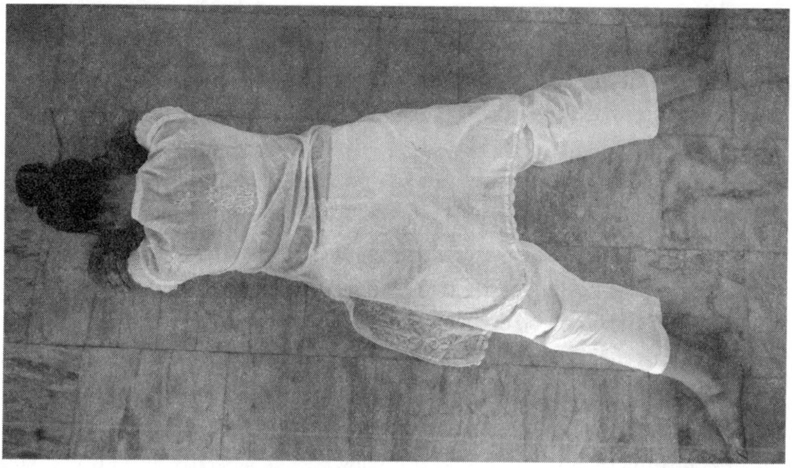

Figure A1.5. Makarāsana, the Crocodile Posture. Do not practice this posture if you are more than three months pregnant (or as soon as you are "showing") or if you have recently had abdominal surgery. Consult your health care provider first if you have an abdominal hernia (in the belly or groin) or any other concerns about this posture's safety for your own mind/body.

Section 2: Exercises for Awareness of Nāḍīs, Cakras, and the Transpersonal Mindfield

These exercises are helpful in developing an initial meditative awareness of the three principal nāḍīs, your cakras, citta, and how they all operate. Nāḍī-śodhana is a particularly powerful prāṇāyāma exercise that helps to relax and center the mind/body very efficiently. Practiced regularly for a long time, it also helps to modulate your emotional reactivity and may help in dealing with trauma. The cakra exercises help you to understand what is happening as the cakras are activated in meditation and can assist you in tracking the relationship between the activity of your cakras and your emotional life. The exercises on meditation and prayer are intended to support your expanding awareness of your connection with other people through the transpersonal mindfield.

Exercise 2.1 *Nāḍī-Śodhana (Anuloma-Viloma)*, Alternate Nostril Breathing

Alternate nostril breathing, also known as *anuloma-viloma* or *nāḍī-śodhana*, "channel purification," is a breathing practice of prāṇāyāma and is one of the most powerful initial Yoga exercises for centering your attention and deepening relaxation. Because this exercise alternately stimulates the contralateral cerebral hemispheres, it balances the influences of each and enhances communication between the hemispheres across the corpus callosum, which connects them. Over a long period of practice, nāḍī-śodhana thus substantially moderates emotional reactivity. In prāṇik terms, it purifies the nāḍīs (energy channels) of the energy body (prāṇa-maya-koṣa) by eliminating knots and warps caused by emotional disturbances.

This exercise is usually performed after āsanas and relaxation and just prior to meditation. It should be done on an empty stomach at least two hours after one's previous meal. It is best done before rather than after meals.

Sit with the head, neck, and trunk aligned in a stable sitting posture. Let the breath become smooth, deep, even, and as pauseless as possible. Form your fingers into *Viṣṇu-mudrā* by placing the tips of your index and middle fingers on the muscle below your thumb. In this position, you can alternately open and close your nostrils with a slight movement using your thumb and ring finger (see Figure A2.1a below). An alternate hand position is to place those same fingers between the eyebrows (Figure A2.1b), which also leaves your thumb and ring finger free to operate your nostrils. When opening and closing the nostrils, let the tips of your fingers rest just below the end of the nasal bone about halfway up your nose. This makes it easy to close and open the nostrils with minimum distortion to the shape of your nasal passages. As you do the exercise, keep the breath flowing smoothly and quietly. Avoid creating any suspension of the breath (sahita-kumbhaka) until the spontaneous suspension (sahaja-kumbhaka) has begun to occur regularly in your meditation. This usually occurs after a number of years of regular practice.

There are many different patterns for alternate nostril breathing (96 in all). Table A2.1a below suggests the pattern for beginning practice. The exercise always begins by exhaling through the active nostril. You can place your fingers below your nostrils or just feel the flow of breath in them to determine which is flowing more freely.

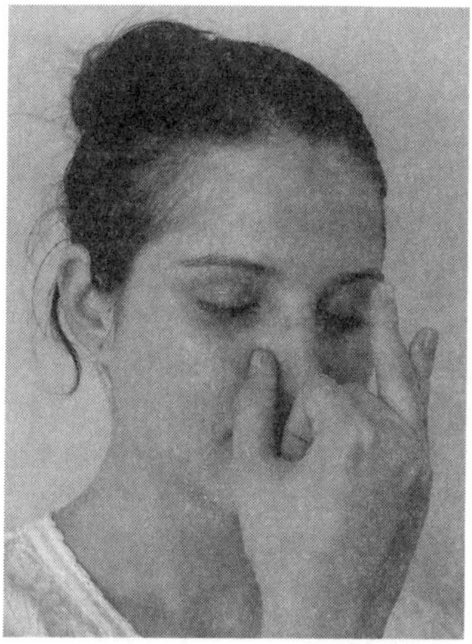

Figure A2.1a. Viṣṇu-Mudrā. Place the tips of your index and middle fingers on the muscle below your thumb to alternately open and close your nostrils using the thumb and ring finger. Let the tips of your fingers rest just below the end of the nasal bone about halfway up your nose, which will allow you to close and open the nostrils with minimum distortion to the shape of your nasal passages.

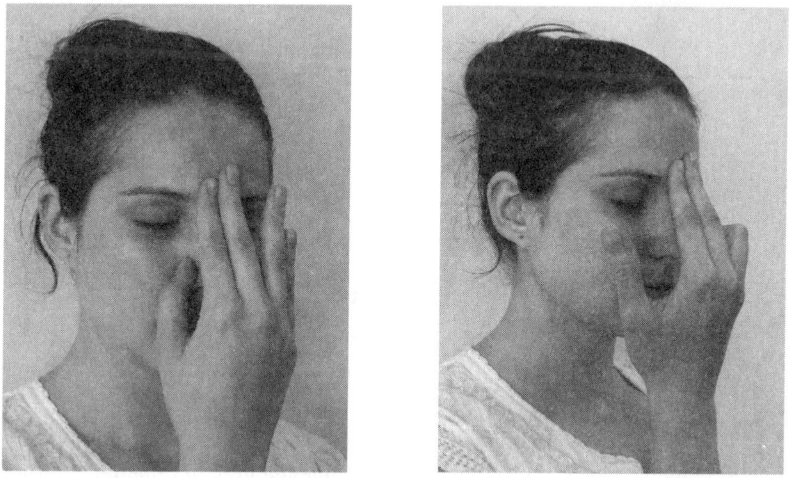

Figure A2.1b. Alternative Mudrā, Fingers Between Eyebrows. Place the tips of your index and middle fingers between the eyebrows. This leaves your thumb and ring finger free to operate your nostrils. Let the tips of your fingers rest just below the end of the nasal bone about halfway up your nose, which will allow you to close and open the nostrils with minimum distortion to the shape of your nasal passages.

Table A2.1a

Alternate Nostril Breathing: Beginning Practice

Exhale	Inhale
Active	Passive
Active	Passive
Active	Passive
Passive	Active
Passive	Active
Passive	Active

Note. This table represents one unit of exercise. A full practice includes three units and alternates the starting nostril each time for a total of 36 breaths. Between units, exhale and inhale three times through both nostrils.

As noted above, Table A2.1a represents one unit of the exercise. Between units, exhale and inhale three times through both nostrils. The usual recommendation is that you practice three units, alternating the starting nostril each time, for a total of 36 breaths, with the exhalation and inhalation each counted as distinct breaths. This takes 5–10 minutes to complete. (The first unit begins by exhaling through the active nostril, the second unit begins by exhaling through the passive nostril, and the third unit begins, again, by exhaling through the active nostril.) When this pattern is quite familiar and natural to you, feel free to continue the pattern, and complete three sets of three units (108 breaths). The second set of three units begins with an exhalation through the passive nostril, and the third set of three units returns to beginning with an exhalation through the active nostril (see Table A2.1b). This takes between 30 and 45 minutes to complete, as the breath will likely slow down as you continue. Nāḍī-śodhana is a very good way to quickly reach a state of profound mental and physical stillness. Done twice a day, it is potent medicine for acute emotional disturbance, especially for those with serious mood disorders. As your concentration improves, try to eliminate the use of your fingers, and change the flow of breath mentally.

Table A2.1b
Alternate Nostril Breathing: 108 Breaths

Exhale	Inhale	Repetitions
Active	**Passive**	**3x (Set 1, Unit 1)**
Passive	Active	3x
Passive	Active	3x (Set 1, Unit 2)
Active	Passive	3x
Active	Passive	3x (Set 1, Unit 3)
Passive	Active	3x
		= 36 breaths
Passive	**Active**	**3x (Set 2, Unit 1)**
Active	Passive	3x
Active	Passive	3x (Set 2, Unit 2)
Passive	Active	3x
Passive	Active	3x (Set 2, Unit 3)
Active	Passive	3x
		= 72 breaths
Active	**Passive**	**3x (Set 3, Unit 1)**
Passive	Active	3x
Passive	Active	3x (Set 3, Unit 2)
Active	Passive	3x
Active	Passive	3x (Set 3, Unit 3)
Passive	Active	3x
		= 108 breaths

Note. 3x = 3 times. Remember to exhale and inhale through both nostrils 3 times between each unit.

Table A2.2

Cakra Locations and Their Mantra Recitation and Pronunciation, Element, Shape, and Color

Cakra	Approximate Location	Elemental Mantra	Mantra Pronunciation	Element	Shape	Color
Mūlādhāra-cakra	Perineum, between anus and genitals	*Laṁ*	"Lum"	Earth	Square	Red-orange
Svādhiṣṭhāna-cakra	Genitals	*Vaṁ*	"Vum"	Water	Crescent moon	White
Maṇipūra-cakra	Around navel	*Raṁ*	"Rum"	Fire	Upward-pointing triangle	Red
Anāhata-cakra	Center of chest	*Yaṁ*	"Yum"	Air	Hexagon	Smokey grey
Viśuddha-cakra	Center of throat	*Haṁ*	"Hum"	Space	Full moon	Deep azure, as in the night sky with a white moon
Ājñā-cakra	Between eyebrows	*Oṁ*	"Aum"	Mind	Still flame	Crystal clear

Note. It is common to feel activity only in the cakras that are most active. The sahasrāra, sometimes referred to as the seventh cakra, is not included on this list because it is not a cakra in the same sense as the lower six. It is typically only accessible meditatively to very advanced practitioners.

Exercise 2.2 Mantra Practice to Experience Your Cakras

This exercise will give you an initial sense of the field of operation (kṣetra) of the cakras in your body and a sense of which cakras are most active. This varies from person to person, and the activity of the elements in the cakras follows a regular progression through the day. For more information on this topic, see Rama (1988) and Muktibodhananda (1999). While activity doesn't imply imbalance, it certainly can point to personality strengths, especially in the three higher cakras: anāhata, viśuddha, and ājñā. For a review of the cakra functions and their relationship to the primary fountains, refer to Table 7.2 on p. 146. When I have done this exercise with groups, almost everyone feels something somewhere, and very few feel something in every location.

Lie on your back in śavāsana (Figure A1.1). Keep a thin pillow under your head, and feel free to cover your body with a light blanket or shawl. If you have problems with your knees or lower back, feel free to use a rolled blanket under your knees. Systematically relax the muscles in your body from head to toe as you would in an ordinary progressive muscle relaxation exercise (see Exercise 1.1). When you are completely relaxed, let your breath flow from head to toe as you exhale and from your toes to your head as you inhale. For a few minutes, feel the sweeping flow of cleansing and nourishing energy in the ceaseless ebb and flow of the wave of breath and prāṇa.

Then, when you are ready to begin, focus your awareness in the region of your perineum, midway between your anus and genitals. As you sense this space in your body, mentally repeat the syllable *laṁ* (pronounced "lum"), the mantra for the earth element, on both the inhalation and the exhalation. If you need a visual stimulus, visualize a square colored red-orange. See where you feel any sensation of subtle tingling or heat. There is no set duration for this exploration; stay long enough to feel something or to be clear that you do not. Next, focus in the general region of your genitals, and as you sense this space, mentally repeat the syllable *vaṁ* (pronounced "vum"), the seed sound for the element water. Visualize a white crescent moon. Again, see where you sense any subtle tingling or heat. Repeat this procedure by moving progressively from one cakra to the next. Table A2.2 includes the body locations, mantra recitations and pronunciations, colors, and shapes for each cakra.

Exercise 2.3 Breathing on a Mirror to Determine the Active Elements in your Cakras

Another way to monitor the activity of the cakras in your moment-to-moment mental functioning comes from the svara science of subtle energy rhythms in the prāṇa-maya-koṣa. Different aspects of any cakra may be active in a given person in the process of gradually working towards all the cakras' inward opening.[1] Activity depends on the precise nature of the knots in one's cakras and nāḍīs due to emotional disturbance and also on one's

[1] There is a lot of questionable teaching about "opening" cakras. Opening them in terms of their outward functions turns practitioners away from the awakening of Kuṇḍalinī. However, containing the outward expression of the energy of the cakra and rechanneling it into the suṣumnā current facilitates a cakra's inward opening towards awakening. For example, the second cakra opens when a person has achieved a comfortable celibacy.

practices, particularly mantra practices. Each petal of each cakra carries a subtle vibration of one letter of the Sanskrit alphabet whose vibrational energy is part of the activity of that cakra. The activity of cakras may—and probably should—shift over a lifetime.

You can deduce which elements operating in the cakras are active in your breath by placing a small mirror about 2 in. (5–6 cm) beneath your nostrils as you breathe out. As the condensation from your breath evaporates, you will notice the moisture pattern of your breath resolving into a geometric shape. Table A2.3 below illustrates which shapes correspond to which active cakras.

Table A2.3
Shapes and Their Active Element/Cakra

Shape	Element	Cakra
Square	Earth	Mūlādhāra-cakra
Crescent moon	Water	Svādhiṣṭhāna-cakra
Triangle	Fire	Maṇipūra-cakra
Hexagon	Air	Anāhata-cakra
Circle or shapeless cloud with dots in it	Space	Viśuddha-cakra

Exercise 2.4 Mantra Meditation

Mantra practice is central to the Himalayan tradition of Yoga meditation and to many other traditions as well. For example, this method is the same one used by Orthodox Christian practitioners of hesychasm with the Jesus prayer, "Lord Jesus Christ have mercy upon me, a sinner." The method is described in the beautiful spiritual classic *The Way of a Pilgrim* (Harvey, 2001) by an unknown author of the nineteenth century.

After settling on your seat with your head, neck, and trunk aligned, withdraw your mind from all other space and time. Feel the breath flowing in your nostrils. Allow your breath to flow. Systematically relax the body, the breath, and the mind. As you move towards inner stillness, feel the breath as if it were sweeping through the whole body for a few moments. Then, when that flow is well established, feel the flow between your navel and your nostrils. Listen within for so *'ham* (*ham* with the exhaling breath, *so* with the inhaling breath), your personal mantra, or a divine name that is close to your heart. If you are not religious, you can simply count the breath, one to five and back. Allow the mantra to arise in your mind in whatever way is easy and natural. Allow the mantra to flow with your breath and your mind, leading your mind inward in meditation towards an experience of the silent presence of the mantra. Continue the practice as long as it is comfortable. Even two minutes can create a noticeable shift in your mood.

Exercise 2.5 Prayers of Loving Intention

Praying for someone is very simple and straightforward. In the transpersonal, inner depths of the mindfield, where words are relatively external, the mindfield doesn't function with words, but with the subtle vibrations that characterize, for example, the deeper levels of mantra japa. Swāmī Veda often explained that when he prayed for someone, he simply held an image of the person in his mind with a concentrated, nonverbal loving intention.

If it helps, you might use a visual intention to wrap the person in the Guru's meditation shawl or just wrap him or her in a shawl of healing light. You could also repeat some of the verbal intentions for loving kindness from the Buddhist practice of metta (maitri) meditation, for example, "May you be safe and secure. May you experience ease of well-being." Or feel free to create your own. (In this practice, these intentions traditionally begin with oneself, extend to a dear loved one, and then to a friend, a neutral person, a challenging person, and to all sentient beings. However, you can focus on just one individual if you wish.) In using these verbal cues, it is not the words themselves that are effective, but the feeling (bhāvanā) and the concentration that they evoke. These exert an effect on others nonlocally that is actually measurable (Schlitz and Braud, 1997).

Exercise 2.6 Tonglen Meditation

Another practice, mentioned in the first pages of this book, is Tonglen meditation from the Tibetan Buddhist tradition. In this practice, you take in the suffering energy in the world around you with the inhaling breath and offer friendliness (*maitri* in Sanskrit, *metta* in Pāli), compassion, joy, and well-being with the exhaling breath. This is a valuable practice, but be aware that until you have already substantially clarified your mindfield, the suffering energies you absorb from the world around you may make you physically or mentally ill. People often asked Swāmī Rāma about how to do healing. He would often say that it is easy to take the suffering of others on yourself, but knowing what to do with that suffering energy so that you don't get sick is a much harder task. Thus, the loving kindness meditation and prayer form in Exercise 2.5 above are recommended until a trusted spiritual guide suggests you are ready for Tonglen.

Section 3: Journaling Exercises

In the process of developing a dialogue with your mind, you may find it useful to work in various ways in a diary or journal. The following are some possible formats for various kinds of experiments. Many of the observations and questions are expressed in tabular form for the sake of this book. Feel free to arrange them and play with them in any way that you find useful on your own path.

Exercise 3.1 Investigating Emotional Patterns Using the Four Components of Emotion: Sensation, Cognition, Motivation, and Saṁskāra

Here you turn your awareness to the four components of emotion whenever an emotion catches your attention. Tracking these in a journal, you may uncover patterns in how your emotions influence your daily life and in how you tend towards certain emotions over time. You may notice positive patterns, such as gratitude and contentment, as well as some of the patterns described in Chapter 8 on journaling and inner dialogue: "What if?" (panic); "If only I'd done *x*, then I'd be okay." (depression); "That's awful-disastrous-catastrophic-terrible-horrible!" (anxiety); "You (*your favorite self-accusation*)!" (shame); and so forth. Your emotions will tell you stories that may or may not always be accurate. These patterns, rather than pointing to the absolute truth of your experience, will nevertheless have something important to tell you or to teach you, often about your basic needs and whether or how well they are being fulfilled.

In this practice, you first tune into your breath and body sensations to provide an "anchor" or a "home base" from which to observe your arising emotion(s). You then track the relationships between how you feel at a given point in time, how your belief(s) are shaping your emotion(s), and how the primary fountain(s) are motivating each. You consider whether and how accurately your belief(s) seem to reflect reality. (Remember "the work" of Byron Katie from Chapter 8.) You ask yourself whether the strength of your emotional response seems proportionate to its stimulus, and you reflect on whether the action suggested by the emotion is skillful. You then decide whether it makes sense to act in that way. If so, proceed. If not, what would be a more skillful action? A more realistic perspective? A more appropriate degree of emotion?

Note that the idea is not to artificially cover over your emotional reactions in any moment, but to see them clearly. In the case of suffering, we acknowledge our pain to manage it within ourselves, act constructively, and let it go—without internalizing it or unloading it onto others. For example, when our emotional response is disproportionate to the facts of a situation, we may become aware of this and choose an appropriate behavioral response. Meanwhile, however, the emotions may continue to bubble up or to seethe under the surface. (Most of us know the phrase *suck it up* and have perhaps responded to a coworker or a family member in a way that we think we "should" rather than in a way that expresses our true needs and feelings.) Often we cannot act out our raw emotions, so to prevent suppressing them, we can acknowledge all their components: sensation, cognition, motivation, and saṁskāra. By experiencing the fullness of an emotion, we can truly convince ourselves of, and make peace with, our response to it.

In this process, it is easy to get caught up in our "story," to allow the cognitive component of emotion to dominate. This includes our interpretation of why a situation is as it is; what it means; how we think it reflects a trait of ourselves or the other person, group, or culture; or how other scenarios seem to relate to or affirm this one. The list could go on. These last two thought patterns are instances of global thinking, and they make us feel good when they relate to positive interpretations and bad when they describe negative ones. In either case, these patterns usually are not realistic, and they reinforce the neural networks that represent them in our brain-nervous-system-body-mind.

To rewire our personality's emotional habit patterns, we must interrupt them. This means disrupting all their components. To this end,

1. Instead of latching onto our story (cognition), we latch onto our awareness. We intentionally tune into our breath (sensation) to slow

the story down.

2. We feel what is going on in our body (sensation), and we attempt to relax the tension patterns that accompany the thoughts. (This is one reason the relaxation training of the first section of this appendix is so important. Each emotional pattern carries with it its own pattern of bodily tension—these are our "postures in life," from Chapter 6. The more we practice body awareness and relaxation, whether by lying on the floor or by moving about in the world, the more easily we can access and alter our sensations during challenging situations. We can thus affect change in the emotion in which our physical tension plays a part.)
3. We allow ourselves to feel the desire(s) that stem from our motivation(s)—hunger, anger, loneliness, tiredness, or food, sleep, sex, self-preservation. These are life-giving to the body when provided in a balanced way (e.g., the middle path of Buddhism). How can we meet our underlying need(s) healthfully?
4. Awareness of the above alters our habitual response (saṁskāra) because awareness itself is incompatible with unconscious, preprogrammed neural behavior.

In this practice, we distinguish between watching a saṁskāra and reinforcing it. As we watch, awareness automatically helps us get our footing back, to step onto more stable emotional ground. When we see our usual story (cognition) reassert itself, it does so in a weakened way because from a more relaxed mind/body (sensation), we are less affected by the neural habit that uses for its fuel the whole tensed-up brain-nervous-system-body-mind pattern. We are thus able to look at a saṁskāra from a new perspective, helping us to revise our motivation in turn.

For example, I once worked somewhere that experienced a serious organizational problem that resulted in a lot of strong emotions and reactivity on the part of everyone involved. When a similar situation arose a few years later, I was in a much better place in terms of my own mindfulness. Rather than react impulsively, I became aware of a familiar feeling of anger arising within me, tuned into my body sensations, relaxed my muscles, and focused on my breath. The sensation of my breath in my more relaxed body became an anchor that stabilized me to explore the anger, rather than to be carried away by it. I could see the emotion within me and knew that it was a realistic response to what had happened both personally and organizationally. I began to examine my beliefs about what should happen to correct the situation, and this allowed me to test in my imagination whether acting on my anger would be constructive in solving the problem. The answer was clearly "no," and suddenly the momentum of the old pattern simply evaporated. This contributed to a more successful resolution with a lot less drama.

In another example, one of my clients had a very psychologically based depression. (That is, his depression was rooted primarily in his thinking, rather than in his biology, even if the repetition of his thoughts had come to alter his biology.) Every week he would begin to tell his tale of woe and begin to cry, and I would start to think about my grocery list. This is usually a sign to me that people are not taking their pain seriously. In cases like these, it may seem that my resonance circuits have temporarily gone offline. But actually I *am* resonating with these clients: They want to appear to want to change when they really don't. I resonate in turn by not wanting to help either! When I recognize this, the compassionate action becomes to find a way to address this with the client. (This phenomenon is tough to acknowledge in our own lives, but the next time you feel that you are not being understood or helped, ask yourself if you are also trying to help yourself. You may find that sometimes your frustrations are justified, while at other times they are less so.) After a few sessions of this, I told my client that I thought his tears were an effort to get me to take care of him rather than to help him change, and he agreed with that. The next week the session began the same way. He began telling his tale of woe, his head dropped as usual, and tears began to fall on his shoes. But then he looked up to see if I was watching, and he met my eyes with a look of, "Caught me!" My face said, "Gotcha!!" And we both howled with laughter. We laughed for five minutes. He caught himself doing the dance of his saṁskāra. This awareness takes some experience to get to on one's own, but we are all capable of it.

Depending on our individual make-up and awareness, we might find that one of the four components of emotion is easier to access than the others. That's okay. We can begin this intervention from any of the four components, as they inevitably lead to the others. Often, the cognitive approaches work best for the in-the-moment work that we do on our own. Just remember to relax your mind/body as you examine your thoughts. You can do this by simply taking a few deep breaths. There's a familiar saying, *Don't believe everything you hear*. A saying in meditation circles is, *Don't believe everything you think*. And don't believe that you are your thoughts. The idea is to question your thoughts, to take a step back to gain perspective.

Let's summarize this exercise with one last example:

- You might observe in yourself feelings of a flushed face, racing heart, and a desire to punch somebody. You conclude that you must be angry (sensation). If you know that you're angry, but your physical sensations are vague, don't worry. Go to the next step.
- Slow your breathing down (sensation). We can all do this. Relax the tension in your body as best you can (sensation, again).
- Okay, what does your anger refer to? You have already begun to introduce some perspective because you have inserted mindful awareness into the anger pattern.
- You now know what you are angry about. And you have started to prepare yourself to look at it objectively. You can ask what you believe about the situation that helps you to feel that way (cognition).
- "This other person should do *x*!" What does that tell you about what you want or need in the situation (motivation)?
- How have you responded to that want or need in the past? Does it make sense in the present (saṁskāra)?
- Depending on how you decide to act on the emotion, how do you feel now? Is it better? How much better? How does your body feel? What happened to your anger?
- Dwell on the positive consequences for 30 seconds or so to integrate them into your neural networks.

During an acutely emotional situation and over time, this process creates a new, more positive story (i.e., a brighter saṁskāra). Beyond this, we can even shift our awareness away from the four components of emotion (still a story) and notice the awareness itself that is noticing the components. This last practice teaches us to rest in pure awareness and is said to be a gateway into enlightenment. Table A3.1 provides a sample template for tracking these responses in your emotional life.

Table A3.1
Tracking Emotional Patterns Using the Four Components of Emotion

Emotion	
Event to Which It Refers	
SENSATION: What is the quality of my breath (e.g., shallow, deep, short, smooth, fast, slow, as if I am gasping for air)?	
How does my body feel (e.g., hot, clammy, tight, choked up, nauseated, amped up, lethargic, at ease)?	
Where does my body feel this way (e.g., at the eyes, throat, neck, shoulders, heart, stomach, back, skin, in particular joints, throughout)?	
How do these sensations change, if at all, as I deepen my breath?	
COGNITION: What beliefs do I have that help me feel the way I do?	
Are these beliefs true? If not, what perspective could I take that might reflect the situation more accurately?	
MOTIVATION: Which primary fountain(s) might be involved (food, sleep, sex, and/or self-preservation)?	
How can I meet these needs appropriately (in balance)?	
Is the intensity of this emotion appropriate, given the above facts of the situation? If not, what intensity would be more appropriate?	
SAṀSKĀRA: How have I acted on this emotion in the past? Does it make sense to act in that way now? Why or why not?	
If not, what other action would be more skillful and why?	
How do I feel now that I have acted?	
If I feel an improvement in my emotional state, what is my experience when I dwell on this feeling for at least 30 seconds?	
What have I learned about one of my emotional tendencies?	

Exercise 3.2 Tracking Rhythms in the Breath

In this exercise, you correlate nostril activity with the activity of the subtle elements in the cakras, with your emotions, and with the motivations for action that your desires provide. Note the time of day and the nostril(s) that are active. Then take a small mirror, and hold it about two inches under your nostrils. Exhale on the mirror, and watch as the moisture evaporates. Notice which geometric shape seems to form: square (earth element), crescent (water), upward triangle (fire), hexagon (air), or diffuse cloud with spots (space). By comparing the activity of the nostrils and the elements with your activity, you can evaluate the ways in which you are acting in harmony with those rhythms and the ways in which you may be in conflict with them. To review the correlation of elements and their activities, refer to Table 7.2 on p. 146. When these are in harmony, your activities seem to flow; when they are in conflict, your activities may feel like a struggle and make you relatively inefficient. This is a way to know "what comes naturally" and

Table A3.2
Tracking the Correlation Between Breath Rhythms and Daily Activities

Time of Day	
Active Nostril	
Elemental Shape	
Element/Cakra	
Emotion	
What am I doing when this nostril is active?	
Is my current activity in harmony with my active element and cakra?	
If not, what could I do instead?	
Motivation and Desired Action (from Four Fountains)	
Are my motivation and desired action in harmony with my active element and cakra?	
If not, what could I do instead?	

to learn to follow the flow of prāṇa. For example, in writing this book, I learned only to write when my left nostril was flowing. If I wrote when the right was active, it was a struggle. Conversely, in editing the book, I waited until the right nostril was open. Table A3.2 provides a model that you might follow as you track these rhythms in yourself.

Exercise 3.3 Tracking Emotional Responses in Āsana Practice

In Chapter 6 on āsana, we discussed how the physical body is a concrete representation of our emotional habits and how we have acted upon them in the past. The chapter described ways in which the body stores emotions in muscle and connective tissue as well as in the brain and nervous system. This journaling exercise asks you to keep a log of your awareness and emotional releases that occur in the practice of āsana (see Table A3.3). In this way, you can begin to inquire into them (ātma-vicāra) and make better decisions about how to act on them in the future as you gradually create your new body/mind.

Table A3.3
Tracking Emotional Responses to Āsana

Āsana	
Time Held	
Sensations Noted	
State of Breath	
Images	
Thoughts	
Memories	
Emotions	
Cakra Implicated	
Changes Over Time	

Exercise 3.4 A Daily Journal of Beauty, Joy, and Wonder

Sometimes one needs to intentionally retrain his or her talented critical mind when it has lost the ability to see what is good and beautiful in life. To do this yourself, carry a notebook with you and note at least once each day something that gives you a sense of beauty, joy, or wonder. Feel free to make more than one entry. Refrain from judging how significant or trivial it seems to be. Just sense its beauty. As you build up a habit of doing this, you will find it much harder to look at your life and say that there is nothing good or beautiful in it. When a person is struggling with depression, this can be lifesaving—because if one knows where to find beauty, it is harder to become utterly hopeless.

Another method along these lines is to keep a journal of gratitude. At the end of each day, note at least one thing that you feel grateful for. Again, it doesn't matter how small. Over time this record of gratitude is something that can help you to remember positive aspects of yourself and your life and help you to prolong your positive emotions.

Exercise 3.5 Journaling About the Relationship Between Emotions and Food

Humans are genetically programmed eating machines. We are wired to store up food for times of scarcity, something that rarely exists for most of us in modern society. For the vast majority of the 400,000 years of our evolutionary history, however, food scarcity was a common experience. In our modern times of relative abundance, we encounter a great deal of difficulty when we try to redirect this genetic programming based on the primary drive for food. Most of this struggle concerns the ways we turn to food to meet other (emotional) needs. The journal exercise in Table A3.5 can help you to sort out your emotional food habits. You might choose to journal when you feel an impulse to eat, or you might journal at set times during the day. Over time you will get a sense of your habits, and this will help you, step by step, to develop a long-term strategy for how to deal with emotionally driven food cravings. Once these quiet down, you may find that you taste your food differently!

Table A3.5
Tracking Emotions and Eating Habits

Date & Time of Impulse to Eat	
What do I crave? (An experience, e.g., to crunch, or a specific food, e.g., chocolate?)	
What is happening around me?	
What do I feel physically? What are the sensations?	
Am I Hungry? Angry? Lonely? Tired? How are the primary fountains involved?	
What does my self (inner child) really need?	
What would genuinely meet that need?	
What did I do, or what will I do, to meet that need?	
Am I truly physically hungry and in need of nourishment? If so, what healthy food option could satisfy my craving for a particular food experience, noted above? Could I also enjoy the less healthy option I desire in a small portion?	
How do I feel now that I have acted?	

Exercise 3.6 Journaling About the Relationship Between the Primary Fountains and Sexual Impulses

Like food, we often turn to sex for a dopamine reward (excitement rush) to try to meet other important emotional needs. Sex can serve any emotional agenda: to express love, hatred, revenge, self-esteem, greed. Understanding your own patterns in this regard can help you to gradually move your sexuality in a more loving and joyful direction, so that you can play sexually when your real intention is to celebrate loving someone or you genuinely want to reproduce or you just want to enjoy a lover's intimate company.

Table A3.6
Tracking Primary Fountain Needs and Sexual Impulses

Date & Time of Sexual Impulse	
What is happening at this moment?	
How do I feel about it physically?	
Am I Hungry? Angry? Lonely? Tired? How are the primary fountains involved?	
What does my emotional state suggest about what I (my inner child) really need? (Maybe it's a sexual experience, and maybe it isn't.)	
What could I do to really meet that need?	
Did I do that? Or what stopped me?	
How do I feel now that I have acted?	

(Or, if another need is underlying a sexual impulse, rather than distract yourself with sex, you can identify and meet that need.) Once your agenda is more clearly loving and joyful, you may find a depth in sexual experience that you didn't expect and that can carry you beyond the physical. Table A3.6 provides a template for building your awareness in this area.

Exercise 3.7 Journaling About the Relationship Between Positive Emotions and Sex

In addition to understanding how you sometimes use sexuality to fulfill other needs (Exercise 3.6), you might also find it helpful to keep a sexual activity journal to explore what you know about your sexuality in a positive way (Table A3.7, below). This might include your play with others or with your own body. We often assume that orgasm is required for an enjoyable experience; this exercise doesn't make that assumption. For more on this, you might read Marla Robinson's (2009) *Cupid's Poisoned Arrow: From Habit to Harmony in Sexual Relationships*.

Table A3.7
Tracking Joy in Sexual Experience

Date & Time of Sexual Activity	
Besides desire, what other feelings were present?	
What did I/we choose to do?	
Was there orgasm?	
More than one? With or without ejaculation (male or female)?	
What was the balance of pleasure versus joy in the experience?	
How did I feel afterwards?	
How did I feel at the end of the day?	

Exercise 3.8 Assessing Spiritual Progress

In the twelve-step method of addressing addictions, one part of that spiritual program of recovery is to "make a searching and fearless moral inventory of ourselves." There are a number of ways that you can do this kind of self-assessment besides (or in addition to) the twelve-step method. One way to do this is to consult the table of the characteristics of a weaker (vyutthāna) versus a stronger (samādhāna) mind on pp. 230–231. In this contemplative exercise, you honestly assess your mind on these dimensions and note which ones seem important for you. You might note where you feel yourself to be now on a continuum from 0–10, with a vyutthāna mind at 0 and a samādhāna mind at 10. Now for the hard part: Once you have created a baseline for yourself in your own experience, prepare a blank form with each of the dimensions you have chosen, and ask someone you trust to give you his or her honest assessment. Once you have received the feedback from your spiritual friend (*kalyāna-mitra*), examine both sets of data. What are the differences between your assessment of yourself and your friend's feedback? How do you account for these? What surprised you in the feedback from the other person? What does this data imply about what you need to play with in yourself in the near future? Feel free to return to this exercise periodically, but not more frequently than once a year. (And make sure to include your kalyāna-mitra, your spiritual friend!)

Even more challenging, pick a span of time during which you have been doing your practice. Conduct a thought experiment. (This is how Einstein discovered general relativity!) Go to an adversary of yours in life, and genuinely ask him or her whether he or she has any feedback for you about how you have seemed to change over a specific period of time. Tell this person you plan only to listen to what he or she has to say. Listen carefully, keep your breath awareness carefully, and don't react at all. When the person is done, thank him or her sincerely. What did you expect from this experiment? How did the experiment violate your expectations—positively? Negatively? How might you relate to this person differently in the future?

Now that you have done this thought experiment, go and do it in reality. What expectations did you have based on your experiment? What surprised you? What disappointed you? Where did you notice yourself most resisting the feedback? What belief or emotion might be at the root of this resistance? Evaluate these results in comparison to the qualities in the chart on pp. 230–231. Does this change your sense of what work/play you need to do with yourself to shift your mind in a more samādhāna (moving towards samādhi) direction?

I gave this as an assignment to a group of Yoga teacher trainees. I thought many of them would feel too afraid to try this. But each one of them did the assignment! And they were amazed at what they learned and at how positive such an experiment could be. In some cases, the relationship with the person's presumed adversary shifted in a more positive direction as a result of his or her respectful and honest request.

Exercise 3.9 Journaling About Pain

As we noted in our description of the primary fountains, the vast majority of pain that we feel in the body is a fear reaction, even when the pain is from an actual physical injury. The more chronic the pain, the more emotionally involved it is. Here you can measure the impact of your efforts to deal with the relationship between emotions and pain. In rating your pain, you can use a scale called *Subjective Units of Distress,* or *SUDS*; rank your pain from 0–10, where 0 is pain free and 10 is the worst pain imaginable. The intervention

Table A3.9 *Journaling About Pain*	
Date & Time	
Location & Type of Pain	
SUDS Rating	
Intervention	
SUDS Rating After Intervention	
SUDS Rating an Hour Later	
What I Believe This Pain May Be Teaching Me	

is up to you. It might be doing some joints and glands exercises[2] or some postures or alternate nostril breathing, or it might be doing a cognitive intervention, such as Exercise 3.1 or something from the work of John Sarno, MD, discussed in Chapter 4 and noted in References. Table A3.9 above can help you identify what works to help you reduce the fear basis of your pain reaction and to note the trend in the effectiveness of your chosen interventions. The more effective the intervention, the better it may be at helping you resolve the underlying emotional cause. Experimenting with different interventions may bring to light what your pain might be "saying" about your emotional life and what your pain has to teach you.

Exercise 3.10 The Sociogram

A sociogram is a way to map the important relationships in your life against a diagram of the important sectors of your life. It helps you see where you may need more social relationships or a different level of intimacy and where you may need less interaction and more solitude. Our sense of solitary self-relationship and our sense of community with others are not opposites; they are complementary. The healthier our solitude, the

---

[2] Joints and glands exercises are a set of exercises that Swāmī Rāma taught to limber the body, stimulate the endocrine system, and mindfully move prāṇa through the body in a systematic way in preparation for āsana or subtle body practices. See Rama (1977) *Joints and Glands Exercises*, included in References. Compared to other editions, this original edition is closer to what Swāmī Rāma actually taught.

richer our community; the more nurturing and vital our community, the better we understand and love ourselves.

First think about the different levels of intimacy in your life. You can define this in any way that works for you. As a starter, I would suggest at least three levels: 1. primary intimates (parents, children, partners); 2. close friends; and 3. acquaintances. If you feel there are more nuances to the levels of intimacy, feel free to use more. And don't leave yourself out: How intimate is your relationship with yourself?!

Now take a sheet of paper and draw a target diagram with yourself at the center, on the bullseye. Make concentric circles, representing as many levels of intimate relationship with you as you feel are appropriate. Then superimpose on this target diagram a pie chart that represents the important sectors of your life. These might include family, work, spirituality, important avocational activities, and any other places where you spend important amounts of time. Now you have the basic format of the sociogram (Figure A3.10a).

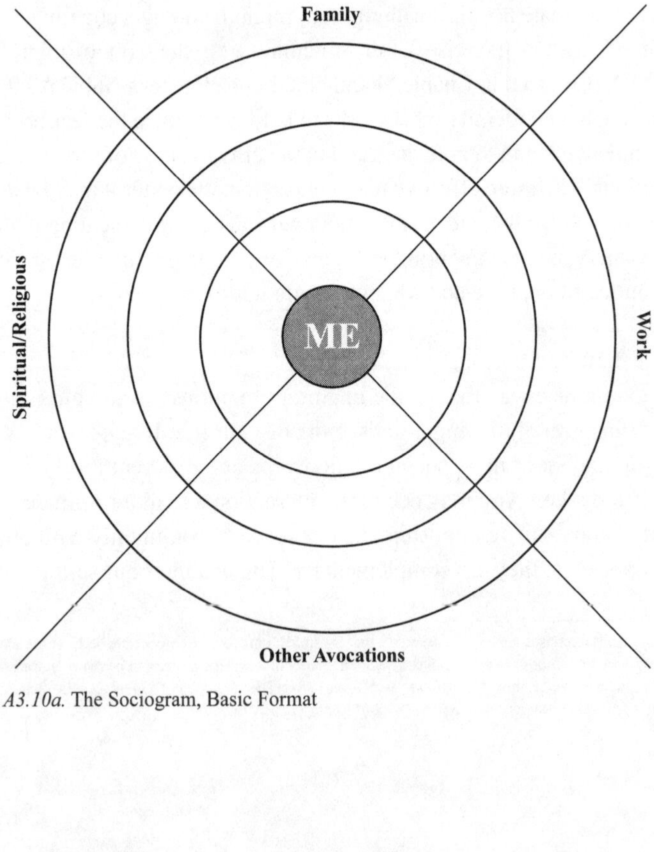

Figure A3.10a. The Sociogram, Basic Format

Next think about how you locate relationships in your life on this map. In which sectors do they occur? Do they occur in more than one? At what level of intimacy do they function? Based on the principle that it is generally a good thing to have some more or less intimate relationships in every sector of your life, where do there appear to be holes? In other words, where do you need to cultivate additional relationships? Given the distribution of people on this map, are there some relationships you would like to make more intimate? Less intimate? You can use arrows to indicate where you would like to move people on the map. You might also want to chart the amount of time you spend with each one. In which cases would you like to spend more time? Less? You might use colored pencils to indicate how each relationship helps you with your relationship with yourself (e.g., Figure A3.10b).

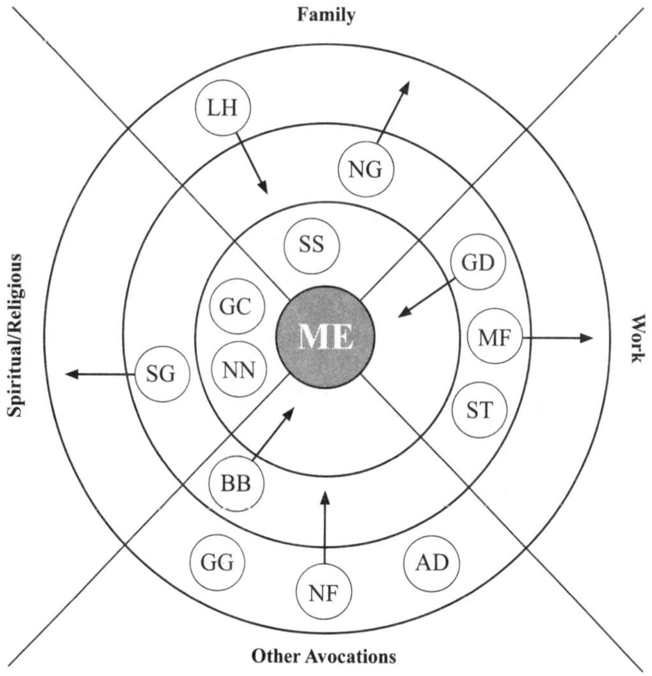

Figure A3.10b. The Completed Sociogram

Our network of relationships is a vital part of maintaining a healthy sense of self and a healthy mind/body. Some ideas that may help you think about what you need in this regard include 1. having relationships of appropriate depth in each major sector of your life and 2. cultivating relationships with people who are different from you in terms of age, race, culture, gender, sexuality, and so forth, so that your ability to cultivate compassion can grow as broadly as possible. (At the same time, this will help you to deepen your self-compassion for parts of yourself that you may have considered to be "not me.")

Exercise 3.11 Using the Yamas and Niyamas to Build Relationship Skills

Once you have identified the relationships in your life that you would like to cultivate or modify (perhaps by using the sociogram in Exercise 3.10), you can use the yamas and niyamas of Yoga to direct your attention and behavior. Chapter 5 discussed the centrality of relationships to our growth and, therefore, to the practice of Yoga: Just as we need others to develop our own psychological self (we borrow our parents' resonance circuits as children), we continue to need other people throughout our lifetimes. Moreover, when we direct our attention outward in relationship, we retrain ourselves to identify not with our limited ahaṁkāra, but with the ātman. Each person is connected to ātman and, through ātman, to us. Remember that our Yoga practice is never just about me and my enlightenment. At every moment we share our realization with others, just as others share theirs with us.

This exercise is designed to increase the joy in your relationships by helping you learn to attune more accurately to, or resonate with, others in your life and to recognize the deeper connections you share. The key ingredient in resonance is empathy, so each practice below is a suggestion for cultivating empathy. Niyamas are traditionally considered *intrapersonal* disciplines and help us to deepen our Self-relationship; yamas are *interpersonal* practices of aspects of empathy (nonviolence) and help us to extend compassion towards other beings in relationship. All of these practices can help you become mindful of patterns of thought and emotion that may be limiting the joy in your interactions with others, and the list below can support you in finding more skillful approaches. You can also implement these exercises for their own sake. And by all means, feel free to invent your own. Be creative, even perhaps (positively) outrageous! Any of these methods will tip your mindfield's balance towards positive saṁskāras.

Choose a suggestion from the list below, and try practicing it every day for a week, a month, or even a year. Pick one that resonates with you, or, again, feel free to create your own. You might also simply look for opportunities to practice one of the yamas or niyamas throughout the day and observe how others implement it in their behavior. The following list of questions and suggestions is intended as a starting point for your exploration:

1. Ahiṁsā, nonviolence. What violent (read *unkind, inconsiderate, judgmental,* etc.) thought pattern or behavior negatively impacts your relationships, and what can you do instead? How can you substitute the opposite attitude (prati-pakṣa-bhāvanā)? What is a nonviolent practice that cultivates empathy? One practice you might consider is to perform "random kindness and senseless acts of beauty," as the bumper sticker recommends. Practice this in a way that no one will know what you did. Make a game of it so that you really feel the joy of this.

2. Satya, truthfulness. What is a common dishonest thought pattern or behavior that negatively influences your relationships, and what can you do instead? When have you used a partial truth to gain power or to wound another? Are there instances of this where it would be healing to the other person and to you to make amends to him or her?

Additionally, consider how honesty is one of our best tools for cultivating empathy. It demonstrates our willingness to be transparent with others. In effect, we are telling the other person that we trust him or her with our feelings because we trust that he or she will be able to relate to us. When someone politely asks you how you are, consider responding with a little more truthful detail than usual, and observe how this impacts the way you feel about yourself and the other person.

3. Asteya, nonstealing. How do you misappropriate, taking for yourself what is not yours? What can you do to relax your sense of what is yours? For example, practice avoiding using the words *I* and *mine* in your communication with others. How does this change your sense of ownership and entitlement towards other people, yourself, your own body? Conversely, when you need to have a fight with someone, make an intention to be rigorous in only speaking from the first person: What is your own perception, your own emotion, your own experience? In other words, never let yourself utter a sentence that begins with the word *you*. How does this change the interaction?

4. Brahmacarya, control of mind and senses. How do you get involved in the sensory world to the detriment of awareness? How do you find awareness of the presence of God at the core of your sensory activities? When eating out, be aware of how much love you feel in the food. How does this change your experience of the meal or those with whom you share it? When eating in general, pause before you begin, and simply ask yourself what you are feeling and what emotions are involved in wanting the food in front of you. Are you truly physically hungry, or are you using food to fill a sense of dissatisfaction in some aspect of your relationship with yourself or with others? How does this awareness change your relationship to the food? To yourself? To others? Even more challenging, ask yourself similar questions about your sexual attractions to others or your desire to pleasure yourself sexually.

5. Aparigraha, nongrasping. What does the "stuff" in your life represent? (In a moment of reluctance to clean out a closet, I once realized that all the clothes I had not worn in five years represented parts of myself that I was not willing to let go of.) What do you have that would make you happier if it were in someone else's hands? Try giving something away the moment another person admires it, and note your reactions to doing this. Was it painful to relinquish the attachment? Did you also feel some joy? How do these interact in your experience?

6. Śauca, purity. How does being physically and emotionally clean also help you to remain calm and steady? Take a bath or a shower right before your meditation time. Note any differences in your meditation when you are clean versus when you just sit down and begin. Do these changes persist beyond your meditation time? Then at some point, try giving yourself a mental shower before you sit down. Does this mental gesture evoke any changes?

With respect to others, give yourself the same mental shower as you prepare to interact with someone. Take a few conscious breaths, and move your awareness away from your agenda, your to-do list, or other concerns so that you will be available to simply listen intently to him or her. How does this change your interaction? You might also clean up your attentional environment: When possible, silence your phone and email notifications. Turn away from your electronic screens. Physically distance yourself from these and other distractions. Close the door, if appropriate. Notice your response. Are you relieved to let these go? Pleased and grateful with the way this improves the quality of your time together? Or do you notice inner resistance? You might ask yourself where any resistance comes from and who you would be (or not be) without it. What does this tell you about your priorities in that moment? You may come to recognize a reasonable need to dedicate more time with yourself, by yourself. How would you give yourself this gift? Or have you found a way to enhance your and another person's joy because you have truly given him or her your attention? How do these polarities interact in your experience?

As another practice, consider the principle of always leaving a place better than you found it. For example, when you use a public restroom alone, clean up some small thing that makes the place more attractive to others: Pick up paper waste, wipe off the counter, and so forth. Again, do this at times when no one is watching. How does this change the way you feel as you leave the restroom?

7. Saṁtoṣa, contentment. What is enough for you—in any domain? How has that changed over time, and how might it change in the future? Experiment with yourself by asking halfway through a meal whether you have had enough. Or choose another sensual pleasure you enjoy. Practice satisfying that desire at one time for pleasure, and at another time using mindful awareness. How does your sense of enough change? Does it change how you relate to others in the same activity? For example, are you more available to focus on them and their experiences, enjoying your own experience more because you can feel their joy as well?

Also consider applying an attitude of saṁtoṣa to your perception of your relationships. Accept that not every relationship will fulfill your every need. While it is realistic to expect your needs to be fulfilled through relationships, it may not be realistic to expect a certain person to fulfill a certain need, given his or her unique personality, interests, abilities, and values. Identify a relationship in which you feel dissatisfaction. What is leaving you unfulfilled? Can you appreciate what the person does bring to your relationship and find a way to fulfill your need in another way, perhaps through a shared activity with this person or through a different relationship? Also ask yourself how well you are fulfilling the other person's needs. Is there a way you can do better?

8. Tapas, enjoyment through concentration. How do you seek satisfaction of desire through pleasurable objects rather than through joyful awareness? How can you see more deeply into the beauty of your experience? For example, consider taking a different primary fountain for a week or a month at a time, and set an intention to practice satisfying those essential desires in the most mindful way that you can, journaling about whatever differences you notice from your ordinary experience of them. In what ways does this change how you understand the people with whom you share these experiences?

9. Svādhyāya, self-study. How do you watch yourself when you are trying to remain aware? Do you watch as a critical judge or as a curious and wondering mother watching her child grow? How do your interactions with others change when you remember that each person is on his or her own path, that other people are also struggling and growing in their own practices of svādhyāya, whether or not they identify them as such? You might also pick one person, and in all your interactions, see him or her as the ātman in disguise. Can you observe this person's actions with a sense of curiosity and love, as a mother watches her growing child?

10. Īśvara-praṇidhāna, ultimate attunement to Great Being (Brahman). How can you feel what another being feels as a way to sense the presence of divinity in others? How can you find where you share your being with an inanimate object and understand the life of that object? How can you feel the progression of life from the stable stillness of a stone to the rooted but upward growing life of a plant, sucking nourishment from the earth, to a simple moving animal, acting according to instinct, to a thinking but not self-aware animal to a conscious human being? Make an intention to practice this contemplation when you leave your house each day for a few minutes before you resume your customary routine. How does this affect the rest of your day?

As another practice, choose someone with whom you are having a disagreement, and intentionally focus on seeing the divinity in him or her and on what divinity might be bringing to you in your interaction with this person. How does this change your behavior? Theirs?

At the end of each day, freewrite a few sentences or phrases based on the prompts in Table A3.11.

Table A3.11
Using the Yamas and Niyamas to Build Relationship Skills

Yama/Niyama	
Person/People with Whom I Interacted	
What I Did	
Effect on Other Person/People	
Effect on Me	
Effect on Our Interaction	
Effect on My Other Interactions, Activities, and Moods Later in the Day	
What I Would Have Done Differently	
What I Learned	
What I Will Do in the Future	

Appendix B

Glossary of Sanskrit Terms

For a very useful and more detailed grammatical analysis of terms from the *Yoga-sūtra*, see Salvatore Zambito's (2010) excellent *Yoga Sūtra Sanskrit-English Dictionary.*

Abhi-dhyāna: Divinity's (Guru's) meditation on us in response to our efforts to meditate and to practice īśvara-praṇidhāna, coming in the form of grace that deepens our meditation and eventually brings us to the highest meditation in samādhi.

Abhiniveśa: Obsession with the bodily dwelling and the belief that the life of the body should never end. It is the source of all fears (YS II.9).

Abhyāsa: Literally, "sit in front." In the Yoga system, it is the word for practice, for when we practice we always sit in front of the Guru, whether or not an embodied person (as guru) is present.

Ahaṁkāra: The function of mind that self-identifies with external objects and people in the process of formulating a psychological sense of self. Ahaṁkāra also maintains the life of the body and the function of the personal mind.

Ahiṁsā: Nonharm, nonviolence; the first and cardinal yama, or moral attitude, of which all the others are specializations. The positive statement of this attitude is compassion (*karuṇā*). When a person becomes established in nonviolence, there is no hostility in his or her presence on the part of any being (YS II.30, 31, 35).

Ajapājapa: When the mental process of repeating a mantra becomes automatic, it is called "nonrepeated repetition," or *ajapājapa*. This term also refers to the breath mantra *so 'ham*, which is repeated automatically with every breath, 21,600 times per day.

A-kliṣṭa: "Unafflicted," the *vṛtti* (mental operation) of samādhi (YS I.5). Vṛttis are said to be of two types: afflicted (*kliṣṭa, kleśa*) and unafflicted (*a-kliṣṭa*).

Ālambana: "Support." An object upon which the mind can form itself as an aid in meditative practices.

Ānanda: Bliss, especially the absolute bliss of the ground of Being, Brahman. The bliss of the ānanda-maya-koṣa, though blissful in comparison to the lower levels of embodiment, is a reduction of the bliss of Brahman.

Ananta, Ānantya: Literally, the adjectives *unending,* and *infinite*, as well as the more abstract concepts of infinitude and endlessness. Swāmī Veda discusses this distinction between variant readings of the *Yoga-sūtra* in his commentary on YS II.47 (Bhāratī, 2001, pp. 581–588).

Ānanta-samāpatti, Ānantya-samāpatti: "Coalescence with Ananta, the endless" or "coalescence with infinitude," respectively. These variant readings of Patañjali's *Yoga-sūtra* II.47 are both correct and have slightly different meanings. The word *samāpatti* is the same term that Patañjali uses in the first chapter of the *Yoga-sūtra* to describe the mental concentrations in the various levels of the lower states of spiritual realization, or *saṁprajñāta-samādhi*s (see Bhāratī, 2001, p. 582).

Antarāya: Obstacle, impediment to spiritual progress (YS I.31). Essentially equivalent to *vi-kṣepa* (disturbance, distraction, YS I.30) and *kleśa* (afflicted mental operation, afflicted vṛtti, YS II.3). See pp. 12–14.

Apāna: The current (*vāyu*) of prāṇa in the body that energizes cleansing and flows downward from the navel to the anus. It governs defecation, urination, and ejaculation and energizes the colon, rectum, kidneys, and genitals.

Aparigraha: Literally, "not grasping about," nongreed, the fifth yama. When this is firmly established, one gains knowledge of the how and why of incarnations (YS II.39).

A-saṁprajñāta-samādhi: Literally, "a-cognitive" samādhi, the highest state of meditation where the activity of the mindfield ceases altogether (*citta-vṛtti-nirodhaḥ*), and the mind enters *niruddha citta-bhūmi.* This is equivalent to *nirvikalpa-samādhi* in the Vedānta system. In this state, the body remains entirely inert and cold without respiration, heartbeat, or brain waves, yet there is said to be a slight warmth around the fontanelle at the crown of the head.

Āsana: Literally, "sitting [still]," as implied by the verb root, √*ās*. Posture. This is not so much holding still with effort as it is settling into a state where one has become stillness itself. Another root, √*sad*, also means "sit" in the sense of settling down. In the latter, there is motion, in the former, none; the practice of āsana as one of the eight limbs of the Rāja-yoga of Patañjali includes both. *Āsana* can also refer to one's meditation seat.

Āśram: Literally, "refuge." It is most often used to denote a place of refuge for spiritual practice, usually carried out under the supervision of a spiritual guide. It can also mean a developmental stage of life: 0–25 years of age *brahmacarya*, celibate student; 25–50 years *gṛhastha*, married householder; 50–75 years *vānaprasthā*, forest dweller living a life of tapas in relative seclusion; and 75+ *sannyāsa*, renunciate.

Aṣṭāṅga-yoga: In modern Yoga, this label is often used to describe the vigorous system of physical practice developed by Paṭṭābhi Jois (1915–2009). Its more literal and classical meaning is the eight-limbed path of practice explained by Patañjali in the *Yoga-sūtra.* It is a synonym for *Rāja-yoga.*

Asteya: Nonstealing, nonmisappropriation, nonmisidentification, the third yama. When this attitude is firmly established in a person, "all treasures attend upon him or her" (YS I.23). This does not refer to material treasures, but to the disembodied Yogis and siddhas who quietly guide aspirants' progress without making themselves known (II.30, 31, 37).

Ātman: The spiritual Self at the core of all beings. It is identical to the great ground of Being, Brahman.

Ātma-tattva-avalokanam: The name in the Vedānta system for the practice of remaining vigilantly alert, seeking the presence of the Self (*ātman*) everywhere around you. In Yoga, the term is *īśvara-praṇidhāna*; in Christian spiritual practice, it is called *the practice of the presence of God* (Brother Lawrence, 1982).

Avidyā: Ignorance, unwisdom, the first kleśa, and thus the cause of all our afflictions. It consists of mistaking the noneternal for the eternal, the impure for the pure, the painful for the joyful, and the non-Self for the Self (YS II.5, 24).

Āyurveda: "The wisdom of long life." The name of the traditional system of medicine in India, which is intimately related to Yoga and was expounded, in part, by Patañjali.

Āyus: "Long life" or length of life. One of the three aspects of one's next incarnation that becomes known at the moment of leaving the current body (YS II.13). (The other two are *jāti*, species of the next body, and *bhoga*, the balance of pain and pleasure in that life, YS II.13.)

Bandha: "Bond" or "lock." These are closures of energy circuits in the subtle energy body that carry the physical body along with them. They happen spontaneously as one reaches a certain depth in practice and can also be practiced physically to prepare the way for subtle experience. For example, many people, when deeply relaxed in meditation, experience a pull of energy that spontaneously lengthens the back of the neck and tucks the chin (*jālandhara-bandha*).

Bhāvanā: To impress a certain attitude or sentiment upon one's own being, not only with the mind but also with the heart. Literally, becoming that attitude. "Creative contemplation" and "transformative meditation" are also useful translations of *bhāvanā*.

Bhāva-śuddhi: Purification of emotions. Another term for *citta-prasādana*.

Bhāvya: Object of concentration upon which bhāvanā is performed.

Bhūmi: A "world" or a level of attainment. In the *Yoga-sūtra* (I.1), the commentator Vyāsa describes the gradual purification of the mindfield in terms of five levels of increasing clarity: *mūḍham,* "stupefied"; *kṣiptam*, "distracted"; *vi-kṣiptam*, "distracted but with moments of concentration"; *ekāgram*, "one-pointed" (lower samādhi); and *niruddham*, "ceased" (higher samādhi).

Bīja: "Seed." The word most often refers to mantras that are monosyllabic and have no dictionary meaning. They are sonar bodies of divine energies.

Bindu: This word can mean "point," "drop," or "seed." Most often it is referred to as the point limit or singularity into which the mind resolves (or dissolves) in the depth of meditation to prepare for entry into samādhi. In some texts, like the *Haṭha-yoga-pradīpikā, bindu* also refers to physical semen.

Bodhi-citta: "Enlightenment mind." One of the great philosophical contributions of the early Mahāyāna Buddhist teacher Śāntideva. His text *Bodhicāryavatāra* (700 CE) elaborates on this concept and the corollary concept of the *bodhisattva*, one who chooses to postpone his or her own enlightenment to work for the liberation of others.

Brahmacarya: Literally, "walking in Brahman." Moving in the awareness of divinity, which requires being able to rechannel the energy of the mind that is usually dissipated through sensory and sensual activity. This is sometimes translated in a limiting way as merely sexual continence or celibacy.

Brahman: "The Vast," "The Expansive," the term in Sanskrit for the ground of Being. It is rather similar to the Judeo–Christian idea of YHWH.

Brahma-vihāra: Literally, "a joy-garden of Brahman," or "a walk in a joy-garden of Brahman." Four attitudes that Patañjali advises as practices to make the mind clear and pleasant (*citta-prasādana*) and that also blossom as *vibhūti*s, natural developments of human potential, in a mind that has become clear and pleasant. They are *maitri, karuṇā, muditā,* and *upekṣā.* They are described identically in Yoga and in Buddhism, and the practices are explained in detail in Chapter 9 of the *Visuddimagga*, the great meditation manual of Buddhaghoṣa (trans. 2011), who lived in the sixth century CE (see also YS I.33, III.24).

Buddhi: The purest layer of the mindfield, having as its functions awareness, decision, discrimination, intention, and intuition. Yet buddhi itself is not conscious. It is simply like a two-way mirror: The mind appears to us to be conscious because the light of the spiritual Self (*ātman, puruṣa*) shines through buddhi over the rest of the mindfield. The activities of the mindfield are also reflected into buddhi for the enjoyment of the Self.

Cakra: Literally, "wheel" or "circle," related to the Latin for *church*. Wherever three or more nāḍīs intersect in the subtle body, this is called a *cakra*. Every joint in the body, for example, is built around a cakra. There are thousands of minor cakras and six major ones that parallel the spine. These are complex energy circuits that tie all the layers of the bodies together and channel the energies of various sounds, elements, deities, and experiences (see Table 7.2 on p. 146 and Table A2.2 on p. 286). They are also referred to as lotuses and are all penetrated by the suṣumnā-nāḍī, which also parallels the spine and guides the ascent of the Kuṇḍalinī. An excellent traditional description of the major cakras is given in Sir John Woodroffe's (1972) excellent work from the early twentieth century, which has been reprinted many times, *The Serpent Power*.

Citta: The mindfield, whether we refer to the great unitary mindfield within which all the universes within universes are held (YS IV.5), or we refer to the unconscious parts of the personal mindfield, which is just a wave in the greater ocean of mind. *Citta* also refers to the material nature of the mindfield, "mind stuff."

Citta-prasādana: Making the mindfield clear and pleasant (see *prasādana* below).

Dahara-vidyā: The wisdom or science of the heart lotus. In the early Upaniṣadic period (ca. 1500–600 BCE), the name for the heart center was *dahara*. This is actually a detailed science of the caves within caves of the heart center. It is mentioned in the *Chāndogya-upaniṣad* (VIII.1.1ff.) and is also described in some detail in the *Maṇḍala-brāhmaṇa-upaniṣad*, but the latter text is intentionally obtuse and requires a qualified guru to really understand the experiences described.

Dhāraṇā: Concentration (YS III.1). Both the everyday state in which the mind settles on a single point of focus, and the sixth limb of Yoga, an advanced state of focus enabled by the fifth limb, pratyāhāra, in which the mind has completely turned away from the senses, thus making external distractions impossible.

Dharma: Often translated as "duty," especially in a religious sense. The law books of Hinduism are called *Dharma-śāstra*, the texts on dharma. Its deeper meaning is the natural pattern of things, similar to the Tao in Chinese philosophy. Dharma is the path of action that develops this natural pattern.

Dharma-megha-samādhi: "The samādhi of the rain cloud of virtues." An experience during the transition from the lower saṁprajñāta-samādhi to the ultimate a-saṁprajñāta-samādhi where one is flooded with omniscience as in a monsoon rainstorm. It is described identically in both the Yoga and the Buddhist traditions of meditation.

Dharma-śāstra: A body of texts that describe how life should be lived. The rule books or law books of Sanātana-dharma, which, in the West, we refer to as Hinduism.

Dhyāna: Meditation. The ability of the mind to hold a single-pointed focus is extended so that the mind produces *pratyaya-eka-tānatā* ("a succession of identical vṛttis"), flowing like an unbroken, steady stream of oil (YS III.2).

Dīkṣā: The process and experience of initiation, where a direct link with Guru-mind is established in the first initiation, and then the Guru periodically raises the disciple's mind to a higher level of experience and understanding through the power of the Guru, *cit-śakti* or *hiraṇyagarbha* ("womb of light"), flowing through the Guru's own mind. This has many degrees, from the initial mantra initiation to final enlightenment.

Doṣa: Literally, "fault" or "flaw." In Āyurveda it represents an imbalance in one's constitution, or *prakṛti*. The three principal doṣas are *vāta* (air), *kapha* (water and earth) and *pitta* (fire). These are rather like the medieval European notion of humors as the basis of one's personality.

Duḥkha: Literally, "bad space," suffering. According to Patañjali, it is caused by aversion (*dveṣa,* YS II.8).

Dveṣa: Aversion, hatred, disgust (YS II.8).

Ekāgram: The *bhūmi,* mental level, where the mindfield becomes literally "one-pointed" and capable of entering saṁprajñāta-samādhi.

Eka-tattva: One principle. In YS I.32 Patañjali advises the practice of one principle, or one reality, as a means to counter the antarāyas (duḥkha, daurmanasya, aṅgamejayatva, śvāsa, and pra-śvāsa, YS I.31) and clarify the mindfield. The practice of a single principle means holding the mind on an object of meditation continuously.

Gāyatrī: The most important mantra of the *Veda*s and of the mantra tradition of meditation practice: *Oṁ bhūr bhuvaḥ svaḥ tat savitur vareṇyam bhargo devasya dhīmahi dhiyo yo naḥ pracodayāt*. It exists in many different variations of this form, and to quote Swāmī Veda (1998) from his unpublished recorded seminar on the subject, "It has six sextillion translations." In addition to this familiar form, there are specialized Gāyatrī mantras addressed to many specific divine energies.

Guṇa: Quality, especially the three interactive qualities of the material universe (*prakṛti*): *tamas*, the quality of inertia; *rajas*, the quality of energy, movement, changeability, and volatility; and *sattva*, the quality of balance, equipoise, and purity.

Guru: This is often translated as "teacher" or "spiritual guide" (lowercase guru). The original Guru, however, is *hiraṇyagarbha,* the "golden womb" or "womb of light," the first devolution of *prakṛti* (the material universe), from its immaterial, unmanifest form, *pradhāna*. In the Śaiva traditions, Śiva, the principle of pure consciousness, is described as the first Guru. Guru carries the power and energy of consciousness, *cit-śakti*. When the Guru works through an embodied person (guru), the energy of consciousness is transmitted by a teacher to a student to a greater or lesser degree. Only when a teacher can move his or her personality entirely out of the way—so that the entire force of the Guru power can be transmitted—can that person really be called a guru. Such people are understandably extremely rare. Also, Guru does not always work through an embodied person but can guide disciples from the subtle world.

Haṭha-yoga: This term is often associated primarily with the physical practices of yoga-āsana and prāṇāyāma. It actually refers to the effort to merge the solar (*ha-*) and lunar (*-ṭha)* aspects of the subtle body to open the suṣumnā channel in meditation to enter the deeper states leading to samādhi.

Iḍā: One of the principal currents of energy, or *nāḍīs,* in the prāṇa-maya-koṣa. It terminates in the left nostril and originates in the *kanda* (a subtle body structure just above the lowest cakra from which all nāḍīs originate, Woodroffe, 1972, p. 115). Some describe the flow of iḍā as parallel to suṣumnā, while others describe it as weaving up the spine in a serpentine manner, intersecting with the piṅgalā and suṣumnā nāḍīs to create each of the six major cakras. Both are true, as these are spatial metaphors for an experience in which there is no space. When this channel is active, it is flowing more predominantly than the right nostril, the right hemisphere of the brain is more active, the body likes to be relaxed or resting, and the mind prefers metaphorical thinking or activities of a creative nature. In the svara science, this flow is called the lunar flow, *candra-svara*.

Indriya: Sensory function. In the symbolic interpretation of the Vedic deities of Hinduism, Indra, the King of Heaven, represents the sensory mind (*manas*), while the king's servants are called *indriya*. So the senses are the servants of the mind. In the Yoga system, there are not only the usual cognitive senses (sight, hearing, taste, touch, and smell) but also a set of senses through which the mind reaches out to the world around it: locomotion in the feet, action in the hands, speech in the tongue, and reproduction and elimination through the genital organs. Sometimes the sensory mind as a whole (manas) is considered the eleventh sense.

Indriya-gupti: Literally, "hiding or protecting the senses." This is the practice of withdrawing the movement of the mind through the senses in the practice of silence and at other times. You keep your eyes focused just in front of your feet as you walk. You focus on listening to your mantra rather than allowing the mind to follow random sounds in the environment. When you eat, you focus your mind on really tasting your food with concentration. It's a lovely practice you can use any time. You will notice when you do that your mind acquires an extra measure of agility and speed.

Īśvara-praṇidhāna: This is often translated as "surrender to the Lord," which is a beginning practice. *Īśvara-praṇidhāna* has a very particular meaning in Yoga, which is to intentionally place your mind as close to divinity as possible at every moment. This is much more like the practice of moment-to-moment mindfulness than it is an exercise in religious devotion. The Christian monk Brother Lawrence (1614–1691) describes it beautifully in his text whose name implies its meaning, *The Practice of the Presence of God* (1982). Establishment of īśvara-praṇidhāna results in samādhi (YS II.45).

Japa: The recitation of mantras in meditation and one of the traditional meanings of *svādhyāya*, self-study. Japa exists on many levels. It can be written (*likhita-japa*), spoken (*vācika*), sung (*kīrtana*), whispered (*upāṁśu*), or mentally repeated (*mānasa*). These comprise the first level of japa: language, or v*aikhari,* "the braying of an ass." In the *madhyama*, or the middle level of japa up to buddhi, the feeling of the mantra continues, and the syllables that are its gross body drop away. Gradually one's concentration gathers the mantra vibration into a singularity, or point-limit called *bindu,* and the mind enters the first stages of samādhi (*saṁprajñāta-samādhi*), sending the meditator into the *paśyanti* level, which transcends the conceptual mind. This is the level of revelation at which the spiritual texts of the world are given to the one-pointed mind of a seer-sage. The final and highest level, *parā*, carries one into *a-saṁprajñāta-samādhi*.

Jihva-mudrā: "Tongue mudrā." In this mudrā, or "gesture," you place the tongue behind your upper teeth and slide it back along the hard palate. This is useful in the practice of silence because you must unfold your tongue to speak, which gives you a couple of seconds to use the fewest words possible or to ask yourself whether you really need to speak at all. Although some practice this mudrā primarily in meditation, those of us disciples living with Swāmī Veda were taught to do this all the time. A very nice habit!

Jñāna-yoga: The path of knowledge or the Yoga of wisdom. This is the path of contemplative practice.

Kaivalya: The term for liberation in Yoga. It is related to the Sanskrit word *kevala*, meaning "solo," which is the source of the Latin *caelibatus* and the English *celibate*, in the sense of perfected interior solitude in contemplation.

Kāma: Desire, and especially sexual desire, because that is the one desire that uses all eleven senses at once (five cognitive senses, five active senses, and the sensory mind itself), bringing the mind to a joyful state of one-pointedness. Kāma is considered one of the legitimate aims of life, and the release we experience from our limited self at the height of sexual experience is often where we begin on the spiritual path. We also awaken to our spirituality during our pursuit of any of the four primary fountains (food, sleep, sex, self-preservation) when we realize that an imbalanced relationship to them leads to suffering, while a balanced relationship, and the choice to gradually reduce our dependence on them, leads to a stabilized mindfield. Additionally, the fountains teach us that no desire provides lasting fulfillment, which we can only attain through realizing our nature as Self.

Kanda: A small, bulblike structure within or proximal to mūlādhāra-cakra from which all the subtle energy channels (*nāḍīs*) originate.

Karma: "Action." The word *karma* is not only action itself, but also often refers to the impressions of action that persist in our unconscious mind in the form of saṁskāras, which become the seeds of our future action. Application of mindful awareness to this process as it operates moment to moment is called *karma-yoga.*

Karmāśaya: "Reservoir of karma," or the accumulation of saṁskāras that are becoming ripe to bear their fruits in the life of our next body. Our karmāśaya arises as we depart the current body and forms a subtle pattern for shaping the next incarnation (YS II.12).

Karuṇā: "Compassion," one of the brahma-vihāra practices that helps to make the mind clear and pleasant. It develops through becoming able to feel others' pain as if it were your own, which motivates you to work to alleviate the suffering of others.

Kevala-kumbhaka: Also called *sahaja-kumbhaka*, or the spontaneous cessation of breath at a certain depth of subtlety in breath awareness. The breath ceases with no anxiety or concern for ever taking another breath. For most people, it lasts a few seconds, but it can last for hours. Its occurrence is the sign that one's nāḍīs and mind are sufficiently purified to practice intentional retention of breath. Before this point, intentional retention strengthens all of one's saṁskāras, according to Swāmī Rāma, and makes the expression of one's karma more intense and the process of clarifying the mindfield more difficult and painful.

Kleśa: "Pain, suffering, affliction," the term used in the second chapter of the *Yoga-sūtra* for the afflicted fluctuations or operations (*vṛtti*s) of the mind (YS II.2–9).

Kliṣṭa: "Afflicted." Mental operations, *vṛtti*s, are classified as afflicted or unafflicted (YS I.5).

Koṣa: "Sheath" or "covering." This is the term for a layer of embodiment in the Vedānta system. There are five koṣas: 1. *anna-maya-koṣa*, the sheath made of food (the physical body); 2. *prāṇa-maya-koṣa*, the sheath made of subtle energy; 3. *mano-maya-koṣa*, the sheath made of the lower sensory mind (*manas*); 4. *vijñāna-maya-koṣa*, the sheath made of the higher mind (*buddhi* and *ahaṁkāra*); and 5. *ānanda-maya-koṣa*, the sheath made of bliss. A parallel system of layers of embodiment exists in the Yoga system (see *śarīra* below).

Kriyā: Practice or process.

Kriyā-yoga: The system of practice prescribed in Chapter 2 of the *Yoga-sūtra* for disciples of the middle level of qualification (*madhyama*, YS I.22) consisting of the last three niyamas: *tapas* (austerity), *svādhyāya* (self-study), and *īśvara-praṇidhāna* (mindful practice of divine presence).

Krodha: Anger, the result of frustrated desire.

Kṣetra: "Field." Each cakra has a field of activity that can be felt in the physical body through relaxed concentration (see Appendix A, Exercise 2.2).

Kṣiptam: The *bhūmi*, mental level, where the mindfield is literally "tossed about," distracted, and therefore unable to concentrate.

Kumbhaka: Suspension of the flow of physical breath. It can be internal (*antara*, i.e., following the inhalation), external (*bāhya*, i.e., following the exhalation), or spontaneous (*kevala, sahaja*).

Kuṇḍalinī: The power of consciousness (*cit-śakti*), which, when awakened, rises along the spine until it reaches the highest point in the system of cakras. For an excellent description of this phenomenon, see Swami Veda Bharati's (2013b) *Kuṇḍalinī: Stilled or Stirred?* and Sir John Woodroffe's (1972) *The Serpent Power*.

Kuṇḍalinī-Śakti: The total power of the Divine Feminine. It is described as an energy using the metaphor of a serpent coiled near the base of the spine in the lowest cakra, *mūlādhāra*. Sir John Woodroffe (1972) translated the term as "The Serpent Power" in the title of his well-known book (see References).

Kūrma-nāḍī: An energy channel along the midline of the body between the heart center and the throat center. Concentration on this location induces stillness of the body, which helps to still the mind (see YS III.31).

Lobha: Greed, the result of the effort to repeat the satisfaction of a desire.

Mada: "Intoxication" (e.g., with pride) or frenzy, generated by too much of something one desires.

Maitri: "Friendliness, amity," (Pāli language, *metta*). One of the brahma-vihāra practices that helps a person to become a friend to all beings, spreading loving kindness in the world.

Makarāsana: The crocodile posture, often used to facilitate diaphragmatic breathing so that a student can get the feeling of the movement and create a physical memory.

Mālā: Garland, rosary, necklace. The alphabet is called *varṇa-mālā,* "garland of letters." *Mālā* often refers to the string of 108 beads used to count the repetitions of mantras (*japa*). One counts 100 repetitions for each round of the mālā, contributing eight repetitions for the Guru to use for the welfare of the universe. A mālā can be made of many different materials, each of which has a different subtle effect.

Manas: The function of mind that is connected to our active and cognitive senses. In addition to its role as sensory mind, it also assists our thinking by raising all sides of an issue, seeking out all the arguments when one is trying to arrive at a decision; however, manas has no power of decision on its own.

Mantra: A word or phrase representing a subtle sound vibration that is given as an object of concentration for meditation and also for gradually changing the nature of the mind (and eventually even the body). Mantra works through the creative impact of the sound vibrations of consciousness.

Marma: A critical point where the subtle body is tied to the physical body. In Āyurveda, marmas are used for healing; in the martial arts, blows are aimed at these points to dislodge the two bodies, causing death.

Matsarya: Jealousy, generated by the belief that something I desire of someone else's is mine. A less intense form is envy, where one simply has a strong wish that the thing in question were one's own.

Moha: Delusion, confusion, stupefaction, sometimes due to a confusion of desires.

Mūḍham: The *bhūmi*, mental level, where the mindfield is literally "stupefied," unable to accurately interpret its environment due to physical or mental illness, intoxication, and so forth. Such a mind has no ability to concentrate.

Muditā: Joyful mindedness, one of the brahma-vihāra practices that helps one to develop an unshakeable sense of joyfulness and a happy mind that influences others.

Mudrā: "Gesture." In Yoga, these are practices like the bandhas that close important energy circuits in the subtle body. They will happen spontaneously at a certain depth in meditation, or they can be done as physical practices to prepare the way for subtle experience. For example, when you apply the tongue lock (*jihva-mudrā*) in meditation, at a certain depth you feel the upward flow of prāṇa along the suṣumnā channel causing the tongue to physically lengthen and reshape itself so that it reaches up into the soft palate where the oral cavity joins the nasal cavity. When this occurs, jihva-mudrā has become *khecari-mudrā*, the meditative experience of "moving in space." Haṭha-yogis try to attain this state physically by gradually severing the frenulum, the membrane under the tongue. This approach is actually unnecessary because when prāṇa flows correctly, the tongue reshapes itself automatically (see Arya, 1985, *Philosophy of Hatha Yoga*). Another example is the consciousness mudrā, *cin-mudrā*. At a certain depth of relaxation, one feels a subtle pull between the thumb and forefinger that gradually draws them together in this familiar gesture of meditation.

Mūla-bandha: The root lock, practiced by gently pulling upward on the pubococcygeus muscle, or PC muscle, in the middle of the abdominal floor, or perineum. This lock closes an energy circuit at the base of the spine and, along with jihva-mudrā, helps to facilitate a smooth and pauseless cycle of breath. As in jihva-mudrā, when prāṇa begins to flow upward along the spine, mūla-bandha will happen spontaneously. It is the same practice recommended by physicians to women for toning the vaginal muscles and to men for maintaining prostate health. It also helps both genders to control incontinence and to redirect sexual energy.

Muni: Literally, "a silent one." An ancient Vedic word for a Yogi.

Nāda: Subtle, nonphysical sound that may appear in a practitioner's mind as one of the signs that he or she has sufficiently purified his or her nāḍīs and is ready to begin the practice of breath retention (*sahita-kumbhaka*, HYP II.20).

Nāḍī: "Tube, current, channel," the Sanskrit name for the pathways along which subtle energy, or prāṇa, flows. In Āyurveda, the nāḍīs are said to have three layers: *mano-vaha*, through which the mind flows; *prāṇa-vaha*, through which prāṇa flows; and *sroto-vaha*, through which "fluids" (blood, lymph, and electrical impulses) flow. The subtler nāḍīs control the grosser ones. Different texts give different accounts of the number of these channels, ranging from 72,000 to 350,000 to a nearly infinite number, depending on the fineness of the resolution of one's discrimination.

Nidrā: "Sleep," especially the deepest kind of sleep called *suṣupti* in Sanskrit, characterized physiologically by the absence of the rapid eye movements of dreaming (REM sleep) and by the production of delta brain waves at a frequency of 0–5 cycles per second (YS I.10, 38).

Niruddham: The *bhūmi*, mental level, where the mindfield has literally "ceased" to operate (*citta-vṛtti-nirodhaḥ*), and one enters a-saṁprajñāta-samādhi.

Niyama: The second of the eight limbs of Yoga. These are personal disciplines, or "practices" that pertain to one's relationship with oneself (śauca, saṁtoṣa, tapas, svādhyāya, and īśvara-praṇidhāna, YS II.32, 40–45).

Paramparā: Literally, "one after the other." This is the word for the personal transmission of Yoga from guru to disciples through the centuries.

Piṅgalā: The nāḍī flowing parallel to the spine, from the kanda near the base of the spine and terminating in the right nostril. (Some describe the flow of piṅgalā as weaving its way up the spine in a serpentine manner, intersecting with the iḍā and suṣumnā nāḍīs to create each of the six major cakras in the suṣumnā. Both are true, as these are spatial metaphors for an experience in which there is no space.) In the svara system, piṅgalā is called the solar rhythm, or *sūrya-svara*. When it is predominant, the left hemisphere of the brain is more active, the body likes to be physically active, and the mind easily performs logical operations.

Prakṛti: *Ur*-nature, root nature, the manifest and unmanifest material universe. In the Sāṃkhya-yoga philosophy, *prakṛti* is distinct from *puruṣa*, which is pure spirit. Prakṛti has three qualities *(guṇa*s*): tamas* (inertia), *rajas* (energy, movement, changeability, volatility), and *sattva* (purity, balance), which continually interact with each other within matter when prakṛti is manifest. In its unmanifest form, with the guṇas in equilibrium, prakṛti is called *pradhāna*.

Prāṇa: The intangible, nonphysical subtle energy that sustains all life. The word *prāṇa* has different meanings at different levels of reference. For example, *Mahāprāṇa* is another name for *cit-śakti* (power of consciousness), or Kuṇḍalinī. At this level, prāṇa is the energy field within which all the universes within universes are sustained. In embodied beings, prāṇa flows in the subtle body through channels called *nāḍī*s. It is felt sometimes in deep states of relaxed awareness as heat or as a subtle tingling, which is sometimes described as feeling like ants crawling on the skin. So prāṇa is both the potential energy of the entire macrocosmic universe in its macrocosmic form, and the power of consciousness as it exists in a microcosmic body. One important principle across the practices of Yoga is that prāṇa does not flow where there is physical or mental tension, hence the importance of *prayatna-śaithilya*, or relaxation of effort (YS II.47), in all practices from āsana onwards. Prāṇa is similar to qi in Chinese medicine, although some levels of qi are physical electricity (most acupuncture meridians, for example). The energy in the central and governor vessels, however, is essentially identical to prāṇa in Yoga. Many other traditions posit this kind of subtle energy system.

Prāṇāyāma: Control and expansion of prāṇa and the exercises that help facilitate this. These comprise the fourth limb of Patañjali's eight-limbed Rāja-yoga (YS II.49–53). See, for example, Appendix A, Exercise 2.1.

Prasāda, Prasādana: From the verb root √*sad*, "settle, sit," and the prefix *pra-* "completely": to clarify, purify, make clear and pleasant. *Prasāda*, a word for grace, is purity that settles down to us from a higher being.

Pra-śvāsa: Ordinary, normal, nonmindful exhalation (YS I.31). Mindful exhalation is called *bāhya* (external, YS II.50), or *recaka*. This is an example of how the meaning of a sūtra is sometimes embedded in grammatical form rather than explained.

Prati-pakṣa-bhāvanā: Impressing on the mind and heart the opposite attitude. This is a method described in YS II.33–34 for countering a painful or dark saṁskāra with the deliberate production of a bright saṁskāra, for example countering a hateful thought about someone with a loving thought. It is the Yogic form of cognitive behavioral therapy (CBT), which deals with using the cognitive component of emotion to redirect an emotion's energy.

Pratyāhāra: The fifth limb of Yoga, which comprises the mind's process of disconnecting from external sensory data in order to enter the inner limbs of Yoga, culminating in samādhi (YS II.54).

Pratyaya: Process of cognition, the flow of thought, presentation of an experience to buddhi (Bhāratī, 2014, p. 808).

Prayatna-śaithilya: Relaxation of effort (YS II.47). In general in Yoga, we begin learning a practice by making an initial effort, which we then gradually relax until the practice becomes *sahaja*, spontaneous, and no tension remains.

Preyas: That which is dear because it is pleasurable. When we act in response to emotion, we often need to choose between what is pleasurable (*preyas,* fulfills a desire) and what is genuinely beautiful, joyous, and beneficial (*śreyas*, from *Śrī*, transcendent beauty and auspiciousness).

Puruṣa: Pure spirit, the pure spiritual Self at the core of every being. It is eternally distinct from matter (*prakṛti*) and is defined in the Sāṃkhya-yoga philosophy as "ever pure, ever enlightened, ever liberated" (*nitya-śuddha-buddha-mukta*) in its true nature.

Rāga: Desire, attraction, that which "colors" the pure crystal of the mind.

Rahasya: "Secret," which in Yoga doesn't mean hidden information so much as it is something that cannot be understood except from a certain depth of experience.

Rajas: The quality (*guṇa*) of energy that represents movement, changeability, and volatility in *prakṛti* (the manifest and unmanifest universe).

Rāja-yoga: The royal path of Yoga, meaning the classical method of practice described by Patañjali in the *Yoga-sūtra*. It encompasses all the other Yoga paths.

Ṛṣi: "Seer," one to whom revelation occurs in the depths of samādhi. Each mantra, for example, has a ṛṣi to whom it was originally revealed.

Sādhanā: From the verb root √*sādh*, "to strive, make effort, and ultimately succeed." So *sādhanā* is the means to succeed in the effort of spiritual practice. One who performs sādhanā is a *sādhaka*.

Sādhu: Also from the verb root √*sādh*, "to strive, make effort, and ultimately succeed." It denotes one who has devoted his or her life to sādhanā. It is also the exclamation for a successful performance, much like the Italian, *Bravo!*

Sahaja: Literally, "born with," natural, spontaneous.

Sahaja-kumbhaka: Also called *kevala-kumbhaka*, or the spontaneous cessation of breath at a certain depth of subtlety in breath awareness (see *kevala-kumbhaka*, above).

Sahasrāra: The center of consciousness that is often depicted at the crown of the head but that is actually twelve finger breadths above. For this reason, in Tāntrik practice it is called *dvādaśānta*, the one whose extent is twelve. This center is often described as a cakra, although it doesn't really function in the same way. It is here that the consciousness of the Yogi rests in the highest samādhi once the Kuṇḍalinī energy has risen, and the Divine Feminine has merged with the Śiva principle of pure consciousness in purest joy, ānanda (see Woodroffe, 1972, p. 16).

Sahita-kumbhaka: This is the voluntary suspension of breath through an effort. It is recommended by Swāmī Rāma and Swāmī Veda Bhāratī that this be practiced only after a spontaneous suspension has begun to occur in a person's meditation. The reason given is that sahita-kumbhaka intensifies all the karmik impressions (*saṁskāra*s), painful as well as pleasant, held in one's unconscious mind. Thus some degree of emotional purification is necessary for the spontaneous suspension to occur. This principle protects the student from creating more unnecessary pain for him- or herself in the process of purifying the mindfield.

Śaiva: The philosophical traditions ascribed to Śiva, the deity whereby all things originate and subside in pure consciousness. These traditions are prominent in South India and in the North in Kashmir. Some of the Śaiva traditions are dualistic, and some are nondualistic. In the philosophical school of Kashmir Śaivism, dating from the eighth century, the nondualistic and Tāntrik paths are merged.

Śakti: "Power," whether potential or actual. The word also denotes the Divine Feminine. In both Indian tradition and in the traditional West, power and capacity are conceived as feminine in nature.

Śakti-pāta: The descent of Śakti. This occurs when the Guru uses the power of His or Her mindfield to directly transmit an experience, which lifts the mind of a disciple to show him or her a new level of being. It is then the task of the disciple to do his or her best to maintain that awareness. Chapter 11 of the *Bhagavad-gītā* describes such an experience on a grand scale.

Samādhāna: From *sam-* + *ā* + √*dhā*, "to place or put together, resolve, harmonize." This is the tendency of the mind to move towards samādhi, along a harmonizing, clarifying, and pacifying trajectory.

Samādhi: The state of ultimate harmonization where one moves beyond ideas, words, and dualistic categories into an experience of singularity. The perceptual triad of object, perceiver, and process of perception has resolved (or dissolved) into a unitary experience that is beyond time (past and future) and occurring in an eternal present. It has two degrees called in Yoga *saṁprajñāta*, "with wisdom," and in Vedānta, *savikalpa*, "with thought." The higher degree in Yoga is called *a-saṁprajñāta*, "a-cognitive" and in Vedānta *nir-vikalpa*, "free of thought." In terms of quantum physics, a-saṁprajñāta (or nir-vikalpa) samādhi is an experience of purest consciousness in its condition "before" it has collapsed probability waves into actual manifest energy and matter (Goswami, 2011). Patañjali explains these levels in YS I.17–21 and I.41–51.

Samāna: The flow (*vāyu*) of prāṇa in the body that assists with assimilation (mental and physical) of nutrition and of right thought. It operates beneath the heart in the region of the navel cakra (*maṇipūra*).

Samāpatti: The process through which one enters the lower samādhi, *saṁprajñāta-samādhi*, "with wisdom." In this stage, the perceptual triad of object, perceiver, and process of perception collapses into an experience of singularity.

Śamathā: The state in Buddhist Vipassanā practice that is equivalent to Yoga's saṁprajñāta-samādhi.

Saṁkalpa: Intention, resolve, commitment. In the West, we might say "will," although the notion of will usually implies force and effort. Saṁkalpa is a very gentle but firm experience in one's buddhi, "like the decision to give oneself in love" (S. V. Bhāratī, personal communication, November 2010). In advanced stages of practice, intention becomes very important in helping a spiritual aspirant (*sādhaka*) avoid getting stuck in the attractions of intense supersensory states of pleasure or bliss.

Sāṃkhya: One of the six schools of orthodox Indian philosophy. Sāṃkhya and Yoga are often spoken of as one system. Sāṃkhya is the metaphysical system on which Yoga is based, and Yoga is the means of practical realization. For an excellent and clear explanation of the basics of Sāṃkhya, see the "Overview of Sāṃkhya-Yoga" in the General Introduction to both Arya (1986) and Bhāratī (2014). Sāṃkhya (and Yoga) are dualistic in outlook because these schools describe the experience of the universe through the mind. (The domain of mind is inherently dualistic, owing its experience to the distinction it perceives between subject and object.) Among the other philosophical schools, Nyāya and Vaiśeṣikā describe our experience of the universe through the senses. Mimāṃsā and Vedānta describe the experience of reality beyond mind and senses. They offer the contemplative skills to harmonize the subject–object dichotomy and move beyond it. In this way, we can say that these philosophies collaborate (rather than compete) with each other by offering a perspective from different levels of experience and realization.

Saṁprajñāta-samādhi: The samādhi "with wisdom," or the lower samādhi. This corresponds to *savikalpa-samādhi* in the Vedānta system. In the Yoga system, it consists of six levels, which are explained in the *Yoga-sūtra* (I.41–50).

Saṁskāra: A subtle mental impression made on the subconscious mind by an action that is motivated by desire. These impressions are often described as "seeds" of future action, which bear their fruit as they arise in the form of emotional momentum to act in a certain way. The word can also mean "a ritual."

Saṁtoṣa: Contentment. This is the ability to be happy with whatever comes in life. It does not mean complacency about one's practice! When established in a practitioner, saṁtoṣa creates in him or her an unexcelled and unshakeable happiness (YS II.32, 42).

Saṁyama: The continuous deepening of concentration and meditation through the stages of dhāraṇā, dhyāna, and samādhi, described in Chapter 3 of the *Yoga-sūtra*. It is thought of as a single process.

Sandhi: Literally, "put together," conjunction. In Sanskrit grammar, this term is used for the rules governing how sounds change when certain sounds are combined (e.g., *i* + *a* = *ya*). In Yoga and Āyurveda, a *sandhi* is the conjunction of two energy channels. In the meditative tradition, sandhi is the conjunction of night and day at dawn and dusk, which are prime times for meditation. This meeting point of night and day mirrors holographically the twilight in the alternating activity of the three principal energy channels. At this time of transition, when dominance shifts between iḍā and piṅgalā, the suṣumnā channel is more likely to be flowing, thus inclining the mind towards meditation.

Śarīra: The word for body in the Yoga system. Literally, it means "that which decomposes." There are three levels of śarīra: *sthūla-śarīra*, the gross physical body; *sūkṣma-śarīra*, the subtle body; and *kāraṇa-śarīra*, the causal body. These correspond to the koṣa system of Vedānta as follows: The sthūla-śarīra corresponds to the anna-maya-koṣa; the sūkṣma-śarīra corresponds to the prāṇa-maya-, mano-maya-, and vijñāna-maya-koṣas; and the kāraṇa-śarīra corresponds to the subtlemost vijñāna-maya- and ānanda-maya-koṣas.

Sati-paṭṭhāna: The Buddhist term in the Pāli language for Yoga's *smṛti-upasthāna*, "the establishment of mindfulness." They are exactly equivalent in meaning and in practice.

Sattva: The quality (*guṇa*) of purity and balance in *prakṛti* (the manifest and unmanifest universe).

Satya: Truthfulness. The pursuit of whole truth, the second of the yamas. Establishment in truthfulness results in all actions and their fruits becoming dependent on the will of the Yogi. In other words, what one speaks will become true (YS II.30–31, 36).

Śauca: The process of obtaining physical and mental purity, which includes both cleanliness of the body and purification of emotions (YS II.32, 40–41).

Śava, Śavāsana: "Corpse," and "posture of the corpse," respectively. The latter refers to the posture done lying on one's back, in which one learns relaxation and other practices that give an experience of the subtle body and, gradually, the ability to move prāṇa with the mind.

Śava-yātra: "Journey of the corpse." This phrase can refer to relaxation practices in general or to a specific exercise. Swāmī Rāma used the term to refer to the 61-point subtle body relaxation exercise (see Appendix A, Exercise 1.3).

Siddha: From the verb root √*sādh*, "to strive, make effort, and ultimately succeed." A *siddha* is one who has succeeded in the effort of *sādhanā*, spiritual practice. Often, siddhas become the gurus and bodhisattvas who quietly guide aspirants' practice without making their presence known.

Siddhi: From the verb root √*sādh*, "to strive, make effort, and ultimately succeed." A *siddhi* denotes a success or an accomplishment, usually in the form of some particular ability (YS IV.1–3), for example telekinesis, clairvoyance, or clairaudience.

Śithali-karaṇa: Literally, "making or doing relaxation." This is the name of a specific practice in the Himalayan tradition of Yoga also known as point-to-point breathing.

Śiva: As a personified deity, Śiva represents the principle of divinity through which all things return to their origin. Popular descriptions of Śiva often describe Him as the principle of destruction, which is not accurate because nothing is ever created or destroyed; it simply comes in and out of manifestation. The iconography depicts Him as an ascetic Yogi with large dreadlocks crowned by a crescent moon and washed by waters of the celestial Ganges (Milky Way) falling to earth via his head. He is festooned with cobras representing Kuṇḍalinī; seated on a deer or tiger skin; and carrying a trident representing all trinities and a *damaru*, the two-headed drum that symbolizes the beat of time. Philosophically, Śiva represents the principle of pure consciousness and the first Guru. His feminine counterpart is Śakti, His power of manifestation of the universe.

Smṛti: Memory, mindfulness. It denotes both the specific *vṛtti*, mental operation, of memory and the general practice of mindful awareness, starting from awareness of the breath (YS I.11).

Smṛti-upasthāna: The Sanskrit term for Buddhism's *sati-paṭṭhāna* (Pāli language), "the establishment of mindfulness." They are exactly equivalent in meaning and in practice.

Spanda: A term from the Kashmir Śaiva philosophy that denotes the first creative vibration in pure consciousness as it moves towards manifestation of energy and matter into form. It is related to the English word *spontaneous.*

Śreyas: That which is genuinely beautiful, joyful, and beneficial. *Śreyas* derives from *Śrī,* the principle of transcendent beauty and beneficence. When we act in response to an emotion, we often need to choose between what is pleasurable (fulfills a desire, *preyas*) and what is genuinely beautiful, joyous, and beneficial (*śreyas*).

Śrī: The universal principle of transcendent beauty and beneficence. It is also the shorter name of a deity named Tripūrasundarī, "the beauty of the three worlds," Earth, Sky, and Heaven (i.e., the whole universe). The spiritual science of this principle is called *Śrī-vidyā* ("the wisdom or science of Śrī"), which comprises several systems of sādhanā in Tantra.

Sthira: "Steady" and "stable"; "steadiness" and "stability."

Sthita-prajñā: A person of steady wisdom whose mindfield has become clear, pleasant, and stable. Such a person is described in the *Bhagavad-gītā* (II.54–72).

Sthiti: "Steadiness, stability."

Sthūla: Gross, physical, the name of the physical body (*sthūla-śarīra*) in the Yoga system.

Sukha: Literally, "good space." The most common meaning is the pleasure that follows the satisfaction of a desire (YS II.7). *Sukha* can also mean "comfortable" (YS II.46). In some texts the word is used as a synonym for *ānanda*, the supreme joy and bliss.

Sūkṣma: "Subtle," the name for the subtle body (*sūkṣma-śarīra*) in the Yoga system (see *śarīra* above).

Śūnya: Voidness, zero. This is one term for the Buddhist experience of enlightenment and is also the word from the svara-yoga system that describes when both nostrils are flowing equally in the suṣumnā-nāḍī (*śūnya-svara*).

Suṣumnā: One of the three principal nāḍīs flowing parallel to the spine, beginning in the kanda near the base of the spine and terminating in the *dvādaśānta* ("the end of twelve"), twelve finger breadths above the crown of the head, the location of the sahasrāra. It is along this path that the Kuṇḍalinī gradually rises towards that highest station, which is why opening this channel is such a priority in the Himalayan Yoga tradition. In the svara system, it is called the void flow, or *śūnya-svara*. When it is predominant, both nostrils flow evenly, the mind enters a spontaneously joyful state, and the mind naturally turns inward in meditation. Swāmī Veda often maintained that neurologically, when suṣumnā is flowing, both hemispheres of the brain are equally active, although I have not seen an empirical test of this hypothesis from the texts of the svara science. According to svara-vidyā, there are only two activities that are appropriate when suṣumnā is flowing: meditation and departing the body at death.

Sūtra: A literary form in Sanskrit most often used to expound the tenets of a school of philosophy in a highly succinct, aphoristic way. The succinctness was of such importance that it was a common saying among grammarians that the elimination of an unnecessary half syllable was worthy of a life's work. The sūtra can thus be one of the most difficult forms of Sanskrit literature to understand and interpret and almost always requires commentaries and an understanding of grammar. In Patañjali's *Yoga-sūtra*, this means that his word choices are always highly intentional, never merely expressive or synonymic. In Buddhist tradition, the word just means, essentially, "text."

Svādhyāya: "Self-study." One of the niyamas, which consists of mindfulness, study of scriptures, and the recitation of mantras. Its establishment in the mind brings direct experience of one's chosen deity (YS II.32, 44).

Svara: The discipline in Yoga that studies rhythms in the prāṇa-maya-koṣa and their relationship to breath and to the activity of the subtle elements in the cakras and in the external world. It is preserved mainly in the oral initiatory tradition of Yoga with very few extant texts. One of these, however, *Śiva-svarodaya*, has been translated by Swami Muktibodhananda (1999) of the Bihar School of Yoga and is listed in References under the title *Swara Yoga*.

Svara-vidyā: The science or wisdom of svara.

Śvāsa: The Sanskrit term for normal, unmindful inhalation (YS I.31). Mindful inhalation is called *abhyantara* (internal, YS II.50), or *pūraka*. This is an example of how the meaning of a sūtra is sometimes embedded in grammatical form rather than explained.

Tamas: The quality (*guṇa*) of inertia and darkness in *prakṛti* (the manifest and unmanifest universe).

Tantra: A system of philosophy and practice that emphasizes the principle that that which binds you is also that which liberates you. There are many Tāntrik systems, some dualistic and some nondualistic, and many scholars argue that they exist distinct from Vedic systems of practice, chiefly because they often use forbidden elements and behaviors to transcend the aversions created by moralism. Actually, the overlap with Vedic systems is very large. The texts of the Tantra tradition most often take the form of a dialogue where Śakti puts a question to Śiva, and they have a conversation to explain the answer to the question. These texts are referred to as *tantra* or *āgama*, literally, "that which has come" to us. Most of these texts are Śaiva, although there are Vaiṣṇava (dedicated to Viṣṇu) forms as well. An excellent introduction can be found in Sir John Woodroffe's (1952/2004) *Introduction to Tantra Śāstra* and other titles by Woodroffe.

Tapas: The third niyama, usually translated as austerity or ascetic practice (fasting, stillness, silence, etc.). However, it is best understood as a process of enjoyment through concentration. The will to obtain pleasure by satisfying desire is supplanted by the mental satisfaction of joy and aesthetic rapture, which then become springboards to higher consciousness. Establishment of tapas yields mastery over the body and senses (YS II.32, 43).

Udāna: The flow (*vāyu*) of prāṇa in the body that energizes coughing, sneezing, vomiting, and speech and is also what a Yogi uses to exit the body at death. It operates from the larynx upward.

Upādhi: Superimposition. In the Vedānta system, these are the illusory understandings we superimpose upon Brahman. Left unchallenged, they can cause *vyādhi*, illness of the body or the mind. They are dissipated by samādhi.

Upekṣā: Literally, "overlook." One of the brahma-vihāra practices that helps one to look beyond someone's current problematic behavior and respond to him or her compassionately based on the person he or she can become once he or she surmounts the current difficulty. Emotional nonreactivity. It also helps us relate to ourselves in this way (YS I.33).

Vāsanā: An accumulation of mental impressions (saṁskāras) of a similar nature that creates a strong karmik momentum in a certain direction. A habit, for example the habit of having a body. Swāmī Rāma used to refer to these as "grooves" in the mind (YS IV.8).

Vāyu: Literally, "wind." Also the name of the deity of the wind in the *Vedas*. When prāṇa flows in a body, it is called *vāyu*. The major prāṇa-vāyus in a human body are prāṇa, apāna, samāna, udāna, and vyāna.

Vedānta: One of the six systems of Indian philosophy. This system of practice has its metaphysical roots in Mimāṃsā and has many schools, again some dualistic and some not. The most prominent school and the one that is thought of most often as synonymous with Vedānta is Advaita (nondual) Vedānta, systematized by the great philosopher and Yogi Śaṅkarācārya in the eighth century. It uses systematic contemplation to lead the mind to ultimate nondualistic knowledge (*jñāna*) through *jñāna-yoga*.

Vibhūti: Often translated as "powers," or as siddhis. The word literally means "varieties of being." So the skills that are described in the *Vibhūti-pāda*, the third chapter of the *Yoga-sūtra*, are developments of normal human potentials made manifest through very, very intensive practice.

Vicāra: Inquiry. Vedāntins advise the practice of *ātma-vicāra,* or self-inquiry, as a contemplative way to recognize and dismiss aspects of our illusory sense of self so that we eventually arrive at an encounter with the genuine Self, *ātman*. At depth, this becomes a deep process of mindful awareness, *ātma-tattva-avalokanam*, "looking around for the essence of Self." This is the primary spiritual method of Ramana Maharshi (1879–1950).

Vikalpa: The mental operation (*vṛtti*) called "imaginary cognition," a thought with no reference point in objective reality (YS I.9).

Vi-kṣepa: Disturbances to the mind or the body (YS I.30). These disturbances result in the mind becoming vi-kṣiptam or kṣiptam and are obstacles to meditation. They include *vyādhi*, "illness" due to imbalances in the body; *styāna*, mental laziness or procrastination; *saṁśaya*, doubt; *pramād*a, negligence in cultivating the means to samādhi; *ālasya*, laziness or sloth due to inertia and heaviness in the mind and body; *avirati*, not turning away from expending mental energy in outward sensuality; *bhrānti-darśana*, wrong views or confusion in one's philosophical map of Yoga practice; *alabdha-bhūmikatva*, failure to achieve a level (*bhūmi*) of realization in one's practice, especially samādhi; and *anavasthitva*, instability or inability to maintain a level of accomplishment that one has attained. *Vi-kṣepa* can be a synonym for *kleśa* (YS II.3). See pp. 12–13.

Vi-kṣiptam: The *bhūmi*, mental level, where the mindfield is generally "tossed about," or distracted, but is beginning to be able to settle into some moments of one-pointed concentration. Meditation then becomes possible.

Viparyaya: Literally, "going awry." False knowledge or false perception, the name for the mental operation (*vṛtti*) of cognition that has no basis in the nature or form of its object (YS I.8).

Vipassanā: In the Pāli language, the name for the Buddhist path of mindfulness meditation common to the Theravāda schools of Southeast Asia in Thailand, Burma, Cambodia, and Śrī Laṅkā. As in Yoga, the principal Vipassanā practice is mindful awareness of breath. Vipassanā practitioners generally don't use mantra as a focus of concentration, so researchers call it an *open focus* method.

Virāṭ: The manifest objective universe as the physical body of divinity. A vision of this was granted to Arjuna in Chapter 11 of the *Bhagavad-gītā.*

Vīrya: Spiritual power or efficacy. The fruit of the establishment of *brahmacarya* (literally, "walking in divinity"); channeling the movement of the mind's energy through the senses. Following the establishment of brahmacarya, the subsequent establishment of vīrya is then what enables a teacher to transmit spiritual knowledge and experience directly into the mind of a disciple in the process of initiation, or *dīkṣā* (YS II.38). *Vīrya*, spiritual power, is also the subtlest form of *bindu*, which exists in gross form in the body physically as semen. In its subtle form, *ojas*, the energy principle of the kapha-doṣa in Āyurveda, is the energetic precursor of the reproductive fluids. The sexual preservation practices of Yoga concern conservation of ojas rather than semen itself, and ojas's eventual transmutation into vīrya.

Vitarka: This word can mean gross thought in relation to the first level of saṁprajñāta-samādhi (YS I.42). It can also mean mistaken logical thinking (violent thought), which accompanies kleśa and is alleviated by impressing the opposite attitude on the mind and heart (*prati-pakṣa-bhāvanā*, YS II.33–34).

Viveka: Discrimination, one of the qualities of buddhi.

Vṛtti: From the verb root √*vṛt*, "turn," as in the English word *vertigo*. These are turnings, operations, or waves in the mindfield (*citta*) that constitute our flow of thoughts and emotions. Cessation of these waves is called Yoga (YS I.2). The vṛttis are described in YS I.5–11.

Vyāna: The flow (*vāyu*) of prāṇa in the body that integrates the systems of the body into a coherent whole, including the skin as well as the skeletal, circulatory, and nervous systems. Vyāna circulates through the whole body.

Vyutthāna: The tendency of the mind towards motion and distraction rather than towards stillness and concentration. This is the opposite of *samādhāna*, above.

Yama: Literally, "restraint, control." The first of the eight limbs of the Rāja-yoga system of practice, usually translated as "ethical restraints" pertaining to relationships. They are ahiṁsā, satya, asteya, brahmacarya, and aparigraha (YS II.30) and are also described as "the great vow" (*mahāvrata*). They apply regardless of birth, time, or place (YS II.31).

Yoga-nidrā: Literally, "Yoga sleep." Conscious entry into deep, dreamless, delta brain wave sleep where one remains both inwardly aware and aware of one's external surroundings without any activity of manas. It is a state of pure awareness that eventually leads one into samādhi by gradually eroding the fragile boundary between deep sleep, which is an unconscious experience of pure being, and samādhi, where the experience of pure being is fully conscious.

About the Author

Stephen Parker (Stoma), PsyD, E-RYT 500, YACEP, met Swāmī Veda Bhāratī, then Dr. Uṣarbudh Ārya, in 1970 at the age of 19. He began studying meditation and was initiated in the Himalayan tradition in 1971. In that year, he first met his guru, Swāmī Rāma of the Himalayas. He studied Sanskrit with Dr. Ārya at the University of Minnesota, earning a Bachelor of Arts degree in South Asian Languages and Literature, *summa cum laude*, in 1975. Dr. Parker was an āśram resident at the Meditation Center in Minneapolis, MN, and began teaching haṭha-yoga and meditation in 1974. In that year, he made a first pilgrimage to India with Swāmī Rāma to attend the Kumbha Mela in Haridwar, India.

Dr. Parker went on to receive a Master of Arts degree in Counseling Psychology in 1982 and a Doctorate of Psychology in 1994, both from the University of St. Thomas, St. Paul, MN. His doctoral advisor was family therapy theorist Bradford P. Keeney, PhD, whose journey with indigenous spirituality and healing traditions is described in his autobiography, *Shaking Out the Spirits*. Licensed as a psychologist since 1985, Dr. Parker maintains a private psychotherapy practice at Northland Therapy Center in St. Paul, MN, and has taught in the graduate psychology programs at the University of St. Thomas and for more than 25 years in the Counseling and Psychological Services Program of Saint Mary's University of Minnesota. He also helped originate the first course on Yoga in an American medical school at the Center for Spirituality and Healing at the University of Minnesota. He has been a guest lecturer at the University of Social Sciences in Warsaw, Poland, in the Peace Studies graduate program at the University of Innsbruck, and in the Indian Psychology Program at the University of Delhi.

Since 1999 Dr. Parker has served as a senior faculty member of the Himalayan Yoga Tradition Teacher Training Program, traveling extensively throughout the world training teachers of Yoga and meditation, leading spiritual retreats, and giving seminars in Europe, Asia, South America, and Africa. He has been a senior faculty member at the Meditation Center in Minneapolis, MN, and at Swāmī Rāma Sādhaka Grāma in Rishikesh, India. In 2007 he took preliminary vows of renunciation in the Daśanāmi order of swāmīs from Swāmī Veda Bhāratī and the Śaṅkarācārya of Karvirapīṭha, and in 2008 he was granted the privilege of receiving mantras in the process of Yoga initiation. "Our only qualification is our master" (Dr. Bettina Bäumer, 2010).

About the Editor

Elizabeth Licht, BFA, RYT 200, is a freelance editor, professional dancer, and Yoga instructor based in Southeastern Wisconsin. Her Bachelor of Fine Arts degree in dance and Honors College degree are from the University of Wisconsin–Milwaukee, where she also studied journalism, Iyengar Yoga, and the Alexander Technique. She is a member of Danceworks Performance Company, a teacher at YogaLoft, and a former UWM Writing Center tutor. Her Yoga certification is from YogaOne Studio. Contact her at http://www.ElizabethLicht.com.

About AHYMSIN

The Association of Himalayan Yoga Meditation Societies International (AHYMSIN) is a world-wide affiliation of centers and initiates. Mahāmaṇḍaleśwara Swāmī Veda Bhāratī, a disciple of H. H. Śrī Swāmī Rāma, provided the impetus for founding AHYMSIN in 2007, when initiates from around the world gathered at Swāmī Rāma Sādhaka Grāma in Rishikesh, India. AHYMSIN's purpose is to teach and make available the knowledge of Yoga meditation within the tradition of the Himalayan masters, as interpreted by Swāmī Rāma of the Himalayas. Activities include teaching the science of Yoga, carrying out research and publication in the field of Yoga and related branches of knowledge, and performing acts of charity for the benefit of humanity. AHYMSIN also has an international teacher training program, including a 200-hour program and a 600-hour program, for certification as a Yoga teacher. AHYMSIN is a registered nonprofit society with the government of India.

About Swāmī Rāma Sādhaka Grāma

Swāmī Rāma Sādhaka Grāma (SRSG) in Rishikesh, India, serves as AHYMSIN world headquarters and as a spiritual retreat center for AHYMSIN members and others. Also located at SRSG are the Swāmī Rāma Dhyāna Gurukulam, the Meditation Research Institute, and Himalayan Yoga Publications Trust. The Dhyāna Gurukulam is an intensive, long-term (three to five years) study program that prepares people for service as spiritual guides. The Meditation Research Institute is a lab that was opened to document the various meditative techniques of the Himalayan tradition and to test their effectiveness with scientific tools and methods. It aims to understand the neural correlates of consciousness and especially brain dynamics during meditation.

Find Us Online

AHYMSIN http://ahymsin.org/
Swāmī Rāma Sādhaka Grāma http://sadhakagrama.org/
Himalayan Yoga Tradition Teacher Training Program
http://www.himalayanyogatradition.com/
The Meditation Center http://www.themeditationcenter.org/